Arguing with Numbers

Arguing with Numbers

Statistics for the Social Sciences

Victor Thiessen

with the assistance of Paul Gingrich

Fernwood Publishing

Editing: Douglas Beall
Cover design: Eric Ourique with Beverley Rach
Design and Layout: Jackie Logan
Printed and bound in Canada.

*Through the abacus, which symbolizes statistics, aspects of reality can be seen.
The view permitted, however, is at best partial.*

A publication of
Fernwood Publishing
Box 9409, Station A
Halifax, NS B3K 5S3

Canadian Cataloguing in Publication Data

Thiessen, Victor

    Arguing with Numbers

    Includes bibliographical references and index.
    ISBN 1-895686-12-1

1. Statistics. 2. Social sciences — Statistical methods. I. Title.

HA29.T44 1993   001.4'22   C93–098536–2

To Meta, my mother,
a strong and wonderful woman.

Table of Contents

List of Figures and Tables

Figures

Tables

Acknowledgements

I failed my first statistics course, which in itself taught me a lot. To now write this book indicates the enormity of my debt to the patience, confidence and support of many.

Tony Davis (St. Francis Xavier University) first encouraged me to revise and complete the work upon seeing a partial manuscript. Shortly thereafter Errol Sharpe, the publisher of Fernwood, casually mentioned his interest in a text on quantitative methods. My needs fulfilled his in this respect.

Errol asked Paul Gingrich (University of Regina) to review the manuscript. My first contact with Paul occurred in the form of receiving thirty- odd typed pages of his reactions to the first draft of *Arguing with Numbers*. His criticisms were sound, his suggestions positive. A respect, and personal relationship grew out of this. Paul's contribution could not be adequately recognized by mere mention in this Acknowledgement.

I would also like to acknowledge the helpful comments from my former students who were exposed to a draft of this text; Wade Kenny and Valerie Pottie Bunge were particularly thorough. A number of colleagues provided detailed criticisms which immensely improved the final manuscript: Tom Barrett (Mount Saint Vincent University), John Benoit (Dalhousie University), Dianne Looker (Acadia University), and Jörg Blasius and Harald Rohlinger (University of Cologne). donalee Moulton applied her skills to find simpler and more elegant ways of expressing some of my pedantic academic prose.

Douglas Beall, the editor, was more than thorough and meticulous. He helped me understand why I sometimes phrased things differently from how he would, and why his way was often better. The number of changes he made warranted retyping the complete manuscript, a tedious task which was superbly handled by Chauna Porter. Jackie Logan spent long hours working on design and layout, and I wish to extend a special thanks to her. Beverley Rach created the abacus on the front cover and served as production co-ordinator. The drawing on the front and back cover was by Eric Ourique.

Finally, I want to thank Barbara Cottrell and Katie Thiessen for their love.

WHAT MAKES A GOOD ARGUMENT?

The Role of Theory, Methods and Statistic in Arguments

For many of us, the prospect of learning statistics seems both boring and frightening. But at the same time, we do enjoy developing and defending certain arguments (usually our own) and destroying others.

As its title implies, this book focuses on constructing and demolishing arguments based on numbers. These are perhaps the two most useful roles for statistics in the social sciences. Statistical manipulations are powerful tools for assessing an argument's strengths and weaknesses, but they can also lead to false conclusions. We need to understand statistical reasoning in enough detail to detect these errors, because they are often far from obvious.

Scholarly arguments are assertions supported by evidence. For example, in social psychology the "similarity-attraction hypothesis" is an argument which asserts that we are attracted to those similar to ourselves, and many empirical studies have been offered as evidence. This documentation takes the form of statistical manipulations of researcher-created numbers. Such manipulations are the realm of statistics. This book is designed to guide you through specific statistical techniques and the general logic of statistical reasoning so you will be able to evaluate the arguments of others and develop numerically based arguments of your own.

Numerically based arguments contain two types of assertions. The first type of assertion is that certain observable events are connected, or related, to each other. It postulates the form or nature of the relationship. A more formal statement of the relationship between similarity and attraction might be: "The higher the proportion of agreements between strangers, the greater the mutual attraction." The second type of assertion provides an interpretation, or a theoretical basis, for the relationship. It answers the question, "Why should the events be related?" We endeavour to understand our social world by offering interpretations of documented events. Thus, some social psychologists interpret the similarity-attraction hypothesis as a support for classical conditioning theory. This theory argues that "stimulus generalization" accounts for the relationship between similarity and attraction. Similarity is, by such an account, an intrinsic "positive reinforcement," and human beings "generalize" their warm response to any object (in this case another individual) in their immediate environment. In the course of this book, we will have occasion to evaluate this and other arguments more carefully.

1

For an argument to be solid, it must pass several tests. Most importantly, it must successfully withstand the challenge of alternative interpretations, for all findings invite plausible alternative interpretations. We can argue, for example, that individuals who happen to be attracted to each other negotiate or construct agreements. This formulation poses a threat to the classical conditioning interpretation. These arguments, and the interpretations they provide, I will call **theories**. I do not make a sharp distinction between numerically based arguments and theory. If there is a difference, it is that theories connect arguments to higher levels of abstraction. That is, theories are couched in general terms and thus provide the basis for expecting a variety of connections among phenomena.

Given the pervasive possibility of alternative interpretations, it is imperative that arguments address and try to refute rival interpretations. One ever-present alternative interpretation to any empirically based argument is that the findings are **methodological artifacts**.[1] Some "facts" turn out to be nothing more than artifacts of the empirical procedures used. Precisely because artifacts are always possible, statistics can be deceptive and can be used to mislead. The most devastating interpretation of any finding is that it is a methodological artifact. Consequently, a prime principle of arguing with numbers is to uncover and remove artifacts. I will provide examples of artifacts throughout this book. We will find a frustrating number of possible artifacts, each of which must be evaluated. The processes of searching for artifacts and minimizing their likelihood are known as **research methods.**

The main ingredients for building social science arguments — theory, methods and statistics—have been introduced. The aim of this book is to hone the skills necessary for developing sound, empirically based arguments. This will involve all three ingredients: (1) formulating one or more theoretical interpretations of observed events, (2) manipulating the observations through a variety of statistical techniques to evaluate the merits of competitive interpretations or theories and (3) searching for and nullifying methodological artifacts.

The Necessity of Expectations

To develop sound arguments, it is essential to formulate concrete expectations. I use the term *expectation* in a number of ways. **Substantive expectations** are theoretically grounded predictions about what our data will reveal. For example, reinforcement psychologists expect that strangers who happen to have similar attitudes will be attracted to each other. Substantive expectations are part of every social science argument.

Hypothetical expectations result from playing a "what if" game. The object of this game is to imagine a possible world that obeys certain rules we create. For example, I can imagine a world in which husbands and wives do not influence each other. This would imply that the beliefs of husbands and wives are no more similar than those of typical strangers. Suppose I had some data on husband-wife pairs in which the beliefs of both were recorded separately. Now suppose that these were accidently mismatched so that the beliefs of the first wife are mistakenly compared with those of the second husband, for example. We would find a certain level of similar beliefs in these fictitious couples. This would be the level of similarity produced by chance, since obviously the fictitious couples could not have influenced each other. At a later point in time, we discover the mismatch mistake and rectify it by computing the correct levels of husband-wife similarity. Were we to find that the correct level of similarity hardly differs from the incorrect one, we would have to conclude that husbands and wives hardly influence each other, at least on these particular issues.

Something similar to this accidental mismatching can be done on purpose through a variety of statistical techniques. In a later chapter, we will learn how to compute the number of "chance" agreements between husbands and wives. These represent how many agreements we could expect in a world where couples do not influence each other and do not strive for common outlooks. We do not know in advance if this possible world characterizes our world. Therefore we compare the expected number of agreements with the actual number of agreements among our couples. If the actual agreements substantially exceed the chance number, we reject the idea that the possible world we created characterizes our world. In general, with hypothetical, or model-induced, expectations we first generate a set of observations which obey certain rules that incorporate a model of a possible world; next we compare our actual cases with those generated by the model; then we evaluate the fit between the actual observations and the model-induced expectations. If the fit is poor, we reject the assumptions and rules on which the model is based, and we conclude that this hypothetical world is not the one in which we live.

Finally, **statistical expectations** are based on certain properties about distributions that have been developed by statisticians. They are expectations, based on statistical theory, concerning the likelihood of various outcomes in the long run. We are all familiar with the statistical expectation that, when flipping a coin, half the time we will get a "tail." The basis for this and other statistical expectations will become clear as the logic of statistical analysis is developed later on in this book.

Uncertainty, Complexity and Ambiguity

The ever-increasing invasion of statistics is now a part of our lives, regardless of how we feel about it. What has prompted this popularity of statistics despite the initial resistance of so many people? First, uncertainty is ubiquitous; doubt about outcomes permeates our existence. It seems as though every idea has an opposite that could be equally valid. Statistical theory addresses this uncertainty.

We can employ statistical analysis to determine the relative plausibility of competitive arguments. For example, I'm sure you could construct quite plausible and logical explanations of why educated soldiers are more likely to suffer psychological breakdowns in military service than those with less education; or why

Southern soldiers in the United States are better equipped to survive the rigours of a tropical climate than Northerners; or why Blacks are less ambitious for promotion than Whites; or why soldiers from rural backgrounds take army hardships better than city soldiers. I am also certain that you could build equally plausible arguments why these statements are false.[2] In science, the sound use of statistics consists of increasing the evidence for one interpretation while decreasing the credibility of competitive ones, and thereby minimizing uncertainty.

A second aspect of modern life is the overwhelming amount of information bombarding our senses. From this complex confusion we must extract what is relevant or critical and ignore the superfluous or trivial.

Statistical analysis enables us to condense information, making it possible to organize, summarize and communicate vast amounts of information that otherwise would overwhelm but not necessarily inform. Of course, the problem of deciding what is important remains. You may have some intuitive notions concerning this, but the material covered in this book should help you to become more adept at deciding what and when something is irrelevant.

An old saw has it that a drunkard uses a lamppost more for support than for light. Unfortunately, statistical manipulations are also frequently used in this way. Therefore, the emphasis in this book is not on statistics as a set of decision-making rules that we must rigorously follow and then passively accept as the verdict. *To make decisions solely on the basis of statistical considerations is appropriate only when no other relevant information is available.* But this is hardly ever the case in scholarly research. The result of a given statistical test is only one of many ingredients we will use for reaching conclusions in our arguments. A review of the literature, for example, is likely to produce relevant information. Additionally, alternative, yet appropriate, statistical techniques can often be applied to the same observations. I will present statistical techniques not so much as tests but as various approaches to organize ideas and information in ways that assess the issues at hand more fully.

Finally, all arguments contain ambiguous assertions. Casting the assertions into statistical terms can help clarify their meaning. Take the sentence, "Typically, men prefer mates two years their junior." The term *typically* permits a variety of meanings, such as:

- Most men prefer a mate two years younger than themselves.
- More men prefer a mate two years younger than themselves than any other age difference.
- Half the men prefer a mate at least two years their junior, and the other half prefer a mate no more than two years their junior.
- The arithmetic average age difference men prefer for their mates is two years younger than themselves.

Moving between verbal and statistical forms of communication helps to clarify and sharpen the intended meaning. The statistical skills we will learn do not relate so much to the ability to calculate tests, as they do to the abilities to translate verbal assertions into statistical equivalents and, conversely, to formulate appropriate verbal conclusions for statistical results.

I wish to emphasize that the results of all numerical manipulations express social constructions: thus their meanings are debatable and need to be assessed carefully. Any given phenomenon may be viewed in multiple ways. And for each approach, a variety of statistical equations might fruitfully be calculated, each of which may highlight some aspects of the phenomenon and hide others. We do not discover social reality; rather, we construct it through our theories and the interpretations we select for our statistical results. Solid arguments develop good constructions. This view of statistics distinguishes social scientists from mathematicians.

Style and Organization

This book addresses itself to serious students who nevertheless approach statistics with some fear and trepidation. I intend therefore to make statistical manipulations more familiar and to make students more skilled in applying these manipulations to arguments. To do this, I have made several choices concerning the style and organization of this book.

1. To find the possible flaws in an argument often requires substantive familiarity with the topic. For this reason, I will return to some of the same arguments at different points in the book. This will permit me to introduce new considerations and build upon previous considerations in the process of developing an argument. The similarity-attraction hypothesis is one of these.
2. I have organized the book in a manner that unfolds and develops the rather simple logic of statistical inquiry. I will focus on statistical logic and therefore will exclude certain variations of statistical formulas developed for special circumstances. Having grasped the overall logic presented here, you should experience little difficulty in using statistical reference books for specific applications.
3. The mathematical derivations and bases of statistics are kept to a minimum. I include them when they pinpoint the nature of the assumptions being made, the violations of which can result in methodological artifacts.
4. Each chapter ends with a summary that captures the highlights of arguing with numbers. This is to make sure that we retain our focus on arguments even while learning the mechanics of statistical calculation.
5. Careful construction of arguments requires analyzing the same data in a variety of sometimes creative ways. Fortunately, with ready access to computer technology, this poses no real difficulties. It does require basic computer literacy and familiarity with some of the statistical software. The Statistical Package for the Social Sciences (SPSS) one widely available software package,

and the one most used in this book. This package, like other software programs, has its own cryptic language to instruct the computer. I have chosen not to provide a thorough introduction to the SPSS language, since good manuals are available which already do this. Instead, I will list the SPSS instructions that produced some of the results given in various examples. These instructions will then be explained step by step in sufficient detail so you can perform similar operations.

6.   The arguments found in social science journals and books are presented as polished products. This gives the impression that the research progressed in an orderly and logical fashion. The frustrating false starts and blind alleys, the often tedious exploration of different ways of capturing the expected relationships, and the groping for interpretations that make sense of the observations remain secret, not necessarily because the researcher wished to hide them, but because publishing constraints require concise treatments. Experienced scholars are well aware of the spurts and sputters; students often are not. To counterbalance the sense of logical progression, I have developed an argument on a topic on which I was truly naive. The topic I chose concerned the images of political parties held by adult Canadians. When I started writing this text, I had not engaged in any research or read extensively on this topic. As the book progresses, I will present my initial expectations and the subsequent considerations that led me to perform each of the statistical manipulations. Some of the steps I took were futile, some of the results were unanticipated and the final answers were far from unquestionable. By including this example, I pay tribute to the frailty of scholarly thought, the fragility of socially produced knowledge, and the frustration inherent in constructing numerically based arguments. Such a tribute is necessary to demystify the nature of scientific investigation.

Notes

1.   I use this term in a broad sense to refer to findings that are more apparent than real. The *Concise Oxford Dictionary* defines an *artifact* as a "thing not naturally present, introduced during preparation or investigation."

2.   By the way, they aren't supported. See Paul F. Lazarsfeld, "The American Soldier: An Expository Review," *Public Opinion Quarterly* 13 (fall 1949): 377-404.

Key Terms

hypothetical expectations: Expectations derived from imagining a possible world that obeys certain rules or laws we impose. They often provide useful comparison points for our observations. Example: We can imagine a world in which parents have no influence on their children's goals. For such a world, we can calculate the proportion of times that children and parents can be expected to have identical goals.

methodological artifacts: Apparent findings that result from the procedures used rather than from the nature of the phenomenon being investigated. Example: Experimental subjects are known to behave in a fashion that supports the substantive expectation, regardless of what this expectation is.

research methods: The procedures used to detect and minimize methodological artifacts. Example: In experiments, to make certain that the person administering the "treatment" does not know the hypothesis being tested.

statistical expectations: Features of events that are premised on statistical properties. Example: In completing a true-false test on a topic about which we know absolutely nothing, the expectation that we will guess correctly on half the items.

substantive expectations: Empirical expectations derived from a theoretical argument. Example: The anticipation that two strangers who happen to agree on many topics will become friends. The complementary expectation is that two strangers who happen to disagree on many topics will find themselves unattracted to each other.

theories: A set of interrelated substantive expectations, together with their interpretation or basis. Theories are scholarly arguments expressed in a general language that is applicable to a wide range of phenomena.

Chapter 1

SETS AND PROBABILITIES: USING STATISTICS TO GRAPPLE WITH OUR SOCIAL WORLD

Scholarly arguments connect **logically independent events** or phenomena. To be logically independent, the connection between the events must not be true simply by definition. To say that children are incorrigible because they continue to get in trouble does not qualify as a rudimentary argument; incorrigibility means nothing more than persistently unacceptable behaviour. Since the statement is true by definition (and therefore a **tautology**), it cannot serve as the main ingredient of a scholarly argument. Or, stated differently, the criterion for admissable arguments is **falsifiability**, which means that the postulated connections between events can be tested empirically, that is, through data obtained via systematic observations (Popper, 1963). At a minimum, we must be able to imagine empirical findings that, were they obtained, would be inconsistent with the argument and would thus weaken it. Assertions are transformed into numerically based arguments when the relevant events and the relationships between these events are defined, interpreted, and subjected to a variety of empirical tests.

At the same time, we should note that social science arguments seldom are dealt a fatal blow (i.e., falsified) through an empirical investigation. Rather, arguments are judged by their relative strength and fruitfulness: the number of substantive expectations that are fulfilled, and the variety of phenomena for which the argument provides a plausible interpretation.

Examples of Arguments

In this chapter, we will take four assertions and begin to transform them into social science arguments. The first three examples have received wide attention in the scholarly literature. The concepts used in that literature are couched in theoretical frameworks which provide the meanings for the terms used. Those frameworks are too elaborate to be summarized here. Hence the initial presentation of the arguments will be quite rudimentary. This will permit participation in the process of refining definitions and propositions. I chose the fourth example precisely because I was unfamiliar with the relevant scholarly literature. It demonstrates an attempt to develop an argument from the very beginning, not knowing where it would lead.

Many ambiguities and contradictions will remain in all four arguments. The reason that scholarly arguments are in a constant state of flux is that no argument is ever the last word. I have given the examples descriptive titles to help me refer to them.

Mate Preference Argument

"Because male reproductive success in humans depends heavily on mating with reproductively capable females, selection over thousands of generations should favor those males who *prefer* to mate with reproductively capable females....*Age* of females is highly correlated with their reproductive capability—youthful females are generally more fecund than older females" (Buss, 1989:3-4). Therefore males should desire young mates. This argument is one implication of a general theoretical framework known as sociobiology. It is an extension and modification of Darwin's theory of evolution to social and cultural phenomena.

Two issues are involved in this argument. First, do men actually prefer young women as mates? Second, if they do, is it because of genetic selection? Assuming for the moment that men do prefer young women, the sociobiological argument constitutes one of many possible interpretations. Some scholars might argue that such age preferences are a reflection of patriarchy: having a younger wife helps perpetuate the unequal division of power between the sexes in favour of men.

Parental Socialization Argument

Parents mould their children's desires to conform with what they want for their children. In sociological terminology, parents socialize their children. Consequently, the educational and occupational plans of children should reflect their parents' desires.

Similarity-Attraction Argument

According to classical conditioning theory, individuals are attracted to others who reward them. Many scholars feel that agreements are intrinsically rewarding. If these scholars are correct, individuals should be attracted to those who agree with them.

Party Imagery Argument

The federal New Democratic Party (NDP) is a left-wing party. Among Canadian adults, only the naive would fail to comprehend this. Therefore, with increasing knowledge, there is an increasing likelihood of perceiving the NDP as left of centre.

Defining Terms Using Set Theory

These examples have a common feature: the assertions are too vague (for example, "left of centre" has little meaning until both "left" and "centre" are defined). We must identify the terms with features of the world that can be comprehended more directly. We will start translating abstract concepts into concrete observables using **set theory** to suggest possible concretizations, or empirical manifestations, for each of the examples. Set theory provides a crude but nevertheless useful initial approach to defining events and their relationships. It has several advantages as a starting point: it forces us to think more clearly about the various events of interest; we can diagram sets and their relations, providing convenient visual images; and the basis of probability theory, essential to statistics, is easier to understand once we have grasped the basics of set theory.

Basic to set theory is the concept of **sets**. A set is simply any well-defined collection of objects. For example, "all humans desiring mates younger than themselves" is a set, as is "all residents of Canada who know the names of a majority of the provincial premiers." An important constraint is the qualification "well-defined." The boundary of the set needs to be clear. Ideally this means we should encounter no difficulty in determining whether someone or something belongs to a particular set. But, when dealing with empirical phenomena, ambiguity often remains. We can reduce ambiguity by modifying the definitions of our sets as necessary. We will tangle with some ambiguities later, when we apply set theory to our examples, and we will see that our conclusions are suspect when our definitions are imprecise.

We impose clarity on events by viewing them from a particular perspective. The decision to define a set in one particular way is not immutable — we can, and ordinarily should, change the definition or look at the same information from a variety of angles. There isn't one correct way, and there may be several fruitful ways. Through differing constructions of our social world, we come to understand it.

Take the concept of unemployment. As used by Statistics Canada, the set "unemployed person" consists of any adult resident of Canada who is not in paid employment, is not self-employed and has reported to a Canada Employment and Immigration office within the past three months.[1] The constraint of reporting to a Canada Employment and Immigration office ostensibly excludes those who are not actively seeking employment. Many observers of unemployment judge this particular social construction to be misleading. They recognize that some people actively seeking a job may nevertheless not report to a Canada Employment and Immigration office. Chief among the reasons for not reporting is a sense of futility of finding work through this avenue.

This example illustrates one of the typical dilemmas in constructing sets: clarity conflicts with suitability. It is clear whether someone has not reported to a Canada Employment Office, but this is unsuitable for determining whether someone is actively seeking a job, never mind someone desiring a job who has given up hope of finding one.

The solution to this dilemma is to construct multiple definitions. A self-definition provides one alternative to the official definition. For this alternative, a person would be classified as unemployed if he or she was not working for pay but claimed to desire paid employment. This is not necessarily a better definition, simply an alternative one. Ultimately, our definitions of events, and any resulting quantitative information, remain social constructions that are judged by their usefulness.

The term *objects* in the definition of a set is intended broadly. Non-physical things are considered objects for the purposes of set theory. For example, the type of political organization of a society, such as democratic, fascist or communist, can be considered a set, as long as each society's type can be ascertained.

The individual objects comprising a set are called **elements**, or members. Thus, each and every male who desires a young mate is a member of the set referred to previously. But we need some way to specify the elements of a set. This is most frequently done by providing rules that are clear enough that one can decide whether a particular object should be included in a given set. In the context of an empirical study, these rules are called **operational definitions**. Let's construct some initial sets for the four arguments.

Mate Selection Sets

In his study of mate selection, Buss (1989) had to provide a rule for deciding whether a young mate was desired. His operational definition consisted of asking males to indicate the preferred age of a mate relative to their own age. Respondents who gave an age less than their own are members of the set. This rule makes it easy to decide whether a given observation fits the definition. Conventionally, a capital letter symbolizes the set, with the rule that specifies the elements of the set enclosed in brackets, as in:

$$Y = \{\text{humans desiring mates younger than themselves}\}.$$

Having defined the set this way, we can use the upper case letter to refer to it.

It is often convenient to think of objects as belonging to some large set, called the **universal set**. This universal set is the universe of discourse. It provides a frame of reference, letting others know the boundaries of what we are talking about. Let's reserve W as the symbol for the universal set to distinguish it from all other sets. In the mate preference example, the universal set could be defined as all humans. This would let the reader know that the argument is restricted to *Homo sapiens*. But Buss makes it clear that his argument pertains only to males, so a more appropriate universal set would be:

$$W = \{\text{human males}\}.$$

Having defined the universal set, all subsequent sets are assumed to be **subsets** of it. To define this term more precisely: for sets A and B, if every element of B is also an element of A, then B is a subset of A. One advantage of set theory is that definitions, such as subsets, can be illustrated by what are known as **Venn diagrams**, named after a mathematician prominent in developing set theory. These diagrams aid comprehension and communication. Let's take the assertions given at the beginning of this chapter and transform aspects of them into Venn diagrams. In Venn diagrams, we first draw the universal set. In our examples below, the universal set will be drawn as a large rectangle. This set will usually be explicitly defined, as in the first example, where the universal set is "human males." Then, within this universal set, various subsets will be defined. The subsets will be drawn within the boundaries of the universal set. I have drawn them as circles, but their shape is actually arbitrary.

Figure 1.1 shows a Venn diagram for the mate preference example. Such diagrams help clarify expectations: thus, in Figure 1.1, the sociobiologists' substantive expectation is for few males to fall outside the set Y. Instances that fall outside the set Y weaken the argument. Ideally, the elements inside the circle would represent instances supporting sociobiological expectations, with those outside the circle weakening the argument. Clearly, supporters of the sociobiological perspective would hope that the area of the circle nearly fills that of the universal set. Their expectation is visually reinforced by making the set Y fill most of the space of the universal set.

Figure 1.1
Mate Preference Venn Diagram

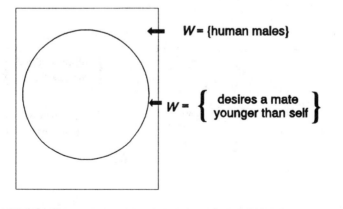

For this example, Buss's operational definition of the set "desires a mate younger than self" is precise enough for his purposes. His rule simplifies the decision of whether a given observation fits the definition. In this sense it is an acceptable set. Yet, in another and very important sense, it is a poor set: it no longer corresponds closely to the argument being made. Remember that "reproductive capability" was the explanation offered for the expectation that males would prefer young mates. A 55-year-old male who prefers a 50-year-old female is, by Buss's definition, a member of the set Y. But a 50-year-old female may have no reproductive capability. Hence cases such as this one should be considered as disconfirming evidence. Buss's definition has the effect of treating this and other similar cases as supporting the argument. A more appropriate rule for "desires a young mate" might include all those who gave a preferred age in the teens. To be useful, our sets must not only be clear but must also correspond closely to the features required by the argument.

This discussion illustrates how the choice of operational definitions alters the apparent support for an argument. If we construe the desire for a young mate the way Buss did, we will obtain evidence which seems to fit better than if we use the construction "desires a mate still in her teens."

Figure 1.2
Parental Socialization Venn Diagram: Father
and Teenager Pairs

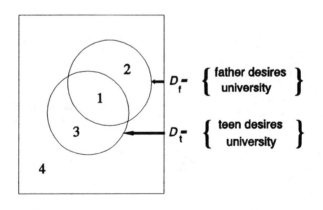

Parental Socialization Sets

The parental socialization argument was presented at such a general level that it did not suggest any specific sets. Our task is to translate these indefinite expectations into one or more specific manifestations, or sets. Let's do this in the context of Looker's (1977) survey of Hamilton, Ontario, high school students. She obtained information from each of three family members — mother, father and their teen-aged child — that provides a possible test of the socialization argument. She asked both parents: "Which of the following paths would you like your son/daughter to take after high school?" The teenager's plans were ascertained by the analogous question: "After you leave high school, which of the following paths would you like to take?" The response alternatives were work; apprenticeship; commercial, business or trade school; community college; teacher's college; or university.

Let's focus for the time being on whether attending university is desired. (We could have chosen a desire other than attending university, but with set theory it is convenient to choose one particular desire). We are now in a position to formulate one possible manifestation of the parental socialization argument: children whose fathers prefer them to attend university are more likely than other children to desire to do so. (We would of course hold a similar expectation with the mothers' preferences.) Figure 1.2 provides a possible diagram. To remind us that we are focusing on the desires of pairs of family members (father and teenager), let's use a subscripted notation. The letter D will signify "desires to attend university" with the subscripts f and t referring to father and teenager, respectively. The two sets are:

D_f = {fathers who want their children to attend university}

D_t = {teenagers from the same families who want to attend university}.

I have numbered the different regions of the Venn diagram to isolate their different meanings. Region 1 consists of those father-teenager pairs (or dyads) where both desire university attendance; region 2 represents instances where the father wants the child to attend university, but the teenager has other plans. Conversely, region 3 is populated by pairs in which the teenager wants to attend university, but the father prefers a different path. Finally, in region 4, neither fathers nor their children have university attendance as their goal. The Venn diagram reminds us of these four possibilities.

Advocates of the parental socialization thesis would expect region 1 to be large relative to regions 2 and 3. How small can region 1 be before we should conclude that the parental socialization thesis is unsupported? Right now we don't know how to define a minimum size, but in subsequent chapters we will be in a position to evaluate how small region 1 can be before we conclude that our substantive expectation was not supported.

Scrutiny of Venn diagrams can lead to additional insights. We have already seen that region 1 should be quite large relative to the second or third region. But what about region 4? Since it includes those father-teenager dyads where both desire a path other than university, the parental socialization theory predicts that this region would also be relatively full. Had we not drawn and labelled the different regions, we might have missed this second implication of the parental socialization argument.

Having succeeded in ferreting out an additional expectation, let's dig even deeper. To be eligible for inclusion in the study, Looker required that the family included a mother, a father and a teenager. Note that this makes the universal set "mother-father-teenager triads residing in Hamilton, Ontario." This permits us to introduce both parents into the picture, giving us Figure 1.3, with the additional set:

$$D_m = \{\text{mothers who want their children to attend university}\}$$

Figure 1.3
Parental Socialization Venn Diagram: Mother, Father and Teenager

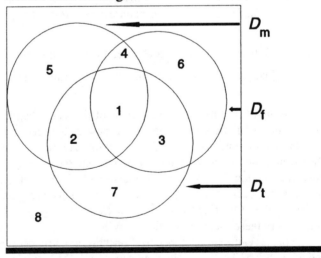

The three sets of interest (choosing the path of attending university for each of mother, father and teenager) create eight distinct regions, each representing a different combination of the desires of the three family members:

Region 1:   All agree that university attendance is desirable.
Region 2:   The mother and teenager agree attending university is desirable, but not the father.
Region 3:   The father and teenager agree attending university is desirable, but not the mother.
Region 4:   The mother and father agree attending university is desirable, but not the teenager.
Region 5:   Only the mother chooses university attendance.
Region 6:   Only the father chooses university attendance.
Region 7:   Only the teenager chooses university attendance.
Region 8:   All choose a path other than university attendance.

These different combinations trigger questions about the parental socialization thesis. What path can teenagers be expected to desire when the parents disagree between themselves? Do the desires of mother and father influence those of the teenager equally, or is one parent more important in this than the other? The value of the Venn diagram is precisely that it depicts these possibilities clearly, helping us to clarify our expectations.[2] We might now refine the parental socialization argument with some additional expectations. First, teenagers are most likely to want to attend university if both parents desire this. Second, teenagers are least likely to want to attend university if neither parent desires this. (Obviously, those teenagers whose parents disagree on this issue should fall between these two extremes.)

Party Imagery Sets
For the political party imagery example, the relevant sets are those who think of the NDP as left of centre and those who are knowledgable. Neither set is clearly defined. Let's begin to rectify that, using the 1984 Canadian National Election Study (CNES) (Lambert, Brown, Curtis, Kay and Wilson, 1986). The set "places the NDP to the left of centre" could be concretized using the following question:

I would like you to use this scale which goes from left to right, with "1" being the most to the left and "7" being the most to the right.

	Left					Right	
Where would you place the federal New Democratic Party?	1	2	3	4	5	6	7

Note that response category 4 is in the centre. This physical cue might suggest to respondents that responses to the left of 4 imply placing the party to the left of centre. Hence responses of 1, 2 or 3 might fulfill the criterion of placing the federal NDP to the left of centre.

The terms *left* and *right* have not been defined, yet we have obtained a set corresponding to those who place the NDP to the left of centre. This was achieved by letting respondents choose their own meaning for "left" and "right." Although such an approach is unsatisfactory, we might agree to it as a starting point. The 1984 CNES participants were asked what the terms *left* and *right* meant to them in the context of politics and political parties. Other research has documented that many Canadians do not think in such terms. Furthermore, where they do, their image of "left" and "right" is often at variance with the academic's use of these words (Lambert et al., 1986). Considerations such as these will require further refinements in this example.

The original formulation of the party imagery argument did not specify what constitutes knowledge. As with all concepts, the term *knowledge* permits an array of possible meanings and, therefore, possible empirical manifestations. Since we would expect party imagery to be particularly strongly connected to knowledge of the political arena, let's begin with such a focus. A second question from the 1984 CNES study can be used to tap political knowledge:

We are interested in how well-known the provincial premiers are across Canada. Can you think of their names?

	Correct	Wrong	Don't Know
1. Newfoundland	1	2	8
2. Nova Scotia	1	2	8
3. Prince Edward Island	1	2	8
4. New Brunswick	1	2	8
5. Quebec	1	2	8
6. Ontario	1	2	8
7. Manitoba	1	2	8
8. Saskatchewan	1	2	8
9. Alberta	1	2	8
10. British Columbia	1	2	8

As the names of each province were read, the interviewer would circle 1 if the respondent correctly named that province's premier, 2 if the name was incorrect, and 8 if respondents replied they didn't know the name of that province's premier. We can calculate the number of correctly named premiers simply by counting the number of 1's. That is, in measuring political knowledge, we construct one piece of information out of the ten separate responses. By doing this, we purposefully ignore other aspects of the responses, such as which particular premiers were named. We judge these other aspects to be irrelevant, at least initially, to our purpose of measuring political knowledge.

Few of us would object to the assumption that the more premiers one can name, the more political knowledge one probably possesses. (Although we could all formulate alternative measures that we might prefer. Indeed, good arguments require multiple measures.) More problematic is the necessity to categorize some respondents as politically knowledgable. We could arbitrarily define as knowledgable those who recalled the names of a majority of the premiers. This example shows a major limitation of set theory: it is ill-equipped to handle events that are matters of degree. Clearly, political knowledge is a matter of degree (as is placing the NDP to the left of centre, although perhaps less obviously so). Respondents who know the names of four premiers are likely to be more knowledgable than those who can name only one. Defining "knowledgable" in set theory terms requires us to make an arbitrary distinction. Since good arguments avoid unnecessary arbitrariness, we would ordinarily not use set theory for the party imagery example. In short, defining events as sets is appropriate when distinctions in kind are made. When distinctions of degree are made, other approaches are more effective.

Figure 1.4
Venn Diagram Showing Political Knowledge as a
Subset of Placing the NDP to the Left of Centre

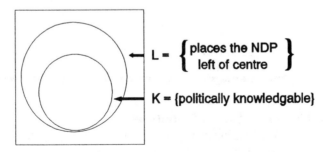

L = { places the NDP
      left of centre }

K = {politically knowledgable}

If we return to the original formulation in the party imagery example, we will find that the expectations are phrased in two somewhat incompatible ways. First I stated that only the naive would fail to place the NDP to the left of centre. This implies that *all* politically knowledgable Canadians would place the NDP to the left of centre. In Figure 1.4, I have drawn K as a subset of L. This conforms to the original assertion that knowledge is a sufficient condition for placing the NDP to the left of centre. But then I stated that knowledge merely *increases the likelihood* of perceiving the NDP as left of centre. In this latter form, it is not necessary for all knowledgable individuals to place the NDP to the left of centre. For this case the diagram should be modified as in Figure 1.5. It is clear from these examples that the Venn diagrams should reflect accurately whether one set is a subset of another.

Figure 1.5
Venn Diagram Showing Political Knowledge as Not a Subset of Placing the NDP to the Left of Centre

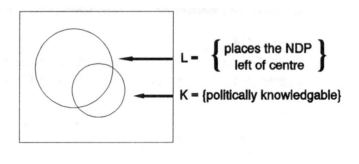

$$L = \left\{ \begin{array}{c} \text{places the NDP} \\ \text{left of centre} \end{array} \right\}$$

$K = \{\text{politically knowledgable}\}$

Null Sets and Units of Analysis
Another kind of set remains to be mentioned: the **null** (or **empty**) **set**, defined as any set having no members. The mate preference example, originally formulated at the level of individual male mate preferences, can be restated at the societal level to provide an example where a null set might be expected. At the level of individuals, the mate preference argument acknowledges that some males prefer older females. The argument at this level predicts only that, over millenia, such males will diminish since they will produce few offspring, thereby decreasing their reproductive fitness.

But, according to Buss's theory (1989), a given society could not survive over time if its male members preferred older, reproductively less capable females. Thus, at the level of societies, to find whole cultures in which males on average prefer older females would constitute a grave challenge to the biosocial interpretation. The newly defined set "societies in which males on average prefer females older than themselves" should be an empty set. This expectation is fulfilled in the thirty-three societies Buss examined.

This example shows an important feature of social science arguments: the expectations at one level of analysis, such as the level of individuals, are not necessarily the same as those at other levels, such as the levels of groups, organizations or societies. These different levels are called **units of analysis**. In the parental socialization example, the unit of analysis was the teenager-father-mother triad. In the party imagery example, the individual constituted the unit of analysis. The mate preference example was formulated at both an individual and a societal level of analysis. The unit of analysis should ordinarily be part of the definition of the event of interest.

Isolating Events with Set Operations

For the parental socialization Venn diagrams, we defined various regions that depicted combinations of matched and unmatched desires. Set operations permit us to isolate and symbolize such possibilities. Each of the four set operations (**intersection, union, complement** and **difference**) creates a new subset, which is part of the universal set. I will illustrate these operations with the parental socialization example. Since these operations are also useful definitional aids, I will define the concept of agreement in the similarity-attraction argument using these operations.

Intersection $(A \cap B)$
The intersection of sets A and B, symbolized as "A and B" or $A \cap B$, is the set of all members simultaneously belonging to *both A and B*. In Figure 1.6, the shaded portion represents the intersection. The intersection of sets D_f and D_t is a new, smaller set consisting only of those father-teenager pairs in which both desire university attendance (this corresponds to region 1 of Figure 1.2).

Union $(A \cup B)$
If we have two sets, A and B, then their union, symbolized as "A or B" or $A \cup B$, is the set of all elements that are members of *either A or B, or both*. As indicated by the shaded area in Figure 1.7, the union of D_f and D_t is a set including all teenagers who would prefer to attend university as well as all fathers who desire such a path.

Figure 1.6
The Intersection of Two Sets

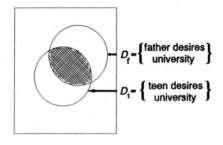

Figure 1.7
The Union of Two Sets

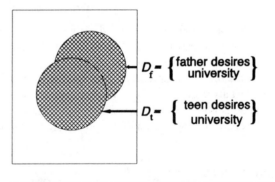

Remember that the critical phrase in intersection was *both A and B*. In union, the critical phrase is *either A or B, or both*. In other words, an intersect includes only those elements that are common to both sets; each element possesses both characteristics. Hence an intersect of A and B is always a subset of their union. That is, the number of elements in the intersection of two sets is always less than or equal to the number of elements in their union.

Complement ($\overline{A}$)

The complement of any set A, symbolized as $\overline{A}$, consists of *all elements in the universal set that are not in A*. The shaded portion of Figure 1.8 represents the complement of the set Y. The complement of Y comprises men who do not desire a younger mate. It should come as no surprise that the union of any set with its complement produces a universal set. To convince yourself of this, look at Figure 1.8 again.

Figure 1.8
The Complement of a Set

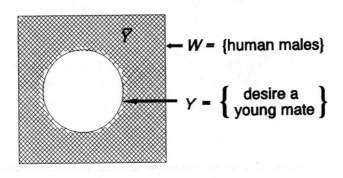

$\leftarrow$ *W* = {human males}

$Y = \left\{ \begin{array}{c} \text{desire a} \\ \text{young mate} \end{array} \right\}$

Difference (A~B)
The final operation in set theory is difference. The difference between any two sets *A* and *B* is the set that includes *all the elements of A that are not elements of B*. The symbol for this is *A~B*. (This symbol should be read as "*A* difference *B*" to keep it distinct from the arithmetic operation of subtraction.)

$D_f \sim D_t$ isolates those dyads in which the father desires his child to attend university but the teenager does not share this desire (this corresponds to region 2 of Figure 1.2). In finding the difference, the order of the two sets matters. That is, as Figure 1.9 shows, $D_f \sim D_t$ differs from $D_t \sim D_f$. In this example, $D_t \sim D_f$ consists of those pairs in which the teenager would like to attend university, but the father wishes his teenager to choose a different path (which corresponds to region 3 of Figure 1.2). Of the operations in set theory we have covered, this is the only one in which the order is critical.

By combining several operations, we could, for example, isolate those pairs in which either the father or the teenager desired university attendance, but not both of them:

$$D = (D_f \cup D_t) \sim (D_f \cap D_t) \qquad (1.1)$$

where *D* would contain the desired elements.

Figure 1.9
The Difference Between Sets

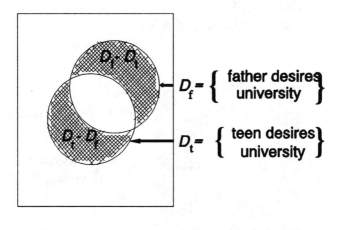

Using Set Operations to Construct Definitions

Intersects provide a possible procedure for defining agreement. Let's draw on a study of marital relations by Laing et al. (1966) for concrete examples. In their study, interest centred on husband-wife agreements and disagreements. Couples were asked to respond separately to a variety of interpersonal issues, such as whether the husband is kind to the wife. The wife was asked to respond (with a "yes" or a "no") to the phrase "He is kind to me." The husband responded to the analogous phrase, "I am kind to her." Laing et al. considered couples to agree if they gave identical responses to an issue. Two forms of agreement are therefore possible: positive agreement (*PA*) occurs when both say "yes" and negative agreement (*NA*) when both say "no." Using the symbols *Y* and *N* to stand for the responses "yes" and "no," respectively, and the subscripts *h* and *w* to distinguish the response of the husband from that of the wife, these combinations can be obtained through the following intersects:

$$PA = \{Y_h \cap Y_w\} \tag{1.2}$$

$$NA = \{N_h \cap N_w\}. \tag{1.3}$$

The first intersect represents agreement that the husband is kind to the wife, while the second represents agreement that the husband is not kind to the wife. Note that the unit of analysis here is the wife-husband dyad.

We can complete the definition of agreement on whether the husband is kind to the wife by obtaining the union of the two forms of agreement defined above. Letting A stand for agreement, we have:

$$A = \{PA \cup NA\}. \tag{1.4}$$

Substituting for PA and NA the particular intersections defined in equations 1.2 and 1.3, we can symbolize agreement as:

$$A = \{(Y_h \cap Y_w) \cup (N_h \cap N_w)\}. \tag{1.5}$$

The complement provides a convenient way to define and isolate disagreement. If we let D symbolize disagreement, we get:

$$D = \overline{A} = (\overline{PA \cup NA}). \tag{1.6}$$

Note the importance of the parentheses in the final expression. These indicate that first we must obtain the union of the two forms of agreement in order to obtain the complement and provide a definition of disagreement.

These equations exemplify some common features of mathematical notation. First, mathematical notation is simply a concise abbreviation for a sequence of operations. Second, subscripts specify particular elements or events from a larger group. Third, parentheses can alter the order in which operations are to be performed. In equation 1.5, the parentheses dictate that the two intersects are to be obtained before the union. Finally, simple set operations can be combined into more complex ones.

These definitions and operations cover the aspects of set theory necessary for our purposes. Now, let's apply set theory to some elementary statistical notions.

From Sets to Probabilities

Probability theory capitalizes on the definitions and operations of set theory. When appropriately applied to empirical events, we can calculate the likelihood of various outcomes.

We attach probabilities only to those empirical events that have been systematically observed under identical circumstances, where each observation represents a single unambiguous outcome. The observations must be infinitely repeatable, at least conceptually, with only one outcome per trial, although the outcome may be different each time. Some examples should suffice to clarify these restrictions:

- Flip a coin three times and record the number of heads obtained. This process can be repeated indefinitely. Each time, one of four unambiguous outcomes will be obtained (0, 1, 2 or 3 heads).
- Residents of Canada are chosen at random[3] and asked to name the provincial premiers. The number correctly identified is recorded. Each time this is done, one of eleven outcomes would be obtained, ranging from 0 to 10 correct responses.
- The Public Archives of Nova Scotia houses the marriage "slips" giving information on each marriage recorded in the province since approximately 1860. Take any marriage slip at random and note whether the bride and groom were born in the same community. These observations can be repeated indefinitely. Each time, one of two outcomes should occur: the bride and groom were born in either the same or different communities.[4]

These three characteristics of observations—systematic procedure, repeatability, and unambiguous outcomes—define events that are amenable to statistical analysis.

Each time we observe an event, a number of outcomes are possible. The number and nature of the outcomes is known in advance; what is unknown is which particular outcome will occur. We can consider each outcome to represent an element of a particular set. We make a congruence between set theory and probability theory by defining all the distinct, possible outcomes as a set. To distinguish this set from others, it is traditionally called the **sample space**. The sample space is to probability theory what the universal set is to set theory.

Keep in mind that we, the researchers, define and create the sample space. For any given phenomenon, a variety of sample spaces are possible. The sample space for party imagery could be the responses of 1 through 7 on the left-right scale (if we exclude from consideration those who did not provide an answer). If our concern is with whether a response was left of centre, we could collapse the sample space of seven possible outcomes so there are only two possible outcomes: left of centre (combining scores of 1 through 3) and its complement (collapsing scores of 4 through 7). Both versions are permissable sample spaces.

The Concept of Probability

Symbols of Equality and Inequality

Symbol	Meaning
=	is equal to
≠	is not equal to
≈	is approximately equal to
<	is less than
≤	is less than or equal to
>	is greater than
≥	is greater than or equal to

Statistical logic is inseparable from the concept of probability. All of us understand, at least loosely, what is meant by probability. We know that when tossing a coin, for example, the **odds** of getting a head is about one in two. This is because there are precisely two outcomes (heads or tails), one of which must occur. Hence the odds of getting a head are one in two (assuming the coin is honest, which means that the two outcomes are equally likely). The odds of "one in two" can be expressed as a ratio, giving us a probability of 0.50. In this next section I will present some of the properties of classical probability theory, to show more clearly what probability means, how it is computed, what it tells us and what it doesn't. We will look at probability within the context of sets, where it refers to the likelihood of an outcome of a particular set occurring. The symbol used to refer to the probability of an event A is *p(A)* and is read as "the probability of A."

Probability theory is based on three axioms, from which other properties can be derived. The first axiom asserts that probabilities are never negative. This is symbolized as:

$$p(A) \geq 0 \tag{1.7}$$

and read as "the probability of A is greater than or equal to zero." This axiom conforms to our basic understanding of probability, that there is no such thing as a negative likelihood. If an outcome is impossible, its probability is zero.

Second, the probability of the sample space S is 1.0:

$$p(S) = 1.0. \tag{1.8}$$

This axiom mathematically expresses the notion that *one* of the possible outcomes in the sample space (of all possible outcomes) *has* to occur.

To understand the third axiom, it is necessary to introduce the concept of **mutually exclusive events**. Two events are mutually exclusive if they cannot occur simultaneously. This idea is perfectly captured in the saying "You can't eat your cake and have it too." In any given election, voting for the Progressive Conservative (PC) candidate, for example, mutually excludes legally voting for any other candidate. The intersect operation can be used to test for mutual exclusiveness. If the intersection of two sets produces the null set, then the two sets are mutually exclusive. That is, if $A \cap B = 0$, then A and B are mutually exclusive. Figure 1.10 illustrates mutually exclusive events.

Figure 1.10
Mutually Exclusive Sets

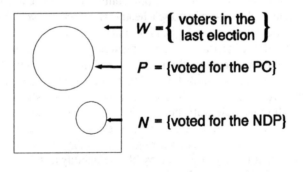

$W = \left\{ \begin{array}{l} \text{voters in the} \\ \text{last election} \end{array} \right\}$

$P = \{\text{voted for the PC}\}$

$N = \{\text{voted for the NDP}\}$

The third axiom states that the probability of the union of mutually exclusive events equals the sum of the probabilities of the individual events. If A mutually excludes B,

$$p(A \cup B) = p(A) + p(B). \tag{1.9}$$

From these formal properties, together with the rules of set theory, we can derive other rules of probability. In this next section I will present a proof for what is known as the **addition rule of probabilities**:

$$p(A \cup B) = p(A) + p(B) - p(A \cap B). \tag{1.10}$$

This is the general formula for finding the probability of the union of sets, regardless of whether they are mutually exclusive. I will now present this proof to provide an example of how statisticians derive rules of probability from the basic axioms. Should that not interest you, this next section can safely be skipped.

Proving the Addition Rule

The third probability axiom gave us a formula for finding the probability of the union of mutually exclusive sets. Using this axiom and a bit of algebra, we will derive the general formula for unions of sets regardless of whether they are mutually exclusive or not. That is, we will prove equation 1.10.

Figure 1.11 illustrates the union of any two sets A and B. Throughout the proof, try to visualize the steps by referring to this figure.

Figure 1.11
Making the Union of Sets Mutually Exclusive

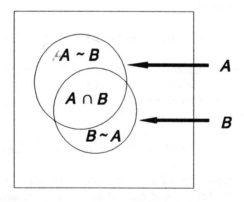

Imagine taking all the elements from A and adding them to B. Notice that if we were to do that, we would have counted the elements contained in $A \cap B$ twice; hence we would have to subtract these elements once. Now let's prove this formally.

From the diagram, we can see that the set A can be described as the union of two mutually exclusive sets, namely $A{\sim}B$ and $A \cap B$. That is,

$$A = (A \sim B) \cup (A \cap B). \qquad (1.11)$$

This now permits us to say that :

$$p(A) = p(A\sim B) + p(A \cap B). \qquad (1.12)$$

Having described the set A as the union of two mutually exclusive components, this assignment of probabilities is correct by the third probability axiom. Again, we are simply expressing the probability of A in a more complex but still accurate way.

Doing precisely the same thing with set B permits us to describe the probability of B as:

$$p(B) = p(B\sim A) + p(A \cap B). \qquad (1.13)$$

Keeping in mind the diagram on the previous page and how we redefined the sets A and B, we see that the union of A and B can now be expressed as the union of the three mutually exclusive sets: $(A\sim B)$, $(A \cap B)$ and $(B\sim A)$. That is,

$$(A \cup B) = (A\sim B) \cup (A \cap B) \cup (B\sim A). \qquad (1.14)$$

Having expressed the union of A and B as the union of three mutually exclusive sets, we can, by the third probability axiom, simply add the probabilities of these three sets, giving us the equation:

$$p(A \cup B) = p(A\sim B) + p(A \cap B) + p(B\sim A). \qquad (1.15)$$

Strange as it may seem at first, to simplify this equation, we must first make it more complex. To do this, let's add $p(A \cap B)$ to both sides of equation 1.15 (remember, whatever we do to one side of the equation, we must do to the other). This gives us:

$$p(A \cup B) + p(A \cap B) = p(A\sim B) + p(A \cap B) + p(B\sim A) + p(A \cap B). \quad (1.16)$$

The right-hand side of this equation now represents the cumbersome way of expressing the probabilities of A and B which we developed at the beginning. So let's substitute them into the equation to get:

$$p(A \cup B) + p(A \cap B) = p(A) + p(B). \qquad (1.17)$$

Finally, subtracting $p(A \cap B)$ back out from both sides of the equation, we get the desired result of equation 1.10.

This equation shows us how to find the probability of the union of any two sets, regardless of whether they are mutually exclusive.[5]

This proof shows that we can derive new probability rules from the basic probability axioms and the rules of set theory. It is now possible to move still closer to the meaning of probability by learning how to attach actual probability statements to events.

Assigning Probabilities to Events

Probability theory was born out of gambling, which involves games of chance. Such games have built-in simplifying features, the most important being that each element in the sample space can be considered equally likely. The probability of any event in such cases is simply the number of outcomes that correspond to the event of interest, over the total number of outcomes. That is,

$$p(A) = \frac{n(A)}{N} \qquad (1.18)$$

where $n(A)$ = number of elements corresponding to the outcome of interest, and
N = total number of outcomes in the sample space.

This is how we arrived at the assertion that the probability of getting a tail is 0.50. When flipping a coin, only two outcomes are possible ($N = 2$), one of which is a tail ($n(A) = 1$). Hence the probability of obtaining a tail in a single flip is 1/2 or 0.50.

This "classical" or theoretical approach to probabilities is seldom useful in developing social science arguments. Fortunately there is an empirical alternative, known as **Bernoulli's Theorem**, for assigning realistic probabilities to the outcomes of experiments.

Bernoulli, a late 17th Century mathematician, postulated a theorem which provides an empirical method of establishing probabilities. He stated that, under certain conditions, the observed **relative frequency** of an event constitutes a reasonable approximation of its probability. The conditions are: (1) the relative frequencies must be based on a large number of observations, (2) the observations must be made independently of each other and (3) they must be made under identical conditions. If we let $f(A)$ denote the frequency of the event A, and N the number of independent observations, then the estimate of the probability of the event A is its relative frequency, which can be written as:

$$p(A) \approx \frac{f(A)}{N}. \qquad (1.19)$$

As equation 1.19 indicates, *relative frequency* is just the proportion of cases in which a particular event occurs. If we flip a coin one thousand times and obtain 480 tails, the estimated probability of obtaining a tail is 480/1,000 or 0.48.

Strangers and Independence

The requirement of **independence** ensures that the outcome in one trial, or case, in no way influences the outcome of any other. Comparing a stranger's opinions with one's own provides an analogy for the concept of independence. By definition, a total stranger cannot have influenced our points of view. We may happen to agree on some topics and disagree on others, but whether we agree on any given topic is "a matter of chance." The two points of view are therefore independent of each other. Ordinarily we agree on more topics with friends than with strangers, since we influence each other's viewpoints. At the same time, however, we probably agree on more topics with a stranger than with an enemy, since incompatible viewpoints is one reason for animosity (if similar others attract, dissimilar others can be expected to repel). Thus the level of similarity we would expect with a perfect stranger captures the statistical meaning of independence.

In order to apply Bernoulli's Theorem, we must conduct empirical studies to get an estimate of the probability of an event. Furthermore, the probability that we assign is only an estimate—it may not be accurate. Fortunately, sound statistical methods can be used to evaluate how good any estimate is likely to be; these methods will be discussed later.

First, let's apply Bernoulli's Theorem to a hypothetical situation that will reveal some of the characteristics of this approach. Suppose we are interested in determining the probability of any Canadian adult knowing the name of their premier. We could obtain systematic information to get an estimate of the probability. This might consist of simply asking an adult to name their current premier. If we repeated the observation five times and found that three adults knew their premier's name, our estimate of the probability would be 3/5 or 0.6. However, we certainly wouldn't put much faith in this estimate. Now let's say that we randomly surveyed 100 Canadians and found that 42 of them knew the name of their premier. This would give us an estimated probability of 42/100 or 0.4.[6] If I repeated the observation 1,074 times and received the correct answer 823 times, then my estimate of the probability would be 823/1,074 or 0.77. I would be more confident of this last estimate since the number of trials is greater; although it is possible that this estimate is less accurate than the first one, it is extremely unlikely. Additionally, the estimate is likely to be more accurate when the sample is more representative of the population being surveyed.

This is the tenuous bridge that Bernoulli's Theorem provides between empirical events and statistical concepts: the relative frequency of empirical events provides an estimate of the statistical concept of probability. For this estimate to be perfectly accurate requires two things: an infinite number of trials or observations, and that these trials be conducted independently under exactly the same conditions. The first of these conditions can never be met. That is one reason no study can ever be said to have proven an assertion. We always remain somewhat uncertain about the accuracy of our answers. But we can make the probable error tolerable by increasing the number of trials. Violation of the second condition is potentially more disastrous in its possible consequences. There are concrete ways to establish how accurate an estimate based on a small number of independent observations is likely to be. However, there is no statistical way to assess the effect of not having independent observations under identical conditions. The purpose of random sampling is precisely to ensure the independence requirement of Bernoulli's Theorem.

Random Sampling

A **sample** is any subset of observations from a population, where the population consists of all possible observations on the topic under discussion. A **random sample** is one obtained in such a manner that the observations are independent. This criterion is satisfied when all elements in the population have a known probability of being included in the sample. Remember that only if the observations are independent can Bernoulli's Theorem be applied. It is to insure independence that techniques of random sampling were developed (although there are additional reasons, such as cost savings and representativeness). Random sampling is designed to produce independent observations. In other words, when we make one observation, we want to make sure that having made that particular observation does not affect which other observations we make. In its simplest form, we list all possible observations pertaining to a given problem (the population), numbering them sequentially. Then we decide how many observations we require (the sample size). Finally, we use a selection procedure to make independent selections from this universe or population. One procedure relies on a table of random numbers. By definition, there are no systematic patterns in random numbers. Since there is no systematic pattern, using them to select a sample of observations results in one observation not influencing the selection of another.

There are many modifications to simple random sampling which were developed for special circumstances such as reducing the cost. However, the basic purpose of all types of random sampling is to enable us to apply Bernoulli's Theorem.

Although random observations are crucial for estimating probabilities, solid arguments rest much more on consistent patterns. That is, we search for alternative ways of assessing a situation of interest. Our confidence is increased to the extent that the alternative assessments reinforce each other.

The Conditional Probability of Joint Events:
Independence and Dependence

At this point we know how to obtain probabilities for any event, and for the union of two events even when they are not mutually exclusive. Our task now is to find the probability of the intersection between events. An intersection can be referred to as a **joint event**.

Two solutions exist, one of which we already know. Remember that an intersection creates a new subset which is part of the sample space. As such, it is no different than any other set; hence its probability could be obtained in exactly the same way as the probability of any event A. Using the relative frequency method, simply count the number of times a particular joint event occurs and divide by the total number of attempts or trials. That is, for any events A and B,

$$p(A \cap B) = \frac{f(A \cap B)}{N}. \tag{1.20}$$

Suppose we wanted to estimate the probability of a Canadian adult knowing both the names of at least half the provincial premiers *and* thinking that the NDP is left of centre. The 1984 CNES survey could be used for this purpose. A total of 1,750 respondents attempted to name the premiers and place the NDP on a left-right continuum. Of these, 579 knew both the names of at least half the premiers and placed the NDP to the left of centre. Therefore, our estimate of the probability of this joint event is 579/1,750 or 0.33.

Before developing a second way of finding the probability of an intersect or joint event, we must introduce the concept of **conditional probability**, which focuses on the probability of an event within a particular subset (for example, the probability of placing the NDP to the left of centre among Canadians who can name at least half the premiers). The symbol for conditional probability is $p(B|A)$, which is read as "the probability of B given A." This concept will provide us with our first formal method of establishing a statistical relationship. Let's estimate the conditional probability of perceiving the NDP as left of centre, given that at least half the premiers can be named.

Originally we postulated that all politically knowledgable Canadians would place the NDP to the left of centre. At this point we don't know whether this proposition is true, so we diagram the general case, permitting it to be false. The set K (from *Knowledge*) consists of Canadians who know the names of at least half the current premiers, while those in set L (from *Left*) place the NDP left of centre. We are interested, however, only in those who are politically knowledgable, i.e., those who know the names of at least half the premiers. Since we are excluding Canadians who are not politically knowledgable, we can ignore all cases contained in $\overline{K}$, the complement of K.

We therefore change our Venn diagram (Figure 1.12) to reflect this **reduced sample space**, which contains only those Canadians who know the names of at least half the premiers (Figure 1.13). *Within this sample space*, those who placed the NDP to the left of centre is given by $K \cap L$. We can therefore apply equation 1.18 to calculate its probability, simply modifying the symbols to reflect that the sample space is the set K and that the subset of interest is the intersect of K and L. Doing this we get:

$$p(L|K) = \frac{f(K \cap L)}{\cdot f(K)}. \qquad (1.21)$$

Figure 1.12
Party Imagery Venn Diagram

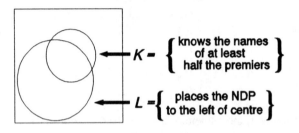

$K = \left\{ \begin{array}{c} \text{knows the names} \\ \text{of at least} \\ \text{half the premiers} \end{array} \right\}$

$L = \left\{ \begin{array}{c} \text{places the NDP} \\ \text{to the left of centre} \end{array} \right\}$

Figure 1.13
Reduced Sample Space

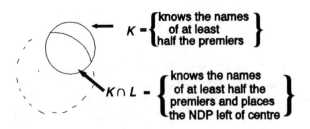

$K = \left\{ \begin{array}{c} \text{knows the names} \\ \text{of at least} \\ \text{half the premiers} \end{array} \right\}$

$K \cap L = \left\{ \begin{array}{c} \text{knows the names} \\ \text{of at least half the} \\ \text{premiers and places} \\ \text{the NDP left of centre} \end{array} \right\}$

A total of 738 Canadians knew the names of at least five premiers, and 579 of them placed the NDP to the left of centre. Therefore, our best estimate of $p(L|K)$ is:

$$p(L|K) = \frac{579}{738} = 0.78.$$

This shows that the likelihood of a politically knowledgable Canadian placing the NDP to the left of centre is high, but more than one in five fail to do so. Being politically knowledgable, as defined here, is not a sufficient condition for always placing the NDP to the left of centre.

Note that in developing the equation for conditional probabilities, we have simply applied an old logic to a new situation and expressed that logic with a set of symbols more appropriate to that situation.

Using the generic symbols A and B, the equation for conditional probabilities becomes:

$$p(A|B) = \frac{f(A \cap B)}{f(B)}.$$

Dividing both the numerator and the denominator of the right-hand side of this equation by N permits us to express the conditional probability as:

$$p(A|B) = \frac{\dfrac{f(A \cap B)}{N}}{\dfrac{f(B)}{N}} = \frac{p(A \cap B)}{p(B)}. \tag{1.22}$$

Since it is arbitrary which of the two sets is labelled A and which B, it follows that the formula above could be rewritten to express the conditional probability of B given A:

$$p(B|A) = \frac{p(A \cap B)}{p(A)}. \tag{1.23}$$

Once we label the sets, which of the two formulas we use is important, because the formulas provide answers to different questions. For example, returning to the party imagery example above, $p(K|L)$ refers to the probability of being politically knowledgable given that the NDP was placed to the left of centre. This differs from $p(L|K)$ which designates the probability of placing the NDP to the left of centre among the politically knowledgable.

These two formulas also provide us with two new ways of obtaining the probability of a joint event or an intersect. Since $p(A \cap B)$ occurs in each of the formulas, all we have to do is solve algebraically for the intersect, which means that we manipulate the formula until we have isolated $p(A \cap B)$ on the left-hand side of the equation. Let's start with equation 1.23,

$$p(B|A) = \frac{p(A \cap B)}{p(A)}.$$

Multiplying both sides of this equation by $p(A)$ and cancelling produces:

$$p(A) \cdot p(B|A) = p(A \cap B). \tag{1.24}$$

Exchanging the two sides of the equation results in:

$$p(A \cap B) = p(A) \cdot p(B|A). \tag{1.25}$$

In the same fashion, we could also show that:

$$p(A \cap B) = p(B) \cdot p(A|B). \tag{1.26}$$

In other words, if we know *either* the probability of A or B *and* the conditional probability of either "A given B" or "B given A," we can also find the probability of the intersect of A and B. We seldom are in a position to use this formula, since we rarely know the conditional probabilities. This method of finding the probability of an intersect is of much greater importance in connection with the concept of **independence**.

Independence

Remember from the discussion of Bernoulli's Theorem that independent events simply do not influence each other: in other words, whether event A occurs does not affect whether or not event B will occur. How can we express this definition statistically? One way is with the concept of conditional probability. If the events A and B do not influence each other, then it must be true that:

$$p(A|B) = p(A) \tag{1.27}$$

and that:

$$p(B|A) = p(B). \tag{1.28}$$

The first equation tells us that knowing that event B has occurred does not change the probability of event A occurring, and the second equation states that knowing that A has occurred does not alter the probability of event B occurring. This captures statistical independence precisely.

Obtaining the probability of a joint event is simple when the events are independent. From equation 1.26, we know that the probability of an intersect is:

$$p(A \cap B) = p(A) \cdot p(B|A). \qquad (1.29)$$

Substituting equation 1.28 into this equation we get:

$$p(A \cap B) = p(A) \cdot p(B) \qquad (1.30)$$

if and only if A and B are independent.

When events are independent, their joint probability equals the product of their individual probabilities. If equation 1.30 does not yield the correct probability of the intersect, then we know that the events in question are **dependent,** and that is precisely what we mean by a statistical relation. If $p(A \cap B) = p(A) \cdot p(B)$ holds true, in other words, then there is no statistical relationship between A and B. Alternatively, if $p(B|A) \neq p(B)$, then there is a relationship between A and B.

Let's return to our political knowledge example. We showed earlier that political knowledge is not a sufficient condition for placing the NDP to the left of centre. We should therefore modify this assertion to state that political knowledge increases the likelihood of placing the NDP to the left of centre; i.e., we expect $p(L|K) > p(L)$, which implies that political knowledge and placing the NDP to the left of centre are dependent events. Previously we calculated $p(L|K)$ to equal 0.78. Since a total of 1,158 out of 1,750 respondents classified the NDP to the left of centre, our best estimate of the probability of L is: $p(L) = 1{,}158/1{,}750 = 0.66$. Assuming that the difference between 0.66 and 0.78 is not due to sampling fluctuations, we conclude that political knowledge increases the probability of placing the NDP to the left of centre.[7]

Extending Arguments

I will devote the remainder of this chapter to elaborating the similarity-attraction argument. As a first step, I will review the empirical literature that addresses this argument. This review will show that the expected relationship between agreement and attraction has been documented in many different studies and that the relationship holds even with different ways of defining and measuring similarity and attraction. Both of these features strengthen the argument considerably. Nevertheless, the literature review also reveals that most of the studies were conducted in laboratory settings between strangers. This is a weakness. To address this weakness, I will, as a second step, test the similarity-attraction hypothesis in ongoing relationships among a sample of married couples. Finally, I will present a rival interpretation for the relationship between similarity and attraction and put it to the test.

Generalization to Different Populations and Measures

A review of the literature reveals that most of the studies on the similarity-attraction hypothesis have used what has become known as "the phantom stranger" design. I will describe this design in detail, both for its ingenious way of measuring agreement and to acquaint you with some of the typical features of laboratory experiments. This experiment consists of a series of steps:

1.   A captive audience[8] (such as university students in a particular class) is invited to participate in a study. The exact purpose of the study is veiled, and simply described as "to determine the extent to which one person can form valid judgments about another person just by knowing a few of his [sic] attitudes" (Byrne, 1971:51).

2.   Those who agree to participate are asked to fill out a "Survey of Attitudes" questionnaire. As the name suggests, this questionnaire contains many attitudinal statements, and respondents are asked to indicate the extent to which they agree with these statements. A typical statement might be, "Racial integration in public schools is a mistake." From the responses, the volunteers' own attitudes are known. An appointment is then made for a laboratory session.

3.   Individual laboratory sessions are scheduled to occur several months after the "Survey of Attitudes" questionnaire has been completed. The time lapse is necessary to minimize the likelihood that the "subjects" (as volunteers in laboratory experiments are usually called) will remember what responses they gave; this is also the reason the questionnaire is lengthier than actually necessary.

4.   When subjects arrive at the laboratory, they are told that the study involves same-sexed pairs and that their partner for this particular session has not yet arrived. While purportedly waiting for the partner to arrive, the subject is handed a brief profile of the partner. In this profile, the partner's attitudes towards a number of issues are described. The attitude statements are a subset of the ones the subject responded to initially.

5.   These profiles have been manipulated so the attitudes endorsed by the partner are identical to those of some subjects and different for others. That is, the partner's profile is constructed to constitute a given level of agreement with the subject's viewpoints. The laboratory assistant is not aware of which "treatment" the subject is given. This decreases the likelihood that the laboratory assistant will unintentionally influence the subject in the next step. Such precautions create "double-blind" experiments, where neither the subject nor the administrator of the experiment is aware of what treatment is being administered in any given instance. The treatments consisted of presenting partners whose attitudes were identical, opposite or somewhere in between when compared with those the subjects had reported several months earlier as their own viewpoints. This becomes the measure of agreement.

6. The subjects are then asked to give their impression of the partner in response to six questions. Two of the items are used to measure attraction: the extent to which the subjects feel they "would probably like this person" and the extent to which they feel they would "enjoy working with this person in an experiment."

7. At this point, the subject is told the true purpose of the experiment and that there is no partner. Because the partner never existed, these studies became known as the "phantom stranger" experiments.

Once all the laboratory sessions are completed, the researchers test whether those subjects who had been presented with an agreeing phantom stranger were more likely to state they "would probably like" or "would enjoy working with" their partner than were those subjects who had been presented with a disagreeing partner. Invariably, the predicted relationship between similarity (attitudinal agreement) and attraction (a combination of stated "liking" and "enjoy working with") was found.

Several important steps were taken to strengthen the similarity-attraction argument. First, the relationship was tested on a variety of different populations: children and adolescents (Byrne and Griffitt, 1966); female clerical workers (Krauss, 1966); hospitalized male schizophrenic and alcoholic patients (Byrne et al., 1969); and adults from other cultures, such as India and Japan (Byrne et al., 1971). Agreement has also been studied in conjunction with varying characteristics of the other, such as the other's sex, race, physical attractiveness and emotional health. An independent agreement effect has generally been found in all these studies.

Second, the predicted relationship has been found using a variety of approaches to measuring agreement. It holds for paper-and-pencil tests (Laing et al., 1966), for audio and visual presentation (Peterson, 1969) and for agreement observed, produced or manipulated in face-to-face interaction (McWhirter and Jecker, 1967). The range of topics on which agreement has been measured ranges from "trivial" opinions to basic values (Byrne, London and Griffitt, 1968), and from impersonal opinions about what others think (Byrne, 1971:112) to personally relevant judgments about self (Clore and Baldridge, 1970). In each, the expected positive relationship between agreement and attraction has been found.

Finally, research on the generality of the attraction response has not been as proliferous as that on agreement. Most studies use a paper-and-pencil measure of attraction. The most frequently used measure is Byrne's (1971) Interpersonal Judgement Scale. This is the two-item scale referred to earlier that requires respondents to indicate how much they like and how much they think they would like to work with a given person. Other measures of attraction that have been used are sociometric choices (Newcomb, 1956), social distance scales (Schwartz, 1966), willingness to help another person (Moss, 1969), and voluntary physical proximity of individuals (Byrne, Baskett and Hodges, 1971). For each of these measures, a relationship between agreement and attraction has been found.

Although there are better and worse definitions and measures of concepts such as attraction, none are perfect. For this reason, arguments must be tested using a variety of measures.

The Parsimony Principle: Generalization to Different Domains

The empirical studies reviewed above constitute an impressive extension of the similarity-attraction hypothesis. Nevertheless, this review also revealed a major weakness. The studies were usually conducted in minimal-information settings such as a laboratory. According to the **parsimony principle**, an argument is more parsimonious when it accounts for a greater variety of phenomena. The similarity-attraction hypothesis is more parsimonious if it can be applied to long-term relationships such as marriage, in addition to first contacts between strangers in minimal-information settings.

Can the similarity-attraction hypothesis be applied to marital relations? To find out, we need to consider how agreement and attraction would manifest themselves within a marriage. Earlier, in the context of defining agreement through set operations, I referred to a study by Laing et al. (1966). In that study, Laing and his co-workers were interested, among other things, in the relationship between interpersonal agreement and marital problems. Their measure of agreement raises no difficulties, since I have already shown that agreement on opinions is the usual method of concretizing similarity. More problematic is the concept of attraction. A reasonable argument can be made that marital difficulties are an expression of low attraction. That is, I could argue that couples who are minimally attracted to each other would experience marital difficulties. Laing's data is relevant here since it consisted of twelve couples who were seeking marital counselling. Laing called these "disturbed" couples. These were matched with ten "non-disturbed" couples who were similar to the disturbed couples in such things as length of marriage, number of children and educational level. However, their family doctor considered them satisfied in their marriage. If we are correct in our assertion that the non-disturbed couples are more attracted to each other than the disturbed couples, then we can test the similarity-attraction hypothesis with this data. We would expect non-disturbed couples to agree more than disturbed ones.

Demolishing Arguments: Rival Interpretations

Every social scientific interpretation of a given event has an equally plausible rival interpretation. To the extent that this statement is true, an undesirable state of affairs exists that we must attempt to rectify. Here I will illustrate part of the process by which this can be done.

Berger and Kellner (1964) provide an interpretation radically different from the reinforcement theory just discussed for the prediction that disturbed couples will exhibit less agreement than non-disturbed couples. They argue that marriage is a process of "joint reality construction." Simplifying somewhat, a joint reality manifests itself in agreements brought about by face-to-face interaction. Part of dyadic, or couple, communication is a negotiation for common definitions and evaluations for a variety of issues. Clearly, this communicative process typifies some couples more than others. Berger and Kellner would argue that "successful" marriages are those where dyadic communication has created a joint reality. Couples who have failed to produce a joint reality (i.e., those characterized by disagreement) should experience marital difficulties. Thus we have rival interpretations: reinforcement theory versus joint reality construction.

Before we explore these alternatives further, we must first show that the predicted relationship between similarity and attraction does in fact hold. That is, first we must show that disagreement and having a disturbed marriage are related, or dependent. If they are related, then (by the definition of dependence) we should find that:

$$p(Agreement|Disturbed) \neq p(Agreement).$$

In the actual data, our best estimate for $p(Agreement|Disturbed)$ is 0.66, while the $p(Agreement)$ is 0.77. If we assume that the difference between these two estimates is not due to sampling fluctuation (and Laing et al. report that it is not), the prediction is fulfilled. Note that the *direction* of the difference is as predicted, with less agreement characterizing the disturbed couples than is generally the case.

Unfortunately, the argument frequently ends here, with the empirical findings remaining consistent with both interpretations. To test the interpretations themselves, it is necessary to examine the joint reality argument more closely. Remember that the specific mechanism that supposedly produced the agreement was dyadic communication. This mechanism logically should produce another outcome, namely greater understanding of one's partner's point of view.

Let's define *understanding* as the ability to "know" what one's partner's point of view is. Taking the same example of the issue "is kind to," one can measure the husband's understanding of the wife's point of view by first asking the wife whether she thinks the husband is kind to her. Then we ask the husband how he thinks his wife would respond to that question. If his prediction of her response matches her response, we would classify this as an instance of understanding; otherwise we would say the husband misunderstands his wife on this issue. And indeed the data corroborate this expectation. The $p(Understanding|Disturbed) = 0.69$; the $p(Understanding) = 0.78$.

The important point is that the joint reality construction interpretation provides us with an additional prediction, namely that understanding is greater among non-disturbed than among disturbed couples. This additional prediction is not immediately derivable from reinforcement theory. This latter interpretation has provided no reason to believe that understanding is intrinsically reinforcing. With respect to marriage, the joint reality interpretation would be more parsimonious than reinforcement theory, in that it would make the additional prediction that:

$$p(Understanding|Disturbed) < p(Understanding).$$

To appreciate the next step of the argument, I need to discuss what I have called the "fallacy of assumed similarity." Ichheiser (1970), among others, argues that humans create an illusion of understanding through the simple device of perceiving significant others as similar to themselves. When others agree with us, we appear to understand their points of view. The observed greater understanding among non-disturbed couples may constitute nothing more than an artifact of the already-documented greater agreement. If that is the case, the finding concerning greater understanding among non-disturbed couples does not constitute additional evidence, and the joint reality construction interpretation would not be more parsimonious. To test whether the fallacy of assumed similarity has any merit, we must test whether understanding is higher for agreements than for disagreements.

For the data of Laing et al., the estimated probability of understanding on issues on which there is agreement is 0.93. On issues on which there is disagreement, however, the probability of understanding is only 0.36. Thus illusory understanding, rather than genuine knowledge, is a plausible interpretation of the observed findings.

We need not stop at mere plausibility. We can devise a more stringent test of the joint reality thesis. If non-disturbed couples communicate more to negotiate a joint reality, then it follows that in the process of their negotiations they would be more likely to uncover and become aware of their disagreements. That is, we must reduce the sample space to include only instances of disagreement. In this reduced sample space, we have the prediction that understanding of disagreements is greater among non-disturbed than among disturbed couples. If we let the abbreviation UD stand for the set "understanding of disagreements," and C_n for the set "non-disturbed couples," the expectation is:

$$p(UD|C_n) > p(UD).$$

The data show the exact opposite to be the case. The probability of understanding disagreement among the non-disturbed couples is 0.27, whereas the overall probability of understanding disagreements was shown earlier to be 0.36. If the assumption that communication generates greater understanding of the other's point of view is reasonable, then this finding severely damages the joint reality construction thesis.

These findings illustrate what has been coined the **fallacy of affirming the consequent**. If a theory predicts a certain result, obtaining that result does not imply that the theory must be correct, because many other theories might predict the same result.

The Absolute Level Fallacy

Let me end this chapter on a cautionary note. Recall that I documented that disturbed couples agree on about two out of three issues (i.e., $p(Agreement|Disturbed = 0.66)$). Some might be tempted to conclude that such a high level of agreement shows that disturbed couples are *not* prone to disagree. In the context of the similarity-attraction argument, this would be a fallacious conclusion, because it treats numbers in an absolute sense. That is, it considers disagreements to be "low" if they constitute less than 50 percent. But the absolute level of agreement is irrelevant. It is the relative level of agreement that is important. Stated differently, the crucial consideration is the proportion of disagreements among disturbed couples relative to non-disturbed couples.

Although the absolute level of agreement is important in a variety of contexts, it is irrelevant to the similarity-attraction hypothesis. Stated boldly, a report of the absolute level of a phenomena in a group can never provide relevant information about the relationship between events.

Summary

- Arguments that postulate connections between events must be translated into terms that permit direct observation. Set theory provides one avenue for this task.
- Sets and the operations of union, intersection, complement and difference are particularly appropriate as definitional aids when the events of interest are qualitative.
- When observations are collected using random sampling techniques, relative frequencies become reasonable estimates of probabilities. This permits the application of probability theory to the observations. The number of observations is therefore of less importance than the manner in which they were collected.
- The statistical concept of conditional probability provides a first approach to assessing whether two events are related. If two events are related, then the conditional probability will differ from the unconditional probability. Conditional probabilities were used to show that political knowledge was related to party imagery; they were also used to show that disturbed couples are less likely to agree than non-disturbed couples.
- No single study is sufficient for any argument. This is one reason a review of the literature is necessary. The review of the empirical literature also shows the different ways events can be viewed. The phantom stranger experiments, for example, provide a novel way of constructing agreements and disagreements.
- The concern in arguments is not so much with whether they ultimately are correct, but with whether they are fruitful. Fruitful arguments are parsimonious. A wide range of phenomena behave as expected from the argument.
- Arguments create expectations that certain events will be related, and they

provide an interpretation for those expected relationships. When a predicted relationship is found, it does *not* imply that the interpretation is also correct (although it increases the plausibility of the argument). To assume that it does would be to commit the fallacy of affirming the consequent because any observed relationship is consistent with many interpretations.

- Since rival interpretations are ever-present, a main ingredient of a good argument is the demolition of its chief competitors. This frequently takes the forms of: (a) inferring additional expectations from the rival interpretation and (b) showing that these additional expectations are not supported. This was done with the joint reality construction interpretation of the relationship between agreement and marital difficulties. It was argued that, if the joint reality construction interpretation had merit, then the non-disturbed couples should understand their disagreements better than the disturbed couples. Since the exact opposite was found, the plausibility of the joint reality construction interpretation was weakened.

Notes

1. The official definition is more elaborate than indicated here. Nevertheless, our definition is sufficiently complete for the purpose at hand.
2. At the same time we must not forget that the sets we draw may blind us to other, perhaps more important, questions. Having drawn the three sets the way we did, for example, hides the possibility that socialization to the path of university attendance may be a gendered phenomenon. The influence of parents on boys' desires to attend university may be different from their influence on girls' desires.
3. To the uninitiated, the concept of random observation might imply haphazard selection. Just the opposite is the case: random selection follows precise rules which remove the possibility of the researcher affecting which particular residents are selected. More detail on this concept is provided later in this chapter.
4. A third outcome is actually possible; namely one where the community of birth is illegible or not recorded. Usually such instances are ignored by treating them as "missing cases." The more of these there are, the more skeptical we should be about subsequent conclusions. We will return to the problem of missing data on several occasions.
5. At this point, try to derive the formula on your own. If you cannot do it, read the proof again and then try.
6. The number of digits that we report for estimated probabilities reflects roughly the level of accuracy. For numbers based on one hundred or fewer observations, I report only one significant digit. For this reason, 42/100 is rounded to 0.4.
7. It is possible that the difference between 0.66 and 0.78 is not a genuine difference, but one that arose out of the sampling fluctuations that always occur

when using empirical estimates of probabilities. In Chapter 5 we will learn how to assess this possibility.

8. Ethical considerations require that members of a captive audience who do not wish to participate in the experiment are free not to. To deal with later ethical concerns, the deception concerning the purpose of the experiment must be rectified at the conclusion of the session. This, in experimental jargon, is known as "debriefing the subject."

Key Terms

absolute level fallacy: To conclude that a quantity is large or small, or that an outcome is common or uncommon, on the basis of a faulty criterion. This fallacy often occurs when we evaluate numbers in an absolute, rather than relative, sense. Example: We conclude that an outcome that occurs less than half the time is infrequent. In contrast, suppose the typical couple disagrees on 10 percent of issues; then a couple that disagrees on 20 percent of issues would properly be described as one that has frequent disagreements, i.e., the appropriate comparison is one that relates the instance at hand to typical cases.

addition rule of probabilities:

$$p(A \cup B) = p(A) + p(B) - p(A \cap B).$$

Bernoulli's Theorem: Essentially, this theorem states that if observations are made independently of each other and under identical conditions, then the long-run relative frequency of the occurrence of an event is a satisfactory estimate of the probability of that event. The impact of this theorem is to link a theoretical statistical concept (probability) to an empirical one (relative frequency). This theorem permits us to apply probability rules to empirical events.

complement ($\bar{A}$): A set theory operation which produces a set whose elements are all those not in a given set. This operation is particularly useful for constructing dichotomies, as in A versus $\bar{A}$.

conditional probability: Refers to the probability of an outcome among a particular subset of cases (referred to as the "reduced sample space") and is used to evaluate whether there is an apparent connection between events:

$$p(A|B) = \frac{p(A \cap B)}{p(B)}.$$

Examples: (1) The probability of cancer among those who smoke; (2) the probability of choosing to attend university given that one's parents desire this.

dependence: Events that are empirically connected. Using probabilities, we say two events are dependent if the occurrence of one alters the probability of the other. That is, if $p(A|B) \neq p(A)$, then dependence characterizes the two events A and B.

difference ($A \sim B$): One of the four set operations. For any two sets A and B, A *difference B* contains all those elements in A that are not in B.

element: In set theory, an element is a member of a set. These elements are either listed, or a rule is provided to determine whether a given observation is a member of a particular set.

fallacy of affirming the consequent: The unwarranted conclusion that if a finding was predicted by a theory, it proves that particular theory. Such a conclusion is unwarranted since the same finding may be consistent with many other arguments. It is more appropriate under these conditions to conclude that a theory has been strengthened.

falsifiability: An expectation or hypothesis that could, in principle, be tested, together with a set of possible empirical outcomes which, if they were to be obtained, would be considered inconsistent with the expectation, thereby weakening the argument on which it is based.

independence: The absence of a relationship between two events (the opposite of *dependence*). In probability terms, two events are independent when one event in no way alters the probability of the other event. If it can be shown that $p(A|B) = p(A)$, then events A and B are independent. In other words, knowing whether B has happened does not reduce the uncertainty about event A.

intersection: One of the operations in set theory. The intersection of sets A and B consists of all elements that belong jointly to *both* A and B. Example: If the set A is defined as all Canadians who can name the ten provincial premiers, and the set B contains all those who consider the Federal NDP to be a party to the right of the Progressive Conservative party, then their intersection includes only those Canadians who can name the ten premiers and also place the NDP to the right of the PCs.

joint event: A term synonymous with the set theory concept of intersection; it refers to outcomes that are elements of two sets. Joint events pinpoint instances that have two or more characteristics in common. Examples: (1) Males who prefer young mates, or (2) Canadians who voted for the Progressive Conservative candidate in the 1988 federal election but oppose free trade with the U.S.

mutually exclusive events: Two sets having no elements in common; i.e., the intersect between the two sets results in the null set.

null set: A set with no elements. This is set theory's way of describing an impossible event.

odds: A way of phrasing the concept of probability, used particularly in betting situations. For example, if an outcome has a probability of 0.25, its odds are 1 in 4.

operational definition: A concretization of a concept into empirical manifestations.

parsimony principle: A criterion for evaluating the relative fruitfulness of theories. If one theory explains a greater range of phenomena than another, it it more parsimonious and therefore generally preferred.

probability theory: A statistical theory that quantifies uncertainty. It is most useful when applied to settings that, in principle, permit infinite replications of observations in which probability statements are attached to outcomes of systematic observations.

random sample: A selection of cases to be observed (and on which information is to be gathered) in which the procedure used provides a known probability for every case to be included. If every case has an equal probability of being included, then it is referred to as a simple random sample. Such procedures require that all eligible cases can be identified.

reduced sample space: The operative sample space when interest focuses on a subset of the universal set. Conditional probabilities always involve reduced sample spaces, since interest focuses on the probability of an outcome among a subset of elements that share a certain characteristic.

relative frequency: The proportion of times a given outcome is obtained in all trials. If the observations are obtained independently of each other and under identical conditions, then the relative frequency of an event serves as an empirical estimate of its probability.

sample: Any selection of cases from the universal set (also called the population). If the sample is not random, then Bernoulli's Theorem, which links observed relative frequencies to probabilities, is not applicable.

sample space: The equivalent in probability theory of the universal set in set theory. The elements of the sample space include all possible outcomes of the events under systematic observation.

set: Any well-defined collection of objects. The main use of sets is to construct categories or instances that have a particular characteristic in common.

set operations: The operations of union, intersect, difference, and complement, which define distinct combinations of groupings of elements. These operations permit precise pinpointing of elements or cases with desired combinations of characteristics.

set theory: A body of mathematics through which elements can be organized into sets having common characteristics, and the relationships between these sets can be described using the set operations of union, intersection, complement, and difference.

subset: A is a subset of B if all of the elements of A are also element of B. The main use of subsets is to define instances that share a feature in addition to the ones that characterize the parent set. Example: "Males who prefer young mates" is a subset of "males." In this example, all elements of the subset share two characteristics: (1) they are male and (2) they prefer young mates. The parent set shares only the first characteristic.

tautology: A connection between two events that is true by definition; tautologies are essentially definitions masquerading as knowledge.

union $(A \cup B)$: A set operation which, for any two sets A and B, includes all the elements of either A or B, or both.

unit of analysis: The unit being described or observed. Some possible units (also called "levels" of analysis) are individuals, dyads, groups, organizations and societies.

universal set: A set that includes all possible elements for a given research topic, used to establish eligibility requirements. When obtaining samples, the universal set is the universe, or population, from which the sample is selected.

Venn diagrams: A way to visualize the relationship between sets. Such diagrams also force one to see all the different regions of the universal set, thereby reminding us of the larger situation.

Chapter 2

SELECTING ASPECTS OF PHENOMENA: VARIABLES AND THEIR DISTRIBUTION

Creating Variables

We cannot make logical sense of our world without classifying selected aspects of the phenomena that interest us. In numerically based arguments, classification frequently takes the form of constructing variables. A **variable** is any aspect of a phenomenon whose value differs from one observation to the next. Let's look at some examples:

Sex: One of the simplest of variables, since it has only two values: female or male.

Education: Individuals differ in how much schooling they have had, and these different amounts or "values" of education range from zero to twenty-plus years.

Preferred age of mate: Humans differ in the age they consider ideal for their mate. Some might prefer a 20-year-old mate, others a 30-year-old mate. What is of interest here is the conception of an ideal age for one's mate. The values are the ages expressed in years.

Post–high school preferences: Looker (1977) uses this variable to assess the parental socialization thesis. Canadian high school students differ in what they would like to do after completing high school. As indicated in Chapter 1, the values of the different observations may comprise: work; apprenticeship; commercial, business or trade school; community college; teachers college; and university.

Variables describe characteristics of specific units. In the examples given above, the variables characterize individuals. We reworked the mate preference argument earlier so the **unit of analysis** became a society. The variable "similarity" in the similarity-attraction hypothesis refers to dyads. That is, similarity does not describe an individual, but rather the relationship between two individuals. The unit of analysis in the parental socialization example is the family (or, alternatively, dyadic parent-child relationships). Birth, death and suicide rates are typical variables where the unit of analysis is a society. Generally the context makes clear to what unit of analysis a variable refers. There have been instances, however, where false conclusions have been reached because the researcher did not pay careful attention to the unit of analysis. We will encounter some examples of this later.

Constructing variables constitutes a first step towards measuring phenomena. We posited that knowing the names of the premiers is one aspect of political knowledge. If this is granted, then representing the number of premiers correctly named with the integers 0 through 10 becomes its measure.

It is customary to distinguish between quantitative and qualitative variables. **Quantitative variables** describe phenomena that differ in degree, or numerical quantity, whereas **qualitative variables** depict differences in kind. The number of premiers correctly named exemplifies differences in amount or degree that are naturally captured by numbers; similarly for years of schooling. In contrast, qualitative distinctions in kind characterize post–high school paths such as work, apprenticeship, business school or university.

The opposite of a variable is a **constant**. A constant exhibits an identical value across all observations in a study.

We do not always know in advance whether an aspect of interest will be a constant or a variable. Suppose the variable "preferred age of mate" is conceptualized as comprising three possibilities: (1) prefers older mates, (2) prefers same-aged mates and (3) prefers younger mates. In the previous chapter it was reported that Buss (1989) did not find a single society in which men, on average, preferred mates older than themselves. Using this criterion and Buss's samples, at the societal level this variable turns out to be a constant.

Confusion between variables and constants sometimes arises out of our linguistic conventions. Take the sentence "Most men prefer young mates," which captures the sociobiological expectation mentioned in Chapter 1. The content of the sentence is admirably clear but the distinction between constant and variable is vague. Did you recognize immediately that the variable is "preferred age of mate"? Furthermore, since sociobiology makes this prediction sex-specific (that is, only males are thought to prefer young mates on average), sex is treated here as a constant. Thus all relevant observations are of males. Hence, in the context of Buss's study, the variable "sex" is treated as the constant "male."

Some variables are less variable than others. Theoretically, if a single society exists where males on average prefer older females, the "constant" would be a variable. Practically though, it remains a constant.

"Maximize the variability" is a common research slogan. Arguments supported by maximally different observations are generally agreed to be better arguments. The rationale for the research maxim cited above can be illustrated with the similarity-attraction hypothesis. Suppose we conducted a study on this topic in a university dormitory and there happened to be no variation in similarity between individuals in the dormitory. This might happen if we had used responses to the question, "Are you basically for or against free speech?" as the issue on which to measure similarity. Conceivably, all members of a dorm might give an identical answer to this question, which would result in a classification of all members of the dorm as equally similar. In such a circumstance, it becomes impossible to test whether similar others are more attracted to each other than dissimilar others. But suppose a handful of members expressed an opposing point of view. Now we would be able to test the proposition, although we would not have much faith in our results because whatever difference in liking is obtained between similar and dissimilar others is based on too few cases for the one value. We can imagine all kinds of reasons, other than dissimilarity, why one, two or three individuals might not be liked. If our comparison rested on two groups of approximately equal size (in which case we would have maximum variability in our measure of similarity) and we found a substantial difference in liking between the two groups, the evidence would be considered stronger.

Although we may accept this research maxim and its rationale, it is not always a prerequisite for sound empirical arguments. The mate preference example can be extended to exemplify this. Buss argued that certain biosocial mechanisms would result, over time, in males preferring young females. He found no society where males on average preferred older mates. This finding might be considered powerful support for the biosocial interpretation.

For the sake of argument, however, let me construct a competing interpretation which I will call the "power thesis." The power thesis has the following components: (1) dominant groups develop strategies to retain their dominance, (2) the younger a mate, the more subordinate that mate is likely to be, (3) members of dominant groups can therefore be expected to prefer younger mates, (4) in patriarchal societies, men, by definition, dominate women and (5) therefore in patriarchal societies men should prefer younger mates.

If all societies Buss reported on were patriarchal, it would be impossible to decide in favour of one or the other interpretation on empirical grounds, because the findings would be perfectly consistent with both interpretations. However, the "power" interpretation suggests a research strategy: find a matriarchal society; for such a society, the power thesis has no grounds for predicting that males will prefer younger mates, but the biosocial thesis does. In contrast, for the matriarchal society, the power thesis has grounds for predicting that females would prefer younger mates. This latter prediction would not be made by the biosocial school of thought. A single case of this kind would provide powerful evidence in favour of one or the other interpretation.

Variables are *not* objective entities simply waiting to be discovered. They are convenient social constructions of researchers who believe that the aspects of a phenomena they have defined are fruitful ways of thinking about the phenomena. Different aspects could be isolated, or the "same" aspect could be isolated in different ways.

As with all classifications, constructing variables pinpoints what is considered important and ignores what is considered irrelevant (at least temporarily). Note that I did not say that variables *actually* focus on important aspects, but only that they focus on what the researcher considers to be important.

It should be illuminating to explore the similarity-attraction proposition in greater depth to reveal the assumptions being made. In the simplest instance, the variable "similarity of attitudes" could be constructed as a dichotomy that results when the opinions of two individuals are compared. They either hold the same opinion (labelled "agreement") or they hold different opinions (labelled "disagreement"). It is important to recognize that from knowing whether two individuals agree, one cannot deduce either of their opinions. The implicit assumption is that the content of their opinions is unimportant. In its place, the interpersonal congruence in their viewpoints is highlighted.

A good case could be made that the content of their opinions should not be ignored. Opinions differ in how socially acceptable they are. Rejection of the statement "I dominate her" is today socially more acceptable than an affirmation. We could construct an alternate similarity variable from the combination of responses of a married male and female couple that has three values that retain this distinction in social acceptability:

- *Disagreement*: one endorses and the other rejects the statement (one partner feels he dominates her; the other partner does not feel he dominates her).
- *Positive agreement*: both partners hold the socially acceptable opinion (they agree that he does not dominate her).
- *Negative agreement*: both partners hold a socially unacceptable opinion (they agree that he dominates her).

This new variable focuses attention on both the content and the congruence of opinions. However, it would not permit us to reconstruct in instances of disagreement which of the two partners, wife or husband, held the socially unacceptable point of view. If we judged it important to know this, then the single value of "disagreement" would have to be split into two values: instances of disagreement where the wife held the unacceptable viewpoint and instances where the husband did.

It is not true that one formulation of a variable is correct and others are incorrect. Rather, we construct variables in a manner we believe will yield a greater understanding of the phenomena of interest. In a solid argument, this belief will be put to the test by comparing results using multiple formulations.

The choice of variables and the method of their construction often reveals hidden assumptions and biases of the researcher. Returning to the three ways of formulating the similarity variable, psychologists and social psychologists would be likely to choose the first way of treating interpersonal agreement. These disciplines emphasize individuals and their interpersonal relationships. Scholars from these disciplines have faith that our deepest understanding of humans and human relations are uncovered by focusing on individuals and their interpersonal dynamics. A sociologist, however, might be skeptical of such an approach, believing instead that we must locate each individual's point of view relative to dominant cultural values; the society defines and limits what is socially acceptable. The second and third formulations of similarity presented permit such comparisons and thus would more likely be used by sociologists.[1]

Criteria for Constructing Variables

Although the choice of variables is frequently a matter of faith, good variables satisfy the following criteria:

1. *Mutual exclusiveness*: The various outcomes or values of the variable must be mutually exclusive. This means that none of our observations simultaneously belongs to two or more defined outcomes. Recall that set theory defines the mutually exclusive criterion precisely: if x_i and x_j represent any two outcomes or values of a variable, and $\emptyset$ the null or empty set, then the mutually exclusive criterion is fulfilled if $x_i \cap x_j = \emptyset$. This criterion permits us to assign any case unambiguously to one particular outcome. It is often possible to create mutually exclusive outcomes in our data even though the phenomena they capture are not mutually exclusive. The variable "post–high school preferences" can be an example. We can force the measure of this variable to be mutually exclusive by asking the respondent to check only one possible path. There is nothing wrong with doing this, provided that most respondents do indeed prefer one path over all others. However, if sizable numbers have either no preferences or desire two or more of the possible paths equally, then the obtained mutual exclusiveness is an artifact of the measurement procedure. In such a situation, it would probably be more fruitful to phrase the question as "Which of the following paths, if any, would you definitely not want to pursue?" Both phrasings would be included for a fuller assessment of teenagers' preferences. Regardless, the fulfillment of the mutual exclusiveness criterion should not create substantive distortions.

2. *Inclusiveness*: The values of the variable taken collectively must be **exhaustive**; all possible values must be included. This criterion ensures that *every* case can be classified into one of the defined possible outcomes. This principle can be fulfilled technically by the simple expedient of including "other" as a residual, or catch-all, response category. This was done, for example, for the post–high school preference variables. For this criterion to be fulfilled meaningfully, only a small proportion of cases should fall into the residual category. In Looker's sample, four percent of the teenagers chose the catch-all category. Although most researchers would consider this acceptable, we should recognize that in the ensuing analysis, the catch-all category is usually excluded. Besides reducing the number of usable cases, such exclusion may result in a less random and representative sample.

3. *Maximal variability:* The values of the variable should be constructed in a fashion that will yield sufficient variation, which means all values of the variable should have sufficient cases for analysis. In the mate preference example, if the values had been "prefer a younger mate," "prefer a mate the same age as myself" and "prefer an older mate," few males would choose the last possibility, thus violating the "maximal variability" principle. Obtaining the preferred numerical age of a mate would improve the variable.

4. *Theoretical isomorphism*: In set theory, an **isomorphism** is said to characterize two sets whenever a one-to-one correspondence between their elements exists, preserving the relationship between these elements. In numeric arguments, theoretical isomorphism exists when the values of the variable correspond to the features of the argument being made. Buss violated this principle when he measured the preferred age of a mate *relative* to the male's own age. The biosocial explanation stipulated an *absolute* preferred age (a preference for mates with highest reproductive potential that is predicated on absolute age). As mentioned in the previous chapter, Buss's method would have the unfortunate result of treating instances of 65-year-old males preferring 60-year-old females as supporting the biosocial interpretation, when clearly these should be considered as disconfirming cases.

5. *Numeric preference*: Where outcomes differ quantitatively, the values of the outcomes should be expressed in numbers that meaningfully capture the differences in quantity. This "numeric preference" principle is one of the reasons why recording the preferred age of a mate is better than using response categories such as "younger" and "older." If we record the absolute ages, it is still possible subsequently to create categories such as "younger" and "older," but the reverse is clearly not true—we cannot reconstruct absolute ages from the categories. If interest centred on the husband's involvement with making meals, a variable that assessed how many times he prepared a meal during a given period of time is preferable to one that ascertained if the husband "usually," "often," "seldom" or "never" prepared or helped prepare meals.

Often exploratory studies, or "**pilot studies**," are conducted to determine whether a given way of measuring a variable is appropriate. Pilot studies are like previews: we obtain a taste prior to a complete showing. In pilot studies, our measurements are pretested on a small, convenient sample that is similar to the population of interest. Ambiguities, difficulties, and violations of the criteria for constructing variables can be detected at this stage.

Constructing Distributions for Variables

Numerically based arguments rest on variables and their distributions. **Distributions** pair the different possible values of variables with their associated frequencies. We construct distributions to show how frequently each of the different outcomes occurred in a given study. Distributions can be presented in columns that associate the different possible outcomes with their absolute and/or **relative frequencies**. Since all the outcomes of a variable are presented in a single table or graph, distributions provide convenient overviews. Table 2.1, for example, presents the distribution of teenagers' post–high school preferences.

Table 2.1
Distribution of Teenagers' Post–High School Preferences

Preference	f	%
Go to work	86	22
Go into an apprenticeship	47	12
Go to a commercial, business or trade school	14	4
Go to a community college	117	29
Go to a teachers college	2	0
Go to university	118	30
Do something else (Other)	14	4
Not ascertained	2	0
TOTAL	400	100[b]

[a]The question asked was: "After you leave high school, which of the following paths would you like to take?"
[b]The percentages do not sum to 100 because of rounding.

Source: Constructed from data collected by Looker (1977).

The values of the variable "post–high school preference" are identified in the first column of the table under the heading "Preference." The second column indicates how many teenagers took each of the choices, i.e., it gives the **absolute frequency** associated with each value of the variable. Attending university was the most popular choice: 118 teenagers indicated this preference. This was closely followed by attending community college, chosen by 117 teenagers. The last column converts the frequencies into **percentages** of teenagers making each choice. Thus, the 118 teenagers who preferred university constitute 30 percent of the total sample.[2]

Frequency distributions show which outcomes are populous and which are not. To be made more vivid, distributions can be presented graphically. **Pie charts** (their shape suggested the name; see Figure 2.1) are particularly appropriate for qualitative variables. Pie charts have no beginning or end, or top or bottom. Both of these features visually reinforce non-hierarchical distinctions in kind. The sizes of the slices are **proportional** to the frequencies, clearly reinforcing the important information for the reader. Pie charts are less desirable for variables with many outcomes. Too many slices produce cumbersome pie charts, and small slices are difficult to present visually. One solution is to collapse or combine categories.

Figure 2.1 is a pie chart of teenagers' post–high school preferences. It contains the same information as Table 2.1, except that the two instances of attending teachers college and community college are combined and the fourteen "Other" preferences are combined with attending commercial, trade or business school.

Figure 2.1
Pie Chart of Teenagers' Post High School Preferences

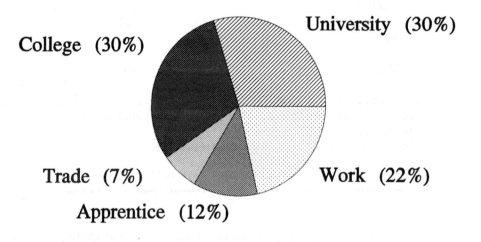

College (30%)

University (30%)

Trade (7%)

Work (22%)

Apprentice (12%)

Source: Data from Looker (1977).

Frequency distributions do more than summarize. Particularly in the context of arguments, they facilitate important comparisons. For this purpose, several distributions are often presented in a single table. Table 2.2, for example, gives the distribution of post–high school preferences that parents desire for their teenager, in addition to the teenager's own preference. Presenting the three distributions in adjacent columns facilitates comparisons. To make the comparisons still easier, I have reorganized the preferences of teenagers from most to least frequently chosen (except for the residual category listed last).

Table 2.2
Distribution of Post–High School Preferences among Hamilton Teenagers and Their Parents (%)[a]

Preference	Teenagers	Mothers	Fathers
University	30	40	42
Community college	29	26	21
Work	22	13	9
Apprenticeship	12	10	12
Commercial, business or trade school	4	6	11
Teachers college	0	0	2
Other	4	4	3
TOTAL	100[b]	100[b]	100[b]
(N[c])	(398)	(327)	(322)

[a]Teenagers were asked: "After you leave high school, which of the following paths would you *like to take*?" Each of the parents was asked: "Which of the following paths would you like your son/daughter to take after high school?"
[b]The percentages may not sum to 100 due to rounding.
[c]The number of cases is less than the total sample size of 400 because of non-responses.

Source: Constructed from data collected by Looker (1977).

Misleading Collapsed Outcomes

Any outcome can be made to appear populous through the simple expedient of combining it with another. To avoid such misleading depictions, it is incumbent to note the precise nature of all collapsing preferably within the table or graph. This includes an indication how many observations were in each category prior to its being combined with another.

We can now see both what the preferred paths are and how similar the distribution of preferences are. When *constructing* tables, the aim is to facilitate making comparisons. When *reading* tables, the aim is to reach verbal conclusions that are supported by the numbers presented.

Figure 2.2 provides possible conclusions on the left, with the supporting evidence garnered from Table 2.2 detailed on the right. Of course, these conclusions are arguable and tentative. They are given here to illustrate how patterns are detected in numbers and then translated into theoretical and substantive conclusions that are supported by the evidence.

Table-reading skills include recognizing what conclusions are not supported, or even addressed, by the table. For example, on the basis of Table 2.2, we cannot assess parental agreement on preferred paths. Although a similar percentage of both parents would like their child to attend university (40 percent and 42 percent for mothers and fathers, respectively), we cannot conclude that parents tend to agree with each other on this topic. We cannot assess agreement because frequency distributions don't show whether mothers holding a given preference are married to a father with an identical preference. To ascertain parental agreement, we would need to evaluate the desires of mothers and fathers simultaneously. Evaluating two variables simultaneously is known as **bivariate analysis,** a topic we will develop in the next chapter. Constructing frequency distributions is an example of a **univariate analysis** technique, because here we analyze only one variable at a time. Note that the *sequential* analysis of the preferences of teenagers, mothers and fathers (as in Table 2.2, for example) remains an example of univariate analysis.

Visual information is generally digested more quickly than numerical information. Graphic aids are particularly advantageous when a wealth of information is presented, as in Table 2.2. Figure 2.3 presents the information contained in Table 2.2 in the form of a **bar graph.** In bar graphs, each bar represents a different outcome, with the length of the bar proportional to the frequency of the outcome. Note how triadic comparisons are facilitated in Figure 2.3.

Frequency distributions are, as a rule, constructed in a way that explicitly shows that the absolute frequencies add up to the total number of cases, and/or that the relative frequencies add up to 100 percent. There is one major class of exceptions to this rule, however. Frequently, variables are constructed with dichotomous outcomes (a dichotomous variable is one with two possible values). These are often constructed out of lists, where each item on the list is either present or absent for a given case. For example, adapting Kohn's (1969) work on class and conformity, Looker asked her Hamiltonian teenagers to choose three characteristics they considered "most important to you in judging yourself as a person" from a list of thirteen. Additionally, these teenagers were asked which three characteristics they felt their mother and their father would feel were "most important in a boy or girl of your age." Table 2.3 provides the results.

Figure 2.2

Conclusions and Evidence Gleaned from Table 2.2

Verbal Conclusions	Numeric Evidence
The relative popularity of paths is similar for teenagers, mothers and fathers.	The most popular post–high school choice among teens, mothers and fathers is going to university, with attending community college the second most frequent choice in all three groups. Attending teachers college is the least frequently mentioned preference in all three distributions.
The overall preferences of parents are more similar to each other than either is to the teenagers' preferences.	Comparing the second and third columns (mothers' preferences with fathers' preferences), it can be seen that in no instance is there more than a five percent difference in the frequency of their respective preferences (five percent more mothers than fathers choose attending community college; conversely, five percent fewer mothers than fathers prefer their child to attend commercial, business or trade school). On the other hand, at least 10 percent more mothers and fathers than teenagers prefer university attendance.
The relative popularity of paths between mothers and teens is more similar than that between fathers and teens.	The rank order of popularity of preferences is identical for mothers and teenagers. That is, the path most frequently chosen by mothers is also the one most frequently chosen by the teenager, the least frequently chosen path among mothers is also the least frequently chosen among teenagers, and the same is true for all other choices in between. This is not the case when comparing fathers and teenagers. For example, going to work is the third most frequently expressed desire among teenagers, but only the fifth most frequent path fathers would choose for their child.
Parents are more likely to believe that deferred gratification is necessary to obtain the best results.	Parents are at least 10 percent more likely than teenagers to choose university attendance as the post–high school path. This means delaying immediate earnings for at least three years. Conversely, parents are about half as likely as teenagers to opt for immediate work as the preferred path after high school (13 percent of mothers

Source: From data collected by Looker (1977).

Figure 2.3

Bar Graph of Post High School Preferences of Teenagers
and Their Parents

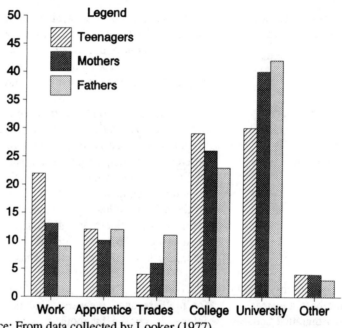

Source: From data collected by Looker (1977).

The first thing to be noted about Table 2.3 is the wealth of information it summarizes. It condenses thirty-nine separate distributions (thirteen dichotomous variables given separately for each teenager's own choice and the choices they think their mothers and their fathers would make). To do this, the table presents only one-half of each distribution, namely the percentage who chose each characteristic. It excludes the percentages who did not choose a characteristic because, for dichotomous variables, this information is redundant. For example, Table 2.3 reveals that 51 percent of the teenagers chose "being responsible" as one of the three most important characteristics. Clearly, 49 percent must not have chosen this characteristic. This latter figure is not presented because readers can easily determine such values for themselves.

Table 2.3
Teenagers' Own Values and What They Think Their Parents Would Prefer (%)

Characteristic	Teen's Report of		
	Own[a]	Father[b]	Mother[b]
Being responsible	51	48	39
Being honest	48	39	43
Having good sense and sound judgment	37	30	24
Being considerate of others	37	13	22
Trying hard to succeed	34	36	23
Having good manners	21	32	40
Having self-control	20	12	11
Being neat and clean	13	16	32
Getting along well with others your age	13	6	9
Obeying your parents well	9	32	25
Being interested in how and why things work	8	4	2
Being a good student	5	18	19
Acting like a boy (or girl) should	4	17	14

[a]The question asked was "Which three of these characteristics would you say are the most important to you in judging yourself as a person?"

[b]The question asked was: "Which three of these characteristics would you say your father (mother) feels are most important in a boy or girl of your age?"

Source: Constructed from data collected by Looker (1977).

Style of Tables

A number of stylistic points should be observed when constructing tables:

- Make the tables self-evident. A reader should not have to study the text to understand the table.

- Number the tables.

- Provide a clear, descriptive title.

- Round percentages to the nearest whole number. Otherwise it suggests greater accuracy than is ordinarily warranted. In the event that the percentages no longer add up to 100 because of rounding, the total should nevertheless be given as 100 (since that is the true total), and a note explaining this should be included (see, for example, note "b" in Table 2.1).

- Report the number of cases on which the percentages are based.

- Acknowledge the source for each table where more than one source of data is drawn upon.

- Organize your tables to highlight the important points.

Presenting the thirty-nine distributions together in one table is an effective way of documenting and comparing the profiles of teenagers' own values and those they think their parents would want them to have. I won't provide detailed interpretations for Table 2.3. Suffice it to say that there are some overall similarities in the values teenagers endorse and those they think their parents would prefer. For example, honesty and responsibility are important to teenagers, and they also think their parents consider them important. At the other end, teenagers seldom consider "being interested in how and why things work" to be important, and seldom do they think either parent would consider this an important characteristic. Despite these similarities, teenagers' perceptions reflect a generation gap on some issues. Not surprisingly, more teenagers feel their parents value obedience than they themselves do. Similarly, fewer teenagers chose being a good student than the number who believe their parents would make this choice. Finally, teenagers' perceptions also reveal some gender stereotypes of the times: that success is more important to fathers than mothers, and that neatness and cleanliness is more important to mothers than fathers.

Reconceptualizing Party Imagery

We must always remember that our variables are not "discovered," but rather that they represent convenient social constructions. As such, many constructions are always possible, each having certain advantages and disadvantages. Developing solid arguments requires an exploration of possible alternative conceptualizations of our variables. Let's do that with party imagery.

The question on the federal NDP's left-right status was part of a series of questions on left-right political orientations. I have reproduced the questions on left-right party images in Figure 2.4.

In the original construction of the left-right image of the federal NDP party, responses of 1, 2 or 3 were defined as belonging to the set "places the NDP to the left of centre." The complement of this set (i.e., scores of 4 through 7) completes the definition of the variable "perceived left/not left status of the federal NDP party."

Figure 2.4
Items for Measuring Left-Right Party Imagery

For the next few questions I would like you to use this scale which goes from left to right, with "1" being the most to the left and "7" being the most to the right.

	Left						Right
[var509[a]] Now, where would you place the federal Liberal Party?	1	2	3	4	5	6	7
[var510] Where would you place the federal Progressive Conservative Party?	1	2	3	4	5	6	7
[var511] And where would you place the federal New Democratic Party?	1	2	3	4	5	6	7

[a]These are the SPSS variable names.

Source: 1984 CNES.

The argument introduced in Chapter 1 was that politically knowledgable Canadians would be likely to place the NDP to the left of centre. The implicit rationale for this argument rested on the assumption that the federal NDP was indeed a left-wing party. Stated differently, placing the federal NDP to the left of centre was thought to represent a correct response, with all other responses being treated as incorrect.

The advantage of this formulation is its simplicity: it produces only two outcomes, one of which might represent a correct, and the other a false, image of the NDP. Nevertheless, this formulation has several disadvantages. The first is that it treats responses of 4 through 7 as equally false. I suggest, and I trust you will agree, that placing the NDP to the extreme right is less correct than placing it dead on centre. One possible solution would be to use the original seven-point response format in its entirety. If we were to assume that the NDP was objectively located to the extreme left (corresponding to a 1 on the left-right response format), we would be able to capture degrees of incorrectness. But there is no consensus among scholars that the NDP is objectively located to the extreme left. Thus, this possible way of treating party imagery is rejected.

A second disadvantage is that this measure implicitly assumes that humans use an absolute scale when forming judgments about political parties; in this case that they use a notion of "dead centre" as an anchoring point for their assessments of parties on a left-right continuum. Dead centre was a score of 4. Note that our original definition of party imagery classified respondents who placed the NDP as left of "dead centre" as having a correct image.

A possible alternative conceptualization minimizes both of these disadvantages. Many social science scholars would argue that the NDP is to the left of certain other parties, such as the Progressive Conservatives (PCs). By conceptualizing party imagery as the left-right position of the NDP *relative* to that of other political parties, we acknowledge the possibility that respondents may not use a "dead centre" anchor. Furthermore, this way of looking at party imagery creates a more meaningful continuum. At a minimum, we would have three meaningful outcomes: "correct" placement (NDP was classified to the left of the PCs), "semi-correct" placement (the NDP was classified as identical to the PCs on a left-right continuum) and "incorrect" placement (the NDP was placed to the right of the PCs). Alternatively, we could retain the full range of relative scores. In that case, our variable has a potential range of –6 (with the NDP placed at a 7 and the PCs at a 1 on the left-right response format) to + 6 (corresponding to placing the NDP at 1 and the PCs at 7). We permit respondents to have their own relative anchors. Suppose one respondent placed the NDP on 4. When this respondent is now asked to place the PCs on the same scale, the respondent has the chance to use a placement position that will indicate how far to the left or right of the NDP they consider the PCs to be. In short, this new variable is created by subtracting the respondent's placement of the NDP from that of the PCs. We would have no difficulty classifying scores of –6 to 1 as being increasingly "correct." Whether scores of 2 through 6 are also increasingly correct is more problematic; that depends on how far to the left relative to the PCs the NDP "really" is.

Figure 2.5

SPSS Produced Bar Graph of the Left-Right Position of the NDP
Relative to the PCs

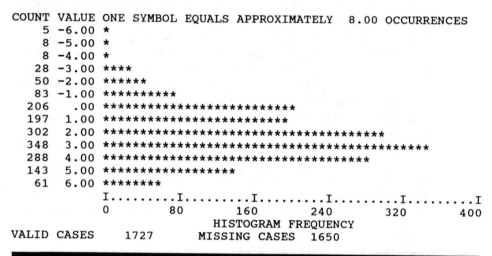

```
COUNT VALUE ONE SYMBOL EQUALS APPROXIMATELY  8.00 OCCURRENCES
    5 -6.00 *
    8 -5.00 *
    8 -4.00 *
   28 -3.00 ****
   50 -2.00 ******
   83 -1.00 **********
  206   .00 ************************
  197  1.00 ***********************
  302  2.00 **************************************
  348  3.00 *******************************************
  288  4.00 ************************************
  143  5.00 ******************
   61  6.00 ********
          I.........I.........I.........I.........I.........I
          0        80       160       240       320      400
                         HISTOGRAM FREQUENCY
VALID CASES      1727     MISSING CASES  1650
```

One way to present these results visually is in the form of a bar graph. Figure 2.5 is a printout of an SPSS-produced bar graph of this newly created variable.

The SPSS form of the bar graph consists of three columns of information. The first column (labelled "COUNT") gives the frequencies associated with each of the values of the variable. The second column (labelled "VALUE") prints the values of the variable, ranging from –6 to +6. The third column is the visual representation of the frequencies. SPSS uses asterisks (*) to represent frequencies. The cryptic phrase "ONE SYMBOL EQUALS APPROXIMATELY 8.00 OCCURRENCES" informs you that each asterisk stands for approximately eight cases. Thus, there is one asterisk to represent the five respondents who placed the NDP to the extreme right and the PCs to the extreme left (resulting in the value of –6 for the variable). Similarly, eighteen asterisks are used to represent the number of Canadians who placed the NDP five units to the left of the PCs. This represents approximately 144 (18 x 8 = 144) cases. Observe (from column 1) that 143 Canadians were in this particular set. Conventionally, bar graphs are presented with the axes reversed in relation to those produced by SPSS.

Looking at the bar graph as a whole, it is easy to see that substantially more Canadians place the NDP to the left of the PCs than to the right; occurences of positive values exceed negative ones by a large margin and the shape of the distribution provides much information at a glance. It is precisely for this reason that graphic representations of distributions often are preferred over numeric ones. We will explore the shape of distributions in greater detail in Chapter 4.

A distinction between **discrete** and **continuous distributions** is traditionally made. In continuous distributions, an infinite and uncountable number of outcomes could occur between any two adjacent recorded outcomes. This is not so for discrete variables, where outcomes other than those presented are considered impossible. Age is a continuous variable, since an infinite number of finer and finer gradations of age are possible. "Post–high school plans" is an example of a discrete variable. There is a finite number of possible preferences. All categorical variables are by definition discrete. Note that although our recorded observations are usually discrete, we may think of the concept itself as continuous. The number of premiers known is a discrete variable, since there are precisely eleven possible outcomes. We think of the concept "political knowledge," however, as a continuous variable. That is, frequently we think of the "underlying" variable as continuous, even though our measure of it is discrete.

When we think of the underlying concept as continuous, we can plot the frequency distribution in a continuous form known as a **histogram**. A histogram is similar to a bar graph in which the spaces between the bars have been deleted and the tops of the bars have been connected with a continuous line. By using a smooth curve, we imply that the variable is a continuous one. Figure 2.6 is a histogram for

Figure 2.6
Histogram of the Perceived Left-Right Position of the PCs
Relative to the NDP

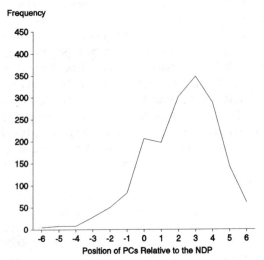

Source: 1984 CNES.

the relative measure of party imagery. When we wish to emphasize the discrete nature of the phenomenon, we should prefer to employ bar charts with the bars separated by spaces, as in Figure 2.5.

Constructing Distributions for Continuous Variables

By definition, continuous variables permit an infinite number of values. This presents a display problem. The solution is to collapse the infinite number of values into a manageable number of classes, usually less than twenty. Figure 2.7 presents the collapsed age distribution of Canadians, as given by Statistics Canada for 1986. Each of the bars contains a class of contiguous outcomes. The first class contains all Canadians who were less than five years old in 1986. The second class contains those Canadians who were between five and nine years old. In this example, the class interval is five years; that is, each bar represents an interval of five years. To avoid visual distortions, the interval selected is constant. The only exception to this is in the first and/or last intervals. In Figure 2.7, the last interval is open-ended, including all Canadians aged 75 and older. It is unfortunate that Statistics Canada has such a large, open-ended age category. When presented in a chart, this category has a misleading effect, because it gives the impression that there is a sudden and large increase in the number of Canadians aged 75 years or more. If Statistics Canada had included a few additional classes (e.g., 75-79, 80-84, 85-89), the visual impression of the age distribution would be less distorted.

Figure 2.7
Population Distribution for Canada, 1986

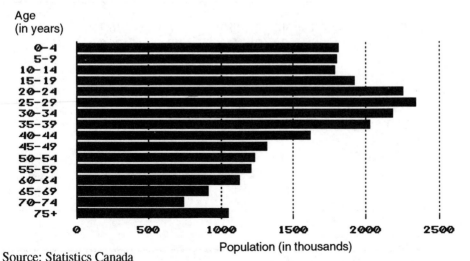

Source: Statistics Canada

Using SPSS to Produce Distributions

SPSS produces frequency distributions in a format that requires some explanation. Table 2.4 provides a frequency distribution of the placement of the federal NDP on an absolute left-right continuum. The two left-most columns of the table reproduce the value labels and their numeric values. These two columns are read together so that the meanings of the values of the variable are kept in mind. In Table 2.4, for example, the value of 1 means that the federal NDP was placed farthest to the left, while a value of 7 signifies that it was placed on the extreme right. No value labels are given for the outcomes in between, since they refer simply to intermediate left-right placements. Note also that respondents who "refused" and those with "no opinion" were given scores of 0 and 8 respectively. The frequency of occurrence of the various outcomes is given in the third column. As one might expect, more Canadians placed the federal NDP to the extreme left than to the extreme right (283 versus 45). Only thirty-five respondents refused to answer this question.[3]   The fourth colun expresses the frequencies as percentages of the total number of cases.

Table 2.4
SPSS-Produced Frequency Distribution of Absolute Left-Right Placement of the Federal NDP

Value Label	Value	Frequency	Percent	Valid Percent	Cum. Percent
LEFT	1	283	8.4	16.2	16.2
	2	458	13.6	26.2	42.3
	3	417	12.3	23.8	66.2
	4	327	9.7	18.7	84.9
	5	145	4.3	8.3	93.1
	6	75	2.2	4.3	97.4
RIGHT	7	45	1.3	2.6	100.0
REFUSED	0	35	1.0	Missing	
NO OPINION	8	1,592	47.1	Missing	
	Total	3,377	100.0	100.0	

Source: 1984 CNES.

For example, the 283 respondents who place the NDP to the extreme left represent 8.4 percent of the total sample of 3,377 cases. The fifth column expresses the frequencies as percentages of the total number of *valid cases*. A valid case is one for which meaningful information was obtained. Relevant information for a given case may not be available, or the information may not be considered meaningful. "Don't Know" responses, for example, are frequently defined as not valid. In SPSS, the codes for such responses are defined as "MISSING VALUES." For this party imagery variable, respondents who were not asked or who refused to answer this question are treated as missing cases. That is, the number of valid cases is 3,377 – (1,592 + 35) = 1,750. Hence the 283 respondents who placed the federal NDP to the extreme left represent 16.2 percent of the 1,750 valid responses. The last column provides a **cumulative percentage distribution.** As the name suggests, cumulative percentages provide the sum of the percentages in the previous rows plus that row's percentage. Cumulative percentages organize the information so we can determine at a glance what percentage of the (valid) outcomes occurred at or below a given point. Here, for example, we conclude that two out of every three respondents (66.2 percent) placed the NDP to the left of centre (assuming that the middle outcome of 4 represents "dead centre").

Introduction to SPSS

When data is collected, it is usually organized into a rectangular (matrix) form. Each row is a case (observation) and each column is a variable, as in Figure 2.8.

Here we have n variables and N cases. The cases might be individuals, dyads, organizations, cultures or time periods. The variables are the characteristics (usually given numeric values, as in the example) of each case that has been selected for the sample. This matrix is frequently called the "raw" data. In the political imagery example, the cases represent a random sample of adult residents of Canada. Information on many characteristics of each respondent, obtained through personal interviews, is recorded as the variables. In the 1984 Canadian

Figure 2.8

A Rectangular Data Matrix

Variables

		1	2	3	.	.	.	.	.	.	.	.	n
	1	2	5	1	.	.	.	.	.	.	.	.	3
	2	1	4	8	.	.	.	.	.	.	.	.	6
	3	9	3	6	.	.	.	.	.	.	.	.	5
Cases	.		.	.	.								.
	.		.	.	.								.
	.		.	.	.								.
	.		.	.	.								
	N	2	9	4	.	.	.	.	.	.	.	.	2

National Election Study, information on over five hundred characteristics for each respondent was recorded—information such as age, sex, party preference and voting behaviour. These are the variables. This information is then entered into a file in machine-readable form. Since this has already been done for the 1984 CNES data, I won't discuss data-entry procedures here. Suffice it to say that the raw data exists on a magnetic tape or disk in a form which can be read by the SPSS program.

Raw data is cumbersome to work with. In recognition of this, the SPSS software has a built-in feature that converts raw data into what is called an SPSS system file. The 1984 data we will use is in this form.

A system file provides additional information about the cases and about each variable. In an SPSS system file, each variable has an associated name. For example, if the first column of numbers refers to a person's sex, then the name attached to the first column of information could be "sex." Frequently, researchers simply name the variables sequentially. That is the case with the 1984 CNES. Here the variable name associated with the left-right status of the NDP was "var511." Additional information, such as VARIABLE LABELS (providing a descriptive phrase for identifying each variable) or values to be considered as MISSING VALUES (which lets the computer know which codes are to be considered "not applicable" or "not ascertained")[4] are also included in the system file.

Frequently the original definitions of variables and their associated values need to be modified. Such modifications are possible through a number of data transformation instructions available in SPSS. Thus one can RECODE values of a variable, and one can COMPUTE new variables as combinations and mathematical transformations of existing ones. These are powerful aids in developing arguments.

Once the data has been appropriately transformed, various statistical procedures are available. For example, the distribution of number of premiers correctly named was obtained with the FREQUENCIES procedure. These procedures perform the tedious calculations. Let's look at the set of instructions shown in Figure 2.9 which produced the political knowledge table.

Figure 2.9
SPSS Instructions for Obtaining a Frequency Distribution and Bar Graph

```
1  GET FILE = "vote84.sys".
2  COUNT premiers= var446 TO var455(1).
3  VARIABLE LABELS premiers "Number of premiers correctly named".
4  FREQUENCIES VARIABLES=premiers
5       /BARGRAPH.
6  FINISH.
```

I will use several conventions in listing SPSS instructions. First, I will number each line. These numbers do not actually appear in the set of SPSS instructions but are entered here simply for ease in referring to specific instructions. The instructions start in the first column, except where I have indented them, as in line 5.[5] Secondly, capitalized words are part of the SPSS language and must be spelled identically, as they appear in the examples. Non-capitalized words are not part of the SPSS language, and within certain restrictions you are permitted to create these words at will. The restrictions are spelled out in the various SPSS manuals. For example, "var511" is an arbitrary name for the variable concerning the left-right status of the NDP. The restrictions on such names are:

- They must start with an alphabetical character.
- They must be composed of only alphabetical and numerical characters (i.e., they can't contain special symbols such as % or /.).
- They cannot contain blanks.
- They cannot be longer than eight characters.

Once an arbitrary name has been given, it must subsequently be spelled precisely that way. I cannot, for example, refer to "var511" as "v511".

The order in which the instructions are entered is important, since the SPSS software processes the instructions in the order in which they are given. Let me now describe what each of these instructions does.

Line 1: The GET FILE command retrieves an SPSS system file. We specify the particular one we want by enclosing the name of the file in single quotation marks. This becomes the "active" file, and all subsequent instructions are performed on the variables contained in this file.

Line 2: This is a data modification instruction. It creates a new variable, to be called "premiers." The variable "premiers" is constructed by counting the number of 1's it finds between "var446" and "var455" inclusive; "var446" to "var455" are the names for the ten variables that contain information on whether each of the ten premiers was identified. A code of 1 in each instance means that the premier of that province was correctly named. This instruction creates our measure of political knowledge.

Line 3: Every time a new variable is created, it is good practice to document the meaning of that variable by giving it an extended (up to forty characters) VARIABLE LABEL. That is what is done here with the newly created variable "premiers." Both the variable name and the contents of the variable labels will be printed to permanently identify the output. This saves much time when reading the printouts.

Line 4: This is a statistical procedures instruction. The keyword FREQUENCIES produces frequency distributions. SPSS can produce many frequency distributions with a single command; it is simply up to the user to indicate for which variables frequency distributions are desired. This instruction produced Table 2.4, for example.

Line 5: This is a subcommand of the previous command. SPSS considers subcommands to be continuations of the main command, and on mainframe versions they are recognized as continuations by being indented one or more spaces. On microcomputer versions, continuations across different lines are recognized by their punctuation; a period is permitted only at the end of a complete command (note that there is no period at the end of line 4). This subcommand produced the bar graph in Figure 2.3, for example.

Line 6: This informs the computer that there are no further instructions. FINISH is an optional command.

Summary

- Creating variables is a more powerful way of defining events than set theory. A variable is a class of events having two or more mutually exclusive and exhaustive values. Variables are appropriate for either qualitative or quantitative events.
- A major advantage of variables over sets is that all possible outcomes are kept in the foreground simultaneously. Frequency distributions of these variables, particularly in the form of bar charts or histograms, show important features of the phenomena under investigation at a glance.
- Variables are constructed rather than discovered. Alternative definitions are therefore always possible, each having its own advantages and disadvantages. For example, the perceived status of the NDP was originally defined on an absolute left-right scale. However, this variable was reconceptualized to focus on the placement of the NDP relative to the PCs. Thus we were able to measure how many units the NDP was placed to the left or right of the PCs. If we assume that the NDP is "objectively" to the left of the PCs, our measure has the desirable feature that the smaller the negative number, the less "correct" is the placement of the NDP.

Notes

1. Note, in addition, that the unit of analysis differs among these formulations. In the original definition, similarity simply describes the dyad. In the second and third formulations, the unit of analysis is more complex, namely the relationship of the dyad to its society.

2. Here's how percentages are calculated:

$$\text{percentage} = 100(f_i / N)$$

where f_i is the frequency of the "ith" value, and N is the total number of cases. For example, the percentage of teenagers who would like to attend university is:

$$100(118/400) = 30\%.$$

3. The large number (1,592) of respondents classified as having no opinion is misleading—these respondents were not asked this question. I am reproducing the labels as they appear in the publicly available data. A more appropriate value label to refer to these cases would be "Not asked."
4. In certain instances, a "Don't know" response might be considered missing data. For the political knowledge measure, it is clear that a response of "Don't know" can be considered the same as providing the wrong name. In other situations, it may be better to treat such responses as missing data. The political party imagery measure is a situation where I would treat a "Don't know" response as missing data.
5. Computer programs use different conventions for signifying the end of a command. For mainframe versions of SPSS, a new command starts in the first column and all continuations (known as "subcommands") are indented, as in line 5. For the microcomputer version, a period serves the same purpose.

Key Terms

absolute frequency: A count of the number of times a given outcome occurred. Absolute frequencies are sometimes given in pie charts and bar graphs, since the areas of the slices and bars already indicate their relative frequency. Example: In one community, 160 (out of 400) residents voted for the Liberals, compared with 240 (out of 500) in another one. Since comparisons such as these are awkward, relative frequencies, in the form of percentages or proportions are usually calculated and reported.

bar graph: A frequency distribution presented in such a way that the outcomes of the variables are represented by bars whose lengths (or heights) are proportional to their relative frequencies. The bars are separated by spaces to emphasize the discreteness of the distribution.

bivariate analyses: Techniques whereby two variables are analyzed jointly or simultaneously to assess whether a relationship between events exists. Example: Conditional probabilities, which refer to the likelihood of one event in the presence of another event.

constant: A universal attribute, or at least a characteristic of an object in a given study that does not vary from one observation to another. Its antonym is a variable. A generally held principle of research is that constants cannot be explained empirically.

continuous distributions: Distributions of quantitative variables; between any two outcomes it is in theory possible to have another one if finer measurements had been taken. Histograms visually emphasize continuity and are the medium of choice for graphing continuous distributions. Examples: Income and chronological age.

cumulative percentage distributions: A way of presenting the distribution of ordinal and metric variables in which the percentage of cases having a score less than or equal to any given value is given.

discrete distributions: Distributions of variables with a countable number of outcomes. Bar graphs, which have a space between adjacent bars, are frequently used to visually accent the discrete nature of a variable. Example: The distribution of the variable defined as "the number of provincial premiers of Canada correctly named," which has eleven discrete outcomes ranging from zero to ten.

distributions: A univariate technique whereby the different values of a variable are presented together with their frequency or probability. Distributions can be presented numerically as frequency, percentage or probability tables, or they can be graphically presented in the form of pie charts, bar graphs or histograms.

exhaustive (inclusive): One of the criteria for constructing variables; it implies that room has been made for all possible outcomes of the variable. This criterion is often fulfilled by including an "Other" category as one of the outcomes. However, this practice is inadvisable if many cases are classified as "Other."

frequency distribution: A univariate technique whereby the distinct values of a variable are associated with their respective frequencies.

histogram: A graphic method of presenting distributions for quantitative and continuous variables, such as age and income. The shape of the distribution is traced by a continuous line such that the area between any two outcomes corresponds to the proportion of cases falling between these two points.

isomorphism: A close correspondence between the outcomes of a variable and the features of the phenomenon germane to the argument being made. Example: The absolute age of a preferred mate is more isomorphic with the biosocial mate preference argument than the relative age. Conversely, the left-right placement of the NDP relative to the PCs or Liberals is more isomorphic to the concept of correct placement than the placement of the NDP on an absolute left-right scale.

mutually exclusive: Events that cannot occur simultaneously. This is one of the criteria for constructing variables: the values of a variable must be mutually exclusive. Example: A list of the candidates' names would provide mutually exclusive response categories appropriate for the question "For which candidate did you vote in the last federal election?"

percentages: Frequencies that have been standardized to a base of 100 to facilitate comparisons. Example: 160 represents 40 percent of 400. This percentage is obtained by dividing 160 by 400 and multiplying by 100.

pie chart: A graphic form of presenting a frequency distribution, where each slice of the pie represents a different outcome and the size of the slice is proportional to its relative frequency. Pie charts effectively communicate information about qualitative variables with not more than about seven outcomes (or slices).

pilot studies: Preliminary observations conducted to detect, assess and alleviate problems in the implementation of an empirical study. They are particularly useful for improving operational definitions of variables.

proportions: Frequencies that have been standardized to a base of 1; also called relative frequencies.

qualitative variables: Characteristics of objects constructed in a way that produces differences in kind. Such variables are usually contrasted with quantitative ones, which contain differences in amount or degree. Examples: Type of occupation, such as white collar or blue collar; preferred political party, such as Liberal, Conservative or NDP.

quantitative variables: Variables constructed in a way that extracts different amounts or degrees of the attribute. Examples: Annual income; number of premiers correctly named.

relative frequency: The proportion of times a given outcome occurs; that is, the absolute frequency of an outcome divided by the total number of observations. Example: The relative frequency of 160 out of 400 is 0.40. This proportion is obtained by dividing 160 by 400. Such proportions are often converted to percentages by multiplying the proportion by 100.

unit of analysis: The objects, or cases, under investigation. These can range from individuals to groups and whole societies. It is important to keep the unit of analysis firmly in mind, since relationships between similar variables may be quite different for different units. For example, Blau (1955) documented that cooperative individuals are less productive than competitive ones. At the same time, groups in which members cooperate are more productive than those where members are competitive.

univariate analyses: Techniques of analysis in which only one variable is considered at a time. Sometimes more than one variable is considered, but if each is considered separately (independently) of the others, the analysis remains univariate. Examples: frequency distributions; averages.

variable: A way of classifying the characteristics of objects being studied that results in two or more mutually exclusive and exhaustive values or outcomes. Variables are constructed to capture what the researcher considers to be possibly important differences between the units, or cases, to be observed.

Chapter 3

DOCUMENTING RELATIONSHIPS:
CONTINGENCY TABLES AND THE
CHI–SQUARE DISTRIBUTION

In the previous chapter, we learned to organize outcomes into variables. To begin to describe phenomena, we calculated the frequency distributions of the variables of interest. Distributions, and their graphic representation, are derived from **univariate analyses**, which focus on only one variable at a time. Questions that ask whether two variables are connected, or related, require us to analyze the two simultaneously. Such techniques are known as **bivariate analyses**.

Even questions that, at first glance, seem to involve only one variable, frequently turn out, on closer inspection, to require bivariate analysis for a proper answer. Take the question "Are men violent?" We might think the answer depends on the proportion of men judged to be violent. Without an appropriate comparison point, however, we would be committing the absolute level fallacy introduced in Chapter 1. Appropriate comparisons are usually found by introducing a second variable. In this example, sex would be an appropriate second variable. The question then becomes: "Are men more violent than women?" Other comparisons could be made as well. For example, we could conceivably compare men's current violence with that of an earlier era, making time period a variable. In either instance, the answer to the question requires us to analyze two variables simultaneously.

This chapter develops the basic logic of bivariate analysis. First, we will create a special type of sample space, known as the **Cartesian product**. The Cartesian product consists of all possible intersects of the values of two variables. Next, we will obtain the frequency distribution of this sample space. Since this is a distribution of all possible combinations of outcomes of two variables, it is an example of bivariate distribution. Such distributions are known as **contingency tables**, or **cross-classification tables**. Finally, we will examine how Bernoulli's Theorem combines with the concept of statistical independence to make use of the **chi-square distribution**.[1] This distribution will permit us to answer the question "What is the probability of a relationship between the two variables?"

Cartesian Products

A Cartesian product (named after the early 17th Century French philosopher and mathematician René Descartes) consists of all possible pairings of the values of two variables, and, conceptually at least, this set is at the heart of much statistical inquiry in the social sciences.

Double Subscripts

A convenient way to organize some information is in a matrix of rows and columns. Cartesian products, for example, are customarily presented this way. When organized in this fashion, double subscripts are used to specify any cell, with the first subscript referring to the row, and the second one to the column. For example, "$Cell_{1,2}$" refers to the entry in the first row, second column, of the matrix in question.

Let's take the parental socialization thesis to illustrate the usefulness of this kind of set. Stated crudely, this thesis holds that parents mould the desires of their children. In the previous chapter we noted that the distribution of the post–high school preferences of parents and their teenaged children were quite similar. We emphasized that such similarity, however, did not constitute evidence supporting the parental socialization thesis. To simplify the discussion, let's focus only on mothers and their teenagers.[2] In this setting, two variables are relevant: the post–high school preferences mothers have for their children, and the corresponding preferences of their teenagers. To simplify even more, we will dichotomize these variables: for both variables, the two outcomes, or values, are whether attending university is preferred or not. When both variables of the Cartesian product are dichotomies, the resulting table is often referred to as a **four-fold table**, as shown in Figure 3.1.

Figure 3.1
Cartesian Product of the Post High School
Preferences of Teenagers and Their Mothers

	Mother's Preference	
Teenager's Preference	Attend University	Other
Attend University	a	b
Other	c	d

Several points should help to clarify Figure 3.1:

- Each column in any Cartesian product represents a unique outcome (value) of one variable. The first column, for example, represents the set "Mother's preference is for the child to attend university."
- Likewise, each row represents a distinct outcome of the second variable. In Figure 3.1, the first row is the set "Teenager desires to attend university."
- The number of cells is obtained by multiplying the number of rows times the number of columns (hence the name Cartesian *product*).
- Each cell in the Cartesian product represents the intersect of a given value of the first variable with a given value of the second variable. In Figure 3.1, the four possible intersects are labelled a, b, c and d. Cell a represents the intersect where both mother and teenager prefer university attendance for the teenager, and cell d shows neither mother nor teenager prefer university.[3]

If the parental socialization thesis has merit, we would expect cells a and d to be relatively full. That is, we expect to find many instances where, if a mother preferred her teenager to attend university, so would the teenager. Similarly, where a mother preferred some other path, the teenager should also prefer this path. Cells b and c should be relatively empty: when mothers want the teenager to attend university, teenagers should relatively infrequently desire some other path. When mothers desire their children to take some path other than university attendance, the teenagers should seldom desire to attend university.

Figure 3.2
Cross-Classification of Post High School
Preferences of Teenagers and Their Mothers

	Mother's Preference		
Teenager's Preference	Attend University	Other	
Attend University	87	14	101
Other	42	182	224
	129	196	325

Source: Data from Looker (1977).

To evaluate these expectations requires us to obtain independent observations on both variables for every case. With such data we can construct the **bivariate frequency distribution** as a cross-classification or contingency table. Figure 3.2 provides such a cross-classification, using the Looker (1977) data.

The expectations derived from the parental socialization thesis seem supported. Note in particular that cells a and d are relatively popular, with 87 and 182 observations in these two cells, respectively. In contrast, cells b and c are sparse, containing, respectively, 14 and 42 cases. Thus teenagers appear to desire for themselves the path their mothers prefer them to take. These numbers contained in Figure 3.2 can be grouped into distinct types, as shown in Figure 3.3.

Figure 3.3
Parts of a Contingency Table

Part	Example from Figure 3.2
• **Row marginals**: The number of observations for each value of the row variable.	There were 101 teenagers who hoped to attend university and 224 who planned to take some other path.
• **Column marginals**: The number of cases for each value of the column variable. The column (and row) marginals are synonymous with the univariate frequency distribution of the column variable.	There were 129 mothers who preferred their children to attend university. An additional 196 mothers preferred some other path for their teenagers. The column marginals add up to the total number of observations, 325. (The same holds true for the sum of the row marginals).
• **Cell frequencies**: The number of observations obtained in each of the cells defined by a particular Cartesian product.	There are 87 instances where both teenagers and their mothers chose university attendance, and another 182 instances where neither chose university attendance. In 14 dyads, the teenager preferred university attendance but the mother did not; in 42 instances the reverse was true.
• **Number of observations**: The total number of cases for which information on both variables is available. The cell frequencies add up to the total number of observations.	The sum of the four cell frequencies is 325, which represents the total number of cases for which information on post– high school preferences for both mother and teenager was available.

Source: From data collected by Looker (1977).

The Logic of Chi-Square

For the numbers in Figure 3.2, it was obvious that our expectations were upheld. But often results are ambiguous. In such situations it is desirable to have a yardstick against which to evaluate the results. The chi-square distribution provides one such yardstick. The logic of chi-square can be expressed more simply in the context of the parental socialization thesis.

Figure 3.4
Marginal Distribution of Post High School Preferences of Teenagers and Their Mothers

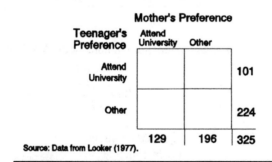

Source: Data from Looker (1977).

In the first step we visualize how our world would look, statistically, if the parental socialization thesis were wrong and parents did not influence their children's desires. Try to imagine a world in which parents and their children were as strangers to each other. Figure 3.4 provides the univariate or **marginal distributions** for the parental socialization thesis. These show that 129 mothers want their teenagers to attend university and 101 teenagers have the same desire. Now, it is empirically possible that none of these 101 teenagers are offspring of the 129 mothers who desire university attendance for their children. It is also possible that all of them are offspring of such mothers. The question then becomes: "What would the cell frequencies be if the data had been collected in a world where parents did not influence their children; where parents and their children were virtual strangers?"

The answer to this question is intimately connected to the concept of statistical **independence**, developed in Chapter 1. There we showed that two events, *A* and

B, are independent of each other if, and only if $p(A \cap B) = p(A) \cdot p(B)$.

This permits us to calculate the frequencies we would expect to find in each cell of Figure 3.3 if the desires of teenagers and their mothers were independent of each other. The **column marginal** for mothers preferring university attendance (D_m) is 129, and the estimated probability of this event is 129/325 or 0.40. The **row marginal** representing the analogous desire for children (D_c) is 101, which yields an estimated probability of 0.31. If the desires of mothers in no way influenced the desires of their children, then

$$p(D_m \cap D_c) = (.40)(.31) = 0.12.$$

If we want to know how many cases we would expect to find in this intersect, we would simply multiply our answer by the total number of cases, 325. Thus we would expect $(.40)(.31)(325) = 40.3$ cases in that particular intersect. Generalizing, the expected frequency in any cell is simply:

$$N\left(\frac{\text{row marginal}}{N}\right)\left(\frac{\text{column marginal}}{N}\right). \qquad (3.1)$$

Cancelling the *N* in the numerator with one of the *N*'s in the denominator, we get:

$$E_{ij} = \frac{(r_i \cdot c_j)}{N}. \qquad (3.2)$$

where: E = **expected frequency**
r = row marginal
c = column marginal
N = total number of cases, and
i and j = subscripts designating any particular row and column, respectively.

Figure 3.5 shows these expected frequencies for all cells. Comparing them with the observed frequencies (Figure 3.2) shows that cells a and d each contain in excess of forty-five cases more than expected. These cells represent instances in which the desires of mothers and their teenagers are congruent. Cells b and c represent instances where the desires of mothers and their teenaged children are incompatible, and these contain correspondingly fewer cases than expected. These results strongly oppose the view that we live in a world where mothers and their children are like strangers to each other. Rather, our world is one where the post–high school preferences of teenagers are related to the preferences of their mothers. Such a pattern is consistent with the parental socialization thesis.

Figure 3.5
Expected Distribution of Post High School Preferences of Teenagers and Their Mothers

Mother's Preference

Teenager's Preference	Attend University	Other	
Attend University	40.1	60.9	101
Other	88.9	135.1	224
	129	196	325

Source: Data from Looker (1977).

We used Bernoulli's Theorem to obtain the expected frequencies in Figure 3.5. However, if we were to obtain additional random samples of 325 mothers each, it is highly unlikely that in each of them exactly 40 percent would desire university attendance for their children. The differences in the percentages that we would find in the different samples are referred to as **sampling fluctuations**. For this reason, we wouldn't expect the observed frequencies to equal precisely the expected frequencies, even if the desires of children were independent of their mothers' desires. We expect some differences simply because of chance fluctuations in our estimates of the various probabilities. Therefore, the crucial question is "How likely is it that the obtained discrepancies are due to chance or sampling fluctuations?" To answer this we need a measure of how large the discrepancies are in Figure 3.5 as a whole. We might be tempted to add up all the discrepancies between the observed (O) and expected (E) frequencies as our measure. Thus we could take $(87 - 40.12)$ $+ (14 - 60.9) + (42 - 88.9) + (182 - 135.1)$. However, were we to do this, we would find that such sums always equal zero. The reason for this is simple. Since the sum of the observed frequencies equals the sum of the expected frequencies, which equal N, the sum of $(O_{ij} - E_{ij})$ will also equal zero.[4] One solution is to square each of these differences; i.e., find $(O - E)^2$ and sum these. This quantity reflects how large a difference we have between expected and observed frequencies. But there is still one drawback: the expected frequencies in some cells are substantially greater than the expected frequencies in other cells. For example, the expected frequency in one cell may equal 10 and the observed frequency may equal 9. A different cell may have an expected frequency of 100 and an observed frequency of 99. In both cases $(O - E)^2 = 1$. However, in the second case, the agreement between the observed and the expected is obviously much closer. (Look at it in terms of percentages: in the first cell there is a 90 percent agreement between observed and expected frequencies, but in the second case there is a 99 percent agreement.) To take this factor into account, we divide each of our squared differences by the expected frequency, which results in a quantity known as chi-square:

$$x^2 = \sum \frac{(O - E)^2}{E}. \tag{3.3}$$

Dividing by E takes into account the differences in the size of the expected frequency in each cell. All other factors being equal (we will see later on what this entails), the larger the computed chi-square value, the less likely it is that A and B are independent. Let's calculate the chi-square value in Table 3.1.

Table 3.1
Calculating a Chi-Square Value

Cell Subscript	Observed (O)	Expected (E)	$(O - E)$	$(O - E)^2$	$\frac{(O - E)^2}{E}$
1,1	87	40.1	46.9	2,199.61	54.85
1,2	14	60.9	-46.9	2,199.61	36.12
2,1	42	88.9	-46.9	2,199.61	24.74
2,2	182	135.1	46.9	2,199.61	16.28
TOTAL	325	325.0	0.0	$\chi^2 =$	131.99

Notice that the sum of the observed frequencies equals the sample size of 325, as does the sum of the expected frequencies. For this reason, the sum of the differences between the observed and the expected equals zero. Finally, the computed chi-square equals 131.99. Although we can get a discrepancy of any possible magnitude just by chance,[5] the question we must answer is "How likely is a discrepancy as large as 131.99 if the desires of children are independent of their parents' aspirations for them?" To answer this question we must introduce the notion of **degrees of freedom** (usually abbreviated as df). Perhaps the simplest way to explain this concept is by example.

Figure 3.6

Determining the Degrees of Freedom

Mother's Preference

Teenager's Preference	Attend University	Other	
Attend University		14	101
Other			224
	129	196	325

Figure 3.6 gives the marginals (row and column subtotals) and the entry in one cell. Convince yourself that, with this information, all of the other cells are completely determined. For example, $cell_{1,1}$ must be 87, otherwise the first row would not add up to 101. Therefore $cell_{2,1}$ must be 42, if the first column is to add up to 129. Similarly, $cell_{2,2}$ must be 182. In other words, we can put an arbitrary number in only one cell of this table: one cell is *free* to take on any value (except of course a value greater than the appropriate row or column marginal). We call this the degrees of freedom of a table. For all tables, the degrees of freedom are found by:

$$df = (r-1)(c-1). \qquad (3.4)$$

where r = the number of rows (excluding the marginal row), and
         c = the number of columns (excluding the marginal column).

Thus, the degrees of freedom for Figure 3.6 is $(2-1)(2-1) = 1$. For each degree of freedom, there is a unique chi-square distribution. The degrees of freedom determine the shape of the chi-square distribution, and such characteristics are called **parameters**. Hence, the parameter of the chi-square distribution is its degree of freedom. Appendix A provides information on chi-square distributions with differing degrees of freedom. At the top of this appendix page are listed the different probabilities of obtaining chi-squares of various magnitudes. For example, for a table with one degree of freedom, the probability of obtaining a chi-square as large as 7.879 is 0.005. That is to say, only once in a thousand times would you get a chi-square as large as 7.879 between the desires of mothers and their children if in fact these two variables were independent. Our computed chi-square was 131.99, so the probability of a chi-square this large is even less than 0.005. This means that we can be quite confident that the post–high school preferences of mothers and children are related. It is extremely unlikely that the discrepancies between the observed and expected values represent sampling or chance fluctuations that occur when relative frequencies are used to estimate probabilities.

Table 3.2
Observed and Expected Frequencies for the Relationship of Post–High School Preferences Between Mothers and Teenagers

Teenagers' Preferences	Mothers' Preferences					
	(1)	(2)	(3)	(4)	(5)	N
1) Work						
Observed	26	7	12	11	11	67
Expected	8.5	2.0	7.2	17.7	26.6	
2) Apprenticeship						
Observed	4	19	5	6	3	37
Expected	4.7	3.9	4.0	9.8	14.7	
3) Commercial, Trade, or Business School[a]						
Observed	6	2	2	6	4	20
Expected	2.5	2.1	2.2	5.3	7.9	
4) Community/Teachers College						
Observed	5	5	11	55	24	100
Expected	12.6	10.5	10.8	26.5	39.7	
5) University						
Observed	0	1	5	8	87	101
Expected	12.7	10.6	10.9	26.7	40.1	
N	41	34	35	86	129	325

[a]Includes "Other" preferences.

Source: Looker (1977).

Up to this point we have dichotomized the post–high school preferences of both mothers and children, primarily to simplify the presentation of contingency table analysis. One major advantage of contingency tables is the detailed descriptions they permit. A cell-by-cell comparison of the observed frequencies with the expected frequencies provides invaluable assistance in detecting patterns of connection between events. Let's look at the connections between the post–high school preferences of mothers and their children in greater detail (Table 3.2).

The largest difference between observed and expected frequencies occurred when both teenager and mother chose university attendance: 87 mother-offspring pairs are located in this cell, more than double the expected number of 40.1. In general, the largest discrepancies occur for those cells indicating mother-offspring agreement in post–high school preferences. That is, the "agreement" cells (which fall along the main diagonal, from the upper left to the lower right corner) are much more populous than expected under the assumption that the preferences of mothers and their children are independent.

In addition, the preference that children express least often (attending commercial, trade or business school) is also the one where mothers and their children are like typical strangers; only two mother-offspring pairs are observed in the agreement cell, about the same as the 2.2 expected. In short, comparing the observed with the expected frequencies in Table 3.2 reveals two patterns: (1) the cells that indicate mother-offspring agreement are substantially more populous than would be expected if mothers did not influence their children, and (2) for the path of attending commercial, trade or business school, the observed frequencies are similar to those we would expect if mothers did not influence their children in this area. Perhaps this is an ambiguous path.

Assumptions in the Test for Independence

Statisticians have shown that equation 3.3 usually obeys the chi-square distribution. There are, however, certain conditions in which our calculations of discrepancies are not approximated very well by the chi-square distribution. One such condition occurs when the expected frequencies in the cells are very small. Consequently, a general rule has been established: don't use the chi-square test if more than 20 percent of the cells have an expected frequency of less than five.[6] Two things to remember here: (1) it is the expected rather than the observed frequencies that should not be less than five, and (2) this is only a general rule and sometimes you may be forced to violate this assumption. Some work has been done showing that chi-square is a **robust test**; that is, it is not too critically affected by violations. Collapsing a table is one way to increase the expected frequencies in cells. The expected frequency is less than five in seven of the twenty-five cells in Table 3.2, which is unacceptable. Hence we would have to collapse, or combine, some of the distinct outcomes. Interpretability is the main criterion for deciding which outcomes should be combined. I would suggest, for instance, that "work" and "apprenticeship" be combined, since neither involves further education. I would keep "university" in a category by itself, partly because it is the single most frequently desired path. Finally, I would combine the remaining two outcomes into a category called "non-university education."[7] In this collapsed version, the lowest expected frequency is 23.3 (see Table 3.3). This permits us to calculate the chi-square value, which is 184.34. With four degrees of freedom, this means there is less than one chance in a thousand that teenagers' desires are independent of their mothers' desires.

Table 3.3
Collapsed Cross-Tabulation of the Post–High School Preferences of Teenagers and Their Mothers

Teenager's Desires	Mother's Desires (1)	(2)	(3)	Total
(1) Work/Apprenticeship				
Observed	56	34	14	
Expected	24.0	38.7	41.3	(104)
(2) Non-university education				
Observed	18	74	28	
Expected	27.7	44.7	47.6	(120)
(3) University education				
Observed	1	13	87	
Expected	23.3	37.6	40.1	(101)
TOTAL	(75)	(121)	(129)	(325)

Source: Looker (1977).

For Table 3.3, it is important to recognize that the major diagonal cells (where the row subscript equals the column subscript; that is, $cell_{1,1}$, $cell_{2,2}$, and $cell_{3,3}$) contain the cases that support the parental socialization argument. In all three of these cells, the observed frequency is substantially higher than what would be expected if mothers' desires did not influence teenagers' desires. In fact, the observed frequencies in these cells add up to about double the expected ones (217 versus 108.8, respectively). This is of greater importance than the size of the chi-square. Chi-square tells us only whether two events are related; it does not reveal the nature of the relationship. Therefore, it is imperative to look at more than just the computed chi-square value. We must make sure that the form of the relationship, as revealed by a cell-by-cell examination of the difference between the expected and observed frequencies, is congruent with the argument being made.

One drawback in chi-square analysis is that the results are intimately connected with the sample size. The larger the sample size, the more likely you are to get answers that are **statistically significant**, all other things being equal. The reason for this is built right into the computation of chi-square. In equation 3.3, the numerator is squared but not the denominator. This results in bigger chi-squares wherever the absolute frequencies are large and discrepant from the expected absolute frequencies. Consequently, chi-square tells us only how confident we can be that a relationship exists; it does not tell us the nature or the strength of the relationship. In Chapter 6, we will develop statistical techniques that are unaffected by sample size and which answer these two questions. For now it will suffice to note that percentages are sometimes satisfactory solutions.

Percentage Tables

By convention, contingency tables are presented in the form of percentages rather than raw numbers. **Percentage tables** provide an alternative method (to that of comparing observed and expected frequencies) for detecting and presenting the relationship between two variables.

The literal meaning of "percent" is "out of every one hundred." The purpose, then, of computing percentages is to circumvent the problem of unequal numbers of cases. With unequal numbers of cases, comparisons are difficult to make. Note in Table 3.4 that 75 respondents could not name any premier, but 242 could name exactly one. To say that 34 of the former and 122 of the latter placed the NDP to the left of centre would not be very helpful. Converting these numbers to percentages ($34/75 \times 100 = 45$ percent; $122/242 \times 100 = 50$ percent) makes the comparison immediately clear. Facilitating comparison is the main purpose of constructing percentage tables.

In Table 3.4, each row of percentages adds to 100 percent. We could have constructed the table so each column adds to 100 percent (or even so all percentages in the table add to 100 percent). The direction in which percentages are calculated depends on which variable is considered the independent, and which the dependent, variable. In the strongest sense, an **independent variable** is the cause and the **dependent variable** is the effect.

Many arguments use causal imagery. When constructing percentage tables, we make this imagery more explicit by making the percentages add to one hundred for each category of the independent variable. In the party imagery example, we argued that political knowledge causes one to see the NDP as left of centre. Conventional wisdom considers the correct left-right status of the NDP to be left of centre. The argument suggests that lack of knowledge blinds individuals from knowing this. Therefore political knowledge causes individuals to place the NDP to the left of centre.

Table 3.4 presents the relationship between political knowledge and party imagery in percentages. It shows that among those who could not name a single premier, less than half (45 percent) placed the NDP to the left of centre. The percentages so classifying the NDP increases with the number of premiers correctly named. Among Canadians identifying seven or more premiers, at least four out of five identify the NDP as a party of the left.

Table 3.4

Percentage of Canadians Placing the NDP to the Left of Centre by Number of Premiers Correctly Named

Number of Premiers Correctly Named	Perceived Left-Right Status of the NDP		
	Left	Not Left	N
0	45	55	75
1	50	50	242
2	53	47	225
3	61	39	240
4	68	32	230
5	71	29	208
6	79	21	188
7	82	18	156
8	81	19	104
9	88	12	49
10	85	15	33

Source: 1984 CNES.

It is sometimes useful to think of the percentages in a contingency table as conditional probabilities that have had their decimal point moved two places to the right. With respect to Table 3.4, we could say that the probability of placing the NDP to the left, given that no premiers can be named, is 0.45; among those who can name nine premiers, the probability of placing the NDP to the left of centre is about double that, at 0.88. The *form* of the relationship can thus be summarized: the more premiers correctly named, the greater the likelihood of classifying the NDP to the left of centre.[8] The *strength* of the relationship is estimated by obtaining the percentage difference between the extreme categories: Canadians who knew the names of all the premiers were about 40 percent more likely to place the NDP to the left of centre than were those who knew none of them (85 percent – 45 percent = 40 percent).

Let me return to the issue of whether a variable is to be considered an independent or dependent one. Whether it is one or the other (or neither) is primarily a matter of the argument being made. Let's illustrate this point using the similarity-attraction hypothesis. Reinforcement theory treats agreement as the independent variable, since agreement is the positive reinforcement that causes individuals to be attracted to each other. The joint reality construction argument treats attraction as the independent variable and it argues that individuals who are attracted to each other will seek to establish a joint reality, that is, to forge agreements. Finally, a third approach, known as balance theory, does not give causal priority to either variable, stating simply that disagreement among friends (as well as agreement among enemies) is psychologically uncomfortable. Individuals will seek to remove the "psychological pain" either by changing their opinion or changing the relationship.

In the parental socialization example, we expect teenagers to desire the path their parents want them to take. Here it is usually argued that parents' desires constitute the independent variable, with the desires of the teenager dependent on that. In the traditional two-parent family, there are two possible independent variables, one being the desires of the mother and the other the desires of the father. Table 3.5 presents the results.

Although Table 3.5 could have been presented as two separate tables, one table makes it easier to compare the relevant percentages. The cross-tabulations reveal a strong and consistent parental socialization effect. With the exception of commercial, trade or business school, a majority of students desire the same path desired by their mothers. The same conclusion holds with respect to the impact of fathers' desires.

Turning to the style of tables, several features should be stressed. Overall, a table should be labelled and documented so a reader can understand it without reading any accompanying text. First, the table should have an appropriate title. Second, each of the variables should be labelled and each of the possible outcomes should be clearly identified. Third, the number of cases (N) on which a percentage is based should be provided. This is done in the third row of the table. These N's help the reader assess the stability of the various percentages and they also make the direction of the percentages clear. Finally, where several sources of data are being used, the specific source of the data should be credited.

Table 3.5
Teenagers' Post–High School Preferences of Their Mothers and Fathers (%)

Parents' Preferences	Teenagers' Preferences					
	(1)	(2)	(3)	(4)	(5)	N
1) Work						
Mother	63	10	15	12	0	(41)
Father	70	0	5	18	7	(56)
2) Apprenticeship						
Mother	21	56	6	14	3	(34)
Father	17	66	3	14	0	(35)
3) Commercial, Trade, or Business School[a]						
Mother	34	14	6	31	14	(35)
Father	39	19	32	7	3	(31)
4) Community/Teachers College						
Mother	13	7	7	64	9	(86)
Father	13	7	5	71	4	(112)
5) University						
Mother	9	2	3	19	67	(101)
Father	8	5	5	13	70	(116)

[a] Includes "Other" preferences.

Source: Constructed from data collected by Looker (1977).

SPSS Instructions

I will comment only on those instructions for obtaining a contingency table (shown in Figure 3.7) that have not been covered in previous examples.

Figure 3.7
SPSS Instructions for Obtaining a Contingency Table

```
1   GET FILE = "vote84.sys".
2   COUNT premiers = var446 TO var455(1).
3   VARIABLE LABELS premiers "Number of premiers correctly named".
4   RECODE  var511 (1 THRU 3=1)(4 THRU 7=2).
5   VALUE LABELS var511
6        1 "Left"
7        2 "Not left".
8   CROSSTABS TABLES= var511 BY premiers
9        /CELLS=COUNT,COLUMN,EXPECTED
10       /STATISTICS=CHISQ.
```

Line 4: This is a data modification instruction. Here we are collapsing the codes for "var511" which classifies respondents' left-right perception of the NDP. Codes of "1 THRU 3" are recoded as 1's and represent left-of-centre views. The remaining codes of "4 THRU 7" are recoded as 2's and represent views of the NDP that are not left of centre.

Lines 5-7: Having recoded "var511," it is good practice to provide accurate "VALUE LABELS" that define what each outcome represents. Here we are recording the fact that a score of 1 means the respondent classified the NDP as left of centre and that a score of 2 means that the respondent did not. These VALUE LABELS will be printed in our output when we obtain the Cartesian product. Thus they too provide permanent identification of the meaning of our variables. Note that lines 11 and 12 are indented, since they are continuations of the VALUE LABELS instruction. On mainframe applications, all continuations must be indented by at least one space. If they are not, the SPSS software assumes they are new instructions, which it subsequently cannot interpret.

Line 8: This is a statistical procedures instruction. The keyword CROSSTABS produces Cartesian products that are the bases for percentage tables. They are also the ones on which chi-square analyses are done. It tells the computer which tables we desire. Here we want only one table, which is the Cartesian product of "var511 BY premiers." The variables listed before the keyword BY will appear as the rows of the table, and the variables listed after the keyword BY will become the columns of the table. Our table will have two rows and eleven columns.

Lines 9-10: Associated with many procedure instructions in SPSS are a variety of subcommands which create greater flexibility and user control of the results. Subcommands are separated from the procedure instruction and other subcommands with a slash (/), as shown at the beginning of lines 9 and 10. The CELLS subcommand requests that the expected and observed (COUNT) frequencies and the column percentages be computed and printed (i.e., the percentages in each column of the table will add up to 100 percent). The STATISTICS subcommand instructs SPSS to calculate and print the chi-square value for any table created.

Summary

- The set of all possible pairings of the values of two variables is a Cartesian product, which forms the logical basis for assessing whether a relationship between two variables exists.
- In cross-tabulations, empirical outcomes are mapped onto a Cartesian product and usually presented as percentage tables. These tables are percentaged in the direction of the independent variable, and the percentages are compared in the direction of the dependent variable. If the columns represent the different outcomes of the independent variable, then the percentages in each column add up to one hundred, while the percentages for a given row are contrasted. Whether a given variable is treated as independent or dependent is a theoretical question, to be answered through argumentation.
- Corresponding to the observed frequencies in a cross-tabulation, a set of expected frequencies can be calculated. These expected frequencies indicate how many cases we would expect in each cell if the two variables were independent of each other. The probability rule for independent events, covered in Chapter 1, is used for these calculations. The expected frequencies provide an estimate of what our world would look like if the two variables in no way influenced each other.
- The discrepancy between the observed and expected frequencies results from either sampling fluctuations (arising from the use of relative frequencies as estimates of probabilities) or from the variables not being independent of each other. A chi-square distribution is used to determine the plausibility of these two possibilities.

Notes

1. Chi (pronounced "*ki* ," which rhymes with "*why* ") is the name for the Greek letter χ.
2. We could just as easily have focused on fathers and their children, but it would complicate the presentation unnecessarily at this point to bring in both parents.
3. Note that the concept of *agreement* is used in the parental socialization example.

        Cells a and d represent agreement between mother and teenager on desired paths, whereas cells b and c indicate disagreement.

4.   For the sake of readability, the subscripts will not be given explicitly in the remainder of this chapter; the summation is always assumed to be over all cells of the Cartesian product.

5.   It is possible, although improbable, to get ten, twenty or thirty heads in a row, even with a fair coin. Some call that luck; statisticians call that sampling, or chance, fluctuation.

6.   Another condition is when the degrees of freedom are small. Especially in a two-by-two table (where $df = 1$), the approximation is not good. Therefore, a correction (called "Yate's correction") is used for such tables. This is done automatically in SPSS.

7.   An alternative to collapsing is elimination of categories. Often "undecided" or "don't know" responses are simply excluded from the chi-square analysis. One might even make the argument for Table 3.3 that the category "commercial, trade or business school" (which also happens to include a few "other" responses) should be eliminated, both because of the ambiguity of the category and the small number of respondents choosing this category.

8.   It is appropriate to ignore small inconsistencies in summary statements. In the case at hand, I would ignore the small decrease in percentage (from 88 percent to 85 percent) that occurs when comparing the party imagery of those who named nine versus ten premiers. These are subjective judgment calls, based primarily on the size of the percentage difference and on the number of cases. In Chapter 5, we will learn to evaluate these inconsistencies using statistical tests of significance.

Key Terms

bivariate analyses: Statistical procedures, such as contingency tables, in which two variables are considered simultaneously. Bivariate analyses permit us to assess whether two variables are statistically dependent; i.e., whether there is a relationship between them. These forms of analysis are crucial ingredients in arguments, because if events are dependent, knowledge of one reduces our uncertainty about the other. For example, in the similarity-attraction argument, knowing how similar two individuals are reduces the uncertainty with respect to the likelihood of their becoming friends.

bivariate frequency distribution: Distributions in which the frequency of each combination of values of two variables is given. Usually bivariate frequency distributions are presented two-dimensionally, with the rows representing the values of the one variable and the columns those of the other. In this form they are usually called contingency or cross-classification tables.

Cartesian product: A set composed of all possible pairings of the elements of two sets. As a consequence, each element of a Cartesian product has two distinct characteristics.

Cartesian products present a visualization of the form of bivariate statistical analysis. This form is two-dimensional, with the rows being the values of one variable and the columns those of the second. Thus each cell formed by intersection of a given row and column locates a joint event with those two characteristics. The number of cells is the product of the number of distinct values in the two parent sets.

chi-square distribution: A family of theoretical statistical distributions whose shape is determined by its degrees of freedom. In the context of bivariate frequency distributions, it is used to assess the probability that discrepancies between observed and expected frequencies (calculated on the assumption that the two variables are independent) could have arisen through chance fluctuations. If the resulting probability is low (conventionally less than 0.05), then we conclude that the two events in question are dependent.

column marginal: The frequency distribution of the column variable in a contingency table. The column marginals should always be supplied in a contingency table, as the last column, if they constitute the base on which percentages have been calculated.

contingency table: A Cartesian product in which the cells contain the frequencies of the joint events they represent. When the purpose of the table is to document or test a relationship between two variables, it is customary to also include percentages which have been calculated so that the percentages in those cells with a given value of the independent variable add to one hundred. Thus, if the rows represent the independent variable, then the percentages in each row sum to one hundred.

cross-classification table: Another name for a contingency table.

degrees of freedom: In contingency tables, the degrees of freedom specify the number of cells in the table that are free to vary, given the marginal distribution. This is captured by the formula:

$$df = (r - 1)(c - 1).$$

where df symbolizes the degrees of freedom, and r and c refer to the number of rows and columns, respectively, of the table. (The marginal row and column are not included in the count of the number of rows and columns.) In a different context, suppose we know that the sum of three numbers is twenty, and that the first number is three and the second is five. Clearly the third number *must* be twelve. Hence only two numbers are free to vary.

dependent variable: When two variables are related, the one that is thought to be the effect of the other. (See *independent variable*.)

expected frequency: In the context of a bivariate frequency distribution, the "expected frequency" is the frequency of any cell that could be expected statistically if the two variables in question were independent of each other. Although we use the term "expected," we usually hope that our results differ markedly from them, since the more they differ, the more the knowledge of the one event reduces uncertainty about the other event.

four-fold table: The simplest of all contingency tables, having precisely two rows and two columns, constructed by cross-classifying two dichotomous variables. Although generally too crude for many arguments, it provides a convenient way to think about relationships. Thus we can conceptualize the connection between smoking and cancer by cross-classifying "smoke/does not smoke" with "cancer/not cancer." To test the connection would require much more refined procedures that take into account the extent of smoking, for example.

independence: The occurrence of one event does not alter the probability of another one. In a chi-square analysis of contingency tables, the expected cell frequencies are calculated on the assumption that the row variable is independent of the column variable. When events are independent, knowledge of one event does not reduce our uncertainty about the other event (since it doesn't alter the likelihood of its occurrence). In most arguments, we don't like to conclude that events are independent, since this usually implies that our explanations or hypotheses are not supported.

independent variable: When two variables are related, the one that is thought to produce the other is called the independent variable. This language suggests a causal imagery and, as such, the independent variable can be thought of as the cause, and the dependent variable as the effect. We need to be cautious of this type of linear thinking. For example, it is plausible that a student's studying causes an improvement in grades. Here "study habits" is the independent variable and "grades" the dependent one. At the same time, symbolic interactionists, among others, would consider that having obtained a good grade acts as a stimulus for studying harder. Now "grades" is the independent variable and "study habits" the dependent one. We might conclude that there is a circular relationship between grades and study habits, such that receiving a good grade causes improved study habits, which cause grades to improve, and so on. Although statistical analysis might depict events in a linear fashion, it does not forbid a circular mode of thought.

marginal distributions: The univariate frequency distributions that represent the row and column totals of a contingency table. These are customarily presented as the last (or marginal) row and column. If the row (or column) percentages are presented, the row (or column) marginal reminds us of the base on which the percentages are calculated, and hence are considered a necessary component of well-constructed contingency tables.

parameters: Characteristics of theoretical distributions that determine the shape of that distribution. For example, the degrees of freedom is a parameter of the chi-square distribution.

percentage tables: Contingency tables where the cell frequencies have been converted to percentages, with the base of the percentage being the row or the column marginals, depending on which is considered the independent variable. Converting the frequencies to such percentages makes it easier to see whether, and in what ways, two variables are related to each other.

robust test: Any statistical procedure in which violation of an assumption on which it is based tends not to distort the finding. The chi-square test of independence is considered a robust test, except when the expected frequencies are small. As a rule, if more than 20 percent of the cells have an expected frequency of less than five, the chi-square test should not be used.

row marginal: The frequency distribution of the row variable in a contingency table. These row totals should be given whenever they constitute the base on which percentages have been calculated.

sampling fluctuation: The variability that occurs when relative frequencies are used to estimate probabilities. In a contingency table, the chi-square distribution can be used to calculate the probability that the discrepancy between the observed and the expected frequencies (assuming that the two variables under consideration are independent of each other) results from sampling fluctuations. Such calculations rest on the assumption that the observations were obtained independently of each other and under identical conditions. Random sampling procedures are used to approximate these conditions. As one might expect, the larger the sample size, the less the sampling fluctuation generally will be.

statistical significance: A shorthand reference to the probability that the difference between the observed and the expected outcomes is the result of sampling fluctuation. In chi-squared analysis of contingency tables, a statistically significant finding implies that the two variables in the cross tabulation are probably related in some way and to some extent; that is, that they are dependent events. Findings that are statistically significant are not necessarily strong or important ones, since even small differences between the observed and the expected outcomes can become statistically significant with a sufficiently large sample.

univariate analyses: Simple forms of statistical analysis, such as calculating frequency distributions, in which one variable is analyzed at a time. Univariate analyses are essential for describing phenomena; they are less directly useful in our efforts to explain them.

Chapter 4

GLEANING INFORMATION FROM DISTRIBUTIONS: MEASURES OF LOCATION, DISPERSION AND SKEWNESS

Now that we have constructed distributions of variables, we can extract summary characteristics of the distributions as a whole. This summary information lets us ignore particular outcomes and focus on more general characteristics of a phenomenon. In this chapter we will learn to glean such general information from distributions. We will find three overall characteristics of distributions useful: measures of location, dispersion and skewness. **Measures of location** (or centrality) answer the question "What is the typical, or average, outcome?" **Measures of dispersion** answer the questions "How typical is the typical outcome?" or "How diverse are the outcomes?" And **measures of skewness** provide the answer to "How symmetrically distributed are the outcomes?"

But before we turn to these measures, we need to consider carefully how we assign numbers to represent the outcomes of variables. In the party imagery example, we use the integers 0 through 10 to designate the number of premiers a respondent could recall. These numbers aptly define and label the various possible outcomes and permit a variety of manipulations. For example, we wouldn't hesitate to say that the respondent who recalled the names of eight premiers recalled twice as many as the respondent who could name only four. In contrast, no numbers spring naturally to mind to designate the various preferred paths, such as apprenticeship or attending university, in the parental socialization example. If we did let numbers represent the different preferred paths, we would be severely limited in the types of arithmetic operations permissible, which brings us to a consideration of **levels of measurement**.

Levels of Measurement

Numbers have certain pleasing characteristics: we can add, multiply and compare them. We can say, for example, that the number 10 is twice as big as the number 5. Attaching numbers to events makes it easier for us to reach conclusions about our social world. However, manipulating these numbers may not produce meaningful information about that world. Of fundamental importance is our ability to translate numerical results into statements about empirical events.

Numbers are more malleable than the events they signify. Although all numbers have the same abstract properties that permit us to add, subtract, compare, and so on, it is not always true that the events in our world have these same properties. Therefore we must always assess the congruence between our numbers and the events they represent. Even though we universally use numbers to represent events, certain mathematical operations are not always warranted. The operations we can perform depend on (1) the nature of the event we are studying and (2) the level of measurement of our observed variables.

There are four levels of measurement: nominal, ordinal, interval and ratio. The "weakest" of these is nominal, the "strongest" is ratio (by "weak" I mean that few mathematical operations are permitted).

A **nominal** (or **categorical**) **measure** simply attaches numbers to events, with different numbers representing discrete categories. Take post–high school preferences as an example. For convenience, we could assign numbers to each of the preferences, as in Table 4.1. But these numbers are quite arbitrary; other sets of numbers could serve equally well, since the numbers assigned to nominal events have none of the usual connotations of numbers. The numbers assigned cannot even be compared to each other to determine which event is larger or smaller. They represent nothing more than convenient symbols for the various sets or outcomes. For this reason, nominal measures are often called **qualitative variables**, where the numbers represent distinctions in kind rather than quantity.

Table 4.1
Nominal Numbers for Post–High School Preferences

Number	Meaning
1	Work
2	Apprenticeship
3	Commercial, Trade or Business School
4	Teachers College
5	Community College
6	University
7	Other

Source: Looker (1977).

Since set theory requires only qualitative distinctions to be made, all set operations can be performed on nominal data. Because the numbers attached to nominal events are simply shorthand names, the only warranted operations are those we could perform on the names of the events themselves. We could compare whether two teenagers have the same desire, or count how many of them want to enter the work force immediately, or get estimates of the probabilities of this event. When we assign numbers to categorical events, the numbers have none of the intrinsic meanings generally associated with numbers.[1]

The next higher level is **ordinal measurement**. Numbers representing ordinal events have a meaningful ordering relative to each other; they represent a relative position, not an absolute one. Relative position simply implies that we can assess whether one event has more of the attribute being measured than another event.

The response format used in the 1984 CNES question on party imagery is a typical ordinal measure. A response of 1 places the NDP further to the left than a response of 2 and, likewise, a response of 6 is more to the right than a score of 5. The higher the number, the more to the right the respondent places the NDP.

We assign numbers at the ordinal level of measurement to reflect the order or inequality we believe characterizes the events. Technically, ordinal numbers must maintain the monotonic character of events. (**Monotonicity** means that, for each outcome, we can determine whether it has more, the same or less of the attribute in question than any other outcome.) We then assign numbers to these outcomes so the numbers reflect this monotonicity. For the original left-right party image variable, theoretically we could have assigned the numbers $-3, -2, -1, 0, 10, 20$ and 30 instead of the numbers 1 to 7. For both sets of numbers, the greater the number, the more to the right the respondent placed the NDP. What we must not do, however, is reverse, for example, the numbers 20 and 30, because such a reversal would violate the monotonicity that we assume characterizes the left-right measure.

With ordinal measures we don't know *how much more* of the characteristic one event has relative to another event. For example, we can't tell how much more to the left the NDP is placed by someone who rates it a 2 rather than a 3. All we know is that it is more.

Equal interval measures are somewhat more absolute in their meaning, although not entirely. The major characteristic of interval measures is that the numbers reflect constant differences. The difference between three and four units of the variable being measured is exactly the same as the difference between five and six units. Our political knowledge variable has this feature: the numbers assigned correspond to the number of names of premiers recalled. The numbers assigned to such outcomes are less arbitrary than ordinal numbers, since interval numbers reflect constant magnitudes. This permits us to add, multiply, subtract and divide such numbers with confidence that these operations will produce information that reflects the phenomena of interest in a meaningful way.

The highest level of measurement is **ratio measurement**, which has the same properties as interval measurement but, in addition, possesses an absolute zero point. This permits us to make statements such as "this score is twice that score." In the social sciences, age and income are examples of ratio measures. A 64-year-old person is twice as old as one who is 32; someone who makes $20,000 a year earns twice as much as someone who makes $10,000.

Levels of Measurement and Permissible Operations

Measurement Level	Permissible Operation
• nominal (categorical)	— count (same, different)
• ordinal	— compare (<, =, >)
• equal interval	— add, multiply
• ratio	— form ratios

How Can We Tell the Level of Measurement?

The level at which a variable is measured often seems straightforward. Few researchers would question that age (measured in years) is a ratio measure, or that religious denomination (measured in categories such as Jewish, Protestant or Catholic) is a nominal variable. Yet the level of measurement can be a matter for debate. For example, **Likert-type scales** are considered prototypical ordinal measures. The monotonic ordering implies that the beliefs of two individuals of whom the first strongly agrees and the other simply agrees with a statement are more similar than the beliefs of two individuals of whom the first strongly agrees and the other strongly disagrees. Nevertheless, a number of scholars have argued that opposing extreme responses of "strongly agree" and "strongly disagree" are similar (both responses being opinionated ones). In this vein, Hoffer (1951) argued that it would be easier to convert fanatics from one camp into an opposing one than to convert moderates. These two views of the nature of Likert scales can be diagrammed through linear and circular representations, as in Figure 4.1. The ordinal level is represented by the straight line; the nominal level by the circle. In the linear representation, "Strongly Agree" and "Strongly Disagree" are maximally separated, but not so in the circular representation.

Bear in mind that the measurement level resides not in the phenomenon itself, but in our treatment of it. For this reason it is important to provide arguments to support the measurement level being assumed. Let's do this for the parental socialization example. So far we have treated the various post–high school preferences as categorical events. Let's develop an argument to transform them into ordinal events. We start our argument by making a distinction between what teenagers expect to do and what they desire to do after high school. Looker (1977) gathered information on both aspects of post–high school plans. Next we introduce a

Likert Scales

In survey research, a common questionnaire format for assessing opinions and attitudes is known as the Likert scale. Typically, a statement is presented and the respondents are asked to indicate the extent to which they agree. One of the statements often used to measure political alienation, for example, is:

"Generally, those elected to Parliament soon loose touch with the people."

A variety of response formats has been used. In the four-point format, the response alternatives are:

Strongly Agree	Agree	Disagree	Strongly Disagree
1	2	3	4

A five-point version permits a neutral, or undecided, option:

Strongly Agree	Agree	Neither Agree nor Disagree	Disagree	Strongly Disagree
1	2	3	4	5

With more than five alternatives, it is customary to label only the end-points:

Strongly Agree						Strongly Disagree
1	2	3	4	5	6	7

Research has been conducted to evaluate whether certain response formats are preferable over others. The tentative conclusions are that an odd number of response alternatives is preferable to an even number, and five or more response categories are preferable to four or fewer.

theoretical assumption, namely that individuals ordinarily strive for the highest things they can reasonably hope to achieve: our goals exceed our grasp. We may expect to achieve something less than we desire, but seldom do we desire something less than we feel we can achieve. To take a specific example, we would not be at all surprised if some high school students were to say that they would like to attend university, but that circumstances compel them to enter the work force instead. We would be more surprised if they were to say that their desired goal was to start work immediately, but they expected to attend university instead (except where students are pressured to attend university). That is, we think of university attendance as a higher goal than immediately entering the work force. In fact, an argument could be made that, with the exception of the rather meaningless option of "Other," the outcomes listed in Table 4.1 represent increasingly higher desires.

Figure 4.1
Nominal versus Ordinal
Representation of Likert Scales

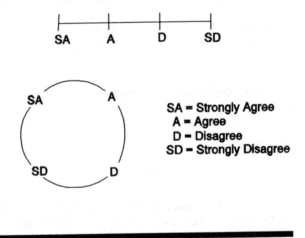

SA = Strongly Agree
A = Agree
D = Disagree
SD = Strongly Disagree

Table 4.2
Testing for Ordinality: Teenagers' Expected and Desired Post–High School Plans

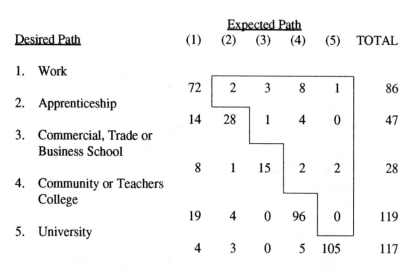

Desired Path	Expected Path (1)	(2)	(3)	(4)	(5)	TOTAL
1. Work	72	2	3	8	1	86
2. Apprenticeship	14	28	1	4	0	47
3. Commercial, Trade or Business School	8	1	15	2	2	28
4. Community or Teachers College	19	4	0	96	0	119
5. University	4	3	0	5	105	117

Source: Looker (1977).

We can cross-tabulate the expected and the desired plans to test whether this is so. Table 4.2 provides the results. This table shows the relationship between the desired and expected post–high school paths among teenagers. The solid lines enclose those instances where the expected path exceeds the desired path. Ideally, these would all be empty sets; instances in these cells weaken the argument that these paths can be considered ordinal. Fortunately for our argument, such instances are not excessive. For example, fourteen of the eighty-six teenagers who desired to go to work nevertheless expected to take a "higher" path. Altogether, Table 4.2 shows that only twenty-three out of almost four hundred student responses do not conform to an assumed ordinality. This constitutes strong evidence in favour of our argument, but we can make it even stronger. Earlier I suggested that some of the twenty-three exceptions may represent instances where students felt pressured to take a path they did not personally desire. Since such pressures would not characterize the desires and expectations of the parents, we would expect even fewer exceptions in their responses. And indeed, among fathers and mothers, the evidence for ordinality is even stronger, with only twelve and nine contrary cases, respectively (see Table 4.3).

Table 4.3

Testing for Ordinality: Post–High School Paths Parents Desire and Expect Their Teenagers to Take

Desired Path	(1)	(2)	Expected Path (3)	(4)	(5)	TOTAL
1. Work						
Father	25	2	0	0	0	27
Mother	39	0	0	1	0	40
2. Apprenticeship						
Father	18	17	1	0	0	36
Mother	12	18	2	2	0	34
3. Commercial, Trade or Business School						
Father	15	4	18	5	2	44
Mother	16	2	12	1	3	34
4. Community or Teachers College						
Father	13	2	4	53	2	74
Mother	13	4	3	64	0	84
5. University						
Father	12	5	7	22	86	132
Mother	11	2	8	20	89	130

Source: Looker (1977).

Ranks and Percentiles

To measure how quickly runners run a mile, we use a stopwatch. If no stopwatch is available, we can simply note which runner came first, second, third and so on. This way of measuring a phenomenon or variable is known as a **rank order**. The numbers assigned reflect the relative position of the observations on the relevant criterion within a particular group or population.

To get the rank, we order each event or outcome from lowest to highest on the variable of interest.[2] Thus the score itself indicates where this event stands relative to others in the frequency distribution.

The maximum number of ranks depends, naturally, on the number of members of the group being rank-ordered. This makes comparative statements somewhat awkward ("She was nineteenth out of forty-seven"). The solution is to compute **percentiles**, which standardize the scores by indicating what percent of the scores are lower than a given score. For example, the 90th percentile means that 90 percent of the observations in the distribution have a score lower than that one.

Percentiles are identical to cumulative percentages in a frequency distribution. Later in this chapter we will learn how to compute percentiles.

Ranks and percentiles are ordinal measures: the difference in time taken between the winner and the runner-up, for example, is usually not the same as the difference in time between any other adjacently ranked runners. Both ranks and percentiles reflect the position of an outcome in the frequency distribution: the scores no longer reveal "how much" of a certain characteristic a particular event has, but rather "how many" events are lower or higher. For instance, when someone tells us she earns $10,000 per year, we know exactly how much she makes. But if someone's income exceeds that of 70 percent of all Canadians, we know only how much this person makes relative to others. This is the major characteristic of ranks and percentiles: they provide information on the *relative* position of a particular outcome.

Several important points may be made in this discussion of measurement:

- Although numbers are universally flexible, in the realm of social research, some numbers flex more than others. In situations where the measures are interval, we can add, multiply, subtract and divide. In other situations, where the measures are nominal, the only meaningful operation is to count the frequencies of various events and then to compare these frequencies.

- We should aim to measure events at a level approximating the features of the events that interest us. If we feel that the important aspect of an event is whether it has a particular characteristic, then a nominal measure is quite appropriate. If our concern is with the relative position within a group, however, then the ordinal measure of rank, or percentile, is most appropriate. But if our interest centres on the actual amount or value of some characteristic, then we would strive for an interval or ratio scale.

- "Higher-order" levels of measurement (ratio is the highest, in the sense that it retains most of the properties of numbers) contain all the properties of lower-order measurements, plus additional properties. Hence, it is always possible to convert interval measures into nominal or ordinal measures. Since higher-level measurements permit more legitimate manipulations and can be converted to lower-order measures, it is advisable to record events at the highest possible level.

- The higher the level of measurement, the more kinds of statistical manipulations are permissable and meaningful. More ways of summarizing, ignoring and condensing can be used with higher-level than with lower-level measures. Not only are *more* statistical techniques permissible, but the techniques warranted for high-level measurements are also often *more powerful* in their capacity to summarize, ignore and condense. Hence, we should strive to create interval or ratio level measures and use these more powerful techniques.

- Although ordinal measures generally are inferior to interval and ratio ones, there are situations in which the ordinal position is the most salient feature. For example, which gorilla is the largest in a group is more important in determining the status structure than how large that gorilla is. Similarly, whether the NDP is ranked to the left of the Liberal party may be more important than how far to the left any of the parties is placed. Where human perception proceeds on the basis of social comparisons rather than absolute judgments, our measures should be comparative.
- At times it is reasonable to treat a lower-order measure as though it possessed higher-level characteristics. Now that we have learned the rule, we can talk about the exceptions. For example, grade-point averages are based on ordinal measures, since the difference between the grades of A and B may not be the same as the difference between D and F. Yet we assign the numbers 4, 3, 2, 1 and 0 to grades to obtain grade-point averages. To get averages we must add and divide, and these operations assume interval data. Nevertheless, despite the fact that we do not have interval events here, the averages do provide a useful summary measure of academic performance for some purposes.

This brings us to a contentious point: fruitful insights can sometimes be derived through operations that might be technically inappropriate. I am not advocating sloppiness or unconcern about assumptions. What I am advocating is an intelligent appraisal of what the assumptions mean and the conditions under which we might be willing to violate them for the sake of useful answers. The more we understand the rules, the better equipped we are to violate them and still obtain valuable insights. If we understand the principle, then occasionally we can break the rule.

The level of measurement is intimately connected with the types of summary information that can be gleaned from distributions. We are now in a position to develop the summary measures of location, dispersion and skewness. Measures of location are also known as measures of **central tendency**.

Measures of Central Tendency

The first way we will want to characterize distributions is by their location, i.e., we want to ascertain the "average" outcome. There are several meanings of "average," namely **mode, median** and **mean**. Since these may result in different answers, we should take a close look at each of them.

Mode

The mode answers the question: "Which outcome occurs most frequently or has the highest probability of occurring?" The mode is determined by inspecting the frequency distribution. In a histogram or bar graph, the mode occurs at the highest point in the chart. Figure 4.2 is a histogram of the age at marriage of a sample of Nova Scotian brides.[3] The modal bridal age is approximately 20 years, since that age corresponds to the highest point in this histogram.

Figure 4.2

Histogram of Bridal Age

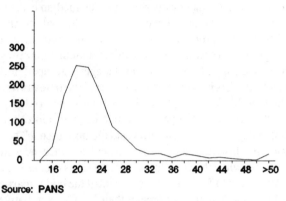

Source: PANS

Figure 4.3 superimposes the grooms' age at marriage on the histogram of the brides' marital age. Note that the modal age of grooms is several years older than that of brides. This is one way of showing that grooms tend to marry younger persons than brides do. Note that, although the distribution of two variables is presented in this figure, it nevertheless remains an example of **univariate analysis**. To make it bivariate, the unit of analysis would have to be the bridal couple. With such a unit, we could compare the ages of the bride and groom in each couple. **Bivariate analysis** of this form would permit us to determine what proportion of grooms married younger brides. This we cannot do with univariate analysis.

Figure 4.3

Histogram of Marital Ages of
Brides and Grooms

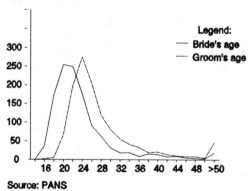

Source: PANS

Median

The median, a second type of average, divides a distribution into two equal halves. To find the median, the outcomes must first be arranged from lowest to highest, as when plotting a frequency distribution. The median is the value below which half the observations fall and above which the other half occur.

Table 4.4 reproduces Figure 4.2 in the form of a frequency distribution. Although age is a **continuous variable**, for tabular purposes, it is treated as a series of discrete classes. In this table, bridal age is grouped in two-year intervals. For grouped data, it is important to keep in mind the **true limits** of each class. The class labelled 19-20, for example, includes brides aged right up to, but not including, those who have turned 21 years. (Remember, we didn't have our first birthday until the 365th day; we remained zero years old until then.) The cumulative percentage column simplifies the calculation of a median, since the median equals the value of the variable when the cumulative percentage is precisely 50 percent.

According to Table 4.4, 38.8 percent of the brides married before they were 21. Clearly the median must be greater than 21. The cumulative frequency by the end of the next interval is 59.5 percent, which surpasses the median. Thus the median is contained somewhere in the interval between 21 and 23 years. To obtain the exact median we must perform a mathematical operation called **interpolation**. We know, by inspecting the table, that 20.7 percent of brides were married in the two-year interval between 21 and 22. However, we need only 11.2 percent to reach 50 percent $(50 - 38.8 = 11.2)$. Hence the median is located at 0.54 of the distance between 21 and 23 $(11.2/20.7 = 0.54)$. This is the same as multiplying 0.54 by 2 years, which works out to be 1.08. Adding 1.08 years to 21 years (the upper bound of the class below the median) gives us the interpolated median of 22.08. In other words, half the brides married before 22.08 years.

Another important feature of Table 4.4 and Figure 4.2 is the open-ended nature of the first and final classes. So few brides married in any of the age groups over 44 that, for convenience in presentation, these have been combined

Table 4.4

Distribution of Bridal Age

Age	f	%	Cum %
<17	38	3.2	3.2
17-18	174	14.5	17.6
19-20	254	21.1	38.8
21-22	249	20.7	59.5
23-24	177	14.7	74.2
25-26	91	7.6	81.8
27-28	63	5.2	87.0
29-30	31	2.6	89.6
31-32	18	1.5	91.1
33-34	19	1.6	92.7
35-36	9	0.7	93.4
37-38	16	1.3	94.8
39-40	14	1.2	95.9
41-42	8	0.7	96.6
43-44	10	0.8	97.4
>44	69	2.6	100.0
Total	1,211	100.0	100.0

Source: PANS.

The Summation Symbol

In statistical calculations, we often add many numbers. It would be convenient to have a shorthand way of expressing such additions. The Greek upper case sigma, Σ, is used for this purpose. Suppose we had three scores for the variable X:

$$x_1 = 3$$
$$x_2 = 6$$
$$x_3 = 2 \ .$$

All of us know we could express the addition operator for this variable as: $x_1 + x_2 + x_3 = 3 + 6 + 2 = 10$. The compact way of expressing this is:

$$\sum_{i=1}^{3} x_i = 10.$$

This summation symbol would be read as: Add the numbers represented by the subscripted variable x, starting with the first case and ending with the third one. The subscripted component of Σ ($i=1$) indicates from which observation we should start adding. The superscripted component indicates to which observation we should add. The summation symbol is sometimes abbreviated to Σ_i (and even simply Σ) when it is clear that the addition is to be performed from the first to the last observation of the variable.

---

into a single, **open-ended class**. Since the median is found in the middle of the distribution, it can be calculated precisely even though the first and last classes are open-ended.

Mean

The most common meaning of average is the **arithmetic mean**. Most of us probably know how to calculate the mean of a set of numbers: we simply add up the values of the outcomes of the variable and divide by the number of observations. In symbolic form, the mean is given by:

$$M = \frac{x_1 + x + \cdots + x_n}{N} = \frac{\sum_{i=1}^{N} x_i}{N} \tag{4.1}$$

where M = the mean

x_i = the symbol for the value of the variable for any given case, and

N = the total number of observations or cases.

When outcomes have been organized into a distribution, the mean can be thought of in a somewhat different way, which captures the notion of expectations.

For any discrete distribution, the **expected value** of the variable X (symbolized as $E(X)$) is:

$$M = E(X) = \sum_{i=1}^{k} x_i p(x_i)$$ (4.2)

where x_i =   the i th value
  $p(x_i)$ =   the probability of that value occurring, and
  k =   the number of values of the variable.

For empirical distributions, this formula provides a quicker method for calculating the mean. In both this and the following equation, the subscript i refers not to a particular case, but to a particular value of the variable.

Remember that, via Bernoulli's Theorem, f_i/N is an estimate of $p(x_i)$. Hence we can rewrite the above equation for empirical distributions as:

$$M = E(X) = \sum_{i=1}^{k} \left(\frac{f_i}{N} \right) x_i.$$ (4.3)

Let's calculate the mean number of premiers named using this equation. Table 4.5 provides the necessary information. The first column of this table gives the eleven possible values of the variable, ranging from 0 (none of the names of the premiers recalled) to 10 (all ten premiers correctly recalled). The second column gives the frequency with which each of these outcomes occurred. The third column is the **relative frequency** (the frequency divided by the total number of observations — if we were to multiply the numbers in this column by 100, we would obtain the percentage of cases falling within each outcome). The fifth column is the product of the value of the variable with its relative frequency (that is, the figures of column 1 multiplied by the corresponding figures in column 3). The sum of this column is the mean of the distribution, which in this example is 3.493.

Column 4 provides the product of the value of the variable with its absolute frequency. Dividing the sum of this column (11,838) by the number of observations (3,377) is often a preferable way of obtaining the mean, since less rounding errors are likely (every time we divide, a rounding error is possible; we divide only once using this method).

While examining this table, let's also calculate its mode and median. An inspection of the column of frequencies shows that 689 respondents could name precisely one premier. This represents a greater number of respondents than is associated with any other specific outcome. Hence the modal number of names of premiers known is one.

Table 4.5
Calculating the Mean Number of Premiers Correctly Named

(1) x	(2) f	(3) f/N	(4) x (f)	(5) x (f/N)
0	246	0.073	0	0.000
1	689	0.204	689	0.204
2	511	0.151	1,022	0.302
3	433	0.128	1,299	0.384
4	382	0.113	1,528	0.452
5	329	0.097	1,645	0.485
6	288	0.085	1,728	0.510
7	233	0.069	1,631	0.483
8	146	0.043	1,168	0.344
9	72	0.021	648	0.189
10	48	0.014	480	0.140
TOTAL	3,377	0.998[a]	11,838	3.493

[a] Except for rounding, this number would be 1.000.

Source: 1984 CNES.

If we ordered the 3,377 respondents on the value of the variable "number of names of premiers known," the median would be the value obtained by the middle (or $N/2$) respondent, who would be the 1,689th respondent. The scores of half the respondents would be greater than this respondent's score. Adding the frequencies, we can see that 1,446 respondents recalled the names of two or fewer premiers (246 + 689 + 511 = 1,446), which is less than we require for the median. But 1,879 respondents recalled three or fewer premiers' names, which is more than we need for the median. Hence the median number of names known is somewhere between two and three. To obtain the precise answer, we could again interpolate. We know that at two names we are 243 observations short of the median (1,689 – 1,446 = 243). But 433 cases fall between two and three names. Hence the median would be estimated to be at 243/433 of the distance between 2.5 and 3.5. When this fraction, calculated at 0.56, is added to 2.5 (the upper bound of the interval 1.5 to 2.5) the result is a median of 3.06.[4] In calculating the median for this distribution, we are treating the number of premiers correctly named as though it were a continuous variable. The discrete outcome "knows the names of two premiers" can then be thought of as containing the continuous outcomes in the interval between 1.5 and

2.5 names. Hence the upper bound of the number 2 would be 2.5. With discrete information, it is a matter of personal choice whether to interpolate to obtain the median. Some researchers prefer to report the median as the closest whole number.

To calculate a median, we must have at least an ordinal level of measurement; otherwise we cannot meaningfully order the outcomes from lowest to highest.

Comparison of Mean, Median and Mode

As stated earlier, the mean, median and mode are different measures of averages. Since they are not necessarily identical, we must decide which measure is most appropriate. There are several criteria for this. The first is the *level of measurement of our observations*. To obtain the mode, we need to determine only which is the most populous outcome. Since this involves nothing more than counting, we can use this measure for nominal data. For the median, we must know the relative position of any outcome: is it higher or lower than any other outcome? Since we need not know how much higher or lower other outcomes are, we can use the median whenever we consider our measures ordinal. Finally, when computing the mean, we add and divide, treating data as though it were interval in nature. Basically, the mode imposes no assumptions about the nature of the data, while the mean imposes the severest assumptions.

A second consideration is the *form of the distribution*. For most symmetric distributions, the mean, median and mode have identical values. Figure 4.4 illustrates this.

Figure 4.4
The Mean, Median and Mode in a
Symmetrical Distribution

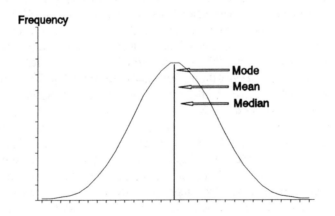

If a distribution is symmetrical, then it is inconsequential which measure of central tendency is computed. Some distributions, however, are **skewed**. By this we mean that one end of the distribution is more extended or drawn out than the other. The more skewed a distribution is, the more discrepant the three measures of central tendency will be. The distribution of marital age of brides is **positively skewed**. Looking at the histogram in Figure 4.5, which locates the mode, median and mean for the distribution of "bride's age at marriage," we can see that it has a tail on the right, or positive, side. As is typical of positively skewed distributions, the median is to the right of the mode, and the mean is even further to the right of the median.

A study of the frequencies of Table 4.5 suggests that the distribution of political knowledge is also positively skewed. Notice how the frequencies mount steeply and then taper slowly. The positive skew is confirmed by the relationship between the three measures of central tendency. Earlier we calculated the mode for this distribution as 1, the median as 3.06 and the mean as 3.49.

In a **negatively skewed distribution**, the exact opposite occurs: the mean is to the left of the median, which is to the left of the mode. An inspection of the distribution of the relative measure of party imagery given in Chapter 2 (Figure 2.6) suggests that it is negatively skewed. Here the frequencies increase slowly up to the mode and then drop rapidly. Again, the negative skew is confirmed by the relative positions of the mean, median and mode, whose values are 2.15, 2.42 and 3, respectively.

Figure 4.5
The Mode, Median and Mean for Bride's
Age at Marriage

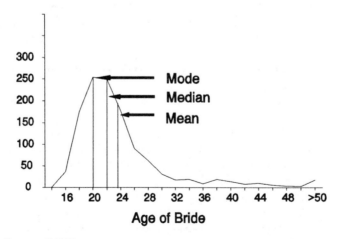

Source: PANS

Third, these three measures also differ in how much they are affected by the *nature of the distribution as a whole*. The mode is least affected by the other values in the distribution. The rest of the distribution could be completely changed, but as long as no other outcome has a higher frequency, the mode remains unchanged. The median incorporates more information about the distribution as a whole. Changing scores that were below the median into scores above the median would obviously change the location of the median. However, the median is insensitive to changes in the tails of the distribution: making the low scores even lower (or the high scores higher) would not affect the value of the median. Finally, the mean is influenced by the value of each observation and thus is affected most by the nature of the whole distribution. The effect of a few extremely high or low scores in the tails of the distribution (known as **outliers**) could alter the value of the mean drastically. For this reason the median is usually preferred to the mean to describe a skewed distribution.

Missing Information and Misleading Results

It is customary when analyzing data to provide numeric values to all cases, even to those where meaningful information is not available. In survey research, the numbers 9 and 99 frequently represent instances where a respondent refused to answer a question. A score of 9 in the party imagery example, for instance, does not signify placing the NDP to the extreme right. Rather, it indicates that the respondent did not answer this question. It is imperative that we exclude these cases when calculating certain statistical information such as the mean. In SPSS, such cases are excluded by defining the value of 9 on this variable as a MISSING VALUE (see the SPSS instructions at the end of this chapter).

Our results could be quite misleading if we failed to exclude such cases. Yet, by excluding them, we introduce a new potential for error: the excluded cases may not be typical. This presents a serious problem whenever information on a variable is missing for a substantial proportion of cases. We will examine this problem in detail in the next chapter.

Finally, the mean, median and mode each correspond to one definition of "best guess" or *expected outcome*. When using the mode, we imply that the best guess as to which outcome will occur is the one that occurs most frequently. Using this definition of expected outcome, we frequently will be exactly right, and we don't worry about how *far* off we are when we are wrong. Using the median as our expected outcome, half the time we will estimate too low and half the time too high. Finally, when using the mean, the sum of our errors will cancel out exactly.

When using the mean as our best guess for any outcome, our average error will always equal zero. Let's see mathematically why this is true.[5] If we use the mean as our best estimate, then, for any given observation, our error will be the difference between the value of the observation and the mean of the distribution. Let's call this difference a **deviation**, and, symbolizing it as d, we get this expression:

$$d = x_i - M. \tag{4.4}$$

Then the sum of all the errors, or deviation, is:

$$\sum_i d_i = \sum_i (x_i - M). \tag{4.5}$$

Removing the parentheses, we get:[6]

$$\sum d_i = \sum x_i - N \cdot M. \tag{4.6}$$

Dividing both sides of the equation by N results in:

$$\frac{\sum d_i}{N} = \frac{\sum x_i}{N} - M. \tag{4.7}$$

But what is x_i / N? It is, of course, the arithmetic mean. By substitution we then get the desired result that the average deviation is zero:

$$\frac{\sum d_i}{N} = M - M = 0. \tag{4.8}$$

Misleading Statistics

Skewed distributions provide an opportunity to mislead, intentionally or otherwise. Thus, if we wanted to convey most dramatically the lack of political knowledge among Canadians, we would report the mode, emphasizing that the most likely number of premiers Canadians can name is one. Conversely, if we wished to suggest high levels of political knowledge, we could report that Canadians, on average, know the names of 3.5 premiers. To avoid these kinds of biases, it is customary to report medians whenever distributions are markedly skewed. Remember that, in skewed distributions, the median is located between the mean and the mode. In this instance the median number of premiers named is 3.06. It would, however, be preferable to report all three measures, since each provides important information.

Conditional Means

In Chapter 1, we defined conditional probabilities. In Chapter 3 we extended the idea of conditional probabilities to percentages in contingency tables, or Cartesian products. Table 4.6, for example, reproduces in part the information given previously in Table 3.4, which shows that the proportion of Canadians placing the NDP to the left of centre increases steadily with the number of premiers identified. Subsequently we noted that this measure of party imagery had certain disadvantages. We therefore developed a relative measure of party imagery. This consisted of the difference in the left-right placement of the NDP compared to the PCs. Here the resulting score could be interpreted as how many units to the left (or right) respondents placed the NDP compared to their placement of the PC party. This new measure ranged from –6 to +6. This relatively large range makes the use of conditional probabilities awkward at best. However, this is precisely a situation where conditional means are appropriate. We can compute the mean left-right difference for those who didn't know the names of any premiers, similarly for those who knew the name of just one premier and so on.[7] We would expect that the more premiers Canadians could name, the further to the right of the NDP they would place the PC party on average.

Before presenting the findings, let's take the argument one step further. Respondents in the 1984 CNES project were also asked to place the federal Liberal party on the same left-right continuum. It is generally thought that the Liberal party is to the left of the PCs but to the right of the NDP. This might make it somewhat harder for respondents to "correctly" place the Liberal party to the right of the NDP, but with increasing political knowledge, we would expect them to increasingly do so. Stated differently, the mean scores should be lower, but the trend with political knowledge should be the same. Table 4.7 presents the findings.

A number of features of this table are worth noting. First, the "total" row shows that Canadians on average place the Liberals just over one unit (on the original

Table 4.6
Proportion Placing the NDP to the Left of Centre by Number of Premiers Correctly Named

Number Named	Proportion	N
0	0.45	75
1	0.50	242
2	0.53	225
3	0.61	240
4	0.68	230
5	0.71	208
6	0.79	188
7	0.82	156
8	0.81	104
9	0.88	49
10	0.85	33

Source: 1984 CNES.

seven-unit measure) to the right of the NDP. That is, *on average*, they place the Liberals in a "correct" position relative to the NDP.[8]

Second, they place the PC party even further to the right (2.15 units to the right of the NDP). Thus they place the Liberals between the NDP and the PCs, which is precisely where conventional wisdom places them. Such unconditional, or overall, means should be included in tables showing conditional means.

Third, even with minimal political knowledge (e.g., not knowing the names of any of the premiers) the above two patterns hold. That is, both the Liberals and the PCs are placed, on average, to the right of the NDP, and the Liberals are placed between the NDP and the PCs.

Fourth, the conditional mean placement of the PC party relative to the NDP mirrors that found in Table 4.7, where an absolute measure of party imagery was used. This "mirroring" is near perfect, even to the small reversal in the general trend that occurs with knowing the names of all ten premiers. (The reversal could be related to the small number of cases at the high end of political knowledge, but we will come back to this point later.) Thus, with increasing political knowledge, Canadians are increasingly likely to place the NDP left of centre in an absolute sense and to see the PCs as increasingly to the right of the NDP.

Fifth, the effect of political knowledge on placement of the Liberals relative to the NDP is less straightforward. Overall there is clearly a trend, with increasing political knowledge, to place the Liberals further to the right. However, many reversals occur in this relationship. For example, a reversal in means occurs between knowing the names of one and two premiers; another between four and five; a third between seven and eight; and finally one between nine and ten. Because these conditional means are calculated on relatively small samples, they are relatively unstable and may represent nothing more than the fluctuations that normally occur in small samples.[9]

These reversals nevertheless pose a theoretical dilemma. Increasing political knowledge should work equally well in helping respondents to place the PCs and the Liberals to the right of the NDP, but the data suggest political knowledge is less strongly related to placing the Liberals "correctly." Could this be because it is "harder" to place the Liberals than the Conservatives to the right of the NDP? Not really, since that should only reduce the mean scores, which it does, but not the relationship to political knowledge. The increased difficulty should make politically knowledgable individuals able to discriminate between the Liberals and the NDP more clearly. Just the opposite occurs: the difference between knowing the names of six and ten premiers shows no consistent impact on placement of the Liberals relative to the NDP. This fact suggests a measurement resolution of the dilemma. Remember that these relative measures, in their current form, implicitly treat higher scores as more correct. Thus a score of 6 is more correct than a score of 5, which is more correct than a score of 4 and so on. Suppose, however, that the "true" position of the Liberals is about 1.5 units to the right of the NDP. Then, with increasing political knowledge, respondents will converge to this placement. If that were true, we would expect the mean scores to rise to this level and remain there.

Table 4.7
Mean Left-Right Image of the Federal Liberal and Progressive
Conservative Parties Relative to the NDP, by Number of Names of
Premiers Known

Mean Location to the Right of the NDP for:

Number of Names of Premiers Known	Liberals	Progressive Conservatives	N^a
0	0.29	1.23	73
1	1.00	1.39	238
2	0.81	1.56	218
3	1.13	1.89	240
4	1.36	2.15	222
5	1.25	2.53	205
6	1.45	2.59	184
7	1.50	2.85	153
8	1.40	3.00	102
9	1.55	3.23	48
10	1.45	2.97	33
TOTAL	1.18	2.15	1,716

[a] Due to missing values, the number of cases differs slightly (by no more than two cases in any row) between the two variables. Where there is a difference, the smaller N is reported.

Source: 1984 CNES.

We could make a similar argument with respect to the PCs. Here, however, let's assume that the true placement of the PCs relative to the NDP is about three units. This would account for the slight reversal noted earlier.

Let me summarize the problem and its tentative resolution. The problem is this: our most knowledgable respondents on average do not place the NDP farther and farther to the left of the Liberals and PCs. Several interpretations of this are possible:

1. Sampling fluctuations caused the repeated reversals in means. This interpretation is not very satisfactory because there are quite a number of reversals and it implies a weak connection between political knowledge and party imagery.

2. The form of the connection between political knowledge and party imagery is complex: naming up to six or seven premiers results in increasingly "correct" party imagery, but additional knowledge has no such effect. Stated more generally, the relationship between political knowledge is characterized by a **ceiling effect** (which occurs when increases in one variable produces progressively smaller consequences). This interpretation is not much better, since no plausible scenario springs to mind that might account for a ceiling effect.

3. Placing the NDP increasingly further to the left of the other two parties does not correspond to having increasingly correct party imagery. This interpretation has promise because, although it is clear that the NDP is to the left of the other two parties, we have no reason to believe that it is an ultra-left party. That is, we know the NDP must be placed to the left of the other parties, but we can't say how far. Hence we have no reason to believe that variation in positive numbers (how far to the left relative to the other parties the NDP is placed) is valid variation (i.e., represents increasingly correct party imagery).

A cautious researcher might conclude that these reversals are nothing more than sampling fluctuations; a bold researcher might argue that these reversals reflect a convergence around a true placement; and a persistent one might construct alternative measurement procedures that could differentiate between these two interpretations. Let's persist.

One such alternative measure would collapse placements of the Liberals one or more points to the right of the NDP to one point. This would treat placements of the Liberals one or more points to the right of the NDP as equally correct. It would at the same time retain the feature that the farther the Liberals were placed to the *left* of the NDP, the more incorrect their responses would be.

A look at the column labelled "Mean Position" in Table 4.8 shows the results to be substantially better than those obtained with uncollapsed measures. Now those who cannot name a single premier on average place the Liberals incorrectly (as revealed by the negative conditional mean). The conditional means rise more or less steadily from this low to a high of 0.73. True, there are several reversals, but these are minor fluctuations (they occur in the second decimal point). We conclude, albeit tentatively, that political knowledge is instrumental in placing both the Liberals and the Conservatives "correctly" to the right of the NDP.[10]

This example illustrates several important features of social science arguments. It demonstrates the necessity of exploring data in multiple ways. This was done here by including the placement of the Liberals as a relevant aspect of party imagery. Such explorations need not be time-consuming, particularly when software such as SPSS is used.

Furthermore, it reveals that underlying many of our variables are implicit or explicit concepts. Underlying the left-right placement of the Liberals relative to the NDP is the concept "extent to which a respondent's left-right placement is congruent with social scientists' placement" (and it is also usually assumed that the social scientists' placement is an objective or "correct" one).

Table 4.8
Mean Left-Right Position of the Federal Liberal Party Relative to the NDP by Number Premiers Named

Mean Location to the Right of the NDP for:

Premiers Identified	Mean Position[a]	Standard Deviation	N
0	–0.32	1.92	73
1	0.12	1.42	238
2	0.17	1.27	218
3	0.25	1.37	240
4	0.46	1.21	222
5	0.43	1.27	205
6	0.63	0.85	184
7	0.67	0.71	153
8	0.66	0.91	102
9	0.73	0.67	49
10	0.73	0.84	33

[a] All positive scores (where the NDP was placed further left than the Liberal Party) were given a value of 1.0.

Source: 1984 CNES.

Improving numerically based arguments requires that we obtain as good a "fit" as possible between the measure and the concept. In this instance, this consideration suggested that we should collapse all positive scores for the Liberals versus the NDP measure, but that we should not collapse the negative scores (which presumably capture increasing degrees of false placement). Without the underlying concept, this would be a most peculiar thing to do. This process of maximizing the fit between measures and their underlying concepts is usually thought of as increasing the **validity** of the measures.

Measures of Dispersion

A second summary characteristic of distributions is the amount of dispersion, or variability, in the outcomes. In some distributions the outcomes cluster together, but in others the outcomes differ substantially from each other. That is, for some variables the outcomes are relatively homogeneous and in others they are more heterogeneous. How can we capture this characteristic in a single summary figure?

A first approach might be to subtract the smallest score from the largest. The difference between these two extreme scores would give us some idea of the amount of variability in the outcomes. We call this difference the **range** of a distribution. For the data on ages of brides at marriage, the youngest bride in the sample was 12, the oldest 79. The range is therefore sixty-seven years. By itself, this measure of dispersion suggests tremendous variability in the age at which women marry.

As a measure of dispersion, the range of a distribution has some severe limitations, the most obvious one being that it is totally dependent on only the two extreme scores. Hence, it is quite unstable and sensitive to the tails of the distribution. In the bridal age data, for example, the second-youngest bride was 16 years old, and the second-oldest bride was 65. Excluding the two most extreme cases, the range is reduced to forty-nine years. But this disadvantage is also an advantage, since the range alerts us to the presence of extreme scores, or **outliers**. The presence of outliers can create misleading results in many statistical analyses. Given that most data analysis is performed using computers, rather than manually, we might fail to notice these outliers if we did not compute the range.

We would like a measure that doesn't put so much emphasis on only two extreme scores. One solution is the interquartile range. Remember that we defined the median as that value which divided a distribution into two halves, each containing half the cases. For this reason, the median is sometimes also referred to as the 50th percentile. Now let's split each of these halves again into two parts, so that each part contains a quarter of the observations. This would give us four **quartiles**. The first quartile is that outcome which includes the first 25 percent of the observations, the second quartile ends at the median, the third quartile includes up to the 75th percentile of the observations, while the last quartile includes all the rest of the observations. The symbols for the values of the variable corresponding to the 25th and 75th percentiles are Q_1 and Q_3, respectively. This is shown in Figure 4.6 for the distribution of bride's age at marriage.

The **interquartile range** is simply the difference between the outcome that corresponds with the third quartile and the outcome corresponding with the first quartile. That is,

$$IQR = Q_3 - Q_1. \qquad (4.9)$$

Obviously, this measure is not as affected by extreme scores. Often the interquartile range is divided in half and called the **semi-interquartile range**:

$$SIQR = \frac{Q_3 - Q_1}{2}. \qquad (4.10)$$

Since the semi-interquartile range is exactly half as large as the interquartile range, it is inconsequential which of these two is used.

But there are still some possible disadvantages to this measure of dispersion. It still reflects only two of the scores in the whole distribution, which makes these measures too arbitrary for anything other than descriptive purposes. Therefore, we need to develop additional measures of dispersion. One way is to use the concept of deviation as defined in equation 4.5. We might be tempted to use the average deviation as a measure of dispersion; however, we already proved that this would always result in a zero. Alternatively, we could take the absolute value of each deviation, add these, and obtain the mean absolute deviation. This is sometimes called the **mean deviation**:

$$Mean\ Deviation\ =\ \frac{\sum |x_i - M|}{N}. \tag{4.11}$$

Figure 4.6
Quartiles for Brides' Age at Marriage

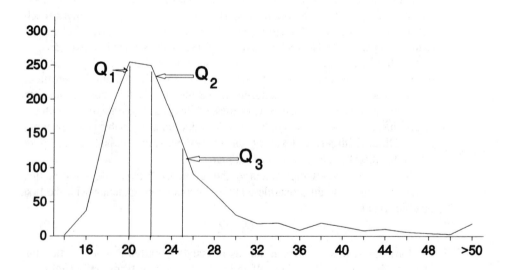

Source: PANS.

Unfortunately, the properties of this measure have not been explored extensively by statisticians. Rather than taking the mean absolute difference, they have preferred to use the mean squared deviation and have called this the **variance**. In symbols, the variance is:

$$Var(X) = \frac{\sum (x_i - M)^2}{N}. \tag{4.12}$$

We can use the language of expectation for the variance as well. The expected value of the squared deviation of a variable from its mean is:

$$E(X - M)^2 = Var(X) = \sum_{i=1}^{k} (x_i - M)^2 \cdot p(x_i). \tag{4.13}$$

In this equation, k refers to the number of values of the variable. Substituting relative frequencies for probabilities we get:

$$E(X - M)^2 = Var(X) = \sum_{i=1}^{k} (x_i - M)^2 \cdot \left(\frac{f_i}{N}\right). \tag{4.14}$$

As in the previous equation, the summation is over the number of values of the variable rather than over the number of cases.

This measure is affected by every value in the distribution. However, since we are adding, squaring and dividing, we are assuming that our observations have interval properties. Notice that the variance equals zero only when there is no dispersion in the distribution. In such a case, the distribution is really a constant where each outcome is also the mean and hence there is no deviation. The more the dispersion, the larger the variance. By squaring the deviations, this measure of dispersion is not in the original units but in squared units of the variable being measured. This is sometimes awkward (for example, how does one think in squared dollars?) and therefore the square root of the variance is often taken to reflect the original units. This measure is called the **standard deviation**, symbolized as s:

$$s = \sqrt{\frac{\sum_{i=1}^{N} (x_i - M)^2}{N}}. \tag{4.15}$$

The variance measures how alike or homogeneous the outcomes in any distribution are, so it can be used as a measure of how good the mean is as an estimate of the expected outcome. If the variance or standard deviation is relatively small, then the mean is a reasonably good estimate of the expected outcome.[11]

The concept of variation is of crucial importance to empirical arguments. Although most social science research focuses on means or their equivalents, in an important sense the variance (or any other measure of variation) is more fundamental to the research process. Formulated as a basic research principle: The greater the observed variance for any variable, the greater its potential in an empirical argument.[12] In the limiting case where the variance is zero (i.e., the "variable" is a constant), its connection to other phenomena cannot even be evaluated. In this context it should also be pointed out that one aim of much research is to explain variation: Why is it that phenomena vary from trial to trial, between different settings, or over time?

When analyzing a set of data, it is therefore advisable that one of the first steps taken is to calculate the distribution and its associated characteristics, such as the mean and the variance.[13]

When designing a research project, the variance principle dictates to a large extent the sampling design. To illustrate, suppose we are interested in persons with a prison record. A simple random sample of residents of any community would likely result in too few cases. One solution would be to obtain two samples: one taken from court records, and a second (of approximately equal size) taken from the residents of the area encompassed by that court. Neither sample by itself would have sufficient variance in the variable of greatest interest: previous incarceration. The two samples taken together, however, should provide reasonable variation in the variables of interest.

In general, for any phenomenon where the natural occurrence of the event in the population has little variation, a sampling design that artificially increases the variance must be used. Doing so will destroy the representativeness of the data, but the variance principle supersedes the representativeness principle. **Representativeness** means that the sample distributions approximate those of the population from which they were taken. Simple random sampling procedures are used to maximize representativeness, but researchers depart from such procedures when they know that it will result in insufficient variation.

Frequently it is possible to maximize the variance and still salvage representativeness. An example of this is the 1984 CNES project. These researchers recognized that a simple random sample would result in low variation on the variable "province of residence," because the population in the Atlantic Provinces is relatively sparse. Since provincial variation in voting patterns and other political phenomena were of prime interest, the researchers used a sampling design that "oversampled" residents of the Atlantic Provinces. However, this sample can be made to be representative again by "weighting" each of the cases to correct for the oversampling. This weighting factor is included in the data file as one of the variables. If we now wished to estimate the mean number of premiers Canadians can name, for example, we would have to use the weighting factor, since otherwise our sample would not be representative of Canadians.

We are now in a position to return to Table 4.8. The third column provides what might be called the conditional standard deviations. They indicate how much variation around the conditional mean there is in each category of number of premiers identified. These too show an important pattern. Note that the standard deviations for groups correctly naming five or less premiers are all higher than those for groups identifying six or more. In other words, the latter groups are more homogeneous than the former ones with respect to the placement of the NDP relative to the Liberals. Thus, with increasing political knowledge, there is increasing *consensus* concerning the relative placement of these two parties. Stated differently, we could reason that individuals with minimal political knowledge essentially guess when asked the left-right position of the parties. To the extent that their responses are guesses, all possible responses are equally likely to be chosen, resulting in a high standard deviation. With increasing political knowledge, the alternatives chosen converge on those representing the conventionally correct party imagery; thus, politically knowledgable people have similar images of the political parties, which logically manifests itself in a low standard deviation. In this context, the standard deviation can be interpreted as a measure of consensus. At the same time, this example sensitizes us to another pervasive source of methodological artifacts: humans, wishing to be cooperative, respond to our questions even when they have little basis for their answers. We must be aware of this threat to validity in our subsequent interpretations of the data.

The phantom stranger studies of similarity and attraction illustrate how a lack of variance can jeopardize the validity of the agreement measure. Remember that the phantom stranger experiments had two phases. In the first phase, subjects filled out an attitudinal questionnaire. In the second phase, which took place some time later, each subject was presented with a short profile of the phantom stranger in the waiting room of the laboratory. (The subject was told that the other subject, whose profile they were reading, was unavoidably going to be somewhat late.) In this profile, the attitudes of the phantom stranger had been manipulated to be similar or dissimilar to those of the subject (whose attitudes are known from the first phase).

To show how the variance of the attitudinal items challenges the validity of the measurement of agreement, we need to discuss briefly the sociological concept of norms. A basic postulate of sociology is that the behaviour, attitudes and values of members of society are constrained by that society. Certain behaviours and attitudes are prescribed and others are proscribed. Individuals who transgress these norms are labelled "deviants." But how might this "normative regulation" manifest itself? One possibility is through curtailed variance. Let's take an extreme example. Cannibalism is proscribed in Western civilizations. Hence the variance for our attitude towards cannibalism in Canada would be zero or close to it, since almost all Canadians will express abhorrence towards this practice. Somewhat more variance might be observed for attitudes towards fascism. In this example, an individual who strongly supports fascist regimes would be a deviant. Finally, at present, attitudes towards abortion are not normatively governed to any large extent and it is increasingly considered a domain in which varying positions are equally legitimate and a matter of personal conscience. This would be reflected by a relatively high variance on this issue, compared to endorsement of fascism. To sum up, the observed variance surrounding any issue is a possible measure of the extent to which that domain is normatively regulated. In those domains that are normatively regulated, individuals whose points of view differ from the normative ones are deviants.

Now back to the phantom stranger. Many of the attitudinal issues used in the phantom stranger studies are normative ones. In fact, Byrne (1971:54) noticed that "the experimental subjects were remarkably homogeneous in responding to most of the attitude items." In statistical terms, the variance in the attitude measures was low. As a result, "A similar stranger not only agreed with the subject but also appeared to be a normal, average, conforming member of the Texas undergraduate culture. A dissimilar stranger, on the other hand, not only disagreed with the subject but also could be seen as a statistically abnormal individual whose viewpoint was extremely deviant in this culture" (ibid.). This raises the question of whether it was the deviancy or the disagreement that was operating on the subjects. Note that disagreement is a concept that characterizes the relationship between two people, whereas deviancy is a concept that characterizes the relationship between individuals and the society in which they live. Hence quite different levels of interpretation are implied in the two terms.

To differentiate between disagreement and deviancy, Byrne (1962) in another study chose seven of the original twenty-six attitudinal items on which there was the highest variance. Those items that had a high variance can be argued to permit a variety of answers, none of which would be seen as particularly deviant. The seven-item stimulus was still significantly related to attraction. He therefore concluded that similarity in and of itself appears to be related to attraction. Unfortunately, what Byrne does not point out is that the strength of the relationship is substantially reduced. In the original twenty-six-item study, the mean difference in liking between the "zero percent similarity" and the "one hundred percent similarity" condition was 8.59 out of a maximum of 12 points. In the seven-item study, the mean difference decreased to 5.15 on the same liking scale. This shows that a significant amount of the variance in the similiarity-attraction relationship is indeed related to something like deviance. Advocates of the similarity-attraction argument have failed to demolish the rival interpretation that it is not interpersonal disagreement but cultural deviance that repels.

Measures of Skewness

In most social statistical analysis, only measures of location and dispersion are used. Hence measures of skewness will not be treated in depth here. As noted earlier, the mean, median and mode of skewed distributions stand in a certain relationship to each other: in negatively skewed distributions, the mean is to the left of the median and the opposite is true for positively skewed distributions. Hence a rough measure of skewness is simply the discrepancy between the values of the mean and the median. A more common measure of skewness involves taking the deviation of each observation from the mean to the third power. Notice the effect this has on the numbers: a negative deviation will remain a negative number, while a positive deviation will remain a positive number, and when we sum these numbers we will get a result of zero only if we have a perfectly symmetrical distribution. If we have a negatively skewed distribution, then the sum of the cubed deviations will be negative in value, and the opposite if we have a positively skewed distribution. The more skewed a distribution, the larger the absolute value of the sum of the cubed deviations. Note also that, by cubing the numbers, we place substantial weight on extreme numbers; that is, the numbers at the tail of a distribution influence this measure more than the more central numbers. To illustrate, although the difference between the numbers 1 and 3 is only 2, the difference in the cubes of these numbers is 26. It is this fact that causes the tails of a distribution to be weighted most heavily in measures of skewness.

The presence of outliers and skewness pose threats to the integrity of empirical arguments. Outliers pose a threat in that a few extreme cases can substantially affect the mean and our findings are unstable to the extent that we have extreme values or outliers. The results may be an artifact of the location of a few observations, which is why all data should be screened for outliers.[14]

If there are extreme outliers, a good case can be made for deleting those cases. For example, in the Atlantic fisheries, a handful of offshore captains, known as highliners, earn an unusually high income. Davis and Thiessen (1986) simply excluded these cases (approximately three percent of the sample) from the analysis. Otherwise they could distort the overall relationships documented.[15]

Many of the statistical techniques of analysis, particularly the more advanced ones, assume that the distribution of the variables is not skewed. Severe violations of this assumption are therefore clearly undesirable. Sometimes a mathematical transformation will help. For a positively skewed distribution such as income, taking the natural log or the square root of income will correct the skew. The disadvantage of this procedure is that it makes communication with a wide audience more difficult.

Outliers and skewness are sources of statistical difficulties and can produce artifactual findings, so we try to remove these undesirable features of distributions. At the same time, they often represent important features of the phenomena under investigation, and artificially removing them may destroy some essential features of the phenomenon being analyzed. It would be dangerous at best, and ludicrous at worst, to permit statistical considerations to take precedence over substantive ones. So, although for statistical reasons we may want to transform data to remove skewness, this should not be done where the skewness itself reveals important aspects of the phenomenon.

Creating Comparable Measurements: Standard Scores

Social science measurements are plagued by two problems. One is that most measurements do not have a meaningful zero point. It's like trying to find the beginning of a pie; it just doesn't have an obvious beginning. We solve the problem by starting in the middle, and we do much the same thing with our variables by measuring them in terms of deviations from the mean. In other words, we describe outcomes in terms of how many units above or below the mean they are. This solves the problem of not having a meaningful starting point.

The second problem is that many of our measurement units are arbitrary. For example, income can be measured in Canadian dollars or German marks. If we kept these original units of measurement, we would not be able to compare findings across different cultures, subject areas, or situations. This problem can be solved by the use of standard deviation units. We create comparable measures by determining how many standard deviations above or below the mean any particular outcome is. That is, we can change raw absolute scores (which we have symbolized as X) in any distribution into relative **standard scores**, which we will symbolize as z. A standard score is simply a raw score converted into standard deviation units. We can obtain z-scores through the formula:

$$z_i = \frac{x_i - M}{s}. \qquad (4.16)$$

This formula is a linear transformation of X into z .[16] In this formula we first subtract any particular score from the mean of that distribution. Then we divide it by the standard deviation of the distribution. The resulting number tells us how many standard deviations above or below the mean any outcome is.

Let's convert some political knowledge scores into standard scores. The mean and standard deviation of the number of premiers' names known are 3.51 and 2.51, respectively. Therefore the standard score of Canadians unable to name any of the premiers is:

$$z = \frac{0 - 3.51}{2.51} = -1.40. \qquad (4.17)$$

In like fashion, Canadians who can recall the names of all ten premiers would obtain a standard score of 2.59.

It may not be immediately apparent, but two important characteristics of z-scores are that their mean always equals zero and their standard deviation always equals one. Of course, to get z-scores you have to treat your measurements as interval in nature because of the arithmetic manipulations involved. However, for those distributions where one can treat the measures as interval, z-scores can be computed to produce comparability across different settings.

For example, we could conceivably compare a Canadian citizen's income with a German citizen's education and determine whose score is "higher." Thus, if a person's income is two standard deviations above the mean and another person's education is 2.5 standard deviations above the mean, we could say that the second person scored higher in education (relative to other people's education) than the first person did on income (relative to other people's income). We could not make such statements if we used raw scores.

SPSS Instructions and Printout[17]

Figure 4.7
SPSS Instructions for Obtaining Conditional Means

```
1  GET FILE = "vote84.sys".
2  COUNT premiers= var446 TO var455(1)
3  VARIABLE LABELS premiers "Number of premiers correctly named"
4  COMPUTE libndp=var509-var511
5  COMPUTE pcndp=var510-var511
6  RECODE libndp,pcndp (2 THRU 6=1)(ELSE=COPY) INTO
7       libndpc,pcndpc
8  VARIABLE LABELS pcndp "Left-right placement of PC rel. to NDP "
9       libndp "Left-right placement of Lib rel. to NDP"
10      pcndpc "Collapsed l-r placement of PC rel. to NDP"
11      libndpc "Collapsed l-r placement of Lib rel. to NDP"
12  MEANS pcndpc,libndpc BY premiers
```

Lines 4-5: These lines in Figure 4.7 COMPUTE two new variables, which will be called "libndp" and "pcndp". Taking the first one as an example, it instructs SPSS to subtract "var511" (left-right placement of the NDP on an absolute scale) from "var509" (left-right placement of the Liberals). This difference is to be stored in a new variable called "libndp". The result of this operation will be the creation of a new variable that shows how far to the left or right of the NDP a respondent places the Liberals.

Lines 6-7: Line 7 is a continuation of line 6. On mainframe versions of SPSS, it would be important to indent line 7 by at least one space. This command is a different form of the RECODE command we encountered earlier. It is used when we wish to RECODE an existing variable, but we also want to retain the original values. This is done by recoding an old variable INTO a new one. The new variable will be the same as the old one except for the recodes that were performed. In this instance we are asking SPSS to RECODE our two party imagery variables ("pcndp" and "libndp") into the two new variables "pcndpc" and "libndpc." Codes of "2 THRU 6" are recoded as 1. All other values remain the same. This is done with the phrase (ELSE=COPY), which simply instructs SPSS to COPY all other values that it encounters INTO the new variables, named "pcndpc" and "libndpc" (I added a "c" to the end of the variable names to remind me that these are the collapsed variables).

Lines 8-11: Four extended VARIABLE LABELS are provided to document more fully the output that will be created in the next instruction.

Line 12: This procedure instruction produces conditional means. A conditional mean will be calculated for every category of the variable following the keyword BY. A separate table of conditional means is produced for each of the variables listed before the keyword BY. These instructions produced the information contained in Table 4.7.

Summary

- Although we usually assign numbers to the values of variables, the outcomes themselves may not possess the properties of numbers. Which arithmetic operations are permissible depends on the level of measurement used. Levels of measurement range from the least flexible (nominal-level measures) to those fully compatible with all arithmetic operations (ratio-level measures). To some extent, the level of measurement is determined by argument. Thus we marshalled an argument to show that post–high school plans could be treated as having ordinal properties. Fruitful insights can sometimes be obtained even when the operations used are known to violate certain assumptions.
- The overall features of a phenomenon can be summarized conveniently through measures of location, dispersion and skewness of distributions. A variety of such measures are available and may produce discrepant results. Taking political knowledge as an example, the modal number of premiers named is only one, but the mean number is greater than three. Which measures should be used depends on both the level of measurement and the shape of the distribution. In skewed distributions, the three measures of location—mode, median and mean—never coincide. This is one reason why statistics can, or can be used to, mislead.
- A further advantage of the relative measure of the left-right status of the NDP is that two measures are made possible. One compares the NDP with the PCs; the other compares the NDP with the Liberal party. We would expect political knowledge to be related similarly to both measures, and such a result would strengthen the argument being made.
- Conditional means, which are analogous to conditional probabilities, provide a useful statistical technique to test this expectation. Conditional means are especially appropriate when the dependent variable can be assumed to be interval. The independent variable needs to be measured at nothing more than a nominal level.

Using the conditional means, the relationship of political knowledge with the two relative measures of party imagery was indeed similar. The findings were also compatible with those obtained using conditional probabilities.

- The conditional means analysis also produced an unexpected "flattening" in the relationship between political knowledge and party imagery at the higher levels of political knowledge. This flattening was particularly pronounced when the NDP was compared with the Liberals. That is, the conditional means showed no consistent pattern when between six and ten premiers' names were known. This result occasioned a closer scrutiny of the party imagery measure.

- Our empirical measures are usually specific manifestations of general, underlying phenomena. The numbers we attach to the empirical measures are intended to maximize the "fit" with the features of the underlying phenomena. For example, no theoretical difficulties are encountered in considering responses that place the Liberals five units to the left of the NDP as less correct than those that place the Liberals only two units to the left of the NDP. The same cannot be said for the reverse situation. That is, it is arguable whether placing the Liberals five units to the right of the NDP is more correct than placing them two units to the right of the NDP. That all depends on how far to the right of the NDP the Liberal party "really" is. This consideration led to a new number-mapping algorithm that treated all outcomes placing the Liberals at least one unit to the right of the NDP as being equally correct.

- A paramount aim in designing research projects is to insure that sufficient variation exists in the main variables of interest. Concern with variation supersedes concern with representativeness. Sometimes weighted random samples that produce maximal variance can be employed while still permitting representativeness to be retained.

- We can never be certain that our variables do indeed measure the intended concepts. Unexpected contaminations can arise that threaten the validity of the measures. **Validity** refers to the congruence between a measure and its concept. Both the presence of skewness and the low variance in the distribution of attitudes in the phantom stranger experiments were shown to jeopardize the validity of the agreement measures used in these experiments. It is difficult to untangle disagreement from deviance on issues where there is low variance or substantial skewness. One attempt to purify the agreement measure was described. The results showed a weakening of the relationship between agreement and attraction when items with low variance were excluded.

- Skewed distributions, as well as the presence of outliers, produce unstable results. This is because the (chance) location of outliers unduly influences the summary statistics. Also, most of the statistical techniques to be developed in later chapters assume that the distributions are not skewed. For these reasons, where outliers exist, the analyses should be repeated with outliers deleted. Various mathematical transformations, such as taking natural logarithms or square roots of measures, can be used to reduce or eliminate skewness.

- Although it may be necessary from a statistical point of view to remove skewness, the presence of such features may itself be an important substantive piece of information.
- Many measures in social science research have no meaningful origin or zero-point. In addition, the scale or unit of measurement is arbitrary. To minimize these drawbacks, measures are frequently converted to standard scores. Standard scores express observations in standard deviation units with the origin being the mean. This permits comparisons across variables, measures, and populations to be made.

Notes

1. Why then bother to assign numbers to categorical events at all? The answer is simply convenience, especially when we use computers to analyze data. It is always permissible to assign numbers to such events, as long as we don't forget that the nature of the events remains categorical.
2. There are two methods of assigning numbers to rank: from highest to lowest, or from lowest to highest. In the first method we assign the number 1 to the highest (fastest, greatest), 2 to the second-highest, and so on. The second method would let a 1 stand for the lowest, a 2 for the second-lowest, and so on.
3. These data were obtained from marriage records housed in the Nova Scotia Public Archives (PANS). The sample consists of all marriages recorded between approximately 1867 and 1914 in four Nova Scotia fishing communities.
4. At first glance, it may seem puzzling to add the fraction to the number 2.5. To explain this feature, recall the discussion of discrete versus continuous variables from Chapter 2.
5. This proof can be skipped without loss of continuity, for those so inclined.
6. To follow this next step, we need to remember the algebraic principle that adding a constant N times is the same as multiplying that constant by N. The mean is, of course, a constant. Hence we can substitute N for Σ.
7. To calculate these means, we are treating this measure *as though* it were an equal-interval measure, which it clearly is not; most researchers would consider it an ordinal measure. Nevertheless, by computing these conditional means, we have a compact summary of the nature of the relationship between our measures of political knowledge and party imagery. Alternative analyses, such as the one given in Table 4.6, can be used to detect patterns caused by methodological artifacts.
8. This mean is based on all 1,716 respondents who answered these party imagery questions. We must keep in mind that the conditional means are less stable because they are computed on a reduced sample space. For example, there were exactly seventy-three respondents who could not name a single premier. The mean scores of 0.29 and 1.23 (for placement of the Liberals and PCs relative to the NDP, respectively) were calculated on just these seventy-three respondents.

9. The statistical evaluation of these fluctuations will be treated in the following chapter.

10. The column labelled "Standard Deviation" will be explained later in this chapter.

11. One of the more important characteristics of this measure of dispersion is that it gives us the smallest possible squared deviation. That is, subtracting each outcome from the mean and squaring it results in a smaller number than if we subtracted the observations from any other point. It is this feature that makes the mean a good measure of the "typical" outcome.

12. It is important to bear in mind that the magnitude of the variance must always be considered in relationship to the unit of measurement. For example, the maximum possible variance for dichotomously measured variables can be shown to be 0.25. Clearly, although this number is close to zero, in this context it represents extreme variability.

13. With SPSS, this is done using the procedures FREQUENCIES and MEANS.

14. In SPSS, they can be detected simply by asking for the minimum and maximum values of all the variables being used. These can be obtained through the default STATISTICS in the procedure FREQUENCIES.

15. One way of deleting extreme cases in SPSS is to use the SELECT IF instruction. For example, if fishing income is recorded in the variable names "fishinc," and fishers whose incomes exceed $200,000 are to be excluded, the command following GET FILE would be SELECT IF (fishinc LT 200000).

16. We use much the same formula when converting Fahrenheit degrees into Celsius degrees: $F° = 9/5 \, C° + 32$.

17. Let me reiterate that the line numbers are not part of the SPSS instructions. Also, I will not comment on instructions explained in earlier chapters.

Key Terms

arithmetic mean: A measure of central tendency obtained by adding up the values of the variable for all cases and dividing that sum by the number of observations. These mathematical operations require us to assume that the variable in question has metric properties. Since many measures are ordinal in nature, using the mean in such instances may produce misleading results. At the same time, if used cautiously, the arithmetic mean can provide useful summarizing information.

bivariate analysis: Any statistical technique in which two variables are evaluated simultaneously. Example: The mean age of brides conditional on groom's age. This would give us the average age of brides married to 20-year-old grooms, the average age of brides of 21-year-old grooms, 22-year-old grooms, and so on.

ceiling effect: The constraint in a relationship between two variables imposed by virtue of the existence of minimum and maximum bounds. The most common impact of this constraint is that the effect becomes weaker as the limiting value is approached.

central tendency: A variety of answers to the question "What is the typical, or average, outcome?" The mean, median and mode are measures of central tendency.

continuous variable: Any metric variable where, between two adjacent outcomes, an uncountable infinity of additional outcomes is theoretically possible. Age is continuous, but family size is discrete. Since our recorded measures are, of necessity, discrete, we usually are interested in whether the "underlying" variable is continuous. In plotting distributions, we prefer histograms for continuous variables and bar graphs or pie charts for discrete ones, to visually reinforce their assumed nature.

deviation: The numeric difference between the value of a particular observation and the mean of the distribution to which it belongs. Symbolically,

$$d_i = x_i - M$$

where d_i stands for the deviation of the particular observation x_i from the mean (M) of the distribution. By definition, the larger this difference, the less adequately the mean represents this observation.

equal interval measures: A metric measure, i.e., a measure in which the quantity contained in one interval at any point in the scale is identical to the quantity contained in the same-sized interval at any other point on the scale. For example, the age difference between a 33 -year old and a 34 -year old is the same as that between a 64 -year old and a 65 -year old, namely, one year. The possibility that mandatory retirement at 65 makes that a more consequential year than previous years is irrelevant to the mathematical properties, although it suggests that often we may wish to measure attributes that are related to chronological age but not coterminous with it.

expected value: The mean of a probability distribution. The concept of an expected value is important in statistical logic in that it refers to the value at which repeated, independent observations should converge.

interpolation: A mathematical procedure for finding a more precise value of a statistic for a continuous variable which falls in between two adjacent values. Interpolation is sometimes necessary for finding the precise value of the median, and for calculating the mean from grouped data.

interquartile range: A measure of dispersion that expresses the distance between the outcomes corresponding to the 25th and 75th percentile:

$$IQR = Q_3 - Q_1 .$$

where Q_3 and Q_1 are the values of the third and first quartiles, respectively, and IQR is the symbol for the interquartile range. Since the interquartile range is not affected by outliers, it is a reasonably stable measure.

level of measurement: The mathematical properties assumed to characterize the numbers used to represent the values of variables. The main levels are nominal, ordinal, interval and ratio. As the term suggests, the level of measurement describes our measures, rather than being an intrinsic feature of the phenomena being measured. Nonsensical statements can result if we do not pay careful attention to the assumed mathematical properties of our measures. At the same time, often useful information can be gleaned, even when it is clear that the measurement level does not permit the operations performed. For example, grade-point averages can provide useful summary information despite requiring addition and division, neither of which are warranted operations for ordinal data, which grade points are.

Likert-type scales: A popular survey research response format that typically ranges from "strongly agree" at one end to "strongly disagree" at the other. The numbers attached to these responses are usually assumed to have ordinal properties.

mean: The usual abbreviation for *arithmetic mean*.

mean deviation: A measure of dispersion in which the absolute deviations in a distribution are added together and divided by the number of cases. Since the mathematical properties of this measure have not been extensively evaluated, it is less frequently used than the standard deviation.

measures of dispersion: Summary measures—such as *standard deviation, variance, range* and *interquartile range*—for describing the variability in outcomes. They answer the question "How typical is the typical outcome?"

measures of location: Any of the measures of *centrality*, such as the *mean, median* and *mode*.

measures of skewness: Summary measures which contain the extent to which distributions are lop-sided or asymmetrical. The most popular measure is based on the cubed deviations from the mean.

median: A measure of central tendency appropriate for ordinal or metric measures; it refers to the value of the outcome at which precisely half the outcomes have a lower value (and the other half a higher one). It is equivalent to the value corresponding to the 50th percentile. The median is the preferred measure of location for any markedly skewed distribution because, unlike the mean, it is unaffected by the tail ends of a distribution.

mode: A measure of central tendency referring to the most frequently occurring outcome. Because counting is the only mathematical operation required to compute the mode, a mode can be used to summarize nominal measures.

monotonicity: A feature of measures such that larger numbers correspond to increasing amounts of the attribute in question.

negatively skewed distribution: A non-symmetrical distribution in which more outcomes occur above the mean than below it. Figuratively, it is as though the lower end of the distribution has been stretched. The distribution of agreements among friends is usually negatively skewed, with most friends agreeing on a majority of topics, and with only a few instances of friends disagreeing on most topics. In markedly skewed distributions, the mean, median and mode will have different values, permitting conclusions that might be misleading. Generally, if a single measure of location is to be given, the median is preferred in these situations.

nominal (or **categorical**) **measure:** The lowest level of measurement, in which numbers represent convenient symbols for discrete outcomes that contain no connotation of rank or quantity. That is, the outcomes differ in kind (quality) rather than degree (quantity). Example: political party preference.

open-ended class: The first (or last) class of a distribution in which outcomes have been grouped to include all lower (or higher) outcomes. Open-ended classes are frequently used when presenting distributions of skewed variables, such as income. Graphical displays in which open-ended classes have been used can give the misleading impression that the lowest (or highest) class of outcomes occurs frequently.

ordinal measures: A level of measurement higher than nominal but lower than interval. Ordinal measures permit a ranking or ordering of outcomes; it is possible to determine whether one outcome is larger than another, but it is not possible to determine how much larger.

outliers: Extreme outcomes in a distribution. In graphical displays such as histograms, outliers are outcomes in which the next-closest outcome is separated by some distance. Sometimes outliers are arbitrarily defined as any value more than three standard deviations removed from the mean. The presence of outliers causes instability in a variety of statistical procedures, and this instability can be a source of misleading information. It should be standard practice to omit the outliers and then to replicate all statistical calculations to determine whether the new results yield consistent information.

percentiles: A numeric transformation of ordinal or metric measures that standardizes the scores to indicate relative position within a given distribution. These positions range from 1 to 100 and are interpreted as the percentage of cases having a lower score than the one in question. For example, a percentile score of 47 indicates that 47 percent of the other outcomes (in the distribution with which it is being compared) were lower, and therefore 53 percent were higher. Percentiles are constructed in the same way as cumulative percentage distributions. The main purpose of percentile scores is to facilitate comparison. Frequently percentiles are used to locate an individual score within the distribution of cases having specific known characteristics, for example, to compare a typist's speed and accuracy with those of a national sample of secretaries.

positively skewed distribution: A non-symmetrical distribution in which the upper tail extends farther than the lower tail. National income distributions are invariably positively skewed, with a few extremely high incomes, and the vast majority being low to moderate. In positively skewed distributions, the mean exceeds the median, with the latter generally considered the less misleading measure of the typical or average outcome.

qualitative variable: Another term for a categorical variable, where the outcomes differ in kind.

quartiles: A procedure in which a distribution is divided into four equal parts, using the 25th, 50th and 75 percentiles as the dividing lines. Quartiles are used primarily to obtain the median and the interquartile range.

range: A measure of dispersion that is the numeric difference between the largest and the smallest outcomes. Because a range is determined by the two extreme scores, it is highly unstable and should be used primarily as a clue to determine the presence of outliers. (Outliers would increase the range unduly.)

rank order: An ordinal number that corresponds to the position of that outcome relative to all other cases included in the particular distribution. For example, in a race, the rank-ordered outcomes range from first, second and third to second to last and last. Rank order measures are particularly appropriate in arguments where the relative position is likely to be more consequential than the absolute amount, as in studies of community power, or status distribution.

ratio measurement: A metric measurement assumed to have a meaningful absolute zero, permitting one to form ratios. For example, a 64 year old is twice as old as a 32 year old, but if the numbers referred to degrees Celsius instead, one could not say that the first temperature was twice as hot as the second.

relative frequency: The observed frequency of an outcome divided by the number of cases in that distribution. This operation yields the proportion of cases with that particular outcome. This form of standardizing scores facilitates comparison. When relative frequencies are multiplied by 100, the result is a percentage.

representativeness: The extent to which sample characteristics mirror the population from which they are drawn. Simple random samples are employed to maximize representativeness. A common practice in survey research is to "oversample" certain groups of cases that are known to occur infrequently in the population. Doing this artificially inflates the variance so that statistical analysis can proceed more efficiently. Representativeness is regained by statistically weighting the responses in proportion to the oversampling fraction.

semi-interquartile range: The interquartile range divided by two.

skewness: Departures from symmetry in the two tails of a distribution, with one tail extending further than the other. Skewed distributions can be the source of a variety of artifacts and misleading information. For example, the mean, median and mode will differ as a function of the amount of skew.

standard deviation: A popular measure of dispersion for distributions of metric variables. It is obtained by:

$$s = \sqrt{\frac{\sum (x_i - M)^2}{N}}.$$

The standard deviation is the square root of the variance, an operation that presents the results in the original unit of measurement. Otherwise, we would be expressing dispersion in units such as squared dollars and squared years, which would not facilitate communication. The standard deviation quantifies how typical the mean outcome is, and it can be interpreted as the average distance of observations from the mean.

standard scores: A unit of measure in which the outcomes are expressed in standard deviation units relative to the mean. Raw scores can be converted to standard scores using the equation:

$$z_i = \frac{x_i - M}{s}.$$

true limits: The lower and upper bounds used when converting discrete (or grouped) data into a continuous form. Under such conditions, the integer 1, for example, is defined to contain the continuous interval bounded by the lower true limit of 0.5 and an upper true limit of 1.5. True limits are important when interpolating for the median.

univariate analysis: Simple forms of statistical analysis, such as measures of location, dispersion, and skewness of distributions. Such univariate analyses are crucial for detecting distributional features of a variable that may create misleading information, confounding substantive conclusions with methodological artifacts.

validity: The extent to which the recorded variation in a variable reflects variation in the phenomenon it was intended to capture. Methodological artifacts are particularly grievous threats to validity. If our measures are not valid, then neither are any conclusions which are based on them. Social desirability (giving responses that reflect what is thought to be acceptable rather than what is personally believed) is likely to be a pervasive threat to validity.

variance: A measure of dispersion consisting of the mean squared deviation. That is,

$$Var(X) = \frac{\sum_i (x_i - M)^2}{N}.$$

Statistically, the variance has many desirable properties but is awkward to interpret verbally because it represents dispersion in squares of the original units.

Chapter 5

HARNESSING INFORMATION: NORMAL DISTRIBUTIONS AND HYPOTHESIS TESTING

The measures of location, dispersion and skewness developed in the last chapter are useful in their own right; and the mean and standard deviation are tools to create standard scores that permitted us to compare findings. In this chapter, we will develop the logic of formal hypothesis testing in conjunction with a particular theoretical distribution: the normal distribution.

We introduced some of the key concepts of hypothesis testing in Chapter 3 when we discussed the chi-square distribution and showed how it could be used to assess the likelihood that two variables are statistically independent of each other. This is one form of hypothesis testing.

Previously we used the chi-square distribution to help decide whether differences between observed and expected cell frequencies in a contingency table indicate a connection between two variables or simply chance fluctuations. On the basis of the chi-square distribution, we were able to calculate the probability that sampling fluctuations caused the discrepancies. Traditionally, if the probability is less than 0.05, researchers conclude that the discrepancies are caused by something other than sampling fluctuations. The term **statistically significant** is used to describe such results.

In this chapter, however, we will see there is much more to testing hypotheses than computing significance tests. This is because, with large sample sizes, trivial findings may reach statistical significance. Conversely, substantively and theoretically important relationships may fail such tests because of small sample sizes. First, though, it is important to understand the logic of hypothesis testing, so we can use this much-abused statistical procedure wisely. We begin by distinguishing between samples and populations.

Samples and Populations

In hypothesis testing, we use information from samples to make inferences about populations. Samples permit us to make reasonable decisions efficiently. For example, if we were interested in the number of premiers Canadians can name, we do not canvass all Canadians; a smaller, **random sample** will suffice. In set terms, a **population** is a specified universal set of interest. When we obtain information on some of the elements in this universal set, this is a **sample**. To perform hypothesis tests, the elements must be obtained through a method of random sampling. (A simple random sample is one where every element in the population has an equal probability of being included in the sample.) However, the sample information may not in any given instance describe the population from which it is taken accurately. For example, it is unlikely that the mean and standard deviation of a sample will be identical to the mean and standard deviation of the population. Hence we must distinguish between characteristics of samples and characteristics of populations by using different symbols for them. Sample means are symbolized as $\overline{X}$ (called an "X bar") and population means by the Greek letter μ (pronounced "mew"). The standard deviation in a sample is abbreviated as s, and its population counterpart as the lower-case sigma, σ. In general, the Roman alphabet designates sample characteristics and the Greek alphabet those of populations. Characteristics of samples, such as their mean and standard deviation, are called **statistics**, while the corresponding characteristics of populations are called **parameters**.

We rarely know the exact value of any parameter, such as σ. Yet when we perform hypotheses tests concerning the population mean, we need a value for the unknown σ. The solution is to use an estimate, one that is both unbiased and stable. An **unbiased estimate** is one that is neither consistently too high nor consistently too low. Statistically, we consider an estimate unbiased if the expected value of the difference between the estimate and the parameter is zero. A **stable estimate** does not give radically different estimates in repeated trials. If we were to use the standard deviation of the sample, s, as the estimate of σ, we would have a biased estimate. Statisticians have discovered that such an estimate would be consistently too small by a factor of $1/\sqrt{N}$. Hence s should not be used as an estimate of σ. Instead, using the symbol $\hat{\sigma}$ (called a "sigma hat") to represent an unbiased estimate of the population standard deviation, we get the following:

$$\hat{\sigma} = \sqrt{\frac{\sum_{i=1}^{N}(x_i - \overline{X})^2}{N-1}}. \qquad (5.1)$$

This expression differs from s only in having $N-1$ rather than N as the denominator, providing a somewhat larger, unbiased estimate of σ.

How stable is $\hat{\sigma}$? Statisticians have found that this estimate is unstable for small sample sizes and thus shouldn't be used in such situations. But for large samples, $\hat{\sigma}$ does provide a stable, unbiased estimate. Again, we take a pragmatic attitude regarding what constitutes a large sample size: sample sizes greater than fifty provide sufficiently stable estimates for most applications.

The Normal Distribution

In contrast to the empirical distributions we constructed in Chapter 2, normal distributions, like chi-square distributions, are **theoretical distributions**. The shape of a theoretical distribution is determined by its parameters. A chi-square distribution's parameter, you may remember, is its degree of freedom. A normal distribution has two parameters: its mean and its standard deviation.

Figure 5.1
A Normal Distribution

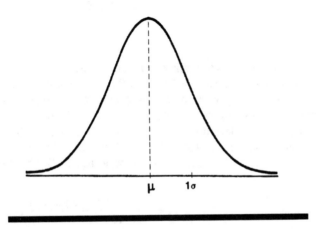

As is evident from Figure 5.1, normal curves are smooth, perfectly symmetrical, unimodal, bell-shaped and continuous distributions. If we folded a normal curve at the mean, the two halves would overlap perfectly. The tails of normal curves approach, but never quite meet, the horizontal or X-axis (also known as the **abscissa**): they stretch to infinity. The possible outcomes of the variable are depicted along the abscissa, or X-axis.

Remember from the discussion of probability axioms in Chapter 1 that the probability of the sample space is 1.0. In theoretical distributions, this axiom is represented by letting the total area of the distribution equal 1.0; doing this, the probabilities of outcomes between any two points on the abscissa correspond to the area of the curve bounded by those outcomes.

In normal distributions the proportion of the area between the mean and one standard deviation above the mean is 0.3413 of the total area. Converting to percentages, we can say that in normal distributions, 34.13 percent of observations occur between the mean and one standard deviation above the mean. Since normal curves are perfectly symmetrical, 68.26 percent of the area (twice 34.13) falls between the two outcomes corresponding to one standard deviation above and below the mean. Similarly, 95.46 percent of the area falls between two standard deviations on either side of the mean. The mean and standard deviation are the parameters of the normal curve, because the precise area (probability) between any two points is a function of these two numbers. Appendix B provides the areas between the mean and any other point on the X-axis for one particular normal curve, the **standard normal curve**, whose mean is zero and standard deviation is one. As discussed in Chapter 4, by converting raw scores into standard or z-scores, we obtain distributions with a mean of zero and a standard deviation of one. The generic formula for doing this, you will remember, is:

$$z_i = \frac{x_i - M}{s}. \tag{5.2}$$

Hence, through this formula, we can convert any normal distribution to the standard normal one. The z-table in Appendix B gives the probability of outcomes between the mean and any other point on the X-axis of the normal distribution. Let's take a few examples. Suppose that IQ scores are normally distributed with a mean of 100 and a standard deviation of 12, as shown in Figure 5.2. What is the probability of having an IQ between 100 and 120? We would find the answer by converting this distribution into the standard normal one, using equation 5.2. In this instance we get:

$$z = \frac{120 - 100}{12} = 1.67.$$

Looking up the area between the mean and a z-score of 1.67, we find that it is 0.4525.[1] That is, the area from the mean to 120 corresponds to 45.25 percent of the total area under the normal curve. If our information about the value of the mean and standard deviation of IQ scores is correct, and if IQ scores are normally distributed, we would conclude that 45.25 percent of the population has an IQ between 110 and 120. What then would be the probability of an IQ greater than 120? Since the normal distribution is perfectly symmetrical, half the area is on either side of the mean. Hence we would subtract 0.4525 from 0.5000, leaving us with a probability of .0475 of observing an IQ greater than 120. As a final example, let's determine the probability of having an IQ between 110 and 120. First, we find the area between the mean and 120 which is 0.4525, as we've already seen. Then we find the area between the mean and 110, which is 0.2967. Subtracting this latter probability from the former (0.4525 – 0.2967) gives us 0.1558. This is the probability of obtaining an IQ between 110 and 120.

Figure 5.2
The Normal Distribution with a Mean of 100
and a Standard Deviation of 12

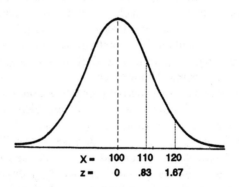

| X = | 100 | 110 | 120 |
| z = | 0 | .83 | 1.67 |

It is important to emphasize that the probabilities we have worked out are only hypothetical. They serve as useful estimates of probabilities only if IQ scores were approximately normally distributed and our estimates of the mean and standard deviation were satisfactory.

However, we seldom use normal curves to estimate the probability of empirical events. We would be more likely to use relative frequencies. Normal curves are used instead, as we will shortly see, for formal hypothesis testing. But, because many statistical techniques assume normality, we need to elaborate what is meant by this.

To start, no empirical variable is ever truly normally distributed. All recorded measures are discrete, with only a limited number of outcomes possible: income is recorded in dollars and cents; age in years; political knowledge in number of premiers correctly named. Yet normal curves are continuous, with an infinite number of possible outcomes. Furthermore, all empirical variables have definite lower and/or upper boundaries. That is, values below a certain number or above another number are impossible: negative incomes aren't defined; no individual lives to 1,000 years; no one can correctly name twenty premiers currently in power. Yet the tails of the normal curve are infinite, having no lower or upper boundaries.

The fact that empirical variables are never perfectly normally distributed should not, in itself, deter us from imposing the normality assumption. Clearly, some empirical distributions approximate the normal distribution better than others. The distributions of some variables, such as age and income, are conceptualized as continuous, even if their practical measurements are discrete. The ranges of certain variables such as income and age are quite large, and by the time we surpass three or four standard deviations from the mean, we would find few instances empirically; and imposing the normal assumption, we would expect few cases statistically.

Then, too, the normality assumption refers not so much to the empirical measure as to the **underlying concept**. Take the example of the number of premiers correctly named. This is an observable variable that is discrete and clearly bounded with only eleven possible outcomes. Furthermore, in the previous chapter we documented that this variable is positively skewed rather than symmetrical. However, we can imagine that the underlying concept, "amount of political knowledge," is continuous, smooth and quite symmetrical, with a wide range. That is, we can imagine that the normal distribution might be an apt analogy for the distribution of political knowledge.

The notion of an underlying or **latent concept** requires us to imagine its distribution. Look again at the normal curve depicted in Figure 5.1. This curve implies that most observations fall near the mean, but the further observations are from the mean, the less frequently they occur. The likelihood of observations at a given distance below the mean is identical to the likelihood of observations the same distance above the mean. There are no sharp discontinuities anywhere in the distribution. Does this not describe the likely distribution of many concepts?

Imagine the distribution of disagreements between couples. The image that comes to mind is closer to a normal curve than a rectangular one, for example. A rectangular distribution of disagreements would mean that the number of couples who never have a disagreement is the same as those who have an average number of disagreements. This doesn't seem a plausible distribution since we expect no more than a handful of couples to never disagree. Assuming a normal distribution is much more plausible for this variable, as it is for political knowledge.

At the same time, one can imagine other phenomena that we definitely would not expect to be normally distributed. In general, behaviours in domains that are normatively regulated are likely to be skewed. Housework, for example, continues to be gender-regulated. Consequently, for the variable "proportion of times a man in the household does the laundry," we would expect to find a pronounced positive skew. Conversely, if the variable is the proportion of times these tasks are performed by a woman, we would expect the mirror image of the former distribution, namely one that is negatively skewed. Similarly, according to sociobiologists, the preferred age of mates among males should be positively skewed, while post–high school preferences should be negatively skewed, since we imagine most people to hold very high preferences, such as university attendance, with only a few having very modest preferences. In these instances we would hesitate to make the normality assumption.

Of course, we do not rely solely on imagination. Prior research may indicate whether a normal curve reasonably approximates the distribution of any concept. Past research suggests that IQ scores are approximately normally distributed, while income is invariably positively skewed.[2]

The observed frequency distribution serves as another guide for the normality assumption. The shape of the histogram will suggest whether the assumption of normality is reasonable. Figure 5.3 reproduces the histogram of party imagery, which is negatively skewed. A normal curve superimposed on this distribution yields inaccuracies that are tolerable for some purposes.[3] In this diagram the dots and colons indicate how the distribution would appear if it were normally distributed.

Figure 5.3
SPSS-Produced Normal Distribution Superimposed on the Histogram of Number of Premiers Named

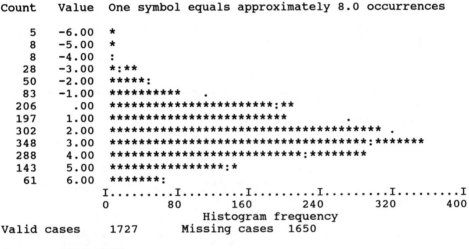

```
Count    Value   One symbol equals approximately 8.0 occurrences

    5    -6.00   *
    8    -5.00   *
    8    -4.00   :
   28    -3.00   *:**
   50    -2.00   ****:
   83    -1.00   *********    .
  206     .00    *********************:**
  197    1.00    ***********************          .
  302    2.00    ************************************ .
  348    3.00    **********************************:*******
  288    4.00    ***************************:********
  143    5.00    ****************:*
   61    6.00    *******:
           I.........I.........I.........I.........I.........I
           0        80       160       240       320       400
                        Histogram frequency
Valid cases    1727     Missing cases   1650
```

Source: 1984 CNES

In short, some error is introduced whenever the assumption of normality is made. It would be wrong to treat statistical answers as precise. Our results are inevitably less precise than statistics suggest. Information on the shape of the distribution should therefore be included in numerically based arguments.

Hypothesis Testing

Statistical hypothesis testing emerged in the context of decision-making. When making decisions, several alternatives are available, one of which must be chosen. The choice is made in an environment of uncertainty, since if one knew which alternative was best, the decision would be a foregone conclusion.

In statistical hypothesis testing, we narrow the choices to precisely two. A "blind date" analogy exemplifies this decision-making feature.

The Blind Date and the Two Errors

Any time a decision has to be made, the possibility of committing two kinds of errors arises. Table 5.1 depicts the blind date dilemma. If we decide to go out and the blind date is incompatible, the evening may be disastrous, constituting one possible error. The other possible error is that we decide not to go, but the date, as it turned out, would have been compatible. In this case, we would have missed a good opportunity. But, given that this is a *blind* date, we have no absolutely certain way of knowing the compatibility of the date in advance.

Table 5.1
The Blind Date and the Two Errors

| | Blind Date is: | |
Decision	compatible	not compatible
Go	have a good time	waste an evening
Not Go	miss a good opportunity	avoid a wasted evening

Table 5.1 captures this fundamental dilemma in decision-making. We start with the assumption that the empirical world has certain unknown characteristics. However, on the basis of statistical evidence, we will decide whether it has a particular characteristic. Classic hypothesis testing is used to determine the probability that we may make a wrong decision. Let's translate this into statistical language.

The Null and Alternative Hypotheses

In statistical language, the dilemma of decision-making is incorporated into two mutually exclusive hypotheses called the **null** (H_0) **hypothesis** and the **alternative** (H_1) **hypothesis**. The null hypothesis always postulates a specific population value of a variable. In this chapter we focus on population means and proportions. For example, if our interest centred on the mean population IQ, the null hypothesis might be stated in the form:

$$H_0: \text{the mean population IQ is 100 } (\mu = 100).$$

The alternative hypothesis is stated in one of two forms. The first is called the two-tailed form, in which the alternative hypothesis is simply:

$$H_1: \text{the mean population IQ is not 100 } (\mu \neq 100).$$

The **two-tailed hypothesis** permits the population value to be *any* number other than the one postulated in the null hypothesis.

The other form is the one-tailed alternative, where we specify that only one direction is permitted. The previous two-tailed hypothesis could, for instance, be changed into the **one-tailed hypothesis**:

$$H_1: \text{the mean population IQ is greater than 100 } (\mu > 100).$$

The null and alternative hypotheses are worded so that they do not violate two characteristics. First, the null hypothesis always provides a *specific* numeric value, such as that the mean IQ is 100. The alternative hypothesis permits a range of other values, such as all values other than 100, or all values greater than 100, or all values less than 100. Second, the null and alternative hypotheses are stated in mutually exclusive terms. If the null hypothesis postulates that the mean IQ is 100, the alternative hypothesis cannot state that the mean is less than or equal to 100, since this would not make the two hypotheses mutually exclusive.

Although we postulate a specific value for the null hypothesis, the number chosen usually represents a substantively important general condition. For the IQ example, we chose 100 for the null hypothesis since this number represents past findings. Stated differently, the decision we have to make is whether IQ has changed, with the null hypothesis being that IQ has not changed and the alternative hypothesis postulating that it has changed.[4] In a one-tailed alternative, we would specify whether the change was an increase or a decrease. Similarly, Buss (1989) measured relative preferred age of mate by subtracting the preferred age from the respondent's own age. The resulting number would be negative whenever the respondent preferred a mate older than himself, and positive whenever the respondent preferred a mate younger than himself. In this example, it would be eminently reasonable to formulate the null and alternative hypothesis as:

$$H_0: \mu = 0$$
$$H_1: \mu > 0.$$

If we decide in favour of the alternative hypothesis, then we have concluded that men, on average, prefer mates younger than themselves. We could, of course, have chosen any other specific number for our null hypothesis. But no other number would correspond to the argument being mounted.

Type I (α) and Type II (β) Errors
The two kinds of errors in decision-making can now be identified and labelled, as in Table 5.2:

Table 5.2
Alpha (α) and Beta (β) Errors

	H_0 is actually:	
We decide that H_0 is:	True	False
True	Correct	Type II or β error
False	Type I or α error	Correct

When the null hypothesis is true but we decide that it is false, we have committed an α error, or **Type I error**. But if the null hypothesis is false and we decide that it is true, we have committed a β error, or **Type II error**. Obviously, we would rather not commit either error, but our knowledge of the empirical world is fallible. Hence we must settle for minimizing the probability of making such errors. At a minimum, we want to know how likely it is that we are making such errors. This is precisely what hypothesis testing does, with the aid of a new type of theoretical distribution, known as the sampling distribution.

Examples of Possible Type I and Type II Errors

Type I

Type II

Parental socialization thesis :
We live in a world where children's views are independent of their parents' views, but we conclude that parents influence their children.

We live in a world in which parents influence their children, but we fail to recognize this.

Mate preference :
A characteristic of our world is that males are unconcerned about reproductive capacity, but we decide they are.

In our world, males prefer younger mates, but we conclude they don't.

Party imagery :
Knowledgable Canadians are no more likely than others to place the NDP to the left of the PCs, but we conclude they are.

Knowledgable Canadians, more than others, view the NDP to the left of the PCs, but we conclude they don't.

Sampling Distributons

A **sampling distribution** is the theoretical distribution of a sample characteristic that would be obtained if an infinite number of samples of a given size were taken. For every kind of sample statistic, such as $\overline{X}$, there is a corresponding theoretical distribution that characterizes that statistic. To illustrate, suppose we had two hundred observations on preferred age of mates, and we computed the sample mean, $\overline{X}$. If we then took another sample of two hundred observations, we would probably obtain a different sample mean. If we repeated this process an infinite number of times, we could construct a distribution of these sample means. This would be the sampling distribution of means based on a sample size of two hundred. It is a theoretical distribution because one never has an infinite number of samples. Note that for every different sample size, there is a unique sampling distribution of the mean. That is, the sampling distribution of the mean of samples of twenty-five, for example, is different from the one based on samples of twenty or thirty.

Fortunately we don't need to obtain sampling distributions, since statisticians have developed theorems that describe the shape of various sampling distributions.

One such theorem, the **Central Limit Theorem**, describes the sampling distribution of sample means. This theorem states that, with increasing sample size, the sampling distribution of the sample means will increasingly approximate the normal distribution, with a mean identical to the population mean, μ, and a standard deviation of $\sigma / \sqrt{N}$, where σ is the population standard deviation and N is the sample size. The effect of this theorem is illustrated in Figure 5.4.

Figure 5.4
Illustration of the Central Limit Theorem

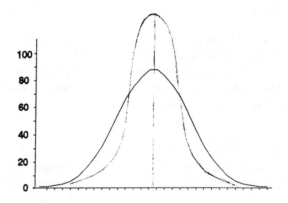

For this figure, assume that the sample means are based on samples of nine observations. Notice that the sampling distribution has the same mean as the population. Its standard deviation, however, is one-third that of the population — because the standard deviation of the sampling distribution is that of the population divided by the square root of nine, the sample size. The standard deviation of the sampling distribution is referred to as the **standard error** of estimate.

The Central Limit Theorem implies that we need not even concern ourselves with the shape of the population distribution if our sample is large. No firm rule defines what constitutes a large sample. Obviously, the less "normal" a population distribution is, the larger the sample needed. It should be noted, however, that the sampling distribution approximates normality even with relatively small samples and generally a sample size greater than fifty is considered sufficient to be relatively unconcerned about the shape of the population. Figure 5.5 illustrates the Central Limit Theorem when the sample size is large. A population distribution has been chosen that is quite unlike a normal distribution: a rectangular distribution where every outcome is equally likely. Yet, with a reasonably large sample size, the sampling distribution approaches normality. Note again that the sampling distribution has the same mean as the population but a smaller standard deviation; with samples of forty-nine, the standard deviation of the sampling distribution is one-seventh that of the population. We are now ready to combine all the concepts developed so far to look at hypothesis testing more comprehensively.

Figure 5.5
Illustration of the Central Limit Theorem
Using a Large Sample Size

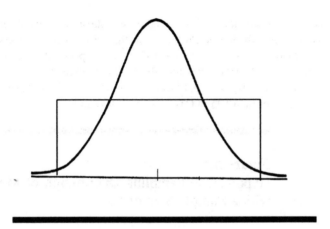

Testing Hypotheses about Population Means

In statistical hypothesis testing, we always make inferences about some population parameter. In this case, we want to make inferences about a population mean, μ. First we take a random sample of observations from the population of interest. Next we compute the sample statistic, $\overline{X}$. We then take a theoretical step by locating this particular sample mean along the continuum of the sampling distribution of the mean. We can do this by applying the Central Limit Theorem, since it describes the sampling distribution of means. This theorem informs us that the sampling distribution will be normally distributed with a mean of μ and a standard deviation of $\sigma / \sqrt{N}$. Using $\hat{\sigma}$ as our estimate of the standard deviation of the population, our only unknown is the value of the population mean, μ. But this is precisely why we conduct a test of hypothesis: to make inferences about the population value of μ. For the null hypothesis we postulate a specific value for μ. The sampling distribution then provides a way of determining how likely various outcomes are, if this were the true value of μ. If the sample mean we get is an unlikely one, we conclude that the null hypothesis is false. Let's take a hypothetical case.

Suppose we are interested in knowing what the mean population IQ is. Past research suggests that the mean IQ is 100, so we use this as the value for our null hypothesis:

$$H_0: \mu = 100.$$

We suspect that the mean IQ has increased over time, so we use a one-tailed alternative hypothesis:

$$H_1: \mu > 100.$$

From our population we take a random sample of, say, fifty observations on IQ. We then calculate the sample mean, $\overline{X}$, and the estimated population standard deviation, $\hat{\sigma}$. Suppose they turned out to be 105 and 17, respectively. If μ were really 100, then the sampling distribution would also have a mean of 100 and an estimated standard error of $17 / \sqrt{50}$, or 2.40. Figure 5.6 shows the probability of obtaining a sample mean greater than 105 in this hypothetical situation.

Figure 5.6
Hypothetical Sampling Distribution of Means with a Sample Size of 50

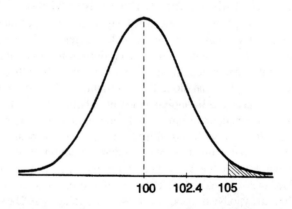

100   102.4   105

The shaded area under the sampling distribution represents the probability of obtaining a sample mean as large as 105, or larger, if the population mean is 100. This diagram indicates that we seldom would obtain a sample mean as high as 105 if the population mean were actually 100. By computing the standard score, we can look up the probability using the table of areas under a normal curve. Remember that to obtain any z-score, we take the distance of the observation from the mean and divide by the standard deviation of that distribution. Using the symbols appropriate for sampling distributions (and substituting $\hat{\sigma}$ for σ) we get:

$$z = \frac{\overline{X} - \mu}{\frac{\hat{\sigma}}{\sqrt{N}}}. \tag{5.3}$$

Substituting the calculated values into this expression we get:

$$z = \frac{105 - 100}{2.40} = 2.08.$$

Looking up the area under the normal curve (Appendix B) that corresponds to this z-score, we obtain the number 0.4812. That is, the area under the sampling distribution from the hypothesized mean of 100 to the observed (sample) mean of 105 includes 0.4812 of the total area. If the true mean were actually 100, then with a sample of fifty the probability of getting an $\overline{X}$ of 105 or larger would be 0.0188 (0.5000 – 0.4812 = 0.0188). Let's state this somewhat differently. The sampling distribution indicates how often we would get various values of $\overline{X}$ from samples of fifty *if* the true population mean were 100. We have found that less than two times in a hundred would we get a sample mean of 105 or larger. Either this disparity between 100 and 105 was produced by chance fluctuations, or the null hypothesis is false. We never know in any given instance which of these two alternatives is the correct one. Instead, we use a decision-making rule for an "acceptable" level of Type I error. By convention, if the probability of a Type I error is less than 0.05, then the null hypothesis can be rejected, and the finding is considered to be statistically significant.[5]

It is important to stress that "statistical significance" simply means that, by rejecting the null hypothesis, the probability of having committed a Type I error is considered to be within acceptable limits. By rejecting the null hypothesis, we reject sampling fluctuation as the explanation for our result.

The findings in our hypothetical example would be considered statistically significant since they satisfy the decision-making rule. Suppose now that we had obtained identical results, but that the sample consisted of only twenty-five observations. In this situation, the standard score would be:

$$z = \frac{105 - 100}{\frac{17}{\sqrt{25}}} = \frac{5}{3.4} = 1.47.$$

The probability of making a Type I error were we to reject the null hypothesis would be 0.0708. By the decision-making rule conventionally used, this finding is not statistically significant. That is, we do not reject the null hypothesis, deciding instead that the evidence in our sample is not sufficiently compelling to conclude that the population mean has increased.

Keep in mind that the two hypothetical examples are identical in every respect, except that the sample size in the second instance is half that of the first. Yet the results were statistically significant in the first instance but not in the second. From a statistical point of view, there is no contradiction: with a smaller sample size, sampling fluctuations are larger and therefore the disparity between the sample mean and the null-hypothesized population value is more likely to have occurred through chance fluctuation. From a substantive point of view, however, these results reveal a dilemma: whether a finding is statistically significant depends to a considerable extent on the sample size. With large sample sizes, small differences may become statistically significant. With small sample sizes, potentially important results may not reach statistical significance. Therefore, in the latter situation, where we cannot reject the null hypothesis, we may be committing a Type II (β) error.

Type II errors are infrequently mentioned in research articles. There are two major reasons for this. First, social scientists never accept the null hypothesis; they simply "fail to reject" it. Since a β error is defined as accepting a null hypothesis when it is actually false, they can never commit such an error. This may sound like a verbal game, but it is more than that. Failing to reject a null hypothesis simply implies that the evidence is not sufficient to reject it. Rather than deciding that the null hypothesis is correct, we suspend judgment. These are the situations in which replication studies might be warranted.

The second reason Type II errors are seldomly reported is because their probability depends on the true value of the population parameter. Since we don't know the true value of the parameter (if we did, we wouldn't conduct tests of hypotheses), we can't compute the Type II error. We could, however, determine how likely it is that we would detect differences of various magnitudes between possible true means and the null hypothesized mean. We could play a "what if" game. What if the true mean IQ were not 100 but really 102? What is the probability that in our test we would detect that the mean is not 100? What if it were actually 105? How likely would we be to reject the null hypothesis in that case?

Although these hypothetical Type II errors are relatively easy to compute, they are seldom reported. For our purposes, it is sufficient to remember that, where a finding does not reach statistical significance, it may be because the sample size is too small to rule out sampling fluctuations.

Hypotheses about Proportions

Proportions are nothing more than means of dichotomous variables. Programs such as SPSS do not require us to distinguish between means and proportions. However, since there are only two possible outcomes for each observation, the calculation of both the mean and the standard deviation is simplified. This permits us to perform **significance tests** with minimal hand calculations. Furthermore, it provides a convenient example of how researchers calculate the optimal sample size in advance of conducting a study.

Let's take one example where the required calculations are so minimal they would ordinarily be done by hand. A political party campaign manager must decide whether to expend more resources on a particular candidate. The electoral district is one that has frequently switched from one party to another, and the candidate in question is a novice. Tests about the proportion of the electorate likely to vote for the candidate would help the decision-making process.

The campaign manager commissions a public opinion polling firm to take a random sample of 625 adult residents in an electoral district. Of these, 340 individuals state they would vote for the candidate. No additional information is necessary to test the hypothesis that this candidate will win.

With only two candidates, the candidate attracting more than 50 percent of the vote will win. Our null hypothesis in such situations is that the proportion of the electorate voting for "our" candidate is 0.50, the highest proportion of votes that would still result in our candidate not winning (50 percent plus one vote is necessary to win). The alternative is that our candidate will win. This will happen whenever the proportion voting for our candidate is greater than 0.50. We therefore phrase the alternative hypothesis as a one-tailed test, namely that the true proportion is greater than 0.50. Stated formally:

$$H_0: P = 0.50 \text{ (our candidate will not win)}$$

$$H_1: P > 0.50 \text{ (our candidate will win)}$$

where P is the population proportion.

It can be shown that, because of the dichotomous nature of our variable, the standard deviation of the sampling distribution of proportions simplifies to:

$$\sigma_P = \sqrt{\frac{P(1-P)}{N}} \tag{5.4}$$

where σ_P = the standard error
   P = the true proportion, and
   N = the sample size.

Of course we don't know the proportion of the population who will vote for our candidate, and hence we cannot calculate the precise standard error. However, this seldom poses a serious problem, since the largest standard error will always be when $P = 0.50$. At this value, multiplying $P (1 - P)$ results in 0.25. Choosing any other value of P will give us a smaller number. For example, $(0.70)(0.30) = 0.21$, and $(0.80)(0.20) = 0.16$. Therefore, if we were to choose 0.50 as our estimate for P, our test would be the most conservative one. If we reject the null hypothesis with this estimate, we can be quite confident that the probability of a Type I error is within acceptable limits. However, if one has reasonable grounds to believe that P should be some other number, one can insert such alternative estimates into the equation. For example, in a three-way race, where the third candidate is expected to attract about 20 percent of the vote (leaving 80 percent to be divided between the remaining two candidates), it would be quite appropriate to use an estimate of 0.40 for P.

Adapting our general formula to the special case of proportions, we get:

$$z = \frac{\frac{f}{N} - P}{\sqrt{\frac{P(1-P)}{N}}}.$$

(5.5)

Substituting our hypothetical results gives us:

$$z = \frac{\frac{340}{625} - 0.50}{\sqrt{\frac{(.5)(.5)}{625}}} = \frac{0.044}{0.02} = 2.20.$$

Our sample results reveal that, even with the most conservative estimate of the standard error, we will be wrong less than five times in a hundred if we predict that our candidate will win the election.

This example contains the features which make formal hypothesis testing appropriate. These are:

- The purpose of the research is not the accumulation of knowledge. Rather, it is to help make a decision (whether to expend more resources on this particular campaign).
- Little prior information is available about the likelihood of the outcome — in this case, the candidate winning. The electoral district was not a "loyal" one and the candidate in question did not have a "proven" record. There is a "natural" population of interest from which it is relatively easy to obtain a random sample and to which we wish to generalize our results. The concern was with the

features of that population, namely the proportion of the population that would vote for our candidate.

- The "fit" between the observed variable (For which candidate do respondents say they will vote?) and the underlying variable of interest (For which candidate will respondents actually vote?) is not particularly problematic.

Nevertheless, some cautions are in order. The prediction might prove wrong for a number of reasons having nothing to do with sampling fluctuations. Most of these are self-evident (such as a volatile electorate where the assumption of a stable proportion voting for a given candidate is inappropriate). Two reasons may be worth mentioning.

First, past research documents a frequent discrepancy on some issues between "words and deeds," as Deutscher (1966) put it. That is, individuals may say they will vote for one candidate, but they actually vote for another. This problem is acute when the issue is a normative one, such as ethnic discrimination. A review of the literature suggests that individuals tend to present themselves as congruent with socially accepted standards, but their behaviour is more likely to be at variance with these standards. The remarkable accuracy of election polls suggests that the words-deeds disparity is usually not a problem in voting studies.[6] At the same time, some polls have produced embarassing predictions, reminding us of the fallibility of the research process.

Second, what have been called "demand characteristics" in experiments often provide artifactual confirmation of desired outcomes. Rosenthal (1976), among others, has documented that where a researcher knows the hypothesis to be tested, unintentional cues are "given off" that tend to make people behave in a manner that confirms the hypothesis (the same principle holds in non-experimental settings). With this in mind, a "double blind" procedure is the safest one. Here, neither the respondent nor the interviewer knows what the "desired" outcome is. This factor dictates that the polling be conducted by an independent organization and that the interviewers do not know which candidate or party sponsored the study.

Calculating the Optimal Sample Size

Particularly when designing a survey study, the researcher must select an appropriate sample size. In certain situations, statistical calculations can help us make this selection.

Returning to our political polling example, the question of sample size can be formulated as: How large a sample is necessary to be 95 percent confident that the *difference* between the observed and true proportion voting for a given candidate does not exceed a certain maximum?

Through a series of algebraic manipulations, we can solve equation 5.5 for N, the sample size. Before showing the result, let me simplify the numerator in equation 5.5. Let's use the symbol *M.E.* (an abbreviation for "maximum error") for the *difference* between the observed proportion and the true proportion. Note that we can express this difference as a single number without knowing the values of its constituent parts, (i.e., f, N and p). With this modification in the symbols, we can rewrite equation 5.5 as:

$$z = \frac{M.E.}{\sqrt{\dfrac{P(1-P)}{N}}}. \tag{5.6}$$

We won't go through the necessary algebraic manipulations here (although you may wish to try them on your own), but the result is:

$$N = \frac{P(1-P)z^2}{(M.E.)^2}. \tag{5.7}$$

Let's choose 0.04 as the maximum error. If we want to be 95 percent confident that our error will not exceed 0.04, we can simply substitute 1.96 for z and 0.04 for M.E. If we use 0.50 as our estimate for P, we will get the most generous estimate of the required sample size; that is, we will get an estimate of the largest sample size required to ensure that 95 percent of the time our error will be less than four percent. The sample size we would need is:

$$N = \frac{(0.5)(0.5)(1.96)^2}{(0.04)^2} \approx 600. \tag{5.8}$$

We would need, at most, a sample of 600 cases to be 95 percent confident that the difference between our observed proportion and the true proportion would be no greater than 0.04. An examination of equation 5.8 reveals that the cost of greater certainty, or a smaller maximum error, is a larger sample size.

Handling Unstable Estimates of σ: The Student's t-Distribution

In a previous section, we learned that when $\hat{\sigma}$ is based on large samples, it is an unbiased and relatively stable estimate of the population σ. The problem remains of what to do when we have small samples, say, under fifty. One partial solution to this problem is called the **Student's t-distribution**. The "Student's t" is a partial solution because it should be applied only to situations in which the population distribution is reasonably normal. With small samples *and* non-normal populations, the results of tests of statistical significance must be treated with caution.

The Student's t is a family of distributions that does not require knowledge of the population standard deviation. Under the conditions described, sample means are characterized by this distribution. Areas under the t-distribution are found in a manner similar to that used for the normal distribution. The t-value is found using equation 5.9:

$$t = \frac{\overline{X} - \mu}{\frac{s}{\sqrt{N}}}$$

(5.9)

with $N-1$ **degrees of freedom**. This equation looks quite similar to that for z-scores for sampling distributions of means. However, there are two differences. First, the sample standard deviation, s, replaces σ. Remember that s is no longer an estimate of the population parameter, σ. It is simply the sample standard deviation.

Additionally, the t-distribution involves the notion of degrees of freedom. Conceptually, the meaning of degrees of freedom for a t-distribution is similar to that discussed for the chi-square distribution. It refers to the number of observations that are free to vary. When computing a mean, $N-1$ numbers are free to vary, while the last one is totally determined by the other numbers and the mean. If the mean of three numbers is four, and two of the numbers are three and seven, then the third number is entirely determined: it must be two; otherwise we couldn't get a mean of four. Since this third number is determined, we don't count it as part of statistical evidence. This is why there are $N-1$ degrees of freedom in this t-test.

Degrees of freedom are important in t-distributions since each degree of freedom produces a different distribution. They differ from the normal distribution in that they are flatter, having more of their area in the tails of the distribution. As the degrees of freedom increase, the t-distribution approaches that of the normal distribution, and they are identical when N is infinity. However, the t and the normal distribution are already quite similar when there are only thirty observations (29 degrees of freedom). In this situation, 95 percent of the area lies within 1.96 standard deviations on either side of the mean in normal distribution. The corresponding t that would include this area is 2.042, which isn't much larger.

In short, a t-value has much the same interpretation as a z-score. However, the area contained between the mean and any given t is not a constant but is dependent on the degrees of freedom. As the degrees of freedom increase, the area corresponding to a given t approaches the area for the identical z. Since there is a different curve for each degree of freedom, the t-table in Appendix C gives only selected probabilities rather than all of them. For example, with nineteen degrees of freedom, a t-score of 2.539 includes 99 percent of the area; a t-score of 2.861 includes 99.5 percent (i.e., the probability of a larger t is 0.005).

The smaller the sample size, the more conservative is the t-test, making it more difficult to reject the null hypothesis using the t-distribution. Clearly, the larger the sample size, the less important it is which of the two tests are used.[7]

Difference of Means Tests: Independent Samples

We have now covered the basic logic of hypothesis testing, as well as several applications for testing hypotheses about the mean and proportion in a single population. We can extend the logic of hypothesis testing to assess the probability that two populations differ in their means (or proportions). The logic of these tests is the same as that just discussed. The main difference is the computing formula.

As with tests concerning the mean of a single population, we assume random samples. However, for the **independent difference-of-means tests,** we need independent random samples from each of two populations. In experimental designs, this is accomplished with **random assignment** into two groups: the experimental and the control. With other data-collection designs, the two populations may be natural ones, such as males and females, or they may be contrived. This involves making an arbitrary but consistent decision as to what the two populations are. For example, we could define all individuals under the age of 45 as one population, and all those 45 or older as the second. In this way, we have constructed two populations, since age is a continuous rather than dichotomous variable.

Once we have a sample from each of the two populations, the question is whether the sample means on some variable of interest differ sufficiently to conclude that the population means differ. Using the subscripts 1 and 2 to refer to the two populations, the null and alternative hypotheses would ordinarily be constructed as:

$$H_0: \mu_1 = \mu_2 \text{ or } \mu_1 - \mu_2 = 0$$
$$H_1: \mu_1 \neq \mu_2 \text{ or } \mu_1 - \mu_2 \neq 0.$$

Earlier we learned that it is always possible to test hypotheses if the sampling distribution of the particular statistic under consideration is known. Therefore the next question is: What is the sampling distribution of the difference between sample means taken from two populations? The answer can be derived from the Central Limit Theorem, together with some information concerning the variance of the difference between two groups. Every time we take samples from two populations, we can compute a statistic called the difference of means, namely $\bar{X}_1 - \bar{X}_2$. For every pair of samples that we draw, we will get some number that is the difference between these two means. For every pair of samples, this difference can be expressed as *one* number. Now we must ask, "If we drew an infinite number of independent pairs of random samples from two populations, what would the distribution of these differences look like?" In other words: What is the shape of the distribution? What is the *average* difference? and What is the standard deviation of the differences in an infinite number of samples? The Central Limit Theorem tells us that the average difference in the sampling distribution will be the same as the true population difference, since we are dealing here with a statement about the *mean* of a sampling distribution. Therefore, all we need to determine is the standard deviation of the differences. It can be shown that, where the two groups are indeed independent of each other, the variance of their difference is equal to the *sum* of their individual variances. Hence the standard deviation of the difference of means is equal to:

$$\sigma_{\bar{x}_1 - \bar{x}_2} = \sqrt{\frac{\sigma_1^2}{N_1} + \frac{\sigma_2^2}{N_2}}. \qquad (5.10)$$

Additionally, the Central Limit Theorem implies that as both N_1 and N_2 (the sample sizes) grow infinitely large, the sampling distribution of the difference between their means approaches a normal distribution, regardless of the form of the original distribution. With these statements, we have succeeded in completely specifying the sampling distribution of the difference of means. Now we return to the general formula for z-scores:

$$z = \frac{\text{distance from observation to (hypothesized) mean}}{\text{standard deviation of the distribution}}.$$

Here our observation is the difference between two means. Thus we have this formula:

$$z = \frac{(\bar{X}_1 - \bar{X}_2) - (\mu_1 - \mu_2)}{\sqrt{\frac{\sigma_1^2}{N_1} + \frac{\sigma_2^2}{N_2}}}. \qquad (5.11)$$

Usually the null hypothesis states:

$$\mu_1 - \mu_2 = 0$$

and therefore this difference drops out of the equation. Let's take several examples where the difference-of-means test can help us reach reasonable decisions.

There are many situations in which researchers must decide whether an unexpected finding represents chance fluctuation or whether it needs to be examined more closely with the goal of developing a substantive explanation for the finding.

Several times in the party imagery example we had unexpected reversals in the proposition that political knowledge is positively related to correct placement of the political parties on a left-right dimension. Some of our earlier attempts to assess this relationship were quite crude, and I argued that the reversals likely resulted from such crudeness. But even in our best effort to date, there are reversals in the expected relationship: the mean left-right placement of the Liberals relative to the NDP drops between knowledge of four and five premiers.[8]

This is an example of a class of situations that is suitably resolved using significance tests, for the reasons presented earlier. Here, a decision has to be made whether the reversal can be ignored. The goal of the hypothesis test is to provide a rule for making this decision, rather than to accumulate knowledge. Furthermore, because the reversal is unexpected, there is no prior or additional information available which can be used to help make the decision.

Although we do not have a natural geographic or substantive population, the relevant question here is: Can we consider the party imagery scores as belonging to one population, or must we treat them as coming from two distinct populations? Our concern is not to generalize to a population but to decide whether we can treat observations that come from two groups (Canadians who know the names of four and five premiers) as nevertheless belonging to one population with respect to their party imagery.

For the null hypothesis, we postulate that the two groups can be treated as being drawn from a single population. That is:

$$H_0: \mu_1 - \mu_2 = 0$$

(the reversal can be ignored) where μ refers to the mean left-right party imagery and the subscripts 1 and 2 refer to Canadians who know the names of four and five premiers, respectively. This null hypothesis incorporates the substantive conclusion that the two groups can be thought of as belonging to one population.

An appropriate alternative hypothesis would be:

$$H_1: \mu_1 - \mu_2 > 0$$

(the reversal requires an interpretation). This one-tailed alternative embodies the conclusion that the two groups should be treated as coming from two separate populations, and that the group knowing the names of five premiers places the NDP in a less correct left-right continuum than do those who know the names of only four premiers. In brief, the alternative hypothesis postulates that the reversal in party imagery between these two groups is sufficiently large that it requires an explanation. Since no plausible explanation comes to mind, we hope that the sampling fluctuation interpretation can be retained.

The required information for performing this test of hypothesis is given in Table 5.3. To test this hypothesis, we simply substitute the appropriate values into equation 5.11:

$$z = \frac{0.4550 - 0.4341}{\sqrt{\dfrac{(1.2128)^2}{222} + \dfrac{(1.2687)^2}{205}}} = 0.17.$$

Table 5.3
Mean and Standard Deviation of Party Imagery by Whether Four or Five Premiers Were Named

	Number of Premiers Named	
	Four	Five
$\bar{X}$	0.4550	0.4341
$\hat{\sigma}$	1.2128	1.2687
N	222	205

Source: 1984 CNES.

The area from the mean to a z-score of 0.17 is 0.0675. Hence the probability of making a Type I error, if we rejected the null hypothesis, is 0.4325. Since this is greater than 0.05, we fail to reject the null hypothesis and conclude that the reversal can be considered to represent chance fluctuations. The region of rejection is diagrammed in Figure 5.7.

Earlier we learned that tests of statistical significance are more useful for making decisions than for accumulating knowledge. Questions about the representativeness of a sample belong in the former domain.

Biased samples jeopardize our ability to generalize findings. Our arguments are strengthened to the extent that we can show the sample is unbiased with respect to the variables of interest. In this next section, we will apply a difference-of-means test to the party imagery example. We will use this test as a decision-making aid in determining whether our sample is representative of adult Canadians.

Figure 5.7
Region of Rejection for a One-Tailed Test

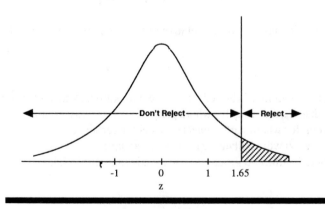

Ideally, sample statistics would mirror population parameters on all variables. In practice, samples accurately reflect populations on some characteristics and not others. But not all biases are alike: some are more disastrous for the argument being made than others. The 1984 CNES project might, for example, provide representative information on party imagery but not on religious affiliation. For the argument being made, the non-representativeness on religious affiliation would not constitute a particularly grave problem, since religious affiliation is not a variable directly involved in the argument.[9] We would be more alarmed if our sample were representative of religious affiliation but biased with respect to party imagery.

You may have noticed in earlier tables that the sample size for the political knowledge variable is about twice that for the party imagery variables. The reason is that only half the sample was asked the questions on left-right party imagery. This raises the possibility that those Canadians asked the party imagery questions are not representative of Canadians as a whole. We would be particularly concerned if they were not representative in the general domain of political knowledge, attitudes and practices. We cannot ascertain with the data at hand whether the sample is representative with respect to left-right placement of the federal parties, because it is precisely the information on these variables that is lacking for half the sample. However, we can determine whether the excluded half differs from the remainder in their political knowledge. If they differ, the half-sample is biased. This would decrease our confidence in the relationship between political knowledge and party imagery previously documented.

The first step is to create two independent groups from the total sample. The first group consists of all those who responded to the party imagery questions. The second group consists of those who did not, almost all of whom were not asked these questions in the first place.

Our basic question is whether the level of political knowledge differs between these two groups. This can be posed in the null and alternative form as:

$$H_0: \mu_A - \mu_{NA} = 0$$

(the half-sample is representative of the population on political knowledge)

$$H_1: \mu_A - \mu_{NA} \neq 0$$

(the half-sample is biased with respect to political knowledge) where the subscript A denotes the group for whom party imagery was ascertained, and NA refers to the group for whom party imagery was not ascertained.

Next we calculate the mean and standard deviation of the numbers of premiers named in the two groups. These are given in Table 5.4.

Table 5.4
Mean and Standard Deviation of Number of Premiers Named by Left-Right Party Imagery Response Status

Party Imagery Status

	Ascertained	Not Ascertained
$\overline{X}$	4.12	2.86
$\hat{\sigma}$	2.50	2.35
N	1,727	1,650

Source: 1984 CNES.

Since this is a two-tailed hypothesis test, we will reject the null hypothesis whenever our calculated z-score is less than -1.96 or greater than $+1.96$, since this would give us a maximum Type I error of 0.05. Substituting the appropriate numbers into equation 5.11, we get:

$$z = \frac{2.86 - 4.12}{\sqrt{\frac{(2.35)^2}{1,650} + \frac{(2.50)^2}{1,727}}} = 15.10.$$

Since this z-score falls in the region where we reject the null hypothesis, we conclude that for reasons yet unknown, those who responded to the left-right party imagery questions are not representative of the Canadian electorate with respect to political knowledge. The difference in mean number of premiers named is so large that it should not be attributed to sampling fluctuations. This is a puzzling fact, since the study design was supposed to create two random half-samples.

One possible methodological source of the differential political knowledge in the two groups is a **reactive measurement effect**: the act of asking humans questions alters the responses obtained. In this context, the half-sample that was asked about left-right party images might have become more sensitized to political issues, permitting them to remember more names of premiers. Such an argument would be plausible only if the question on names of premiers followed, rather than preceded, those on party imagery. Such was indeed the case.[10]

An "unexpected" finding, such as the non-representativeness documented here, frequently spurs researchers to cast their nets more widely. This in turn sometimes changes the focus of the research in ways not initially anticipated. Before we do that here, however, we must remember that non-representativeness is not a problem in itself. It is a problem only when we are estimating population parameters. If our aim were to estimate what proportion of the Canadian electorate places the NDP to the left of the PCs, our estimate would likely be biased; we would probably overestimate the proportion who actually do so.

This deduction is based on the following argument chain: (1) Politically knowledgable Canadians are more likely to consider the NDP a left-wing party than are Canadians in general (this was documented in several ways in previous chapters). (2) Respondents providing party imagery information are, on average, more knowledgable than those who did not (this relationship was discovered in the difference-of-means test discussed above). (3) Therefore respondents to the party imagery questions are more likely to view the NDP as a left-wing party than non-respondents (this is a fallible deduction; i.e., the conclusion is *not necessarily* true, because, when premises are probabilistic, so are conclusions).

In addition, for our conclusion to hold, we must assume that the relationship between political knowledge and party imagery previously documented also holds for the non-respondents. This assumption unfortunately cannot be tested directly. Since we cannot test this assumption directly, we search for indirect but nevertheless relevant tests. A reasonable start is to search for alternate party imagery variables that were asked of everyone rather than just of the half-sample. And indeed a set of questions on the social class bias of the federal political parties meets these criteria (see Figure 5.8).

Our first task is to evaluate whether these questions are analogous to the left-right ones on a conceptual level. This translates to: Is there a "correct" class favouritism position of the NDP relative to the other federal parties? In the 1984 election the NDP campaign focused on "the ordinary Canadian." In addition, it can be argued that the platform of the NDP favours a variety of programs that aid the lower class more than the middle or upper class. Consequently, the NDP should be placed closer than the other parties to favouring the lower class.

Conceptually then, the placement of the NDP on a lower-upper class dimension should be similar to placing them on a left-right scale. That is, the lower-upper class placement of the NDP relative to the other political parties can tentatively be considered as an alternative measure of "correct" party imagery.

If lower-upper class placement is indeed an alternative measure, then it should show the same relation to political knowledge as that found for the left-right aspect. This expectation can be formulated as the **external consistency** criterion. To treat multiple measures as indicators of the "same" concept, they must have similar relationships to other variables (this principle will be discussed in greater depth in Chapter 7).

Our second task is to establish whether the external consistency principle is upheld for our alternative measures. Table 5.5 shows the class placement of the NDP relative to the PCs and the Liberals.

Figure 5.8

Measures of Political Parties' Perceived Class Favouritism

Some people believe that political parties favour particular social classes over other social classes. Here is a scale for describing each of the federal parties. The closer to 1, the more a party favours the lower social classes, and the closer to 7, the more a party favours the higher social classes.

	Lower						Higher	No Opinion
Where would you place the federal Liberal party on this scale?	1	2	3	4	5	6	7	8
Where would you place the federal Progressive Conservative party?	1	2	3	4	5	6	7	8
Where would you place the federal NDP?	1	2	3	4	5	6	7	8

Source: 1984 CNES.

A number of features stand out in this table. Most importantly, the external consistency criterion seems, on the whole, to be fulfilled: with increasing political knowledge, the class position party imagery is increasingly "correct." More precisely, respondents who can name more premiers are more likely to consider the NDP than the PCs as favouring the lower class. The same holds true for placing the NDP relative to the Liberals.

A second feature is that the relationship of political knowledge to class favouritism appears weaker than that for left-right placement. This can be seen by the number of reversals in the conditional means. Two possibilities suggest themselves. The first is that the class favouritism question is more ambiguous to Canadians than the left-right one. This would weaken the relationship between political knowledge and this measure of party imagery. The second is that the relationship is weakened by the addition of those cases for whom the left-right placement was not ascertained. This latter possibility is better tested with correlation and regression techniques which we will cover in later chapters.

Table 5.5
Mean Perceived Class Favouritism of the Federal NDP
Relative to the Liberal and Progressive Conservative Parties,
by Number of Names of Premiers Known

Mean Lower Class Orientation of the NDP Relative to:

Number of Names of Premiers Known	Liberals[a]	Progressive Conservatives[a]	N[b]
0	0.23	0.26	154
1	0.39	0.51	470
2	0.52	0.56	414
3	0.66	0.73	357
4	0.72	0.72	341
5	0.70	0.80	301
6	0.78	0.84	266
7	0.84	0.83	207
8	0.80	0.79	137
9	0.90	0.81	59
10	0.86	0.75	44
TOTAL	0.62	0.67	2,750

[a] The respondents' placement of the NDP on class favouritism was subtracted from their placement of the Liberal and Conservative parties, respectively. A positive result indicates the NDP was judged to be more sympathetic to the lower classes than was the other political party. All instances where the NDP are considered as favouring the lower classes more than the other parties were recoded as 1.
[b] Because of missing values, the number of cases differs slightly (by no more than seven cases in any row) between the two variables. Where there is a difference, the N reported is always the smaller one.

Source: 1984 CNES.

Previously we documented a clear left-right progression for the three federal parties, with the NDP most to the left, the PCs furthest to the right and the Liberals in the middle. This was so for every level of political knowledge. To a considerable extent, this progression disintegrates for the class favouritism measure. There is but a slight tendency to place the PCs more towards the upper classes than the Liberals. Stated differently, the NDP is placed closer to favouring the lower class than either the Liberals or the Conservatives, but little distinction is made between the Liberals and the Conservatives. This is an indication that the class favouritism measure is in some respects not analogous to the left-right measure.

Finally, a sizable number of respondents, although asked, would not place the parties on the class scale. Therefore there is still some possible non-representativeness in the remaining sample, but this problem is substantially less severe now.

Introducing the class favouritism measure of party imagery strengthened our argument in a number of ways. It has broadened the concept of "correct" party imagery. We can begin to think in terms of "underlying" concepts and their observed (measured) indicators. In this case, the latent concept could be labelled "correctness of party imagery" for which we now have four indicators:

1. left-right placement of the NDP relative to the Liberals,
2. left-right placement of the NDP relative to the PCs,
3. class favouritism of the NDP relative to the Liberals, and
4. class favouritism of the NDP relative to the PCs.

Consideration of class favouritism has permitted two additional tests of the political knowledge–correct party placement hypothesis. Since the class favouritism measures "passed" the two tests, our confidence in the merit of the hypothesis rises. Additionally, passing the external consistency criterion reinforces our belief that it is meaningful to think of the class favouritism and left-right position measures as indicators of a common concept. This increases the parsimony of the argument.

The class favouritism questions were asked of the total sample. This permitted us to test the knowledge and correct party imagery proposition on a more representative sample, greatly reducing the possibility that the finding was not generalizable to the Canadian electorate as a whole.

We realized previously that estimates of the left-right position of the NDP would likely be biased in this data, based on the discovery that those who were not asked the left-right questions had less political knowledge. Using our new measures, let's test that possibility. To do this, we repeat the difference-of-means test, substituting the class position measures for the political knowledge measures as the dependent variables. If the half-sample is biased with respect to party imagery, then we should find a significant difference on the class position measures between those who responded to the left-right questions and those who did not. And indeed, for both comparisons (NDP compared to Liberals and to Conservatives), there is a substantial and statistically significant difference between these two groups (the data for this test are not shown). This finding reinforces the conclusion that the half-sample is not representative of the Canadian electorate on party imagery.

Difference of Means Tests: Correlated Samples

The previous section developed the logic and the equations for testing whether the means of a single variable in two populations can be considered equal. In some situations we may be interested in testing whether the means of two variables in a single population can be treated as equal. For example, we may be interested in assessing whether the mean value of a variable has changed over time. Panel studies, where observations on the same cases are measured at two or more points in time, would provide appropriate data. Similarly, our unit of analysis may be dyads (pairs) of related individuals. The unit of analysis in the parental socialization study was the triad, consisting of the mother, father and teen-aged child. That is, a single case consisted of the responses of these three related individuals.

In both situations, a relationship between the two variables is likely, making the assumption of independent observations untenable. That is, in panel studies the scores at the second time point are likely to be strongly influenced by the scores at the first time point. Likewise, a similarity in the scores of the mothers and fathers is likely on any variable of interest. In such situations, the variance of the differences in scores is lower than if the observations came from independent samples. This reduced variance is incorporated in what is called the **correlated difference-of-means test**. Let's perform such a test on the parental socialization data.

In assessing the parental socialization argument, one important question is the extent to which parents have similar aspirations for their child. The assessment of the parental socialization argument becomes more complex if they disagree on the path they would like their child to take after high school. Clearly, if one parent has high aspirations for the child, and the other has low aspirations, it becomes difficult to make concrete predictions about what the child's aspirations will be. The correlated difference-of-means test can be used to evaluate whether the aspirations of one parent are on average different from those of the other. The null and alternative hypotheses would be:

$$H_0: \mu_m - \mu_f = 0$$
$$H_1: \mu_m - \mu_f \neq 0.$$

The subscripts m and f refer to mothers and fathers, respectively.[11] The mean difference between mothers and fathers is 0.11. With a standard score of 1.35, this difference is not statistically significant. Thus we can conclude that, on average, the desired paths of mothers and fathers are similar. This does not mean that individual parents necessarily agree on the desired path for their child. We will return to this distinction in the next chapter.

Two additional points should be mentioned about this example. First, by computing the average desired path, we are treating these variables as though they were interval. In Chapter 3, we found empirical evidence to support the contention that this variable can be treated as ordinal. To consider them interval measures is, however, patently not tenable. To do so introduces a source of error other than sampling fluctuations. The question is whether this additional error is tolerable. We could test this by collapsing these variables so that only two outcomes are possible, and then performing a difference-of-proportions test. Since the modal path desired by both mothers and fathers is for their child to attend university, we could recode their preferences so that:

$$0 = \text{does not desire university attendance}$$
$$1 = \text{desires university attendance.}$$

A difference-of-proportions test on the recoded variables supports the conclusion reached originally. This increases our confidence that the error introduced by considering the variables as interval is tolerable.

A second point is that there was no a priori reason to think that the null hypothesis was false. It is this feature that made the test of hypothesis useful.

SPSS Instructions

Figure 5.9
SPSS t-Test for Independent Groups

```
1  GET FILE = "vote84.sys".
2  COUNT premiers= var446 TO var455(1).
3  COMPUTE pcndp=var510-var511.
4  RECODE pcndp (-6 THRU 6=1)(ELSE=0) INTO polrep.
5  VARIABLE LABELS polrep "NA status on Left-right party imagery"
6       premiers "Number of premiers correctly named".
7  T-TEST GROUPS=polrep(0,1)
8       /VAR=premiers.
```

Line 4 (Figure 5.9): This instruction creates a new dichotomous variable, "polrep", out of the previously created variable "pcndp". It does this by collapsing all legitimate scores into a 1. The remaining cases (that is, all cases that originally either did not give a valid response or were not asked the question out of which the variable "pcndp" was created) are recoded as a 0.

Lines 5-6: We have covered VARIABLE LABELS before; I have simply included the labels for two variables on one instruction. Two cautions are necessary here. First, when the labels for several variables are included in one instruction, the second and subsequent lines of the instruction must be indented for mainframe versions, since they are continuations of the VARIABLE LABELS instruction. For the PC version, the period must be at the end of line 6. Secondly, the VARIABLE LABELS instruction cannot include labels for any variables that have not been defined prior to that point in the sequence of SPSS instructions. That is why I have placed this instruction after I have defined both variables being labelled.

Lines 7-8: This instruction invokes the T-TEST procedure for independent groups. The two groups are defined by the phrase GROUPS=polrep(0,1). This tells SPSS that the independent groups are contained in the variable named "polrep" and that the first group consists of those observations that have a score of 0 and the second group consists of those that have a score of 1 on the variable "polrep". Line 8 specifies the dependent variables on which the tests of hypothesis are to be performed. Here we are asking for only one test, on the variable "premiers".

The results of these instructions are given in Figure 5.10. I have divided the printout into three blocks. In the first block, SPSS repeats the definition of the two independent groups. This permits us to check that the definition corresponds to our intention. In this case, GROUP 1 is defined as all those observations that had a score of 0 on the variable "polrep". These are the cases for which we have no valid party imagery information. GROUP 2 is the remainder of the sample, which includes all cases that responded to the left-right placement questions for both the PCs and the NDP.

The second block provides information about the two groups. It identifies the dependent variable, by both its abbreviated name and its full label. We have specified the variable "premiers" ("Number of premiers correctly named") as the dependent variable. The first column gives the sample sizes for the two groups. In GROUP 1, for example (where party imagery was not ascertained), there were 1,650 cases.

The second column shows the conditional means for the two groups. On average, respondents for whom party imagery information is available can name just over four premiers. In contrast, respondents for whom party imagery information is not available can name less than three premiers. This by itself suggests that the two groups are dissimilar with respect to political knowledge, which in turn implies that the group for which we have party imagery data is not representative of the Canadian electorate.

The third column provides the conditional standard deviations. The standard deviation for the group for which we do not have party imagery information has a somewhat lower standard deviation on the political knowledge variable.

The final column, labelled STANDARD ERROR, is simply the standard deviation divided by the square root of the corresponding sample size.

The third block provides three separate tests of significance, separated by columns of asterisks. SPSS first tests whether it is reasonable to assume that the population variances in the two groups are equal. There are two methods for

Figure 5.10
SPSS t-Test Results for Independent Samples

BLOCK 1

FILE: The Canadian National Election Study
— — — — — — — — — — T - T E S T — — — — — — — — — — —

GROUP 1 - POLREP EQ   .00
GROUP 2 - POLREP EQ   1.00

BLOCK 2

VARIABLE	NUMBER OF CASES	MEAN	STANDARD DEVIATION	STANDARD ERROR
PREMIERS Number of premiers correctly named				
GROUP 1	1650	2.8642	2.350	0.058
GROUP 2	1727	4.1181	2.501	0.060

BLOCK 3

		* POOLED	VARIANCE	ESTIMATE	*SEPARATE	VARIANCE	ESTIMATE
F VALUE	2-TAIL PROB.	* T * VALUE	DEGREES OF FREEDOM	2-TAIL PROB.	* T * VALUE	DEGREES OF FREEDOM	2-TAIL PROB.
1.13	0.011	* -15.00	3375	0.000	* -15.02	3374.07	0.000

estimating the population variances of the two groups. One method assumes that the two populations have equal variances, permitting us to obtain a pooled estimate of the common variance. Where the assumption of equal variance is untenable, we use separate variance estimates. How can we tell whether the equal variance assumption is unreasonable? We perform a separate test of hypothesis for the equality of variances. This is done with the help of a new type of theoretical distribution, known as the F-distribution. The F-distribution provides a test for the equality of two variances:

$$F = \frac{s_1^2}{s_2^2} \tag{5.12}$$

where s_1^2 and s_2^2 are the larger and the smaller sample variances, respectively.

Using this equation, SPSS computes the F-value and the associated two-tailed probability. This probability is a Type I error should we reject the null hypothesis that the two variances are equal. The calculated probability of 0.011 implies that we should reject the hypothesis of equal variances. Hence we should *not* use a *pooled* estimate of the "common" variance.

The second test of significance, labelled POOLED VARIANCE ESTIMATE provides the results we would obtain if we assumed a common population standard deviation for the two groups. Since we have rejected a common variance, we ignore this test. Stated differently, we use the pooled variance estimate test whenever we fail to reject the prior hypothesis of equal variance. Where we reject the hypothesis of equal variance, we do not use the pooled variance estimate test.

The third test of significance, labelled SEPARATE VARIANCE ESTIMATE, provides a satisfactory difference of means test where, as in our case, the notion of a common variance cannot be retained. This estimation procedure results in calculated degrees of freedom which are usually not a whole number. Here the degrees of freedom is 3374.04. With a calculated t-value of 15.02, the probability of a Type I error if we reject the null hypothesis of equal means is less than 0.000. Hence we reject the hypothesis that the two groups have identical levels of political knowledge.

Summary

- The normal curve has properties that make it appropriate as an ideal-typical distribution for many empirical phenomena. The normality assumption refers to the distribution of the underlying conceptual variable of interest. The shape of such underlying variables is determined primarily through reasoning and imagination, although certain empirical checks, such as histograms, are also useful.
- If the sampling distribution of a statistic is known, then tests of significance can be computed. The Central Limit Theorem describes the sampling distribution of sample means, as well as the sampling distribution of the difference between means.
- Hypothesis testing is more appropriate in a decision-making context than in a knowledge-production context. In a decision-making context, little relevant information about the issue under investigation is available, and the results of a single empirical test determine the decision to be made. In a knowledge-production context, many previous studies bear on the issue, and decisions are made by sifting through and weighing the results of numerous tests.

- A statistically significant result may not be substantively or theoretically important. Tests of statistical significance evaluate the likelihood that a given finding is an artifact of sampling fluctuations. In making this assessment, the sample size plays a dominant role. With large samples, small differences may reach statistical significance.

- Statistical hypothesis testing is most appropriate in numerically based arguments where there is no strong reason for believing that the null hypothesis is false. There are two situations where statistical hypothesis testing is often warranted: (1) where evaluating possibly peculiar features of a sample or variable or (2) where justifying the use of simplifying assumptions.

- Tests of significance can be used as a guide to assess certain features of a given sample or measured variable. Flawed samples reduce our confidence in any of the findings based on such samples. Thus, a difference-of-means test was conducted on the 1984 CNES data. This test revealed that the available information on left-right placement of political parties was probably not representative of the Canadian electorate as a whole. As a consequence, the previously documented relationship between political knowledge and party imagery had to be treated as tentative. A related use of hypothesis testing in this data was to assess the equality of variance assumption in a measure. That is, a decision had to be made whether it was reasonable to consider the variance in political knowledge to be equal in two populations (those for whom party imagery information was available and those for whom it was not). There is no relevant information about this issue available, and therefore it is appropriate to make the decision strictly on the basis of a single statistical test.

- The second use of statistical hypothesis testing is as a guide to making simplifying assumptions. One way to produce parsimony is to show that, in a given sample, certain empirical features can be ignored. In the party imagery example, a number of reversals in the relationship between political knowledge and party imagery were found. It would simplify matters if these reversals could be reasonably attributed to sampling fluctuation.

- Unexpected findings spur scholars to construct additional tests for their arguments. The finding of non-representativeness was one stimulus for searching for alternative measures of party imagery. For this particular instance, the alternative measure was asked of the total sample, thus removing the original source of concern. The process of constructing sound arguments includes finding alternative tests that do not share a previously identified weakness or flaw.

Notes

1. To find this number, we go down the rows until we find the z-score of 1.6. Then we go across the columns to find the second digit of z, which in this case is 0.07.
2. Certain mathematical transformations, such as the square root or natural log of

       income, for example, reduce the skew. The disadvantage of such transformations is that the resulting units of measurement often lack appeal, because few of us can think in "logged" dollars.

3.   SPSS will superimpose the normal curve on the histogram of any variable with the subcommand /HISTOGRAM = NORMAL attached to the FREQUENCIES command. Figure 5.3 was produced with this command.

4.   We might also use this test to help decide whether a given sample is representative of a particular population, or whether it is biased with respect to the characteristic of interest.

5.   The convention of considering a Type I error of less than 0.05 as acceptable may not always be appropriate. Nevertheless, it is the convention most often used in academic/scientific contexts. With sample sizes larger than 100, 0.01 might be more appropriate, and 0.001 for samples exceeding 1,000. We shall soon see that sample size and statistical significance are intimately connected. In applied contexts, different levels still might be preferable, depending to a large extent on the relative costs involved in committing Type I and Type II errors.

6.   The words-deeds disparity nevertheless manifests itself in post-election studies, such as the 1984 CNES. Typically, in such studies, a higher number claim to have voted for the winning candidate than is borne out by the election results.

7.   For this reason, SPSS treats all such tests of significance as instances of a t-test.

8.   A second reversal occurs between knowing the names of nine and ten premiers. Since this latter reversal is smaller and based on fewer cases, we will focus on the first reversal. If sampling fluctuation is an acceptable interpretation for that reversal, it will also be acceptable for the second reversal. This example is taken from Table 4.6.

9.   There are some situations in which non-representativeness on religious affiliation would be quite problematic even for the topic at hand. In Chapter 8 we will learn the conditions under which non-representativeness in variables not directly relevant nevertheless create difficulties for proper interpretation.

10.   I am indebted to Harald Rohlinger for alerting me to this interpretation.

11.   The SPSS instruction for obtaining this correlated difference of means test is: T-TEST PAIRS = var777 WITH var1177. The variables "var777" and "var1177" contain the responses of the mother and father, respectively, to the question, "Which of the following paths would you like your son/daughter to take after high school?" The response categories and their numeric codes are identical to those shown in Table 3.6.

Key Words

abscissa: In graphical displays, the horizontal or X-axis. In plotting distributions, values of the variable are located on the abscissa, while frequencies (or probabilities) associated with these values are represented by the height of the distribution on the vertical axis (also called the *ordinate*).

alternative hypothesis: In statistical decision-making contexts, the hypothesis that a population parameter is within some *range* of values other than the specific value of the null hypothesis with which it is paired. For example,

$$H_1: \mu_m - \mu_f \neq 0$$

where μ_m and μ_f represent the population "mean number of premiers correctly named," for men and women, respectively, could symbolize the alternative hypothesis that the sexes differ in their ability to recall the names of provincial premiers. Note that the alternative hypothesis always specifies a range of values for the parameter.

Central Limit Theorem: A theorem which postulates that the sampling distribution of sample means will tend to be normally distributed, with the same mean as the population and a standard deviation that is smaller than the population standard deviation by the fraction $1/\sqrt{N}$. The larger the sample size, the more normally distributed is the sampling distribution of the sample mean, and the smaller is the standard deviation of the sample mean relative to the population standard deviation. This theorem provides the statistical rationale for tests of hypothesis concerning means and proportions.

correlated difference-of-means test: A procedure for testing whether two dependent groups have the same mean. Groups are dependent if they are the same cases measured at two different points in time or on two different variables; or if, in the sample selection process, they are paired with each other (as when sampling wife-husband, parent-child, or employer-employee dyads). The main impact of the pairing procedure is to the standard deviation of the differences. Usually the pairing procedure makes the outcomes of the pair more similar than would be found in two randomly selected cases.

degrees of freedom: In general, the number of quantities that are free to vary before the remainder of them are determined. In a simple Student's t-test, the degrees of freedom are one less than the sample size (that is, $N - 1$). If the Student's t-test is used for a difference-of-means test, the degrees of freedom are two less than the sum of the sample sizes (that is, $N_1 + N_2 - 2$).

external consistency: A criterion for assessing whether different measures can be considered as alternative indicators of a single latent concept. This criterion is fulfilled to the extent that the different measures are similarly related to other (external) variables. If an indicator is measuring the intended concept, its relationship to other variables will be similar to that of all other indicators that we postulate are measuring the same concept.

independent difference-of-means test: A form of statistical hypothesis testing concerning the relative magnitude of the means of two populations. The observations in the two samples must be obtained independently of each other. This test answers the question of whether two groups can be thought of as belonging to the "same" population with respect to the mean of the characteristic being investigated.

latent concept: The unmeasured phenomenon with which our empirical indicators are hopefully reasonably isomorphic. The underlying concept is always more than any possible indicator. For example, *attraction* as an underlying concept might be indicated by how close two people stand to each other when talking, or it might be indicated by a response to the question, "With whom in this room would you like to spend more time?" Underlying concepts, to the extent that they are fruitful, are one route to parsimony, since they provide the promise of explaining a variety of different phenomena that are considered to be various manifestations of the same theoretical concept.

null hypothesis: In decision-making contexts, the hypothesis which postulates a *specific* value for a population parameter. For example, the hypothesis that men and women do not differ in the number of premiers they can name could be formulated as the null hypothesis:

$$H_0: \mu_m - \mu_f = 0$$

where μ_m and μ_f refers to the population "mean number of premiers," named by men and women, respectively. The term *null* emerged because frequently, particularly in the context of difference-of-means tests, the hypothesized value was null or zero, as in this example. The null hypothesis is always paired with an alternative hypothesis, and the decision involves choosing one of them as correct.

one-tailed hypothesis: In statistical hypothesis testing, a form for the alternative hypothesis which stipulates that the parameter is either greater than or less than (but not both) the value specified in the null hypothesis. Better than wrestling with whether to use a one- or two-tailed test is to report the observed value of the statistic and its standard error.

parameter: An attribute of a population, such as the median income of all Canadian residents. The value of parameters is ordinarily unknown and is estimated on the basis of information from a random sample.

population: The setting(s) to which we wish to generalize our sample findings. To justify the generalization on statistical grounds requires that a sample be selected from the population in such a way that every case has a known probability of being included. In scholarly arguments, the relevant settings are typically too diffuse to satisfy this criterion. For example, the relevant population for the similarity-attraction hypothesis might be "all interaction sequences among prior strangers." For such populations, there are no technical solutions to achieve the goal of generalization. A strategy of maximally different information gathering domains is used as an alternative, such as strangers in different cultures or in different settings.

random assignment: A procedure used in experimental design which ensures that the researcher in no way influences which subjects will receive treatments and which ones will not. This is considered the most effective way to insure comparability in the two groups prior to the administration of the experimental treatment.

random sample: A set of observations using procedures that make the selection of cases independent of each other. This implies that every case in the population has a known probability of being included in the sample. Random sampling procedures are a hallmark of sound survey design and are essential for statistically based estimations of population parameters.

reactive measurement effect: The very act of measuring an event alters the event. This possibility is so pervasive that we may consider it a reasonable first interpretation for any finding. A critical stance towards all findings is essential when arguing with numbers.

sample: Cost and time considerations dictate that we restrict our observations to some fraction of the population. In the estimation of population parameters, the sample selection procedure is more consequential than the size of the sample. Large samples where the observations are not independent are inferior to smaller samples where random sampling procedures were employed. Indeed, no statistical rationale exists for classical hypothesis testing using non-random samples of any size.

sampling distribution: A theoretical distribution that refers to how a sample statistic would be distributed if an infinite number of samples of a given size were taken. The importance of sampling distributions is that statisticians have developed theorems concerning their shape and parameters, permitting us to perform tests of statistical significance. For example, the Central Limit Theorem describes the shape (normal), the mean (μ) and standard deviation ($\sigma / \sqrt{N}$) of the sampling distribution of sample means taken from large samples. Of particular practical importance is that the standard deviation of the sampling distribution decreases (by the $\sqrt{N}$) as the sample size increases. The result is that minor differences can be detected with massive samples, not always a happy state of affairs.

significance test: Any of a variety of equations that assesses the probability that an observed discrepancy between a sample statistic and a null-hypothesized parameter could be the result of sampling fluctuation. Less technically, significance tests quantify the permissibility of generalizing sample results to the population from which they were taken. Examples: (1) Student's t-test and (2) the chi-square test of independence.

standard error: The standard deviation of a statistic in the sampling distribution of that statistic. For example, the Central Limit Theorem informs us that the standard error of sample means (based on N observations) is $\sigma / \sqrt{N}$. Standard errors are employed in all tests of statistical significance and can be thought of as a measure of the consistency of our sample statistics.

standard normal curve: A normal distribution that has been standardized to have a mean of zero and a standard deviation of one. This is accomplished by expressing outcomes in standard scores (z-scores) rather than raw scores. Tables showing the areas under the standard normal curve are customarily included in statistics texts. This permits us to determine the probability of any normally distributed outcome between any two standard scores simply be looking up their corresponding areas in the table (see Appendix B).

statistic: An attribute of a sample, such as the sample mean of a variable. The corresponding attribute in the population from which the sample was taken is called a *parameter*.

statistical significance: An assessment of the probability that sampling fluctuation produced the obtained discrepancy between a (sample) statistic and a null-hypothesized (population) parameter. Whether a sample result is statistically significant depends on the size of the discrepancy between the sample statistic and the hypothesized parameter, and on the size of the sample. With large samples, even trivial differences reach statistical significance; conversely, with small samples, substantively important differences may not be detected using conventional criteria. It is poor practice to rely on statistical significance to answer substantive questions whenever other information is available. Reporting the size of the discrepancy and the standard error of the statistic is considered to be superior to reporting statistical significance.

Student's t-distribution: A family of distributions (one for each unique sample size) that are used instead of the normal distribution to test hypotheses about population means when the sample sizes are small, such as less than fifty. As the sample size increases, the Student's t-distribution increasingly approximates the normal.

theoretical distribution: Distributions whose shape is determined by equations rather than by empirical methods. These theoretical distributions have known properties that permit us to calculate or estimate a variety of probabilities, such as the probability that two discrete events are independent. Examples: The chi-square and the normal distribution.

two-tailed hypothesis: In hypothesis testing, a form that expresses the alternative hypothesis as simply different from the value postulated by the null hypothesis: it could be larger or it could be smaller. The two-tailed hypothesis contrasts with its one-tailed counterpart, which phrases the alternative hypothesis as being greater (or less) than the value provided in the null hypothesis. Increasingly, the practice is simply to report the standard error of the statistic, thereby avoiding the one- and two-tailed distinction.

Type I (α) error: The rather lacklustre name given to the error that would have been committed if we rejected a correct null hypothesis. In statistically based arguments, if the probability of a Type I error is less than 0.05 or 0.01, by convention it is tolerable. The blind use of such conventions often makes the review of the empirical literature appear less consistent than it may be, since sample size is a major determinant of the ability to reject the null hypothesis. That is, with small samples, findings that are substantively consistent with other findings may not be statistically significant. For this reason, it is better to report the value of the statistic and its standard error, rather than the Type I error.

Type II (β) error: The error of failing to reject a null hypothesis that is false. This type of error cannot be calculated since its probability depends on the (unknown) value of the parameter. In scholarly arguments, the cost of committing this error usually is that we fail to detect a relationship between two variables. Of course, the stronger the relationship, the less likely that we will fail to detect it.

unbiased estimate: An estimate of a population parameter based on a statistic for which, in the long run, the expected value of the discrepancy between the estimate and the population value is zero. For example, statisticians have shown that the mean of a variable in a random sample of observations is an unbiased estimate of the population mean. That is, if repeated samples were taken from the population, we expect the mean of the (many) sample means to approach to population mean. In contrast, the sample variance constitutes a biased estimate of the population variance, because it underestimates the variance by the fraction $1/N$, where N is the sample size.

underlying concept: See *latent concept*.

Chapter 6

ESTIMATING THE STRENGTH OF RELATIONSHIPS: MEASURES OF ASSOCIATION

Some events are intimately connected to others, some exhibit only a modest relationship, and some are unconnected to, or independent of, each other. In this chapter, we will develop techniques to assess and quantify statements such as:

- "The influence of mothers on their children's aspirations is no greater than that of fathers," and
- "The left-right placement of major Canadian political parties is more strongly related to political knowledge than are evaluations of class favouritism."

Establishing the strength of the relationship between events is a major goal in social science arguments. The equations that quantify the strength of relationships are called **measures of association** and **correlation coefficients**. However, we already have some tools for assessing the strength of relationships less formally: (1) percentage differences in contingency tables; (2) conditional means; and (3) conditional proportions. These techniques have certain descriptive advantages over measures of association and should not be underestimated.

The particular advantage of percentages is that they make few assumptions about the level of measurement or shape of the distribution. Furthermore, they permit a close scrutiny of the form and nature of the relationship. As a result, they are less dangerous than correlation techniques, and the conclusions based on contingency tables (or conditional means and proportions) are less likely to be artifactual. Let's start with the parental socialization example to compare a variety of approaches.

Table 6.1 shows the relationship between the post-high school preferences of teenagers and mothers in percentages. For such tables, percentage differences are customarily calculated to suggest the strength of the relationship.

Focusing on the work path, we could say: "In homes where mothers want their children to join the labour market immediately after school, 63 percent of teenagers report the same preference. In contrast, only nine percent of teenagers desire to find work if their mothers prefer them to attend university. Thus, preferences of mothers make a difference of as much as 54 percent on whether teenagers prefer to join the labour market."

Table 6.1
Post-High School Preferences of Teenagers by Preferences of Mothers (%)

	Preferences of Mothers				
Preferences of Teenagers	(1)	(2)	(3)	(4)	(5)
1) Work	63	21	34	13	9
2) Apprenticeship	10	56	14	7	2
3) Commercial, Trade					
or Business School[a]	15	6	6	7	3
4) Community/Teachers					
College	12	14	31	64	19
5) University	0	3	14	9	67
N	(41)	(34)	(35)	(86)	(129)

---

[a] Includes "Other" preferences.

Source: Looker (1977).

If we focus on university attendance, we could say: "If mothers want their teenagers to join the labour market, then none of the children in our sample expressed a desire to attend university. But 67 percent of teenagers want to attend university if that is their mother's desire. When it comes to the topic of attending university, the preferences of mothers make a difference of as much as 67 percent."

We could make similar statements about each of the three remaining paths. Reporting the largest percentage difference is the most typical way of expressing the strength of a relationship. We might call this the *maximum difference method*, since the largest percentage is compared with the smallest.

A second way of expressing the strength might be called the *minimum difference method*, in which the largest percentage is compared with the second largest. Using the minimal difference method, we could say: (1) "The preferences of mothers make at least a 29 percent difference in whether teenagers desire to join the labour market immediately after high school" (63 – 34 = 29), and (2) "Mothers' preferences make a difference of at least 53 percent on teenagers' desire to attend university" (67 – 14 = 53).

Of course, we could report the results of both methods: "With respect to joining the labour market immediately after high school, mothers' own preferences make a difference of *at least* 29 percent and *as much* as 54 percent on the teenagers' preference."

For both the minimum and the maximum difference method, one principle must not be violated: if the column percentages add up to 100 percent (as they do in Table 6.1), then the percentages to be compared must come from a single row. If the row percentages total 100, then the percentages to be compared must come from the same column.

The example so far makes it clear that percentage differences permit many different summary statements of the strength of a relationship. One way to reduce complexity is simply to ignore some differences. Previously we did this by creating a dichotomy for the post-high school preference variable and by ignoring the differences between the first four paths (all non-university paths). This is identical to reporting only the fifth row of Table 6.1. Moving the decimal point two places to the left, we would have conditional proportions. If the main focus of the study concerned university attendance, this would constitute an appropriate simplification.

Another way to reduce complexity is to make simplifying assumptions. In an earlier chapter, we developed an argument to support treating post-high school preferences as an ordinal measure. If we tentatively treat the different paths as representing equal intervals, we could compute conditional means. These are reported in Table 6.2.

We would now summarize the strength of the relationship with statements such as: "In homes where mothers prefer their teenagers to join the labour market, the teenagers report preferences that, on average, lie between immediate work and apprenticeship. In contrast, in homes where mothers want their children to attend university, the teenagers report desires that, on average, lie betwen attending college and attending university." In a still more compact way, we could also state that an increase of one path among mothers is associated with an average increase of about half a path among the teenagers. That is, adjacent conditional means in Table 6.2 differ by approximately 0.5 units.

Table 6.2
Mean Post-High School Preferences of Teenagers by Preferences of Mothers

Preferences of Mothers	Mean	N
1) Work	1.76	41
2) Apprenticeship	2.24	34
3) Commercial, Trade or Business School[a]	2.77	35
4) Community/Teachers College	3.50	86
5) University	4.33	129

[a]Includes "other" preferences.

Source: Looker (1977).

The conditional means in Table 6.2 retain the distinctions between work and apprenticeship, for example, but impose the severe assumption that the distinction between these two paths was of the same magnitude, as that between any other two adjacent paths.

Although useful and effective in some situations, percentage differences and conditional means suffer some drawbacks as estimates of the strength of relationships. As our example demonstrated, often a large variety of summary figures could be reported, and the impressions of the strength of the relationship gleaned from them can be quite disparate.

One reason estimated strengths can differ substantially is that the calculations are based on row or column marginals rather than on the total sample and are consequently more susceptible to sampling fluctuations. Each cell in a table represents a separate estimate of a conditional probability. Thus the "effective N" is the particular row or column marginal, rather than the total sample size, making the calculated percentages prone to larger fluctuations. For example, in Table 6.1 there were only thirty-four instances where mothers preferred an apprenticeship path for their child. With such few cases, the obtained percentages are quite unstable, making it sometimes difficult to differentiate between substance and sampling artifact.

Despite these drawbacks, where the number of observations permit the computation of percentages and conditional means, this should be done. We should study these results prior to calculating the more exacting techniques covered in this and the following chapters. By using these techniques, we can compensate for smaller sample sizes by making more stringent assumptions about the level of measurement.

Levels of Measurement and Measures of Association

In numerical arguments, we generally must trade severity of assumptions for power of techniques: the more stringent the assumptions, the more powerful the techniques that can be used. This trade-off is important enough that a further illustration is warranted. Our party imagery example will serve this purpose. When we computed the conditional means in Chapter 4, we assumed that it was meaningful to treat the dependent variable (left-right party imagery) as having interval properties. Making this assumption permitted us to summarize the relationship between political knowledge and party imagery with eleven conditional means — one for each value of the independent variable ("number of premiers correctly named").

We were not forced to assume an interval-level dependent variable. We could have treated the dependent variable as nothing more than a collection of unordered categories. (By definition, any measure is at least categorical or nominal.) Then we could have "summarized" the relationship between political knowledge and party imagery with a detailed contingency table. Assuming we collapse all positive scores into one category, as we did in the final conditional means analysis, we would still have a total of eighty-eight cells in such a table (eleven categories of the independent variable by eight categories of the dependent variable). With this many cells, we might find it difficult to see the overall relationship. Furthermore, it would be a tedious process to decide which differences in percentages are "facts" that warrant an explanation and which are sampling fluctuation artifacts and should therefore not be interpreted substantively.

A temporary compromise is to collapse the dependent variable into two categories that represent "correct" and "false" party imagery. We previously collapsed all positive values into one group, which could be labelled "correct" party images. We could now collapse the remaining negative and zero values into a single category to represent "false" party imagery. This would transform our analysis into an example of conditional proportions. This is analogous to what we did with the initial "absolute" measure of the left-right location of the NDP. The result of this temporary compromise reveals a similar positive relationship between political knowledge and party imagery (data not shown). That is, the more premiers named, the higher the proportion holding "correct" party images.

Some researchers would argue that the temporary compromise should be a permanent one, since it avoids making the assumption that the party imagery indicators constitute interval measures. There is some legitimacy to this view. The other side of the coin, however, is that we then forfeit the ability to analyze degrees of correctness in party imagery. In the compromise solution, we are treating those who placed the NDP six units to the right of the Liberals as being identical to someone who saw no difference between the Liberals and the NDP. Clearly, our uncollapsed measure contains information, however imprecise, on degrees of false images. By collapsing the measure, we lose this information.

By treating the dependent variable as a nominal variable, we disregard the potentially useful information that scores of −6 are lower than scores of zero. This limits our analysis to cumbersome contingency tables, which makes it difficult to summarize the relationship. By treating the dependent variable as an interval measure, the numbers attached to the various outcomes (from −6 to 1) are assumed to contain important information. In particular, the numbers are considered to represent increasingly correct party images.[1] Further, the difference between, say −6 and −5 is considered to represent the "same" difference in correctness as that between −1 and 0 (and this difference in turn is assumed to be the same as that between any other adjacent pairs of integers). Clearly this assumes more than can be justified. Should we therefore not compute conditional means on this data?

The criterion I prefer to use for answering this question is not whether the assumption can be shown to be incorrect, but rather, "Will making this assumption lead to a false conclusion about the nature and strength of the relationship between political knowledge and party imagery?"

To answer this question, we need to explore the relationship in a number of different ways, a practice that, in any event, is essential for the development of solid arguments. Hence, we would first treat the dependent variable as a collapsed nominal variable. This would show somewhat crudely the relationship between political knowledge and party imagery. Then we would treat the dependent variable as an ordinal and an interval measure. If the results of treating the dependent variable in these different ways point to the same conclusion, we gain confidence that our conclusion is not an artifact of violated assumptions.

An additional disadvantage of percentage differences and conditional means for assessing the strength of a relationship is that these techniques, although descriptively useful, are awkward for comparative purposes. We showed before (Table 4.7) that the mean left-right placement of the NDP relative to the PCs progressed from a low of 1.23 to a high of 3.23 between different levels of political knowledge. Some reversals in means were found, but even if we ignore them, it is difficult to state precisely how strong this relationship is. Comparing this relationship with that found for class favouritism (Table 5.5), I suggested the latter relationship appeared weaker. Without standard comparison points, however, it is difficult to document such a possible difference.

A related disadvantage is that describing the conditional means or percentage difference is cumbersome. Usually several percentages or means are required to describe the nature and strength of the relationship.

The measures of association that we will develop in this chapter avoid these particular disadvantages. However, they exact the price of more stringent assumptions. Violation of these assumptions can lead to artifacts and therefore must be evaluated carefully in every application.

We would like measures of association that are unaffected by sample size and that summarize the strength of the overall relationship with a single number. Many measures of association besides the ones covered in this chapter are available. Each is more appropriate in some situations than in others. We will see that both the assumed level of measurement and the shape of the distribution of the variables constrain the usefulness of particular measures. The basic logic of the many measures of association is nevertheless quite similar. For this reason, we will focus more on the common logic than on the diverse formulas.

Each measure summarizes the strength (and sometimes the "direction") of the relationship with a single number. This number will usually have limiting values of –1 and +1. A value of 1.0 symbolizes a perfect "positive" relationship and a value of –1.0 denotes a perfect negative relationship. In a **positive relationship**, increasing values of one variable are associated with increasing values of the other variable. A **negative relationship** is one where increasing values of one variable are associated with decreasing values of the other. Numbers in between these two extremes reflect varying strengths of relationships. The closer to 0.0, the weaker the relationship is said to be. Let's start with the simplest measures, **Yule's Q** and the **phi coefficient**.

Yule's Q and the Phi Coefficient

Both Yule's Q and the phi coefficient are used when the variables of interest are treated as dichotomies. Although this limits their applicability, they are useful for developing the logic of measures of association.

Let's continue with the parental socialization data given in Table 6.1. To calculate Yule's Q, the various post-high school preferences must be dichotomized. Since the modal desired path is university attendance (and since that also represents the "highest" path), let's keep this path separate and combine all other paths. Figure 6.1 shows the relationship between the dichotomized desires of mothers and teenagers. The labels a, b, c and d identify each of the four cells of the table. Keeping this labelling in mind, the computation of Yule's Q is simply:

$$Yule's\ Q = \frac{ad - bc}{ad + bc}. \tag{6.1}$$

For the post-high school preferences data, this works out to:

$$Yule's\ Q = \frac{(87)(182) - (14)(42)}{(87)(182) + (14)(42)} = 0.93.$$

Figure 6.1
Cross-Tabulation of Dichotomized Post High School Preferences of Mothers and Teenagers

	Mother's Preference		
Teenager's Preference	Attend University	Other	
	a	b	
Attend University	87	14	101
	c	d	
Other	42	182	224
	129	196	325

Source: Looker (1977)

Yule's Q is particularly appropriate in situations where one event is considered a **necessary but not sufficient condition** for another event. In such situations, the "cause" is more prevalent than the "effect." Figure 6.1 documents that mothers are more likely than their teenagers to desire the path of university attendance (129 vs. 101, respectively). If the mother does not want her teenager to attend university, then the teenager rarely desires to attend university. Out of 196 instances where mothers did not desire their teenagers to attend university, only fourteen teenagers nevertheless wanted to go to university. However, a substantial number of teenagers (42 out of 129) did not want to attend university even though their mothers wanted them to. The absolute value of Yule's Q is high whenever one of the four cells in a four-fold table contains few cases. We would expect precisely one cell to be relatively empty whenever one event is a necessary but not sufficient condition for the other event.

In situations of **unequal marginal distributions**, as in Figure 6.1, Yule's Q is unstable, because small sampling fluctuations can produce quite different estimates of the strength of the relationship. For this reason, the phi coefficient is usually preferred. The computation of phi (ϕ) is similar to that of Yule's Q:

$$\phi = \frac{ad - bc}{\sqrt{(a+b)(c+d)(a+c)(b+d)}}. \qquad (6.2)$$

The numerator for phi is identical to that for Yule's Q. The denominator for phi adjusts for unequal marginal distributions, which is why the computed phi is substantially smaller than Yule's Q (0.64 vs. 0.93, respectively).

Many measures of association are anchored in the concept of **covariation**: the extent to which variation in one variable coincides with variation in the other. One way of capturing covariation is through **cross-products.** If we label the variables of interest as X and Y, then their cross-product is the X-value multiplied by the Y-value. Let's develop a hypothetical cross-product measure of association for the data in Figure 6.1 that will illustrate some important features.

Cross-products require that both variables have numeric values. For reasons that will become clear shortly, let's assign the values of -1 to non-university paths, and $+1$ to the path of attending university. If we label mother's preference the X-variable, and teenager's preference the Y-variable, the cross-product information would be as given in Table 6.3.

If we compute the cross-product of our two variables, as they have been recoded in Table 6.3, it is clear that the product of X and Y for any observation in cell a would be $+1.0$, since multiplying 1 by 1 equals 1.0. Similarly, the product of X and Y for any case in cell d would be $+1.0$, since the product of two negative values always results in a positive number. The product of X and Y for cases in either of the two remaining cells (b and c) would be -1.0.

Table 6.3
The Cross-Product of Dichotomized Post-High School Preferences of Mothers (X) and Teenagers (Y)

Cell[a]	X	Y	XY	f
a	+1	+1	+1	87
b	-1	+1	-1	14
c	+1	-1	-1	42
d	-1	-1	+1	182

[a] The cell labels refer to those used in Figure 6.1.

Source: Looker (1977).

For the data in Table 6.3, the average cross-product would be:[2]

$$\frac{\Sigma XY}{N} = \frac{(182+87)-(14+42)}{325} = 0.66.$$

If all the cases had been in cells a and d, the average cross-product would have been +1.0, i.e., there would be a perfect positive relationship between the measures of the post-high school preferences of teenagers and their mothers. Likewise, if all the cases had been in cells b and c, the average cross-product would have been –1.0. Finally, if the number of cases in cells a and d had equalled those in cells b and c, the average cross-product would have been 0.0, signifying that teenagers were not influenced by their mother's preferences. The actual computed average cross-product for the data in Table 6.3 was 0.66, indicating a strong positive association.

This seems a reasonable measure of the association between two variables, since the closer to 1.0 (or –1.0) the result is, the stronger or more perfect the relationship. However, there is one problem with this hypothetical measure: we would also get a result of +1.0 (or –1.0) if all of the cases fell in just *one* cell. Mathematically, if all mothers and their children in the sample desired university attendance, the result would be 1.0 using the above method, but we have *not* shown a relationship to exist. In order for us to state that there is a relationship, we must also show that whenever X is absent, Y is absent. This we have not shown.

The general problem exemplified here is one of unequal marginal distributions. Note that less than a third of the teenagers preferred to attend university, while about two-thirds desired some other path. This is an unequal row marginal distribution. The more unequal marginal distributions are, the more problematic any of the measures of association will be. Yule's Q and the phi coefficient represent somewhat different solutions to the problem of unequal marginal distributions.

Coefficient phi will give us the same answer as our hypothetical cross-product measure whenever

$$(a + c) = (b + d) = (a + b) = (c + d).$$

The more unequal they are, the *smaller* will be the answer we get from this formula, compared with what we would get using $\Sigma XY / N$. In other words, the formula above *adjusts* our answer for the effect of unequal marginal distributions, and this is exactly what we want. In short, for a 2 x 2 table, we generally use the phi coefficient.

We have argued that the average cross-product would be a reasonable measure of the strength of a relationship only when we can be assured that the negative values of the variables balanced the positive ones. In the next section, an expansion of the hypothetical measure will show that, in a modified form, it produces the Pearson correlation coefficient.

The Pearson Correlation Coefficient

As stated earlier, Yule's Q and the phi coefficient apply to events that are (or are forced to be) dichotomous. In most instances, the events of interest are more complex, requiring alternative measures of association. In the parental socialization example, for instance, there are a number of possible post-high school paths besides attending university, such as work, apprenticeship and community college. Measures of association that relate quantified (numeric) variables are called correlation coefficients. The most common of these is known as the **Pearson product-moment correlation coefficient**. The "product-moment" part of the name refers to the fact that the measure is based on the standardized cross-product of two variables, much like our hypothetical measure of association.

In Chapter 4 we learned that converting observations into standard scores produces distributions with a mean of 0.0. The value of any standard score indicates its relative location in terms of the number of standard deviations above or below the mean. Negative values fall below the mean, positive numbers fall above. In addition, we learned that for normally distributed variables, half the observations fall below, and the other half above, the mean. Consequently, half the scores would be negative and half positive. This suggests that a possible formula for a correlation coefficient might be one that expresses the relationship in terms of the product of their z-scores. This is precisely how Pearson correlations are defined:

$$r = \frac{\Sigma Z_x Z_y}{N}. \qquad\qquad (6.3)$$

Note that this equation is identical to our hypothetical one, except that the variables X and Y are expressed in their standard score equivalents. Pearson correlations measure the extent to which the scores of one variable co-vary with those of the other variable.[3]

Before expanding equation 6.3 into a form directly appropriate for raw data, several features of this equation that can be the source of artifacts should be noted:

- To calculate z-scores, we need to compute the means of the corresponding X and Y variables. The arithmetic operations involved in such calculations require us to treat the observations as possessing interval-level measurement properties. This in itself is frequently problematic and can therefore be the source of artifactual findings.
- An intrinsic feature of cross-products is that extreme numbers result in doubly extreme cross-products. Scores that are extremely high (or low) relative to other scores are called **outliers**. Take, for example, scores that are three standard deviations above the mean. Their cross-product is nine. Compare that with the cross-product of scores that are half a standard deviation above the mean, which is 0.25. Since we compute the *average* cross-product, one instance of the former scores has the same "weight" as thirty-six instances of the latter $[(36) \cdot (0.25) = 9]$. It is this feature that makes the Pearson correlation coefficient particularly sensitive to outliers. Extreme scores can distort the Pearson correlation and become the source of artifacts. As we learned in Chapter 2, such problems can be detected by carefully examining the univariate distributions.
- Measures of association that are based on cross-products are sensitive to the variance and skewness of the variables. This is one of the reasons why it is necessary to assume that the variables are normally distributed. Actually, the assumption being made is that the distribution of X and Y is bivariate normal. This means that X and Y are normally distributed about each other. Stated differently, for any given value of X, Y should be normally distributed around that X, and vice versa. If the distribution of X and Y is bivariate normal, then it is also true that both X and Y are univariate normal. Hence, a good indicator of potential problems is when either X or Y seriously departs from normality.

Having defined and described the Pearson correlation coefficient, we will now develop alternative equations for this coefficient. These will exhibit some additional features of the Pearson coefficient and permit us to calculate such coefficients by hand.

Computing the Pearson Correlation Coefficient from Raw Data

Equation 6.3 defined the Pearson correlation coefficient as the average cross-product of the standard scores of X and Y. When computing such correlations by hand, it would be unnecessarily tedious to first convert each observation into its standard score equivalent. Through a series of substitutions and algebraic manipulations, we can transform equation 6.3 into a form that would permit calculation of the coefficient directly from raw data.

I won't go through all the substitution steps. Instead, let me provide several forms of the Pearson correlation coefficient. In Chapter 4, we learned how to calculate standard scores. Altering the symbols to reflect that standard scores for both the X and the Y variables are required, we get:

$$r = \frac{1}{N} \cdot \frac{\Sigma(X - \bar{X})(Y - \bar{Y})}{(s_x)(s_y)}. \tag{6.4}$$

This form of the equation shows that the numerator consists of the cross-product of X and Y, where both variables are expressed as deviations from their respective means. The denominator consists of two parts: the number of cases and the standard deviation of X and Y. Dividing by N gives us the average cross-product. The average cross-product is also called the covariance of X and Y, and is symbolized as $Cov(X,Y)$. Thus, we can express the Pearson correlation coefficient as:

$$r = \frac{Cov(X,Y)}{(s_x)(s_y)}. \tag{6.5}$$

Dividing the covariance by the standard deviation of X and Y results in the production of coefficients that are always bounded by -1 and $+1$. Expansion of equation 6.5 results in:

$$r = \frac{\Sigma(X - \bar{X})(Y - \bar{Y})}{\sqrt{\Sigma(X - \bar{X})^2(Y - \bar{Y})^2}}. \tag{6.6}$$

This is the usual "definitional" formula for the Pearson correlation coefficient.

Finally, through algebraic manipulation of equation 6.6 we arrive at the "computational" equation:

$$r = \frac{N\Sigma XY - (\Sigma X)(\Sigma Y)}{\sqrt{[N\Sigma X^2 - (\Sigma X)^2][N\Sigma Y^2 - (\Sigma Y^2)]}}. \tag{6.7}$$

Although this formula looks complex, a worksheet example will show that it is quite straightforward. (Table 6.4 in the next section provides an example worksheet for calculating the Pearson correlation coefficient by hand for a small data set. The data in this worksheet is relevant to the debate on the advantages of specialization versus flexibility in the Atlantic Canadian small-boat fishery.) Before turning to the data itself, it is appropriate to provide a brief introduction to the arguments to which it is relevant.

Specialization versus Flexibility

Two competing viewpoints have emerged regarding the desirability of a specialization of fishing effort. One view maintains that specialization is the most rational way to manage the fishing industry. Specialization consists of fishers restricting their efforts to pursuing a small number of species. This currently forms the backbone of fisheries management policies in the form of limited entry licensing. Purportedly, limiting licenses was introduced to control the small-boat fishing industry and to manage it in the best interests of the industry as a whole. The argument is basically that by limiting licenses, two positive results will materialize. First, both the total number of fishers, as well as the number of fishers pursuing a particular species, would be reduced. This should give rise to the second consequence, namely that the remaining enterprises would enjoy enhanced viability. That is, over a period of time, the remaining fishing enterprises should become more efficient. Empirically, if this viewpoint is valid, one would expect to find a negative relationship between fishing capacity and number of species pursued. That is, larger vessel capacity should be associated with fewer licenses. The underlying dynamics are seen as a continual "weeding out" of the less efficient, lower capacity enterprises populated by fishers who have not specialized.

A competing viewpoint maintains that a viable small-boat fishery requires access to numerous ocean resources. In the small-boat fishery, possessing numerous licenses permits a longer and more flexible pursuit of different species of fish. Stated differently, because of the vagaries of fish stocks and fish movements, successful small-boat fishers must be generalists who adapt to these vagaries through a flexible approach to fishing. When cod are plentiful, they pursue cod, when herring are running, they switch to these. In this way they can extend the fishing season and create greater stability in their livelihood efforts. This should increase the possibility of sufficient capital accumulation to purchase and maintain vessels with greater fishing capacity. In the context of the Department of Fisheries and Oceans (DFO) program of limited entry licensing (LEL), this requires that fishers obtain and retain a large variety of licenses. Those who for whatever reason are able to obtain or retain licenses are expected to be the more successful fishers. Thus, in this view, one would postulate a positive relationship between fishing capacity and the number of species pursued.

In the Nova Scotian context, most small-boat coastal zone fishing enterprises, almost by definition, fish in geographically limited areas. That is, the usual distances from port to fishing grounds are necessarily short. Small-boat, coastal zone fishers from geographically distant ports tend to fish geographically separate grounds. There is a tacit territoriality of fishing grounds which is not often violated. In light of this, the specialization argument can be examined at the port level with the expectation that those fishing communities that have specialized the most would be the most viable. That is, ports that hold the fewest average licenses per vessel should have the greatest fishing capacity.

As a first step in evaluating these competing arguments, we must obtain information on both vessel capacity and variety of species pursued. For each vessel, DFO records information on the community in which the vessel is registered; vessel name, length, horsepower (Bhp) and tonnage; and the specific commercial licenses held. The number of commercial fishing licenses held could provide a measure of the number of species pursued that reflects the extent of specialization-diversification. Vessel length, horsepower or tonnage could each be considered an indicator of vessel capacity, which in turn is an indicator of enterprise viability. To keep things manageable, let's restrict our attention initially to the relationship between number of licenses and vessel length. Table 6.4 presents the data on these two variables for twelve predominantly small-boat Nova Scotian ports representing 360 individually owned vessels, all under 65 feet.

Table 6.4
Worksheet for Computing the Pearson Correlation Coefficient

	Mean Number of Licenses (X)	Mean Vessel Length (Y)	XY	X^2	Y^2
Little Dover	3.07	23.46	72.02	9.42	550.37
White Point	2.07	26.00	53.82	4.28	676.00
Neil's Harbour	2.95	26.58	78.41	8.61	706.49
New Haven	2.95	27.79	81.98	8.70	772.28
Petit de Gras	3.58	29.23	104.64	12.81	854.39
Whale Cove	2.22	29.67	65.86	4.92	880.30
Canso	4.07	29.86	121.53	16.56	891.61
Dingwall	2.15	31.37	67.44	4.62	984.07
Sandy Cove	3.00	35.63	106.89	9.00	1,269.49
Little River	1.80	37.93	68.27	3.24	1,438.68
Woods Harbour	2.15	38.75	83.31	4.62	1,501.56
East Ferry	1.88	39.00	73.32	3.53	1,521.00
TOTALS	31.89	375.27	977.49	90.31	12,046.24

Source: Compliled from DFO vessel registration data, September, 1988.

The first column indicates the mean number of licenses for the fishing enterprises in each of the twelve communities. This is the independent variable X. Note the variation in the extent of specialization among the ports. In some ports there is a high degree of specialization, as revealed by a low average number of licenses per vessel. Little River and East Ferry are the most specialized, with fewer than two licenses per vessel. Least specialization occurs in Canso, where the average is about four licenses per vessel.

The second column of Table 6.4 shows the mean vessel length for the same communities. This is the dependent variable Y. Vessel length constitutes our initial indicator of vessel capacity. The three communities of East Ferry, Little River and Woods Harbour stand out as having on average the greatest vessel capacity. That is, the boats in these communities are the longest. Least capacity is found in the communities of Little Dover, White Point and Neil's Harbour: the vessels in these communities are the shortest.

An examination of the first two columns of Table 6.4 suggests that the specialization thesis has some empirical support. This can be documented more precisely by computing the Pearson correlation coefficient between mean vessel length and mean number of licenses for the twelve communities. Columns 1 and 2 of Table 6.4 provide the raw data. To compute the Pearson correlation coefficient, we must calculate the three sets of numbers that are given in columns 3 to 5. Column 3 is the product of the X and Y scores for each community, column 4 is the square of the independent variable and column 5 gives the square of the dependent variable. The sums of each of the columns of Table 6.4 provide the necessary information for computing the Pearson correlation coefficient. Substituting these sums into equation 6.7, we get:

$$r = \frac{12(977.49) - (31.89)(375.27)}{\sqrt{[12(90.31) - (31.89)(31.89)][12(12,046.24) - (375.27)(375.27)]}}$$

$$= \frac{11,729.88 - 11,967.36}{\sqrt{(1,083.72 - 1,016.97)(144,554.88 - 140,827.57)}}$$

$$= \frac{-237.48}{\sqrt{(66.75)(3,727.31}} = -0.48.$$

The calculated coefficient of -0.48 suggests moderate support for the specialization argument. Of course, vessel length is not the only possible measure of fishing capacity. As noted earlier, DFO records also include information on tonnage and horsepower. The correlations between these measures and mean number of licenses can be computed in a fashion similar to that above. The results corroborate the negative relationship (data not shown).

In computing these coefficients, we must assume that our measures are interval and that the respective bivariate distributions are normal. To check whether these assumptions have produced misleading results, let's develop another measure of association, the **Spearman rank order correlation coefficient** (symbolized as r_s). The only requirement for the Spearman coefficient is that the two variables can be rank-ordered. The first two columns of Table 6.5 show the rank order of the twelve communities on the two variables "mean vessel length" and "mean number of licenses," respectively. The ranks in this table are computed directly from the corresponding raw scores in Table 6.4. For example, the mean vessel length of boats registered to the port of Little Dover is 23.46 feet. Vessels in this community are, on average, shorter than those in any of the other ports. Therefore the rank of 1 is assigned to this community. White Point has the second shortest boats and therefore is assigned the rank of 2, and so on. Turning to the licenses variable, Little River has the fewest number of licenses per vessel, giving it a rank of 1 on this variable. East Ferry has the second fewest average number of licenses and consequently it is given a rank of 2 on this variable. The Spearman rank order correlation coefficient is a reasonable measure of association to use when, as in the data being used here, there are few **tied observations**. Observations are tied when they have identical scores on a given variable. In Table 6.5, there are no ties for vessel length, but there are several ties for mean number of licenses. When observations are tied, they are given a rank halfway between the next lower and the next higher observation. For example, Dingwall and Woods Harbour are both given ranks of 4.5 on mean number of licenses, since this number is halfway between the next lower rank of 3 and the next higher rank of 6.

The Spearman correlation coefficient is based on the squared difference between the ranks of the observations on the two variables. It compares the computed squared difference in ranks to the maximum possible squared rank difference. A perfect positive coefficient results when the ranks of the observations on the two variables are identical. A perfect negative coefficient occurs when the computed squared difference in ranks equals the maximum possible rank difference. The equation for the Spearman rank order coefficient is:

$$r_s = 1 - \frac{6\Sigma D^2}{N(N^2 - 1)}. \tag{6.8}$$

Substituting the numbers from Table 6.5 we get:

$$r_s = 1 - \frac{6(411)}{12(144 - 1)} = -0.44.$$

Table 6.5
Worksheet for Computing the Spearman Rank-Order
Correlation Coefficient

	Rank on Vessel Length	Rank on Licenses	Difference (D)	D^2
Little Dover	1	10	-9	81
White Point	2	3	-1	1
Neil's Harbour	3	7.5	-4.5	20.25
New Haven	4	7.5	-3.5	12.25
Petit de Gras	5	11	-6	36
White Cove	6	6	0	0
Canso	7	12	-5	25
Dingwall	8	4.5	3.5	12.25
Sandy Cove	9	9	0	0
Little River	10	1	9	81
Woods Harbour	11	4.5	6.5	42.25
East Ferry	12	2	10	100

$$\Sigma D^2 = 411.00$$

Source: Compiled from DFO vessel registration data, September 1988.

The twelve sites were rank-ordered by mean number of licenses and then by each of the measures of fishing capacity to compute the Spearman correlation coefficients. These correlations are all negative: the Spearman correlations for number of licenses with vessel length, tonnage and horsepower is –0.44, –0.45 and –0.83, respectively. This shows that for all measures, communities with greater average vessel capacity also are licensed to fish for fewer species. These findings too seem to support the specialization thesis. Before we accept this conclusion, however, we must turn to the issue of the appropriate unit of analysis. This will show that the issue is more complex and points to a different conclusion.

The Unit of Analysis

The negative relationship between number of licenses and fishing capacity holds at the community level of analysis. It shows that those communities that have the greatest average fishing capacity are licensed to pursue the fewest species of fish and consequently are the most specialized.

The correlations computed above are at the aggregate community level. As already stated, they show that those communities with the greatest average fishing capacity are also most specialized: they have the fewest mean number of limited entry licenses. It cannot be concluded that the largest vessels (i.e., those of greatest length, tonnage or horsepower) hold the fewest licenses. To jump to such a conclusion would be to commit the **ecological correlation fallacy** (Robinson, 1955), which occurs when associations found at an aggregate level are assumed to be consequences of individual characteristics.

To test whether the largest vessels hold the fewest licenses, it is necessary to move to the individual level of analysis, as is done in Table 6.6. The first row of this table gives the correlations between number of licenses and the various measures of fishing capacity for the total population. In contrast to the previous finding, these correlations are positive, albeit very modest ones, ranging from 0.09 to 0.10. From this we could conclude that there is a slight tendency for vessels with greater fishing capacity to hold more licenses. The overall relationship is so weak, however, that for all practical purposes it would be best to conclude that there is no noteworthy relationship among these variables.

A third possibility exists. This is that the variability in lucrativeness of fishing grounds found in the different communities distorts the relationship between number of licenses and fishing capacity. One way to test this would be to compute the correlations between number of licenses and fishing capacity separately for each of the ports. These correlations are reported in the remainder of Table 6.6. Two conclusions emerge from this table. First, the relationship between number of licenses and fishing capacity is highly variable: in some ports, there is no significant relationship, in others a moderate positive relationship, and in still others a strong positive relationship.[4] Part of this variability is an artifact of the instability of the correlations resulting from sampling fluctuations incurred with the small sample sizes. To compensate partially for this instability, an overall measure of fishing capacity was constructed for each vessel by summing the standard scores of vessel length, tonnage and horsepower. As previously noted, these three variables are highly intercorrelated and should be a more stable estimate of fishing capacity. The correlation of number of licenses with this scale are found in the second to last column of Table 6.6. As expected, they do reduce the overall variability in the coefficients, but even here the coefficients range between –0.06 (Neil's Harbour) and 0.72 (Sandy Cove). Second, in most ports there is nevertheless a moderate to strong positive relationship between number of licenses and fishing capacity. This supports the conclusion that the least specialized fishers are the most successful ones, if one can view the possession of a large and powerful vessel as an indicator of fishing success.

The lesson to be learned from the specialist-generalist example is that the unit of analysis must match the unit of interpretation. When the concern is with the behaviour of individual fishers, then it is inappropriate to use aggregated data at the community level. Contradictory conclusions can sometimes be reconciled by paying close attention to the units of analysis involved.

Table 6.6
Pearson Correlation Between Number of Licenses and Fishing Capacity

Correlation of Number of Licenses with:

Community	Vessel Length	Tonnage	Horsepower	Fishing Capacity[a]	N
Total	0.09	0.10	0.10	0.11	360
Woods Harbour	0.39	0.38	0.35	0.40	92
Petit de Gras	0.11	0.01	0.18	0.11	40
Canso	0.22	0.26	0.11	0.23	59
Little Dover	0.54	0.67	0.59	0.64	28
Dingwall	0.55	0.56	0.26	0.54	41
Neil's Harbour	0.20	−0.16	0.42	0.18	19
New Haven	−0.17	0.06	−0.01	−0.06	19
White Point	0.24	−0.01	0.46	0.28	14
Little River	0.16	0.15	−0.00	0.11	15
Sandy Cove	0.70	0.80	0.56	0.72	16
Whale Cove	0.21	0.17	−0.18	0.08	9
East Ferry	0.61	0.67	0.72	0.69	8

[a] The index "Fishing Capacity" was constructed by summing the standard scores of vessel length, tonnage and horsepower.

Source: Compiled from information supplied by DFO, September 1988.

Let's take another example where this is the case. Take the question "Does cooperation among workers result in greater productivity?" When phrased this way, it is not immediately clear what the appropriate unit of analysis would be. At an organizational level, the question could be transformed to: "Are organizations whose members cooperate with each other the most productive ones?" At an individual level, the analogous question would be: "Are cooperative individuals the most productive ones?" There is no intrinsic reason why the answer to the first question must be the same as the answer to the second question. That is, the productive consequences of cooperation for organizations may be quite different from such consequences for individuals. That is precisely what Blau (1954) found. At an organizational level, cooperation enhanced productivity; for individuals, the cost of cooperation was reduced productivity. Thus the question of the relationship between cooperation and productivity cannot be answered unambiguously unless the unit of analysis is clearly specified.

One final caution about units of analysis needs to be mentioned. Frequently averages are used in situations that require evidence for association. It is irrelevant for the parental socialization hypothesis whether children *on average* desire the same post-high school path as parents do. It would be an error to conclude that if these desires have an identical mean that the hypothesis is supported. Conversely, it would also be an error to conclude that the hypothesis is weakened if the average desire of parents is different from that of the teenagers. Averages refer to aggregates, but the parental socialization hypothesis requires an analysis of dyads. That is, we must show that the desires of parents and their children co-vary, rather than that the average desires coincide.

Comparing Measures of Association

Although the assumptions underlying Pearson correlations are restrictive, we sometimes prefer this measure even when we know that the assumptions are being violated. One primary reason for using this measure is that it forms an integral component of regression analysis. This latter technique, covered in Chapters 7 and 9, lets us address important questions about the nature of the interrelationships among two or more variables. Hence, we often proceed to submit our variables to such analysis after having compared the results of a variety of measures.

Take, for example, the variables measuring post-high school preferences of parents and teenagers. Their distribution suggests severe violation of the normality assumption. Note from the marginal totals of Table 6.1, for example, that the mode occurs at the highest score ("attend university"). In a normal distribution, the mode would be in the middle. Furthermore, the scores representing the different possible paths are ordinal at best. Either of these facts could be considered sufficient grounds for avoiding the Pearson correlation for this data. Still, in an exploratory sense we could hazard using techniques that assume both normality and interval-level measures. If we do this, it is imperative that we compare such results with those obtained using other techniques, as in Table 6.7.[5]

The first half of this table gives the measures of association between the preferences of mothers and teenagers; the second half between fathers and teenagers. As evidenced by this table, many measures of association are available. The particular features and calculation formulas for these can be found in most introductory social science statistics texts. To some extent, the measure used is a matter of preference and depends upon what assumptions are made. Thus, Cramer's V, the contingency coefficient, lambda, and the uncertainty coefficient require only nominal-level measurement; Kendall's tau, gamma, and Somers's D assume ordinality; eta treats the dependent variable as interval, but the independent variable as only nominal; and Pearson's r assumes both variables are interval and that the distribution is bivariate normal.

Table 6.7
Measures of Association Between Preferences of Teenagers and Their Parents Produced by SPSS CROSSTABS Procedure

A.   Measures of Association Between Preferences of Mothers and Teenagers

CRAMER'S V = .45187
CONTINGENCY COEFFICIENT = .67049
LAMBDA (ASYMMETRIC) = .43750 WITH VAR275 DEPENDENT.
LAMBDA (SYMMETRIC) = .38571
UNCERTAINTY COEFFICIENT (ASYMMETRIC) = .24684 WITH VAR275 DEPENDENT.
UNCERTAINTY COEFFICIENT (SYMMETRIC) = .24806
KENDALL'S TAU B = .56670   SIGNIFICANCE = .0000
KENDALL'S TAU C = .52540   SIGNIFICANCE = .0000
GAMMA = .69204
SOMER'S D (ASYMMETRIC) = .57266 WITH VAR275 DEPENDENT.
SOMER'S D (SYMMETRIC) = .56667
ETA = .64025 WITH VAR275 DEPENDENT.
PEARSON'S R = .63948 SIGNIFICANCE = .0000

B.   Measures of Association Between Preferences of Fathers and Teenagers

CRAMER'S V = .45009
CONTINGENCY COEFFICIENT = .66904
LAMBDA (ASYMMETRIC) = .42342 WITH VAR275 DEPENDENT.
LAMBDA (SYMMETRIC) = .34804
UNCERTAINTY COEFFICIENT (ASYMMETRIC) = .24120 WITH VAR275 DEPENDENT.
UNCERTAINTY COEFFICIENT (SYMMETRIC) = .24371
KENDALL'S TAU B = .53148   SIGNIFICANCE = .0000
KENDALL'S TAU C = .49104   SIGNIFICANCE = .0000
GAMMA = .65504
SOMER'S D (ASYMMETRIC) = .54002 WITH VAR275 DEPENDENT.
SOMER'S D (SYMMETRIC) = .53142
ETA = .61467 WITH VAR275 DEPENDENT.
PEARSON'S R = .61283 SIGNIFICANCE = .0000

Source: Looker (1977).

A number of features about this table should be noted. First, we would conclude that a strong positive relationship exists between the preferred path of parents and their children, regardless of which measure of association we used. The uncertainty coefficient yields the lowest numeric value for the strength of the relationship. Yet even this measure indicates that knowledge of a parent's preferred path reduces the error in predicting the teenager's preferred path by approximately 25 percent. (The uncertainty coefficient has a "proportionate reduction in error" interpretation.) By usual standards this would be considered a powerful relationship.

Second, all measures show that the influence of the mother is at least as great as that of the father. This can be seen by comparing the coefficients in the first half of the table with the corresponding coefficients in the second. Thus the conclusion reached about the relative influence of the parents is identical, regardless of the measure used. The important lesson here is that, within a given analysis, the same measure should be used whenever several relationships are compared. The parental socialization literature provides no clear-cut guidance concerning the relative influence of mothers and fathers on their children's post-high school preferences. There is no strong reason to expect the relationship between mothers' and children's preferences to be substantially different from that between the preferences of fathers and children. The phi coefficient for the relationship between the preferences of fathers and teenagers is 0.62. The analogous coefficient between mothers and teenagers is 0.66. This indicates that the desires of mothers and fathers are about equally strongly related to their children's desires. In certain families, the father's preferences may be more decisive than those of the mother; in other families the reverse may be true. On average, however, the influence of mothers and fathers is approximately equal.

Finally, for these measures, imposing ordinality or intervalness assumptions does not alter systematically the estimate of the strength of the relationships. Note in particular that despite the severe violation of the normality assumption documented earlier, the Pearson correlations of the preferences of mothers and fathers with the preferences of their teenager is 0.64 and 0.61, respectively. These results are similar to those produced by the other measures of association. That is, we reach the same conclusions about the parental socialization hypothesis using Pearson correlations as we do using measures which do not assume normality. If the Pearson coefficients had led to conclusions conflicting with the other measures, we would probably abandon the use of techniques that require us to assume normality and interval-level measures.

Agreement, Negativity and Marital Attraction

Correlation coefficients provide a convenient method for assessing the *relative* strengths of relationships. Invariably, in our arguments we entertain several possible causes of a phenomenon. In a solid argument, the relative contribution of each of these possible causes is assessed. In this section, I will use Pearson correlation coefficients to show the relative effects of two independent variables—agreement and negativity—on the dependent variable, marital attraction.

In Chapter 2, we argued that the "phantom stranger" approach to measures of agreement was problematic in that the measurement procedure confounded deviance with disagreement. Disagreeing strangers were intrinsically ones who could be characterized as holding undesirable views—undesirable in the sense that they were incongruent with dominant societal views. Furthermore, in the discussion of Laing's data, it became clear that two types of agreements were possible: positive and negative agreements. Positive agreements are ones in which both partners hold culturally desirable viewpoints, such as that the husband cherishes the wife. Negative agreements are ones where both partners state, for the same example, that he does not cherish her. I argued that these two types of agreement should be treated as distinct concepts since marital difficulty was likely to be differentially related to these two forms of agreement. This expectation could not be evaluated with the information Laing provided. A different data set, collected by Fogarty, Rapoport and Rapoport (1971) permits further exploration of this argument.

The data to be described here were part of a large survey conducted in 1969 of English university graduates of 1960. Within the sample, 205 married couples were identified.[6] In all cases, it was the first marriage for both spouses. Of these, 169 couples were parents at the time of the study. I will use this data to explore the relationship of marital attraction to both agreement and negativity in the context of the feelings the new parents had after the birth of their first child. To do this, we need to develop measures of marital attraction, agreement and negativity.

Two questions on marital happiness were used as measures of attraction. The first was, "Taking things together, how do you really feel about your marriage?" The response categories ranged along a five-point continuum from "very happy" (5) to "unhappy" (1). The second measure of marital harmony was "Do you ever feel that you married the wrong kind of person?" Response categories were "yes—often" (1), "yes—occasionally" (2) and "no" (3).

The birth of a first child is an important event for new parents. A variety of feelings are aroused or heightened by this event. Knowing how one's partner feels (i.e., to agree) should produce marital attraction. The feelings of the new mother and father were elicited from the question contained in Table 6.8.

Since both partners independently answered these questions, it is possible to create measures of husband-wife agreement on their feelings. Two separate agreement scores were calculated: agreement on the husband's feelings and agreement on the wife's feelings. To measure agreement on the father's feelings, the husband's report of his own feelings with the wife's report of her husband's feelings were compared. Similarly, agreement on the mother's feelings required a comparison of the wife's report of her own feelings with the husband's report of her feelings. The agreement scores were calculated in a manner logically identical to those of Byrne (1971). This involved taking the absolute difference between the viewpoints of the husband and the wife on each of ten emotions. For example, if the wife said she felt competent and the husband said she felt competent, then on this issue they agreed. Similarly, if the wife said she did not feel competent and the husband said she did not feel competent, they also agreed. The difference between the husband's and the wife's answer in both these cases would be zero. In cases of disagreement there would be a one unit difference. These difference scores were summed across the ten items, yielding a score ranging from zero to ten on the wife's feelings, and a second score with the same possible range for the husband's feelings. The characteristics of these measurements are like those of Byrne. That is, on each issue there is either agreement or a disagreement, and the extent of the disparity on a given issue is ignored. Second, since the number of issues is a constant, the scores are statistically equivalent to a "proportion of agreements" interpretation. And third, an overall measure of agreement is calculated which is the sum of the agreement scores for the feelings of the husband and the wife.

Table 6.8
Wording and Format of the Items Used to Measure Parents' Feelings After the Birth of Their First Child

During the period at home immediately after the birth of your first child, describe the feelings of the new mother and the new father as you recall them.

Circle "Yes" or "No" for each of these feelings.
("Yes" if it were present in a prominent way)

	New Mother		New Father	
	Yes	No	Yes	No
Helpless	1	2	1	2
Proud	1	2	1	2
Anxious	1	2	1	2
Competent	1	2	1	2
Passive	1	2	1	2
Confused	1	2	1	2
Exhausted	1	2	1	2
Happy	1	2	1	2
Depressed	1	2	1	2
Excited	1	2	1	2

Source: Fogarty, Rapoport and Rapoport (1971) and Baylin (1970).

Since disagreement is an interpersonal concept, the effects should be manifest on both the husband and the wife. Most of the laboratory studies used a hypothetical stranger. Hence the impact of agreement could be assessed only for the subject. Here the effect of disagreement on both the husband and the wife will be assessed.

The measures of agreement constructed here are no better than those used in either the phantom stranger experiments or by Laing. That is, the measures do not separate positive from negative agreements. In the context of the feelings after the birth of the first child, a positive agreement would be one where both partners state, for example, that the wife was not depressed. The couple would have a negative agreement on this issue if both stated the wife was depressed. The difficulty is that positive agreements are likely to be more frequent than negative agreements. To take another example, most couples are likely to state that the new father was proud; few will admit to the "negative" feeling of not being proud. This creates an interpretive dilemma: Is the marriage a happy one because the couple agrees or is it a happy one because the birth of the first child was a gratifying experience? Stated in more theoretical terms, is marital attraction caused by agreement or by positive experiences?

To begin to separate the agreement effect from the negativity effect, we must construct indicators for negativity. By looking at the feelings from a different perspective, we can obtain measures of negativity that are logically independent of agreement. The key insight is to recognize that none of the words in the list of feelings in Table 6.8 is neutral. Each feeling has positive or negative connotations. Thus, for example, when a new father says he feels helpless, he is saying that he is experiencing a negative emotion. Should he say he feels competent, he is expressing a positive emotion. The assumed negative direction of each of the items is as follows: helpless, not proud, anxious, not competent, passive, confused, exhausted, not happy, depressd, not excited. Evidence to support this assumed direction was obtained by asking a sample of Canadian university students which they would rather be, helpless or not helpless, and so on, if they were a new parent. Overwhelmingly (from 73 percent to 100 percent), students endorsed the assumed directions given above. Note that this does not pertain to what they would expect to feel, but rather what they consider to be more desirable feelings.

Four separate negativity scores were created: (1) the number of negative feelings that the father attributed or perceived in the mother, (2) the number of negative feelings the father used to describe himself at that time, (3) the number of negative felings the mother used to describe herself, and (4) the number she attributed to the father. In addition, an overall negativity measure was constructed that was the sum of the four separate negativity scores.

Table 6.9 supports the agreement-attraction hypothesis. All twelve correlations are in the right direction, showing a positive relationship between agreement and marital attraction. The correlations range from a modest 0.09 to a moderately strong 0.31.

Table 6.9
Pearson Correlations of Agreement Scores with Marital Attraction

| | Agreement on: | | |
	Wife's Feelings	Husband's Feelings	TOTAL
Husband felt:			
1) married wrong person	0.09	0.14	0.13
2) happy in marriage	0.27	0.26	0.31
Wife felt:			
3) married wrong person	0.25	0.13	0.23
4) happy in marriage	0.28	0.22	0.29

(N = 148).

Source: Fogarty, Rapoport and Rapoport (1971) and Baylin (1970).

The results shown in Table 6.9 advance the similarity-attraction argument in several ways. First, as noted earlier, most studies on the agreement-attraction relationship were conducted in laboratory settings using strangers as subjects. This study provides evidence that the agreement-attraction connection also applies to established intimate relationships.

Second, it shows that the effect of agreement on marital attraction is a mutual or interpersonal one. The greater the proportion of agreements, the more likely *both* partners are to report that they are happy in their marriage and that they do not feel they married the wrong person.

Third, most of the previous studies focused on *attitudinal* or value agreements. Table 6.9 shows that agreement on the *emotions* experienced by each spouse is related to marital attraction. This extends the range of issues on which agreement is found to be relevant to attraction.

Finally, a review of the similarity-attraction literature suggests that the strength of the agreement-attraction relationship depends on the importance of the issues involved. Agreement on salient issues apparently produces greater attraction than agreement on more trivial ones. Indirect support for this salience hypothesis is provided in this table. Assume that, on average, agreements concerning the husbands feelings are more salient to the husband than the wife, and vice versa. Then agreement on the husband's feelings should be related more strongly with the husband's feelings of marital harmony than agreement on the wife's feelings would be. Similarly, agreement on the wife's feelings should be related more strongly with her report of marital attraction than agreement on the husband's feelings. This is generally the case.

Table 6.10
Pearson Correlations of Negative Feelings with Marital Attraction

	Husband felt:		Wife felt:	
	Married Wrong[a]	Happy	Married Wrong[a]	Happy
Negative feelings reported by wife concerning:				
Herself	–0.09	–0.25	–0.17	–0.29
Her husband	–0.32	–0.36	–0.17	–0.32
Negative feelings reported by husband concerning:				
Himself	–0.13	–0.26	–0.17	–0.25
His wife	–0.10	–0.18	–0.21	–0.18
Total Negativity	–0.27	–0.40	–0.31	–0.41

[a] Scoring reversed so that a low score indicates the spouse felt he or she had married wrong.

(N = 148).

Source: Fogarty, Rapoport and Rapoport (1971) and Baylin (1970).

Table 6.10 shows that negative feelings after the birth of the first child is, as expected, inversely related to marital attraction. In every instance, the greater the number of negative feelings, the lower the marital attraction. The relationship appears to be at least as strong as that found for agreement, ranging from a low of –0.09 to a high of –0.41. Note that negativity too has strong interpersonal effects. For example, how many negative feelings the wife attributed to her husband has a strong effect on how happily married the husband reported himself to be.

To summarize, this analysis provided additional support for the agreement-attraction hypothesis. In particular, husband-wife agreement about the feelings each had was shown to be consistently related to reported marital attraction. At the same time, it was argued that these feelings varied along a negative-positive continuum and that recalling negative feelings surrounding the birth of the first child consistently weakened the marital bond. This raises the question of whether it is agreement or positive feelings (or both) that is related to marital attraction. This question is best addressed with multivariate analysis techniques. These will be covered in Chapter 9.

SPSS Instructions

Line 1 (Figure 6.2): The data for this analysis is on an SPSS system file called "couples.sys".

Lines 2-10: Extended VARIABLE LABELS should be included to identify the meaning of any newly created permanent variables. It is important that these instructions are located after the instructions that created these variables; otherwise SPSS would report that errors were encountered in the instructions and would terminate the execution of the instructions.

Lines 11-12: This instruction will compute a total of sixteen Pearson correlation coefficients. These consist of the two measures of marital attraction ("happy" and "wrong") with the three measures of agreement and the five measures of negativity. These instructions produced the correlations that are reported in Tables 6.9 and 6.10.

Figure 6.2
SPSS Instructions for Obtaining Pearson Correlations

```
1   GET FILE = "couples.sys".
2   VARIABLE LABELS
3         hagree "Agreement on husband's feelings"
4         wagree "Agreement on wife's feelings"
5         agree "Agreement on couple's feelings"
6         neghf "Negative feelings—husband's report of father"
7         neghm "Negative feelings—husband's report of mother"
8         negwm "Negative feelings—wife's report of mother"
9         negwf "Negative feelings—wife's report of father"
10        neg "Total negativity score".
11  CORRELATIONS happy,wrong WITH hagree,wagree,agree
12        neghm,neghf,negwm,negwf,neg.
```

Summary

- Many arguments document covariation among different events. A variety of measures of association are available to facilitate this task. These measures summarize with a single number the strength of the relationship between two variables. This feature makes measures of association preferable to reporting percentage differences or differences in conditional means and proportions.
- The measure of association that should be used depends on two features of the variables in question. The first is the level of measurement we are willing to assume. Some measures are most appropriate for nominal variables, others for ordinal variables, and still others for interval-level variables. The second feature is the shape of the distribution of the variables. Skewed distribution or the presence of outliers pose difficulties for the most commonly used measure: the Pearson correlation coefficient. And the existence of numerous "ties" creates difficulties for coefficients based on ranks, such as the Spearman r_s.
- When Pearson correlations are used, it is important to assess the impact of violation of assumptions of normality and interval-level measures by replicating the analysis with alternate measures of association. If the various measures point to similar conclusions, confidence in continued use of the more exacting measures of association is enhanced.
- The nature and strength of relationships may depend on the unit of analysis employed. If interest centres on the behaviour of individuals, then it is inappropriate to measure the variables at an aggregate level such as groups or communities. Using aggregate data in such situations may result in the ecological correlation fallacy. Analysis of data on the benefits of specialization versus flexibility in fishing strategy exemplified this caution.
- Raw observations can be combined in different ways to construct plausible indicators of different concepts. The feelings of new parents after the birth of their first child were manipulated to create measures of agreement as well as measures of negativity. Pearson correlations showed that agreement and negativity were both related to marital attraction. This raises the possibility that the observed relationship between agreement and marital attraction is an artifact of negativity. Chapter 9 will develop the necessary tools to test this possibility.

Notes

1. Scores from 1 to 6 are unlikely to contain valuable information, since we have little reason to believe that they correspond to increasing "correct" party images. For this reason, we collapse all positive scores to 1.0.
2. All summations are from 1 to N unless specifically noted otherwise. Hence subscripts will not be shown in the equations.
3. A full interpretation of the Pearson coefficient requires an understanding of

linear regression analysis, which is the topic of the next chapter. Our main purpose here is to provide an intuitive understanding of its logic.

4. I postpone discussion of significance tests for Pearson correlation coefficients to Chapter 8.

5. Adding the subcommand STATISTICS ALL to the CROSSTABS procedure causes SPSS to compute a variety of measures of association. These, without the corresponding contingency tables, are given in Table 6.7.

6. I would like to thank Lotte Baylin, who identified the married couples in the data set (see Baylin, 1970).

Key Terms

correlation coefficients: Measures of association whose calculation requires assuming ordinal or interval measures; partly because of this, these measures permit us to specify the *direction* of the relationship. This is because correlation coefficients have a lower bound of –1.0 and an upper bound of +1.0. Positive and negative coefficients designate positive and negative relationships, respectively. For example, in an empirical test of the hypothesis that the force of attraction between two individuals varies *directly* (positively) with their similarity, we would expect a positive correlation. Examples: The Pearson correlation coefficient and the Spearman rank order correlation coefficient.

covariation: The generic term used to designate that two variables vary together; i.e., as the value of one changes, so does the other. Covariation is the weak, statistical counterpart to the philosophical concept of cause; if events do not co-vary, then one cannot be held to be the cause of the other. But if events co-vary, this does not imply that one causes the other; the connection may be fortuitous.

cross-products: The mathematical quantity that results when the value of one variable is multiplied by the value of another variable. Cross-products are at the heart of correlation coefficients, particularly the Pearson correlation coefficient. Indeed, the Pearson correlation coefficient can be defined as the average cross-product of standardized scores (z-scores).

measures of association: A variety of statistical techniques that estimate the strength of the relationship between two variables. Part of the variety of measures results from the variety of assumptions that one may or may not be willing to impose. In particular, some measures are appropriate for nominal measures (Cramer's V; the uncertainty coefficient), others for ordinal measures (Kendall's tau; Spearman rank order coefficient), some for interval measures (Pearson correlation coefficient) and some for a combination, such as a nominal independent but interval dependent variable (eta). The particular advantage of most of these measures is that they are independent of sample size. Consequently, a statistically significant result may nevertheless represent a disappointingly weak relationship, and a relatively strong relationship may prove not to be statistically significant. The former result could obtain when large sample sizes are used, and the latter result when small sample sizes are used. Most measures of association have the convenient characteristic that zero designates the absence of a relationship. In many of these measures, the maximum value is 1.0, representing a perfect relationship.

necessary but not sufficient condition: A logical condition in which the absence of the cause necessarily ensures the absence of the effect, but the presence of the cause does not necessarily produce the effect. Yule's Q would be appropriate for dichotomously measured variables that purportedly stand in this type of relationship to each other. The causal imagery contained in this term surpasses the ability of measures of association to capture; it remains a theoretical and philosophical concept that helps us to think about events.

negative relationship: A connection between two events measured at an ordinal or metric level, such that increasing one decreases the other. Such relationships are also called "inverse relations." In free market economic settings, it is generally argued that an inverse relationship characterizes supply and prices: the greater the supply, the lower the prices, and the more restricted the supply, the higher the prices.

outliers: Extremely high (or low) scores, which, in the context of Pearson correlation coefficients, can have an undue influence on its sign and magnitude. For this reason, such coefficients should be recalculated with outliers removed, to evaluate if the results are comparable.

Pearson product-moment correlation coefficient: The most popular metric correlation coefficient, named after the statistician Karl Pearson. This coefficient assumes metric measures for both variables and can be defined as the average cross-product of scores measured as deviations from the mean and expressed in standard deviation units (i.e., z-scores).

phi coefficient: A measure of association appropriate for four-fold tables. It is in some respects superior to Yule's Q, since it adjusts to some extent the effect of unequal marginal distributions, resulting in a more stable measure.

positive relationship: The relationship between two quantified variables in which large values of one are associated with large values of the other; conversely, the smaller the values of the one variable, the smaller the values of the other. Ordinarily, a positive correlation is the same as a positive relation. To avoid confusion, the variables being measured should be coded so that the larger the number, the greater the quantity of the phenomenon being measured. Examples: (1) The relationship between years of education and income is moderately positive: individuals with more years of education tend to have higher incomes than those with less education. (2) The "similarity-attraction" hypothesis postulates a positive relationship between similarity and attraction. In one version of this thesis, the greater the proportion of agreements between two individuals, the more attracted to each other they are likely to be. (3) The greater the demand, the higher the price. (4) The more cooperative the members of a work group are, the more productive the group.

Spearman rank order correlation coefficient: A popular correlation coefficient, appropriate when the unit of measure for both variables is its rank.

tied observations: With ranked data, two or more observations that have the same rank.

unequal marginal distributions: In bivariate distributions, a situation in which the univariate row and column distributions are discrepant. For example, if a positively skewed variable is cross-tabulated with a negatively skewed variable, the resulting marginal distributions will be unequal. Unequal marginal distributions affect some of the measures of association by depressing the maximum possible value; the more unequal the marginal distribution, the lower the maximum possible value for the measure of association. Example: For two dichotomous variables, when one has a 50-50 split and the other a 20-80 split.

Yule's Q: A simple measure of association that can be used only when both variables are treated as dichotomies. It results in a high value even when only one cell is sparsely populated. For this reason, Yule's Q is appropriate when one event is thought of as a necessary or as a sufficient (but not as a necessary and sufficient) condition for the other. Stated differently, Yule's Q is appropriate where, on theoretical grounds, one expects unequal marginal distributions between the two variables.

Chapter 7

DATA QUALITY: EVALUATING MEASURES

Theoretical and Measurement Models

So far we have directed our effort towards documenting the substantive relationships expected by our arguments. We assessed, for example, connections between similarity and attraction. In like fashion, we explored the relationships between political knowledge and party imagery. The establishment and interpretation of relationships such as these are linked to arguments and theories. Exploring such questions can produce a feeling of generating knowledge. Consequently, the exciting part of research is generally considered to reside in this aspect of argumentation.

An equally important but often neglected aspect of numerically based arguments concerns measurement models. Here the focus is on developing better measures of the phenomena under investigation. Measurement evaluation is typically treated as a necessary evil, part of the unwelcome drudgery of doing social research. And, indeed, by divorcing questions of measurement from questions of theory, these exercises are dreary, mechanical and frequently unproductive. For many social science topics, questions of measurement are vacuous outside the context of the argument being developed. The reason is that the "same" events can be considered from many vantage points. Consequently, sound research is based upon the construction of fruitful vantage points from which to assess social events. Measurements that are illuminating for one purpose may be unrevealing for another. In this sense, there is no correct way to treat a given set of observations. In the context of a specific argument, it may make sense to combine certain events. Combining these same events in the context of a different argument may produce nonsense. To a large extent, our purpose will dictate our measurement procedures.

One view of the relationship between theoretical and measurement models is diagrammed in Figure 7.1. The top part of the diagram depicts the theoretical model. The theoretical model defines concepts and postulates the nature of the relationships between these concepts. In one form of the similarity-attraction argument, these two concepts are causally connected, with similarity producing attraction. Arrows conventionally symbolize causation, with the head pointing to the effect. In the simplified form of Figure 7.1, X is the cause of Y.

Figure 7.1
Theoretical and Measurement Models

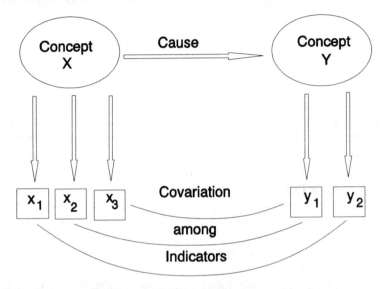

Good concepts produce numerous empirical manifestations, called **indicators** here and enclosed in boxes in Figure 7.1. The postulated links between theoretical concepts (or **latent concepts**) and empirical manifestations are known as a **measurement model.** These postulated links are themselves arguments. Attraction arguably causes diverse manifestations such as: standing closer to, preferring the company of, disclosing more about oneself to, and engaging in a greater variety of activities with the other person. The measures of these manifestations are the indicators of X and Y. These indicators are the data that are analyzed. They are expected to co-vary because the corresponding concepts are causally connected. The numeric evaluation of the data comprises the statistical model.

The top half of Figure 7.1 is the realm of theory, the bottom half the statistical domain, and the bridge connecting the two is methodology. In the absence of theory, methodology is meaningless. Methodological issues are ones that address and assess the fit between theoretical assertions and empirical manifestations. True, techniques such as public opinion polling exist independently of theory. But whether such sampling techniques are appropriate is a methodological question; the answer depends on theoretical considerations, as Blumer (1948) eloquently pointed out.

One may ask, why not simplify matters by discarding the theoretical level altogether and focusing solely on the empirical level? Is the theoretical level unnecessary baggage? There are two reasons why this is not a feasible strategy in the context of scholarly arguments. The first reason is the quest for understanding. The theoretical level postulates answers to the question of why certain events are connected. A fundamental task of scholarly arguments is to produce such explanations.

The second reason the theoretical level cannot be abandoned concerns the **parsimony principle**. Note in Figure 7.1 that a single causal relationship can be expected to produce a multitude of empirical statistical associations. A single theoretical rationale explains the myriad manifestations. Theory allows us to organize human knowledge.

Let's return to the party imagery example to exemplify some aspects of Figure 7.1.

Measurement of Party Imagery

Our interest in party imagery was grounded in the theoretical assumption that certain images are correct and others are not. We described the "correct" image as one which placed the NDP furthest to the left, the PCs furthest to the right and the Liberal party somewhere in between. This description nevertheless remains a theoretical assumption that can never be proven through empirical data. This is one of the reasons we say that conceptual knowledge is constructed rather than discovered. We cannot show that our description of correct party positions is a true one. The best we can do is to rely on authorities, such as social commentators and social scientists, coupled with an examination of the platforms of the parties. The relevant question then becomes whether our description of the parties leads to fruitful inquiry. Only after having made this assumption and, it is hoped, convinced our audience that such an assumption is potentially fruitful, did it become meaningful to explore the factors that lead to correct imagery.

This theoretical assumption had several immediate measurement implications. First, it dictated that party imagery had to be measured on a relative rather than absolute scale. This meant that the questions on party imagery and the response categories provided in the interview (as reproduced in Figure 7.2) could not be used in their original form. In that form, respondents located each party separately on a left-right scale. These absolute measures cannot be easily evaluated for their fit with the assumed correct location, i.e., they lack **theoretical isomorphism**. For example, if a respondent circled a 2 for the NDP, we do not know whether this is an instance of correct placement. If that respondent placed the PCs and/or the Liberals at 1 then the party imagery is wrong. But if the respondent placed the PCs and the Liberal party at 3 or higher, then the placement is indeed correct. Compare b and c in Figure 7.3. The NDP is placed identically in the two hypothetical placements. Yet in b the imagery is correct whereas in c it is false. To obtain the relative scores necessary to capture the concept, we subtracted the placement of the NDP from the placement of the PC and Liberal parties. Without a theoretical concept of correct party imagery, this operation would have been neither necessary nor meaningful.

Figure 7.2
Items for Measuring Left-Right Party Imagery

For the next few questions I would like you to use this scale which goes from left to right, with 1 being the most to the left and 7 being the most to the right.

	Left						Right
Now, where would you place the federal Liberal party?	1	2	3	4	5	6	7
Where would you place the federal Progressive Conservative party?	1	2	3	4	5	6	7
And where would you place the federal New Democratic Party?	1	2	3	4	5	6	7

Source: 1984 CNES.

A second implication of our theoretical assumption was that positive scores in the relative measure were more problematic than negative scores. That is, it was clear that the further to the right the NDP was placed relative to either of the other two parties, the more incorrect was the imagery. But it was not necessarily true that placing the NDP further and further to the left of the other parties resulted in increasingly correct imagery. Figure 7.3 provides examples of varying party imagery. In that diagram, it is clear that the party imagery is more false in d than in c. At the same time, it is not at all clear that the imagery in a is more correct than that in b. That all depends on how far to the left of the other parties the NDP "actually" is. Conventional wisdom has not produced a numeric answer, but our theoretical assumption alerted us to the problem. It suggested that we collapse the positive numbers in the relative scales. By doing this, we consider to be *equally correct* all placements of the PC party of at least one point to the right of the NDP. Collapsing the positive values of responses but not the negative ones would be most peculiar outside the context of the argument being developed.

Figure 7.3
Correct and Incorrect Party Images

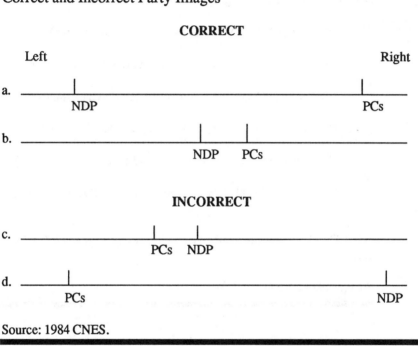

Source: 1984 CNES.

Third, the theoretical concept of correct party imagery stimulated us to find other aspects of party imagery that could be treated as being correct or incorrect. Two sets of party imagery questions in addition to the left-right aspect became candidates for extending the concept of correct party placement. One set elicited images on party favouritism towards lower versus upper classes. The other set elicited responses on party bias in favour of the working versus the middle class. This generates the six measures of party imagery listed in Figure 7.4.

Our argument rests on the assumption that for each of these measures there is a correct party placement. We assume that the correct placement of the NDP is to the left, and towards favouring the lower and working classes, when compared to the Liberals and Conservatives. Further, we expect that respondents who placed the NDP correctly on one measure would be more likely to place the NDP correctly on the other measures. That is, we expect the six measures to be positively correlated, since we assume that they are all manifestations of the single concept, correctness of party imagery. For this reason we expect these measures to show **internal consistency**.

Figure 7.4

Measures of Party Imagery

- NDP versus PC party on left-right orientation (PCNDPLR)

- NDP versus Liberal party on left-right orientation (LIBNDPLR)

- NDP versus PC party on lower-upper class favouritism (PCNDPLU)

- NDP versus Liberal party on lower-upper class favouritism (LIBNDPLU)

- NDP versus PC party on working-middle class bias (PCNDPWM)

- NDP versus Liberal party on working-middle class bias (LIBNDPWM)

Note: The SPSS variable names used in the instructions and in Table 7.1 are enclosed in parentheses.

Source: 1984 CNES.

Finally, we would expect that factors leading to a correct placement of the parties on one aspect of party imagery should also produce correct imagery for the other aspects. Stated differently, there is no compelling theoretical reason to expect political knowledge, for example, to be related to correct left-right placement but not to working class–middle class party bias. Just the opposite is the case: the theoretical model provides the rationale for expecting political knowledge to be positively correlated with all six measures of party imagery. This expectation stems from the **external consistency** principle.

These are the main expectations created by our theoretical assumption. With these expectations in mind, we can now develop the mathematical foundations of approaches to measurement.

Classical Measurement Theory

In **classical measurement theory**, the observed value for any variable is considered to be composed of two parts: the **true score** for that case, and the **measurement error.** That is,

$$O = T + e \tag{7.1}$$

where O =   observed score,
      T =   "true" score, and
      e =   measurement error for that case.

This equation is true by definition, since any number can be expressed as the sum of two numbers. Hence, the important issue is the fruitfulness of this conceptualization. In this formulation, we imagine that any observed score is composed of two parts and that these two parts have distinctly different meanings. In certain situations, this seems eminently reasonable. Taking age as an example, we can easily conceive of someone's reported age as being composed of that individual's true biological age and a certain amount of measurement error. When these two components are added, they constitute that individual's age as recorded in the data. Measurement error in this case would be produced by all those respondent characteristics that lead any individual to report an age other than their true age. These include things such as social desirability (e.g., wanting to appear younger than one is) or imperfect memory. An additional source is instrument/ researcher characteristics which produce an incorrect recording of the reported age. A third source of error is the level of measurement precision in recording age; it could, for example, be recorded in decades or years.

The distinction between true and error components is more problematic for variables such as the number of names of premiers known. It is problematic to the extent that the concept of knowledge itself is problematic. One can imagine that the number of names of premiers any individual can recall varies by time and circumstance; on some days, in certain situations, we can identify more names of premiers than on others. This renders the notion of a "true" number of names known problematic. At the same time, one can readily imagine that individuals do differ in the number of names "really" known. This makes the distinction between true and error components potentially fruitful.

For some concepts, the distinction between true and error components may be inappropriate altogether. In the party imagery example, we assume that the Canadian electorate distinguishes political parties on a left-right dimension. To the extent that the left-right dimension is a salient one for the electorate, this assumption will be fruitful and the distinction between true and error components useful. To the extent that this is not a salient dimension, there may not be any imagery that corresponds to this verbal distinction. Similarly, in attitude studies, the public may not have any attitude on a given topic, making the notion of a "true" score inappropriate. In short, decomposing observed scores into true and error components is more meaningful in some instances than in others. As we will see later in this chapter, it may be unwise to always treat observations in this way.

Having found a conceptualization of measurement error that is applicable in many situations, we must now develop ways to implement this approach. The first step is to recognize that the amount of measurement error likely differs from case to case. However, our concern is not with the magnitude of the error component for any one case but rather for the sample as a whole. To obtain an estimate of the magnitude of measurement error overall, we express equation 7.1 in terms of the variances implied:

$$Var(O) = Var(T + e). \qquad (7.2)$$

Remember from high school algebra that:

$$(x + y)^2 = x^2 + 2xy + y^2.$$

Without going through the steps, we note that the same holds true when obtaining the variance of such quantities: the squares are replaced by the variances, and the cross-product by the covariances, as in equation 7.3:

$$Var(O) = Var(T) + 2Cov(T, e) + Var(e). \qquad (7.3)$$

Equation 7.3 shows that the observed variance can be considered as composed of three parts: the **true variance**, the **error variance** and (twice) the covariance between the true and error components. Since variances are composed of squared numbers, their value is always positive. However, remember (from Chapter 6) that covariances express the correlation between two variables. Hence the covariance can take on a positive or a negative value. Consequently, although equation 7.3 theoretically quantifies measurement error, the presence of the covariance term makes it of little practical value. Like magicians, statisticians have their ways to make unwanted quantities disappear. One technique is to make simplifying assumptions. We assume for the time being that the covariance between true and error scores is zero. When true and error scores are uncorrelated, **random measurement error** is the only kind of measurement error in our data; our error is not systematically related to the true score. Where we are willing to make this assumption, equation 7.3 simplifies to:

$$Var(O) = Var(T) + Var(e). \qquad (7.4)$$

Manipulating equation 7.4, we can express the true variance as:

$$Var(T) = Var(O) - Var(e). \qquad (7.5)$$

This formulation reveals that the true variance is always less than or equal to the observed variance (since variances are always greater than or equal to zero). This fact permits us to draw the following conclusion: For any two sets of data that contain comparable information on a given variable, the quality of the data is better in that set where the variance of the variable in question is lower (all things being equal). Occasionally this fact can be informative in assessing different data sets.

The concept of the **reliability** of a measure is usually expressed as the proportion of the observed variance that is true variance. That is, by definition:

$$Reliability = \frac{Var(T)}{Var(O)}.$$ (7.6)

Traditionally, the reliability of a measure is symbolized as r_{xx}. At first this may appear an odd choice, since r_{xx} expresses the correlation of a variable with itself. Clearly, such a correlation would always be perfect, except for the presence of measurement error. But it is precisely the presence of measurement error we wish to symbolize. Hence it becomes an appropriate symbol for reliability.

Through the simple expedient of dividing both sides of equation 7.5 by the observed variance, we have a solution for the reliability of a measure:

$$\frac{Var(T)}{Var(O)} = \frac{Var(O)}{Var(O)} - \frac{Var(e)}{Var(O)}.$$ (7.7)

Since the left side of this equation is the definition of reliability, we get:

$$r_{xx} = 1 - \frac{Var(e)}{Var(O)}.$$ (7.8)

Equation 7.8 expresses reliability as the proportion of observed variance that is *not* the result of measurement error. We must remember that equations 7.4 to 7.8 are tenable only if the true scores are uncorrelated with measurement error; that is, if our measurement error is purely random.

Assumption of Random Measurement Error

The possibility of neatly partitioning the observed variance of a measure into two components—true and error variance—is enticing. Let's look more closely at the random error assumption which makes this partitioning possible. With random measurement error, we specifically recognize that some observed scores are too high and others are too low. If they are truly random, then the expected value of the signed errors is zero. That is, cases of overestimation are balanced by instances of underestimation. Mathematically, we get:

$$E(e) = 0.$$ (7.9)

When equation 7.9 holds, as it will when all measurement error is random, then measurement error will not affect the mean of the variable. Taking age as the example, if random measurement error is the only type of error present, then the mean observed age is identical to the true mean age. Hence random measurement error does not bias our estimates of the mean of any variable. Stated in the form of an equation, if measurement error is random, then:

$$E(O) = E(T). \tag{7.10}$$

However, random measurement error inflates the observed variance:

$$Var(O) > Var(T). \tag{7.11}$$

The ratio of true to observed variance is, as stated earlier, our estimate of the reliability of a measure.

The conclusions contained in equations 7.9 to 7.11 hold whenever measurement error is purely random. Conversely, none of these conclusions holds in the face of correlated or systematic measurement error. The reason is that the correlation between true and error components can be either positive or negative and this could inflate or deflate our estimates of the mean and the variance.

Systematic or **correlated measurement error** exists when the magnitude of the (signed) error is related to the magnitude of the true score. Let's again take age as our example. Suppose we live in a society where youthfulness is cherished. In such a society we could imagine that older respondents would be tempted to underreport their age. This would cause a negative correlation between chronological age and measurement error. Hence both the mean observed age and the variance of age would be too low. The likelihood and severity of systematic error must therefore be carefully evaluated in any numerically based argument.

Most importantly, systematic measurement error is likely in all normative domains. Let's call this the *normative congruence principle*: the less congruent the "true" response is with cultural norms, the greater the likelihood that the reported response will minimize this incongruence. Countless examples of this principle can be found in the social science literature. It accounts, for example, for why the estimates of the proportion of citizens who voted is higher in surveys than the actual turnout; even the proportion who claim to have voted for the winner is higher. The error is systematic in that the proportion who falsely claim to have voted is higher than the proportion who falsely report not having voted. For any normative issue, we can expect a bias in the direction of congruence with the socially desirable outcome.

Let's return to wife-husband agreement as an example. Imagine a husband who holds a socially undesirable view on some issue, but his wife does not. Clearly such a couple disagrees on this issue. However, the normative congruence principle predicts that such husbands will be tempted to understate their incongruent viewpoints. Consequently, we will overestimate the amount of agreement. Later we will examine some research in greater detail to explore the impact of systematic measurement error in such situations. We will see that the presence of systematic measurement error threatens what is usually called the **validity** of a measure. That is, it diminishes the plausibility that we are measuring what we intended to measure.

Reliability Coefficients: Cronbach's Alpha

Equation 7.8 forms the backbone of most discussions of reliability. That is, reliability is most often thought of as the proportion of observed variance not attributable to error variance. That equation presupposes that we can separate error from true variance. But if we have but one measure of a concept, this cannot be done. However, with two or more measures, this becomes possible. When we administer the same measure on two or more occasions, or we have alternate measures of the "same" concept, we can obtain an estimate of the error variance and hence the reliability of the measure. A **repeated measures** approach is known as **test-retest reliability**, whereas a multiple indicators approach is called **internal consistency reliability**. Multiple measures of a single concept should intercorrelate perfectly. We attribute failures to do so to measurement error.

In Chapter 8 we will show that the **coefficient of determination** (the square of the Pearson correlation coefficient) can be thought of as the proportion of variance in one variable that is "explained" by the other variable. This formulation provides an easy transition to internal consistency approaches to reliability. The "trick" is to correlate one measure of a concept with a second measure of the "same" concept. Let's work through an internal consistency approach with the party imagery measures. We have two ways to assess whether the NDP is placed correctly on a left-right dimension. One measure compares the Liberals with the NDP on a common left-right scale; the second compares the Conservatives with the NDP on the same scale.

The placement of the NDP relative to the PCs should determine the placement of the NDP relative to the Liberals. In the absence of random measurement error, the correlation would be perfect. This is because we are correlating correct party imagery with itself, simply using two alternate measures. Consequently, the coefficient of determination could serve as an estimate of the reliability of a party imagery concept based on these two measures.

This logic has been extended to measures based on any number of indicators. **Cronbach's alpha** is the most commonly used coefficient of reliability for multiple measures. Technically, Cronbach's alpha is the average of all possible split-half coefficients. Our six measures, for example, would be split into all possible pairs, the coefficient of determination between each pair would be computed and the average of all these coefficients would represent Cronbach's alpha. In this fashion, a single measure of internal consistency can be produced with any number of indicators.

Correlation Matrices

A matrix is a set of numbers organized into rows and columns. A correlation matrix provides the intercorrelation of every pair of variables in a list of variables. Each position in the matrix contains the correlation between the two variables defined by the row and column. The symbol r_{ij} (where i refers to the row, and j to the column location) is used to identify the correlation between any two variables. Thus the correlation between the second and third variable in the list of variables ($r_{3,2}$) is found in the third row, second column. In Table 7.1, it contains the correlation between PCNDPLR and LIBNDPLR. These refer to the left-right placement of the PC party relative to the NDP, and the left-right placement of the Liberal party relative to the NDP, respectively. Correlation matrices are symmetrical. That is, $r_{3,2}$ refers to the correlations of the same two variables as $r_{2,3}$. For this reason usually only the coefficients below the main diagonal (the main diagonal is defined as those cells where $i = j$) are given in Table 7.1.

We are now in a position to evaluate our expectations concerning the internal consistency of our six measures of party imagery and their relation to political knowledge. Table 7.1 presents a **correlation matrix** of Pearson coefficients (the SPSS instructions which produced the information for this table are provided in Figure 7.5.)

Table 7.1
Pearson Correlations among Party Imagery Indicators and with Political Knowledge

	PREMIERS	PCNDPLR	LIBNDPLR	PCNDPWM	LIBNDPWM	PCNDPLH	LIBNDPLH
PREMIERS	1.00						
PCNDPLR	0.23	1.00					
LIBNDPLR	0.19	0.50	1.00				
PCNDPWM	0.23	0.17	0.17	1.00			
LIBNDPWM	0.21	0.11	0.10	0.70	1.00		
PCNDPLH	0.25	0.23	0.18	0.33	0.19	1.00	
LIBNDPLH	0.17	0.13	0.11	0.22	0.24	0.56	1.00

Source: 1984 CNES.

The vertical line after the first column was added to emphasize that the first column of correlations has a different logical meaning from the remainder. The first column of correlations tests the expectation of a consistent relationship between political knowledge and every indicator of party imagery, i.e., the external consistency criterion. The correlations of political knowledge (abbreviated as premiers in Table 7.1) with measures of party imagery are moderately low, ranging from 0.17 to 0.25. Nevertheless, the relationships are consistent, fulfilling our first measurement criterion and expectation. In short, the more premiers named, the more accurate is every aspect of party imagery.

The remainder of Table 7.1 provides information on the second set of expectations: the internal consistency of the six measures of party imagery. Here the results are less gratifying. Although all of the correlations are positive, many of them are disappointingly low. For example, respondents who "correctly" place the Liberals to the right of the NDP are only slightly more likely to "correctly" place the Liberals as more biased than the NDP towards the middle classes. The same holds true for a number of other placements. For the majority of the Canadian electorate, there appears to be little connection between a party's left-right leanings and its bias towards the lower or working classes. Contrary to our expectations, these are to a large extent considered to be independent of the positions of Canadian parties.

Several patterns among the indicators of party imagery are worth mentioning. First, if the Liberal party is placed correctly relative to the NDP on a given aspect, then the Conservative party is also likely to be placed correctly on that aspect. These correlations are 0.50, 0.70 and 0.56 for left-right, working-middle and lower-higher aspects, respectively. The magnitude of these correlations is partially a methodological artifact. The artifact results from constrained boundaries in the response categories available to the respondents. That is, the lowest score an individual could give on any of the items is a 1 and the highest a 7. Suppose a respondent scores the NDP as 1 or 2. Such a respondent almost has to place both the Liberals and the Conservatives correctly (i.e., numerically higher) on that dimension, since most of the available response categories would result in a correct placement. Conversely, a respondent who places the NDP at a 6 or a 7 would, even if she or he gave a random response to the Liberals and the Conservatives, be likely to have placed both of them incorrectly. Thus the constrained boundaries produce an inflated correlation.

Secondly, the correlations among the final four measures of party imagery are higher than between these four measures and the first two. This is likely because of the fact that the term *classes* was common to the last four measures.

Finally, placement of the Liberals on any of the three measures shows weaker relationships than placement of the Conservatives. This provides a modicum of comfort, because it was expected that the correct placement of the NDP relative to the Liberals would be more difficult than its placement relative to the Conservatives.

Index Construction

Given the results discussed above, the question is whether the six measures of party imagery can or should be combined into one overall measure. Whenever several measures of a common concept are available, it is desirable to combine them, by taking either their sum or calculating the mean response. By so doing, we obtain a more reliable measure, i.e., one where the proportion of error variance has been reduced. The mean of several fallible measures is less fallible than any of the individual measures.

Earlier in this chapter we learned that, under the assumption of random measurement error, the true variance is always less than or equal to the observed variance. This implies that increasing the reliability reduces the observed variance. The observed variance is always reduced when means of several measures of the same concept are used. The Central Limit Theorem from Chapter 5 can be used to reach this conclusion. This theorem stated that the standard deviation of the sample means is smaller than that of the individual observations by a factor of the square root of the sample size ($\sqrt{N}$). In the context of hypothesis testing, N referred to the number of observations in the sample. In the context of reliability, N refers to the number of measures of a common concept. If we assume a random sample of measures, then the variance of the mean of these measures will be less than the variance of the individual measures. Using the mean reduces the proportion of the error variance. Furthermore, the Central Limit Theorem in this context yields the conclusion that the greater the number of measures combined, the lower the proportion of measurement error. Obviously, we would like to have measures with minimal error variance. Hence we ordinarily are tempted to combine numerous measures.

The rub is that we must assume that the various indicators are indeed indicators of a common concept. Otherwise we would be adding noncomparable indicators, resulting in uninterpretable measures. Increasing the number of items to be combined increases the reliability of the measure but potentially decreases the interpretability of the resulting measure. We may gain reliability but risk validity.

Cronbach's alpha for the six-item measure of party imagery is 0.65. By conventional standards, this is acceptable. At the same time, the pattern of correlations found among the indicators suggests that the three aspects of party imagery are to a large extent independent of each other. However, all of the indicators were related to political knowledge in a consistent fashion. Perhaps the following rules can be used to decide whether an index should be constructed out of several indicators:

1.   Where both the internal and external consistency criteria are met, it is desirable to construct an index. Reliabilities in excess of 0.60 are often considered to have met the internal consistency criterion. The external consistency criterion is met when alternate measures of a common concept are similarly related, within the bounds of sampling fluctuation, to the other variables under investigation.

2. Whenever the external consistency criterion is violated, an index should not be constructed or used, regardless of how well the internal consistency criterion is met. If, for example, political knowledge were positively correlated to one indicator of party imagery, but negatively correlated with a second indicator of party imagery, it would not be helpful to combine the two indicators, because we would then not be in a position to uncover either the positive or the negative relationship. Combining the indicators would clearly be fruitless. Instead, we would in such circumstances be forced to abandon the concept that led us to consider combining the indicators in the first place. Had we found inconsistent effects between party imagery indicators and political knowledge, it is almost a foregone conclusion that we would have had to terminate the investigation of "correct" party imagery.

3. If the internal consistency criterion is violated, but the external consistency criterion is upheld, it is possible, with caution, to use a summary index.

I would consider the findings in Table 7.1 to place us in this last category, even though Cronbach's alpha exceeds 0.60.

Given the findings presented in Table 7.1, it would be sensible to replicate further analysis using three different indices of party imagery. The first index consists of a respondent's mean score on the six indicators. This measure has a reliability of 0.65 but is composed of three mainly independent (from the viewpoint of the electorate) aspects of party imagery. The advantage of this measure is that it uses all indicators, thereby being potentially more parsimonious. The disadvantage is that the meaning of any score is somewhat vague. A score of -1, for example, would indicate that on average both the Liberals and the Conservatives were placed one unit lower than the NDP on all three aspects. But such an average could have been produced by placing both the Liberals and the Conservatives correctly on two of the three aspects and extremely incorrectly on the third aspect.

The second index also uses all six indicators, but they are recoded in a manner which renders the resulting score less ambiguous. This involves computing the proportion of correct placements. That is, for each indicator, we consider all positive scores as instances of a correct placement and all other scores as instances of incorrect placements. The mean of these recoded responses can then be interpreted as the proportion of correct placements. These scores will range from zero (all six placements were incorrect) to 1 (all six placements were correct). Cronbach's alpha for this index of party imagery is 0.72, a slight increase from the uncollapsed version.

A third alternative is to create three separate measures, one for each aspect of party imagery. The advantage of this approach is that it retains the integrity of the respondents' viewpoints. That is, the electorate has indicated that the three aspects of party imagery are to a large extent independent of each other. By treating the three aspects separately, we do not violate their subjective experience. The most serious disadvantages are that we undermine the notion of a correct party placement with this approach and we are less parsimonious. Cronbach's alpha for the two-item measures ranges between 0.68 and 0.79.

By replicating further analysis with all three measurement treatments, we retain the possibility of parsimony. At the same time we permit the experiences of the electorate to correct our conclusion if additional analysis shows that the external consistency principle no longer holds when other variables are introduced.

Measurement Error and Attenuated Correlations

Previously I stated that the coefficient of determination (r^2) can be interpreted as the proportion of the variance in one variable that is accounted for by the variance in another variable. By definition, variation that results from random error cannot be "explained." As a direct consequence, we always underestimate the strength of the relationship between any two variables whenever random measurement error occurs in our indicators. Using the Greek letter rho (ρ) to represent the true correlation, we can symbolize this conclusion as:

$$\rho_{xy} \geq r_{xy}. \tag{7.12}$$

Equation 7.12 provides an additional expectation: to the extent that an index succeeds in reducing the proportion of measurement error, the correlation of a given variable with the index should be stronger than with that of the items constituting the index. This expectation is fulfilled in the party imagery example. The correlation between political knowledge and the six constituent aspects of party imagery ranges between 0.17 and 0.25 (see the first column of Table 7.1). The analogous correlation with the summated measure of party imagery is 0.28.

Correlated Measurement Error

To summarize, the nature of a variety of effects of random measurement error is known. We know that random measurement error has no effect on the estimated mean of our variables, increases the variance of our variables and decreases the estimated strength of the association between variables. Knowing the nature of these effects, we can place boundaries on our findings. For example, we can state that the observed variance is likely a maximum estimate of the true variance, and that the observed correlation is a minimum estimate of the true strength of the relationship. Because the nature of its effects is known in advance, random measurement error does not pose a major threat to our arguments. Certainly it is desirable to purify our measures of such error, but its presence is seldom a source of a fatal flaw in our conclusions. Furthermore, where several measures of a concept are available, the impact of random measurement error can be taken into account and minimized.

Unfortunately, the effect of systematic or correlated measurement error cannot be stated in advance. It can increase or decrease the mean, maximize or minimize the variance, and produce associations where none exist or mask associations that are actually present. In short, correlated measurement errors can be "fatal," and they are often difficult to detect.

A good case can be made for the conclusion that correlated measurement error constitutes a fatal flaw for the Laing data. Laing employed a test-retest format to establish that his instrument was sufficiently reliable. With a four- to six-week interval between two administrations of the instrument, Laing found that approximately 85 percent of the responses were identical on retest. This is a respectable reliability. However, he presented information on the test-retest reliability separately for the disturbed and the non-disturbed couples, and a comparison of the results shows that the reliability was 89 percent and 81 percent, respectively, for the non-disturbed and the disturbed samples. This differential reliability is the source of a potentially "fatal" flaw. The "fatal" flaw argument is somewhat complicated, so let me spell it out step by step.

1. Keep in mind that Laing measured agreement as the sum of the absolute differences between the responses of husbands and wives on sixty issues. A couple was considered to agree on an issue if both partners responded "yes" or both responded "no" to that issue; otherwise they disagreed.
2. Suppose a couple "actually" agrees on an issue. In that instance, measurement error on the responses of one or the other (but not both) spouses would result in that couple being wrongly classified as disagreeing.
3. Suppose a couple "really" disagreed. In that case, measurement error in the responses of one or the other spouse (again, not both) would cause that couple to be incorrectly classified as agreeing.
4. The probability of measurement error simultaneously occurring for *both* partners is low whenever the reliability of the instrument is high (i.e., greater than 50 percent). As indicated before, the test-retest reliability for the Laing data is approximately 85 percent. That is, on average, in 85 percent of the instances, a respondent gave identical responses in the two separate administrations of the instrument. Using the multiplication rule for independent events, the probability of measurement error occurring for *both* partners simultaneously on any issue is 0.02 [(1-.85)(1-.85) = 0.02]. Clearly, in most instances, if measurement error exists, it will affect only one or the other partner's measure, but not both. Hence, the fact that we stipulated "not both" in steps 2 and 3 above is usually fulfilled.
5. So far, measurement error is not problematic since instances of step 3 will act to counterbalance instances of step 2. However, in this step we will show that measurement error will, in Laing's data, act to inflate the estimate of the prevalence of disagreement. Remember that Laing's couples were shown to agree on average on over three-quarters of the issues. Whenever the "true" percentage of agreement is greater than 50 percent, measurement error will inflate the estimate of disagreement. This is because there are more instances

of true agreement than of genuine disagreement. Consequently, there are more instances where measurement error will result in a true agreement being recorded as a disagreement than there will be instances of valid disagreements being recorded as agreements. In short, for Laing's data, the impact of measurement error is to inflate the overall estimate of disagreement.

6.   But measurement error is higher in the disturbed sample than in the non-disturbed sample.

7.   Therefore, measurement error will result in disturbed couples *appearing* to disagree more than non-disturbed. This calls into question one of Laing's major findings (that disturbed couples disagree more than non-disturbed couples). This finding could be an artifact of the differential levels of reliability reported for the two groups. That is, the finding that measurement error on agreement-disagreement was correlated with marital difficulty could account for the observed differential levels of agreement between disturbed and non-disturbed couples.

Having shown the potential impact of correlated measurement error on Laing's conclusion, we could move to other concerns. However, I would like to pause and deliberate on this exercise a little longer. Laing treated the test-retest data as purely a measurement issue. I have shown that this "measurement" problem had a profound impact on his substantive conclusions. Now I want to suggest that the correlated measurement error in this data is perhaps better conceptualized as providing an alternative theoretical interpretation to the overall findings.

The question that must be asked is why the responses of the disturbed couples are less "reliable" than the nondisturbed. Stated differently, what are the factors that induce respondents to give contradictory responses on salient issues over a rather brief period of time?   Is it a matter of measurement error, or is it perhaps a manifestation of uncertainty? I suggest that uncertainty is a plausible alternative reconceptualization of the meaning of unstable responses concerning the marital relationship. That is, if someone is unsure about a topic, it is reasonable to expect that their responses on that topic would fluctuate over relatively short periods of time. The responses of the disturbed couples were more likely to fluctuate than those of the nondisturbed. Such fluctuations are classically treated as measurement error. However, I know of no compelling reason why the responses of spouses in disturbed marriages should exhibit more measurement error than those of other spouses. But I can imagine theoretical reasons why disturbed couples might be less certain about the characteristics of their relationship than nondisturbed couples.

Ironically, the methodological finding of correlated measurement error may be an "artifact" of a substantive/theoretical relationship between uncertainty and marital harmony. This is ironic because invariably we suspect that substantive findings may be methodological artifacts; rarely do we suspect that a method-ological finding may be substantively genuine.

SPSS Instructions

Figure 7.5
SPSS Instructions for Pearson Correlations and
Reliability Analysis

```
1   GET FILE = "vote84.sys".
2   COUNT premiers= var446 TO var455(1).
3   COMPUTE pcndplr=var510-var511.
4   COMPUTE libndplr=var509-var511.
5   COMPUTE pbndpwm=var063-var064.
6   COMPUTE libndpwm=var062-var064.
7   COMPUTE pcndplh=var312-var313.
8   COMPUTE libndplh=var311-var313.
9   VARIABLE LABELS premiers "Number of premiers correctly named"
10          pcndplr "Left-right placement of PC rel. to NDP"
11          libndplr "Left-right placement of LIB. rel. to NDP"
12          pcndplh "Lo-hi class placement of PC vs. NDP"
13          libndplh "Lo-hi class placement of LIB. vs. NDP"
14          pcndpwm "Working-middle class bias of PC vs. NDP"
15          libndpwm "Working-middle class bias of LIB. vs. NDP".
16  RECODE pcndplr TO libndplh (2 THRU 6=1).
17  CORRELATION premiers, pcndplr TO libndplh
18          /PRINT=NOSIG.
19  RELIABILITY VAR=pcndplr TO libndplh
20          /SCALE(partyim)=pcndplr TO libndplh.
21  STATISTICS ALL.
```

Line 2: This instruction in Figure 7.5 counts the number of times the value 1 occurred in the variables named "var446" to "var455" inclusive. These variables contain the information concerning the names of the ten premiers. A score of 1 in any of these ten variables indicated the respondent had correctly named the premier of the province corresponding to that variable. The result of this count manipulation is to be stored in a new variable named "premiers".

Lines 3-8: These instructions compute the six relative measures of party imagery. Note that I have not declared any values of these newly created party imagery variables as missing. In SPSS, newly created variables will be given the "system missing" value if any of the variables used in constructing the new variable have missing values.

Lines 9-15: Each of the relative measures of party imagery created above are given extended labels to document the printouts more fully.

Line 16: All positive values of the relative measures are collapsed. As long as the NDP is placed to the left of the other two parties, the image is treated as correct.

Line 17: This instruction produces a Pearson correlation matrix. After the keyword CORRELATION, the variables for which intercorrelations are desired are listed. When new variables are created in SPSS, they are stored sequentially at the end of each case in the order in which they were encountered in the instruction file. This feature permitted me to use the TO convention in listing the new variables. I could have listed the variables as "premiers TO libndplh" with identical results. This procedure produced the information contained in Table 7.1.

Line 18: This optional subcommand controls how the correlations are printed. PRINT=NOSIG informs SPSS that I do not wish the number of cases and the significance level of each pair of correlation coefficients to be printed. By default, the correlation procedure treats missing cases in a "pairwise" fashion. That is, any case in which information is available for both variables is included, even if information on the other variables on the variable list is missing. Such "pairwise" treatment of missing cases results in the possibility of a different number of cases for the various coefficients.

Lines 19-21: These three lines produced the output which follows below. The keyword RELIABILITY invokes the reliability procedure. This keyword must be followed by a list of all the variables that will be used in any of the associated SCALE subcommands. The phrase "VAR=pcndplr TO libndplh" does this. A word of caution is necessary here. The reliability procedure deletes cases on a "listwise" basis. That is, if information on any one of the variables included in the variable list is missing, that case is deleted altogether. For this reason, it is ordinarily a good practice to keep the variables listed in the reliability procedure at a minimum. After the variables are listed, one or more SCALE subcommands are required. For each scale subcommand, the keyword SCALE is followed by an arbitrary scale name enclosed in parentheses. I have called the party imagery scale "partyim". The name of the scale is followed by a list of the variables that comprise that scale. Finally, line 22 requests all statistics associated with the reliability procedure to be calculated and printed.

Reliability Procedure Output

Figure 7.6 is a partial printout of the results produced by the SPSS commands given above:

Figure 7.6
SPSS-Produced Reliability Output

File: The Canadian National Election Study

RELIABILITY ANALYSIS - SCALE (PARTYIM)

1. PCNDPLR   Left-right placement of PC rel. to NDP
2. LIBNDPLR   Left-right placement of LIB. rel. to NDP
3. PCNDPWM   Working-middle class bias of PC vs. NDP
4. LIBNDPWM   Working-middle class bias of LIB. vs. NDP
5. PCNDPLH   Lo-hi class placement of PC vs. NDP
6. LIBNDPLH   Lo-hi class placement of LIB. vs. NDP

		MEAN	STD DEV	CASES
1.	PCNDPLR	.5935	1.0141	1358.0
2.	LIBNDPLR	.3984	1.2145	1358.0
3.	PCNDPWM	.5987	1.0633	1358.0
4.	LIBNDPWM	.6399	.9881	1358.0
5.	PCNDPLH	.7791	.6736	1358.0
6.	LIBNDPLH	.7857	.6849	1358.0

COVARIANCE MATRIX

	PCNDPLR	LIBNDPLR	PCNDPWM	LIBNDPWM	PCNDPLH	LIBNDPLH
PCNDPLR	1.0285					
LIBNDPLR	.6049	1.4749				
PCNDPWM	.1573	.1880	1.1306			
LIBNDPWM	.0871	.1089	.6910	.9764		
PCNDPLH	.0936	.0969	.2348	.1260	.4537	
LIBNDPLH	.0573	.0766	.1475	.1468	.2452	.4692

CORRELATION MATRIX

	PCNDPLR	LIBNDPLR	PCNDPWM	LIBNDPWM	PCNDPLH	LIBNDPLH
PCNDPLR	1.0000					
LIBNDPLR	.4912	1.0000				
PCNDPWM	.1459	.1456	1.0000			
LIBNDPWM	.0869	.0908	.6577	1.0000		
PCNDPLH	.1371	.1185	.3278	.1893	1.0000	
LIBNDPLH	.0824	.0921	.2026	.2169	.5314	1.0000

				# OF	
STATISTICS FOR		MEAN	VARIANCE	STD DEV	VARIABLES
SCALE		3.7953	11.6574	3.4143	6

ITEM						
MEANS	MEAN	MINIMUM	MAXIMUM	RANGE	MAX/MIN	VARIANCE
	.6325	.3984	.7857	.3873	1.9723	.0205

ITEM						
VARIANCES	MEAN	MINIMUM	MAXIMUM	RANGE	MAX/MIN	VARIANCE
	.9222	.4537	1.4749	1.0212	3.2506	.1576

INTER-ITEM						
COVARIANCES	MEAN	MINIMUM	MAXIMUM	RANGE	MAX/MIN	VARIANCE
	.2041	.0573	.6910	.6338	12.0667	.0345

INTER-ITEM						
CORRELATIONS	MEAN	MINIMUM	MAXIMUM	RANGE	MAX/MIN	VARIANCE
	.2344	.0824	.6577	.5753	7.9776	.0324

ITEM-TOTAL STATISTICS

	SCALE MEAN IF ITEM DELETED	SCALE VARIANCE IF ITEM DELETED	CORRECTED ITEM- TOTAL CORRELATION	SQUARED MULTIPLE CORRELATION	ALPHA IF ITEM DELETED
PCNDPLR	3.2018	8.6284	.3358	.2504	.5974
LIBNDPLR	3.3969	8.0317	.3124	.2484	.6184
PCNDPWM	3.1966	7.6894	.4811	.4839	.5343
LIBNDPWM	3.1554	8.3612	.4060	.4467	.5687
PCNDPLH	3.0162	9.6106	.3814	.3450	.5893
LIBNDPLH	3.0096	9.8415	.3134	.3008	.6068

RELIABILITY COEFFICIENTS   6 ITEMS
ALPHA = .6304   STANDARDIZED ITEM ALPHA = .6475

Summary

- In scholarly research, the measurement of phenomena has no rationale outside the context of a given theory and its associated concepts.
- A major task in any scholarly argument is to assess and improve the fit between theoretical concepts and empirical phenomena.

- Traditionally, the fit between concepts and measures has been addressed by the twin topics of reliability and validity. Reliability refers to the extent to which a measure produces consistent scores; validity refers to whether a measure captures the *intended* concept.
- All human observation, including scientific observation, is fallible, i.e., it is contaminated with error. At the measurement level, such error may be random or systematic.
- The effects of random measurement error are well understood: they do not affect the mean; they increase the variance and they attenuate (or weaken) the observed relationship. Reliability coefficients estimate the proportion of random measurement error. Since their effects are known, they generally are not the source of grievous difficulties in empirically based arguments.
- The effects of systematic measurement error cannot be stated in advance. Systematic, or correlated, measurement error may create overestimates and underestimates of the mean; it may magnify or minimize the variance; it may inflate or deflate the observed strength, reverse the direction, or distort the form, of relationships. In short, systematic measurement error is hazardous to arguments and is *always* a source of invalidity.
- Systematic measurement error is likely in all normatively regulated domains. In general, the more incongruent with normative guidelines a given behaviour or cognition is, the more likely that the *reported* behaviour or cognition will minimize the discrepancy.
- If there are several indicators of a common concept, then indices composed of their sums or means contain a lower proportion of random measurement error than do the individual indicators. Hence, indices ordinarily are preferable to individual indicators.
- The constituent indicators of a concept should possess high internal and external consistency. Internal consistency is synonymous with reliability. The external consistency criterion requires that every indicator of a concept be related similarly to all other variables involved in an argument. External consistency is more crucial to sound arguments than is internal consistency. If measures are not externally consistent, then they cannot be valid measures of a single concept.

Key Terms

classical measurement theory: An approach to measurement that conceptualizes the measured quantity of a variable as being composed of two logically distinct parts: the true amount and the measurement error. This approach forms the backbone of the internal consistency view of reliability, which defines reliability as the proportion of variance in a measure that is not error variance.

coefficient of determination: The square of the Pearson correlation coefficient. Technically, the coefficient of determination is the ratio of the covariance of two variables to their variances. It is often interpreted as the proportion of the variance in the dependent variable that is "explained" by the independent variables. Since the magnitude of the coefficient of determination has this simple meaning, it should be reported rather than the Pearson coefficient.

correlated measurement error: Errors in measurements that are not independent of the true quantities. Compared to *random measurement error*, this type of error is malignant and can be fatal in evaluating a theoretical argument.

correlation matrix: A table of correlation coefficients between every pair of variables arranged in a row by column format. The row and column locations identify the pair of variables. Thus, the coefficient appearing in the second row, third column (symbolized as r_{23}), is the correlation between the second and third variable. Placing short descriptive labels at the top of each column and in the left-most position of each row makes it easy to identify each pair of variables.

Cronbach's alpha: A popular measure of internal consistency among multiple indicators of what the researcher considers to be a common underlying theoretical concept. A common use is in constructing overall measures of attitude (or value or belief) from a number of individual attitude items on a given topic. Coefficients less than approximately 0.7 are problematic. That is, it might be better not to obtain an overall summated measure but to use the items (or some subset of them) individually.

error variance: In classical measurement theory, that part of the observed variance of a measure that results from random measurement error. If it is assumed that the true score is uncorrelated with the error component, then the remainder of the variance is attributed to true differences in the cases being investigated.

external consistency: The criterion that the indicators of a common concept have similar connections to other events. That is, if one of the indicators shows a positive connection to some event, then the other indicators of the concept must also be positively related to that event. Example: If standing close to and desiring to spend time with a particular other person are to be considered indicators of the concept "attraction," then if one of them is positively related to interpersonal agreement, then so must the other be.

indicator: An empirical event that, under defined conditions, is argued to be a manifestation of a particular concept. Example: In Durkheim's theory of suicide, marital status, number of children and religious affiliation are argued to be indicators of anomie (with single people, childless couples, and Protestants being structurally in a more anomic condition than their respective counterparts).

internal consistency: When creating summated measures, the requirement that the individual scale items co-vary. Internal consistency is one approach to quantifying the reliability of a measure. It requires us to have two or more simultaneous alternate measures of a latent concept. If the two indicators are indeed measures of a single concept, then, in the absence of measurement error, the correlation between the two would be 1.0, indicating perfect internal consistency. Usually the correlations are much lower, because the variation in any given indicator results from a multitude of factors in addition to the theoretical concept.

internal consistency reliability: Any of a variety of measures of reliability that are based on the covariance of two or more indicators of a presumed common concept. The symbol for such reliability is r_{xx}. This properly indicates the correlation of a variable with (another measure of) itself and captures the notion of internal consistency. Example: Cronbach's alpha.

latent concept: The underlying theoretical factor that we postulate to cause our empirical indicators to vary. Thinking in terms of a broad theoretical concept that has many empirical manifestations is one device for achieving parsimony. Hence latent concepts are social constructions that postulate a commonality among seemingly disparate phenomena. Example: Attraction is a latent concept; choosing to spend time with and physical closeness when speaking to a particular person are two possible indicators.

measurement error: The discrepancy between the measured value and the "true" value of an observation. All sources of unreliability and invalidity produce measurement error. Two types of measurement error are distinguished: random and systematic. *Random measurement error* decreases the reliability of a measure, and *systematic measurement error* decreases the validity. The latter form of measurement error is particularly pernicious for theoretical arguments.

measurement model: The case made for connecting certain empirical measures with a given latent concept. Measurement models make auxiliary assumptions concerning the meaning of the empirical phenomena. Thus, if we use physical distance while speaking to another person as a manifestation of attraction, we assume that both members of the pair have a shared sense of personal space that they protect from invasion from non-intimates. This assumption is often violated when the members of the dyad are from different cultures. Measurement models create a serious dilemma for the falsifiability criterion in theory testing: if an empirical result does not support a theoretical expectation, either the theory is wrong *or* the measurement model is deficient. Invariably the culprit is seen to be the measurement model, permitting us to retain our favourite theories. The path out of this morass involves greater attention to the measurement model.

measurement precision: The exactness with which a phenomenon is measured. Example: Income may be recorded in dollars and rounded to the nearest thousand dollars. The latter measure is less precise.

parsimony principle: A criterion for evaluating the merits of a theory. This principle pays premiums for simplicity and generality: the less assumptions that need to be made and the more phenomena that are potentially explained by a given theory, the greater its parsimony. Within a given theory, parsimony also refers to the complexity of additional assumptions that are invoked to account for the phenomenon at hand.

random measurement error: Measurement error that is uncorrelated with the true score. In repeated measures, such error would be expected to have a mean of zero in the long run, with instances of overestimating balanced by those of underestimating the true score. It is a "benign" error since many of its effects are known in advance: it does not bias our estimate of the population mean, for example, but it does inflate our estimate of the population standard deviation. Measurement error that is not random is called *systematic or correlated error*. It is tempting to assume that all measurement error is random, since this simplifying assumption permits convenient formulas for quantifying reliability. This temptation must be resisted.

reliability: The extent to which repeated or multiple measures of a variable are consistent. When quantified, it is measured either as test-retest consistency or as internal consistency. In both situations the reliability is defined as the extent to which the measures co-vary; that is, the ratio of the covariance of the measures to their variances represents reliability. Hence the reliability coefficient can range from 0.0 to 1.0. Cronbach's alpha is the most popular measure of reliability.

repeated measures reliability: Also known as "test-retest," repeated measures are one of two main approaches to assessing the reliability of an indicator (the other is the internal consistency approach). As the name suggests, a measure is obtained at two points in time. The time interval between the two measures must be long enough to insure independence between the test and the retest (i.e., long enough that participants cannot recall the response they provided initially) and yet not so long that genuine change has occurred. The main advantage of repeated measures is that there is no danger of adding apples to oranges (we have a *single* indicator at two points in time). The difficulty with this approach is to separate measurement error from true change. It would seem to be the preferred approach for stable phenomena, where major change would not be expected on a daily or weekly basis.

test-retest reliability: Another term for *repeated measures reliability*.

theoretical isomorphism: The criterion for a good indicator which stipulates that the features of the measures possess the same properties as the theoretical features of the concept.

true score: In classical measurement theory, the belief that a true amount of the variable in question characterizes an object. This belief is more useful in some contexts than in others. In particular, for certain external, physical features this belief is unproblematic. For more fluid features, such as the level of agreement between two people, it may not be as useful an approach. In the classical measurement approach, the true score is that part of the observed score that does not result from measurement error.

true variance: In the classical approach to measurement, that part of the observed variance that is attributed to true differences in values among the cases being studied. If it is assumed that the true and error components are uncorrelated, then the remaining variance is defined as error variance. The concept of true variance is meaningful in those situations in which it is meaningful to conceptualize the observed score as having true and error components.

validity: The term used to refer to whether a given indicator captures the intended concept. Establishing validity is a most difficult task, because it presupposes that the theoretical link between the concept and a particular empirical manifestation is known. *Correlated measurement error* is a major threat to the validity of measures.

Chapter 8

REGRESSION ANALYSIS

The statistical technique known as regression analysis condenses massive amounts of information into simple and powerful equations. It accomplishes this by imposing a variety of simplifying assumptions on the data. However, because violation of these assumptions can produce nonsense, it is also a potentially dangerous technique. Two things can be done in advance to minimize the danger. First, regression analysis should be undertaken only after extensive preliminary analysis, using the techniques developed in the previous chapters. Such preliminary analysis often reveals certain danger signals, such as the presence of outliers; distributions that are far from normal; minimal variation; or an excessive number of "missing cases."

Secondly, when the number of observations (cases) is not too large, **scatter plots** can be extremely useful.[1] Scatter plots provide a visual representation of the relationship between two variables. Figure 8.1 provides such a plot for vessel length and number of fishing licenses. Conventionally, the independent variable is plotted along the horizontal axis, and the dependent variable is plotted along the vertical axis. In Figure 8.1, the horizontal axis represents the mean number of licenses; the vertical axis indicates the mean length of the vessels. Each point in the plot represents the scores for one community. I have identified one of the communities: White Point. The X-score for this community is 2.07 and the Y-score is 26, and the two scores together determine the location of this data point on the plot.[2]

An examination of the scatter plot frequently points to possible difficulties. Outliers show up as points along the edges of the plot, distanced from the next closest point. Lack of variability reveals itself by a dense clustering of points on either axis. Unlikely *combinations* of values appear as isolated points in regions where there are few points. For example, if the ages of brides and grooms were plotted, the combination where the groom is 22 years of age and his bride is 40 years of age, although possible, is unlikely. Such points would show up quite starkly in the scatter plot, even though they would not show up in the univariate analysis, since it is not uncommon to have brides aged 40 and grooms aged 22; it is the combination of these two characteristics that is unusual. Such cases should be examined closely since they may represent nothing more than data entry error (for example, a bride's age was actually 20 but was erroneously entered as 40). Such deviant cases can exert an undue influence on the regression results. Finally, the form of the relationship is suggested by visualizing the "curve" of the plotted points.

Figure 8.1
Scatter Plot of Mean Number of Fishing
Licenses by Vessel Length

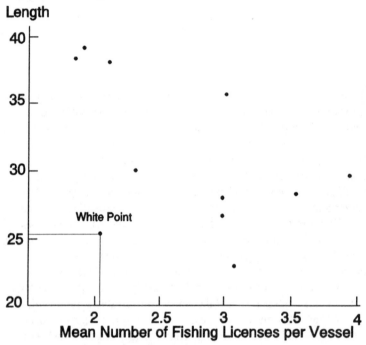

Source: Constructed from data supplied by DFO, 1988.

A reminder about assumptions: the very act of plotting the points in a two-dimensional space treats the variables of interest as though they had interval numeric properties. This is the most basic assumption of regression analysis. It would be absurd to perform regression analysis on categorical data. At the same time, most social scientists would consider applying regression techniques to ordinal data, but with caution.

Figure 8.1 shows that there are no outliers and that sufficient variability exists. Visualizing the form of the relationship is more difficult, since the points do not form a clear line. This is not unusual for several reasons. First, it is unrealistic to think that the number of licenses is the sole, or even the most important, determinant of vessel length. It is simply one of a number of possible determinants. This problem will be addressed in Chapter 9, when we will be in a position to look at the simultaneous effects of several independent variables on a given dependent variable.

Secondly, each of the variables contains measurement error. Our measures are often considered imperfect indicators of underlying or latent concepts. The concepts may be closely related to each other, but the indicators only loosely so. Vessel length, for example, is one possible indicator of the concept "fishing capacity." This concept cannot be measured directly. We can imagine that fishing capacity is more systematically and strongly related to number of commercial fishing licenses held than is vessel length. In Chapter 7, we saw that such measurement error weakens the observed relationship.

A standard strategy in theoretical arguments is to express relationships among events in the simplest fashion possible. This is another aspect of the parsimony principle. A **linear equation** is the simplest mathematical form of the relationship between two variables. Hence, in examining scatter plots, we focus on whether a straight line would describe the relationship reasonably well. Stated differently, does the scatter plot indicate that a form more complex than a linear one is necessary to describe the relationship? We will see below how well a straight line captures the relationship for the data plotted in Figure 8.1.

Obtaining the Least-Squares Regression Equation

Remember from high school geometry that any straight line can be expressed as:

$$Y = bX + a \tag{8.1}$$

where b is the **slope** of the line and a is the **Y-intercept**. The slope informs how much change in Y is associated with one unit of change in X. The Y-intercept is the value of Y when X equals zero. Take, for example, the linear equation which converts temperature from a Celsius to a Fahrenheit scale:

$$F = 1.8C + 32.$$

The slope indicates that one Celsius degree (C) is worth 1.8 Fahrenheit degrees (F). The Y-intercept reveals that a temperature of 0°C translates to 32°F. Using this equation, we know that 20°C is the same as 68°F $[(1.8)(20) + 32 = 68]$. In like manner, all other temperatures can be converted.

The distinction between dependent and independent variables is used in a variety of contexts that carry different connotations. In the most restrictive sense, the independent variable is the presumed cause of change in the value of the dependent variable. From an experimental-design point of view, the independent variable is the "treatment" being given, and the dependent variable is the observed "effect" this treatment has. In this context, it is usually assumed that the treatment causes the effect. In survey research, the dependent variable is the one whose variation we want to explain, while the independent variable is the one being used to explain. In regression analysis, the dependent variable is simply the one that appears on the left side of the equation. That is, conventionally the Y variable is called the dependent variable and the X variable is called the independent variable. Since we used number of fishing licenses to predict vessel length, the latter is the dependent variable.

Although linear equations are simple, the concept of **regression analysis** is less so. It involves finding the "best" straight line to express the relationship between X and Y. Our first task is to define what is meant by the "best" line.

Since observed relationships are rarely, if ever, perfect, the observed values of Y generally do not equal those predicted by the regression equation. To avoid confusion, the symbol Y is used for the observed value, and the symbol $\hat{Y}$ for the predicted value of the dependent variable. To clarify this, let's draw our scatter plot again, this time including a possible straight line to summarize the relationship between X and Y.

The straight line drawn in Figure 8.2 captures the relation between number of licenses and vessel length moderately well. Each point on this straight line represents a particular $\hat{Y}$, since it is the **predicted value of Y** for observations having that particular X-score. The vertical distances between the data points and the prediction line (i.e., $Y - \hat{Y}$) represent error if we were to use this particular line. It represents the deviations of the predicted Y from the observed Y. In other words, the distances $(Y - \hat{Y})$ capture the amount of error incurred in expressing Y as a linear function of X.

Figure 8.2
Fitting a Line Through a Scatter Plot

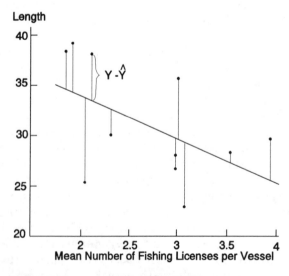

Source: Constructed from data supplied by DFO, 1988.

We might be tempted to define the best straight line as the one which minimizes these distances. However, we encounter the same problem we met in constructing measures of dispersion: negative and positive deviations cancel each other. Since some of our predictions overestimate and others underestimate, we have both negative and positive errors, which would cancel each other and would not provide a useful measure. We therefore apply the same solution we used for defining variance, namely to square the distances. We consider the best straight line the one which minimizes the average *squared* error. This line, known as the **least-squares regression equation**, minimizes the following:

$$\frac{\sum (Y - \hat{Y})^2}{N}. \tag{8.2}$$

Note the conceptual and symbolic similarities of this expression with the concept of the variance of a variable. Remember that one way of interpreting variance is that it represents the average squared error when the mean is used as the "best guess" for any outcome. Similarly, the above expression can be thought of as the variance around the regression line. This variance around the regression line represents the average squared error when the least regression equation is used as the "best guess" for any outcome.

Remember also that we took the square root of the variance to approximate the original unsquared units of measurement. For the same reason, the square root is taken of the variance around the regression equation and called the **standard error of estimate** of Y (abbreviated as s_e). That is,

$$s_e = \sqrt{\frac{\sum (Y - \hat{Y})^2}{N - 2}}. \tag{8.3}$$

The denominator is $N - 2$ rather than N since two degrees of freedom are lost when calculating $\hat{Y}$, corresponding to the sample estimates of the slope and Y - intercept.[3] The next task is to find those values of b and a that will minimize these squared errors. It turns out that b is the ratio of the covariance of X and Y divided by the variance of X . That is:

$$b = \frac{Cov(X,Y)}{Var(X)} \tag{8.4}$$

and the Y -intercept is given by:

$$a = \bar{Y} - b\bar{X}. \tag{8.5}$$

The definitional equation for the slope is:

$$b = \frac{\sum(X - \overline{X})(Y - \overline{Y})}{\sum(X - \overline{X})^2}. \qquad (8.6)$$

To compute the slope manually, use:

$$b = \frac{N\sum XY - (\sum X)(\sum Y)}{[N\sum X^2 - (\sum X)^2]}. \qquad (8.7)$$

Note the similarity of these equations with those for the Pearson correlation coefficient. The numerator is identical, whereas the denominator contains only the variance of X rather than the standard deviation of both X and Y. This implies a close connection between least-squares regression and Pearson correlations, which indeed there is. The similarity can be expressed as:

$$r = b\left(\frac{s_x}{s_y}\right). \qquad (8.8)$$

We learned in Chapter 3 that many measures of concepts in the social sciences do not have a meaningful zero. The value of the Y-intercept (the predicted value of Y when X has a value of zero) is consequently also often meaningless. It is therefore sometimes preferable to express the X-scores in terms of deviations from the mean of X, as in equation 8.9:

$$\hat{Y} = b(X - \overline{X}) + \overline{Y}. \qquad (8.9)$$

Note that, in this form, the Y-intercept simplifies to the mean of Y.

The worksheet used for calculating the correlation between vessel length and number of licenses can also be used for calculating the regression coefficients. Table 8.1 reproduces the worksheet previously given in Table 6.4. Substituting the appropriate numbers for b into equation 8.6 we get:

$$b = \frac{12(977.49) - (31.89)(375.27)}{12(90.31) - (31.89)(31.89)} = -3.56.$$

Table 8.1
Worksheet for Computing the Least-Squares Regression Coefficients

	Mean Number of Licenses (X)	Mean Vessel Length (Y)	XY	X²	Y²
Little Dover	3.07	23.46	72.02	9.42	550.37
White Point	2.07	26.00	53.82	4.28	676.00
Neil's Harbour	2.95	26.58	78.41	8.61	706.49
New Haven	2.95	2.79	81.98	8.70	772.28
Petit de Gras	3.58	29.23	104.64	12.81	854.39
Whale Cove	2.22	29.67	65.86	4.92	880.30
Canso	4.07	29.86	121.53	16.56	891.61
Dingwall	2.15	31.37	67.44	4.62	984.07
Sandy Cove	3.00	35.63	106.89	9.00	1,269.49
Little River	1.80	37.93	68.27	3.24	1,438.68
Woods Harbour	2.15	38.75	83.31	4.62	1,501.56
East Ferry	1.88	39.00	73.32	3.53	1,521.00
TOTALS	31.89	375.27	977.49	90.31	12,046.24

Source: Compiled from data supplied by DFO, September 1988.

According to equation 8.8, our Y-intercept is:[4]

$$a = 31.27 - (-3.56)(2.66) = 40.7.$$

With these solutions, the complete regression equation is:

$$\hat{Y} = -3.56X + 40.7.$$

Taking two examples, for any community in which the number of licenses per vessel is two, we would predict an average vessel length of:

$$\hat{Y} = -3.56(2) + 40.74 = 33.6.$$

That is, we predict a vessel length of 33.6 feet. Similarly, we predict an average vessel length of 26.5 feet for any community which averaged four licenses per vessel. We predict only in the sense of projecting the observed relationship between X and Y onto additional cases not observed.

A caution is necessary here. In any application, the computed regression equation is valid only within the range of the values of X actually encountered. The average number of licenses in the communities represented in Table 8.1 ranged from about two to four. It would be unwarranted to predict the vessel size for communities with an average of six licenses, since it has not been established that the calculated relationship would extend to communities with such a high number of licenses per vessel.

A second way to read this equation is to state the "worth" of licenses in terms of length of boats. That is, the slope indicates how many feet a license is worth on average. In our example, a license is "worth" approximately three and a half additional feet of vessel length.

Where regression analysis is used primarily to describe the relationship between X and Y in the sample, it would be somewhat misleading to call the Y the "predicted" Y. However, sample data is sometimes used to make predictions about population relationships. For example, we might use sample data to predict how much additional income is likely to accrue for each additional year of education. In such situations, it is quite proper to think of $\hat{Y}$ as a predicted value of Y.

Evaluating the Least-Squares Regression Equation

Earlier in this chapter, the similarity in equations between the least-squares slope and the Pearson correlation coefficient was noted. This section expands on the connection to show that the square of the Pearson correlation coefficient (r^2) may be used to evaluate how well the least-squares equation fits the data.

To do this, we must recall two aspects of distributions discussed in Chapter 3. The first is that, in the absence of any additional information, the mean of a distribution can be considered the best guess for any case since the average signed error always equals zero. The second is that the variance of a distribution informs us how good an estimate the mean is. Stated differently, the variance tells how much (squared) error there will be on average if we use the mean as the predicted value. Both of these ideas are intimately involved in the interpretation of the correlation coefficient and the linear regression equation.

In essence, we pit two estimation models against each other. The first model, which acts as a comparison base, predicts that any score is equal to the mean score for that variable. That is:

$$\hat{Y} = \overline{Y}.$$

We seldom actually expect our observations to equal Y. Why then would we set up this model? The answer is that, in the absence of additional information, this is the best prediction for the value of any Y. Furthermore, the variance around Y quantifies how good this base model is, since it is a measure of the average squared error. The base model acts as a minimum standard against which we will evaluate alternative models. Our predictions are always at least as good as those offered by this model. It is the simplest model and, in line with the parsimony principle, would be used when alternative models being considered do not appreciably improve on it.

How can we tell whether the regression model is better? Notice that the linear model degenerates to the base model whenever the slope is zero, since the regression equation under such a condition simplifies to $\hat{Y} = \overline{Y}$, through the following steps:

$$\hat{Y} = b(X - \overline{X}) + \overline{Y}.$$

This model predicts a value of Y on the basis of a linear relationship between X and Y. This is the second-simplest model. Remember that this model does not test whether there is a linear relation; it simply predicts values of Y on the basis of the best linear relation. Since this model is more complex than the base model (we need to know the value of X in order to predict Y), we would not use this model if it did not lead to appreciably better predictions than the base model.

How can we tell whether the regression model is better? Notice that the linear model degenerates to the base model whenever the slope is zero, since the regression equation under such a condition simplifies to $\hat{Y} = \overline{Y}$, through the following steps:

$$\hat{Y} = b(X - \overline{X}) + \overline{Y}.$$

Setting the slope to zero:

$$\hat{Y} = O(X - \overline{X}) + \overline{Y}.$$

And since multiplying any number by zero results in zero:

$$\hat{Y} = \overline{Y}.$$

In the regression model, the criterion for the linear relation to be found is that it results in the smallest variance around the predicted value. That is, our criterion is that the variance around the prediction line be a minimum. As a result, the variance around the regression line can't exceed the variance around the mean. At worst, the two will be identical, and this will happen when the best linear equation is simply the horizontal line representing $\overline{Y}$. In such situations, the slope b is zero.[5]

Our next problem is to quantify the fit of the regression model relative to the base model. The **coefficient of determination** (r^2) serves such a purpose by comparing the variance around the regression equation with the variance around the mean of Y. The predicted value of Y in the regression equation is symbolized as $\hat{Y}$, while in the base model it is $\overline{Y}$. Thus the two variances that will be compared are:

base model: $$\frac{\sum (Y - \bar{Y})^2}{N}.$$

regression model: $$\frac{\sum (Y - \hat{Y})^2}{N}.$$

The difference between these two models is illustrated in Figure 8.3. The least-squares regression line for this set of data is $\hat{Y} = -3.56X + 40.7$. Each point on the regression line is the predicted mean vessel length for that number of licenses. Different vessel lengths are predicted for different mean number of licenses. Remember that under the base model only one vessel length is predicted, namely the mean vessel length for the entire sample under study. But note that for any given number of licenses, only one vessel length is predicted. In other words, all communities with an average of two licenses per vessel are predicted to have an average vessel length of 33.62 feet. Of course, few communities do, and this is why observed vessel lengths seldom fall on the regression line.

Figure 8.3
Partitioning "Error" Distances

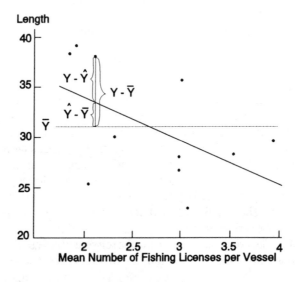

Source: Constructed from data supplied by DFO, 1988.

The dotted horizontal line above the the X-axis represents $\bar{Y}$, the prediction "line" based on the base model. This line indicates that regardless of the number of licenses per vessel, we predict the vessel length to be the mean vessel length.

To increase our understanding of the meaning of the correlation coefficient and its relationship to the regression line, let's look at the scatter plot from a different point of view. What we will do is to come up with a numerical estimate of the magnitude of "error" in the base model and the regression model. In Figure 8.3, three points, Y, $\hat{Y}$ and $\bar{Y}$, are labelled and a vertical line from Y to $\bar{Y}$ is drawn; Y is the observed outcome for one case and $\bar{Y}$ is the average score, as well as the score predicted from the base model. Hence the distances $Y-\bar{Y}$ are the "errors" using the base model. In like fashion, the error using the regression model is the distance $Y-\hat{Y}$. The total distance $Y-\bar{Y}$ can now be expressed as the sum of two components: (1) the distance from the observed value of Y to the regression line, $Y-\hat{Y}$, and (2) the distance from the regression line to the mean, $\hat{Y}-\bar{Y}$:

$$Y - \bar{Y} = (Y - \hat{Y}) + (\hat{Y} - \bar{Y}). \tag{8.10}$$

We have just noted that the distance $Y - \hat{Y}$ is the error using the regression model. Hence the distance $\hat{Y} - \bar{Y}$ must be the distance "explained" by the regression equation which is left unexplained by the base model. Stated differently, the distance $\hat{Y} - \bar{Y}$ represents the improvement of the regression model over the base model. We cannot use these distances directly, since their sum is always zero. As might be expected by now, we solve the problem by squaring the deviations:

$$(Y - \bar{Y})^2 = (Y - \hat{Y})^2 + 2(Y - \hat{Y})(\hat{Y} - \bar{Y}) + (\hat{Y} - \bar{Y})^2. \tag{8.11}$$

Having squared both sides, we have an unwanted middle term which is the cross-product between the "explained" and the "unexplained" distances. Earlier we showed that cross-products are really measures of correlation. Hence this term would disappear if the correlation between the explained and unexplained distances was zero. Stated differently, if the error in prediction using the regression equation is not correlated with the value of X, then the middle term cancels out. Hence we will have to assume that the errors are uncorrelated. This means that we assume that for any level of X, the positive errors cancel the negative errors. Expressing equation 8.11 in terms of the implied variances (and assuming uncorrelated errors), we get:

Total Variance = Explained Variance + Unexplained Variance.

If the variance around the regression line is almost as large as the variance of Y, then the regression model is not much better than the base model. What we'd like is a measure of *how much* better the regression model is. The solution is to calculate the *proportionate reduction* in variance using the regression model as compared to the base model. This is obtained by forming the ratio of the explained variance to the total variance. In terms of the error variance, this is equivalent to:

$$1 - \frac{\Sigma(Y - \hat{Y})^2}{\Sigma(Y - \bar{Y})^2}. \qquad (8.12)$$

Under the condition of uncorrelated error, the above formula is another way of expressing the coefficient of determination, r^2. For the data in Figure 8.1, $r = -0.43$, and $r^2 = 0.18$. Thus, just under one-fifth of the variance in mean vessel length is accounted for or explained by the variance in mean number of licenses.

Standardized Regression Coefficients

As stated previously, the slope is defined as the amount of change in a dependent variable (Y) associated with one unit of change in the independent variable (X). Where the units of measurement for X and Y are meaningful, such an interpretation of the slopes provides substantial information. Thus we were able to express the worth of licenses in terms of vessel length. Equations using the original units of measures are called **raw equations**.

Frequently the units of our measures do not correspond to any consensually established "yardsticks." The units in Likert scales are arbitrary in that sense. In such situations, the **raw slopes** are not very satisfactory, since their magnitude is a function of the arbitrary units of measurement. This makes substantive comparison of slopes difficult. To overcome this disadvantage, the regression equations are standardized. That is, the relationship is expressed using standard deviations as the unit of measurement. Such equations are called **standardized equations**, and the slopes of such equations are called **standardized slopes** or, interchangeably, **beta weights**. This makes it easier to compare slopes from different equations and with different independent variables, since they now use comparable units of measurement: the standard deviations. In standardized form, the slope indicates how many standard deviations of change in the dependent variable are associated with one standard deviation of change in the independent variable.

It is not necessary to convert raw scores into standard scores to obtain the standardized regression equation. Instead, it can be shown that, in the bivariate case, the standardized slope is identical to the Pearson correlation coefficient:

$$\hat{z}_y = rz_x. \qquad (8.13)$$

Substituting equation 8.8 for the Pearson correlation coefficient, the standardized regression equation can also be expressed as:

$$\hat{z}_y = b\left(\frac{s_x}{s_y}\right). \qquad (8.14)$$

That is, the standardized slope can be obtained by multiplying the raw slope by the ratio of the standard deviation of X to the standard deviation of Y. Different standardized slopes can be compared to provide estimates of the relative importance of several different independent variables.

Evaluating Linearity

When using regression and correlation techniques, it is often difficult to distinguish exciting from discouraging results. More often than not, the initial results provide some, but not compelling, support for the argument. A number of procedures can help us evaluate and improve the findings. Chapter 7 showed, for example, how measurement error weakens observed relationships and how index construction can improve the fit. Here, we will assess one other possible source of discouraging results: non-linear relationships.

Keep in mind that an important goal of social science arguments is to organize our treatment of events in such a way that irrelevant aspects are ignored. Our aim is to provide succinct statements of the relevant aspects of a given situation. In other words, we want to describe events as simply as possible, but also as accurately as necessary for evaluating our argument.

The statistical techniques developed so far represent increasingly sophisticated ways of doing this. In every technique, certain features are considered irrelevant, at least temporarily. In regression analysis we describe the relationship between two variables as though the connection between them were linear. Take the relationship between the number of premiers a respondent can name, and the left-right placement of the PCs relative to the NDP. The results of the REGRESSION procedure indicates that the slope is 0.12 and that r^2 is 0.05. The calculated slope indicates that each additional premier a respondent can name results in placing the NDP 0.12 units further to the left of the PCs. The coefficient of determination reveals that our measure of political knowledge accounts for five percent of the variance in this measure of party imagery. In Chapter 7 we documented that even when using a more reliable summated index for party imagery, less than eight percent of the variance in party imagery was explained by political knowledge. This was less than hoped for. The question here is whether the observed relationship is weak because of non-linearity. Is the relationship between political knowledge and party imagery more complex than postulated? The regression equation described the association between political knowledge and party imagery as a simple linear relationship. But the world is sometimes more complex than this (which prompted the Peanuts cartoon to exclaim one day: "Happiness is a linear relationship"). As developed so far, regression analysis treats events as though they were linear, even when they patently are not. Sometimes we can ignore non-linearities as irrelevant abberations. Usually we do this when we have no plausible interpretation for non-linearities. But we must be careful that this doesn't paint a misleading picture. This requires us to evaluate the extent to which the relationship deviates from a linear one.

A simple visual way to capture departures from linearity involves plotting the conditional means. In Chapter 3, we calculated the mean relative left-right placement of the PCs separately for every number of premiers known.

An important feature of the least-squares regression line is that it passes through the conditional means if and only if the most accurate description of the relationship is indeed a linear one. This permits a very simple geometric check for linearity: see to what extent the conditional means can be connected by a straight line. If they depart widely, then some non-linear form would be substantially better to use. If they do not depart widely, then the linear form is perhaps the best one that can be used to describe the relationship. Figure 8.4 provides the plot of the conditional means for the party imagery example. Clearly, imposing a linear relationship on this data is eminently reasonable and not the cause for the low explained variance.

Figure 8.4
Plot of Conditional Means

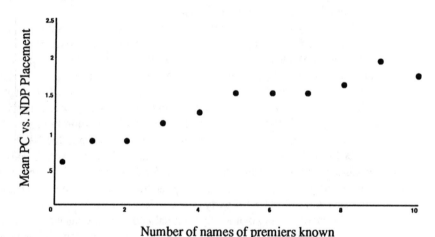

Number of names of premiers known

Source: 1984 CNES

Making Inferences about Population Parameters

Regression techniques can be used to describe a relationship in the sample, as well as to predict outcomes for cases not contained in the sample. For the descriptive use, no assumptions other than those already discussed are necessary. To review, these assumptions are that:

- It is meaningful to treat the variables under consideration as though they possessed interval-level characteristics.

- It is a tolerable simplification to treat the relationship between X and Y as linear.
- The calculated slope was not unduly influenced by the location of outliers.
- The prediction errors are uncorrelated with the values of X (this assumption was explored in depth in Chapter 7).

If we use sample data to make inferences about population parameters, a number of additional assumptions must be made. Before discussing these, let's look at the context in which inferences about populations are made in regression analysis.

Continuing to use Greek letters to represent population parameters, the letter β (beta) is conventionally used to represent the population slope. Similarly, α (alpha) is used to represent the population Y-intercept.

It is seldom the case that the population Y-intercept is of interest, since a meaningful Y-intercept presupposes meaningful zero values for both X and Y variables. However, the value of the population slope, β, is of vital importance in many examples of social science research. It is used to pit the base model against the regression model. Remember that the regression model degenerates to the base model when the slope is zero. The concern is not whether the sample slope is zero, but rather whether the population slope is zero. We want to be reasonably certain that the population slope, β, is not zero before we conclude that the linear model improves on the base model.

The logic of hypotheses testing, as developed in Chapter 5, is used for this purpose. Under certain conditions, the Student's t-distribution can be used to test hypotheses concerning the population slope. The equation is:

$$t = \frac{b - \beta}{s_b} \tag{8.15}$$

where t = computed value of Student's t
b = computed slope from sample data
β = null-hypothesized population slope (usually 0), and
s_b = standard error of b.

Statisticians have shown that under certain conditions, the standard error of b is given by:

$$s_b = \frac{s_e}{\sqrt{\sum (X - \bar{X})^2}}. \tag{8.16}$$

We can now test whether the regression model is significantly better statistically than the base model. In simple (bivariate) regression, such tests of significance do not add much information to the argument. In the context of multiple regression, however, these tests of significance can be very useful. Let's therefore delay applications of these tests until Chapter 9.

Note that, in simple regression, testing the hypothesis that the population slope is zero is the same as testing that the population Pearson correlation coefficient is zero. That is, the decision that the population slope is zero is synonymous with the conclusion that the population correlation is zero. Conversely, the decision that β is not equal to zero is coterminous with the conclusion that there is a non-zero correlation between X and Y. Increasingly in the social science literature, the concern is more with slopes than with correlations. Since tests for slopes provide the necessary information to make conclusions about correlations, I will not provide the equations used to test the correlations directly.

When sample statistics are used to make statements about population parameters, several additional restrictive assumptions must be made. These additional assumptions are necessary to ensure that the inferences being made about the population are valid.

The first restriction is known technically as the **homoscedasticity** assumption (the word is more frightening than the concept). Homoscedasticity is the assumption that the variance of Y is the same for every value of X. Figure 8.5 contrasts a distribution where the assumption of homoscedasticity is violated with one where it is not.

Figure 8.5
The Homoscedasticity Assumption

Homoscedasticity   Homoscedasticity
Fulfilled   Violated

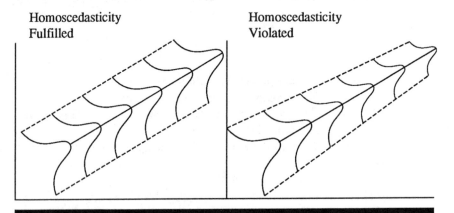

Why is the assumption of homoscedasticity necessary? Remember that the standard error of estimate of Y (s_e) is the average error in predicting Y. This standard error of estimate is a central ingredient in regression hypothesis testing (see equation 8.15). When the assumption of homoscedasticity is fulfilled, the amount of error in predicting Y is the same regardless of the value of X. But when the assumption of homoscedasticity is violated, the average error in predicting Y differs, depending on the value of X. In the case depicted in Figure 8.5, the average error in predicting Y decreases as X increases. That is, there is no single value of s_e appropriate for all values of X. Yet the significance test requires a single value. As a result, the confidence one has that the true slope is some particular number depends on where (at what value of X) the test is taken. In Figure 8.5, the range of likely values for β is much smaller at high values of X than at low values of X. Thus, tests concerning the population value of β should not be taken too literally when the homoscedasticity assumption is violated.

Conditional variances can be used to assess the homoscedasticity assumption informally. Let's return to the party imagery example. Look at the column labelled "Standard Deviation" in Table 4.8. Remembering that variances are nothing more than the squares of standard deviations, the conditional standard deviations reveal a clear violation of the homoscedasticity assumption. These conditional standard deviations start at a high of 1.92 and decrease to 0.71. Were we to create a scatter plot of the relationship between political knowledge and party imagery, the results would appear analogous to those in the right half of Figure 8.5.

This finding might seem discouraging because it indicates clearly that all tests of significance involving these variables will be problematic. That is, the results will contain a relatively high margin of error. At the same time, from the point of view of the argument that was being developed about party imagery, we might have been more devastated had homoscedasticity been found. Let me elaborate.

The argument being developed was that party imagery would be increasingly correct with increasing political knowledge. Up to this point in the argument, the focus has been on the conditional means. Our expectation that politically knowledgable individuals would be more likely to place the NDP to the left of the other federal parties was fulfilled. This empirical expectation, however, was derived from a more abstract hypothesis, namely that the party imagery of politically knowledgable individuals would be more correct than the imagery of those less knowledgable. From this more abstract, theoretical point of view, a second consequence should follow: with increasing political knowledge, party imagery should be less variable. There are many possible false party images, but only one correct one. Therefore the variation in imagery among the uninformed should be greater than among the knowledgable. At the lowest extreme of political knowledge, some individuals will place the NDP to the extreme right, others will place it to the extreme left. They can be expected to do the same for the PC party. Such apparently random placement of the parties relative to each other would result in high between-individual variation of party imagery among the politically uninformed.

At the other extreme, the party imagery of the politically knowledgable should be much closer to a constant, where everybody correctly sees the NDP as located to the left of the two other major federal parties. In short, if placing the NDP to the left of the PCs is the correct placement, and if political knowledge increases the likelihood of correct placement, then increasing political knowledge should result in decreasing variability in party imagery. That is precisely what the data shows.

Conditional normality is the final assumption. This is the assumption that Y is normally distributed around the conditional means of Y (that is, conditional on X). I have attempted to draw this assumption in Figure 8.5. To the extent that the normality assumption is violated, the calculated standard error of the slopes may be in error. There is unfortunately no simple way to test this assumption. The best we can do is to determine whether Y is univariately normal. This is of some help since a necessary (but not sufficient) condition for the fulfilment of the conditional normality assumption is that the distribution of Y is univariate normal. If Y is not normally distributed, then it is certain that this final assumption is violated.

Where Y is not normally distributed, it is sometimes possible to apply a transformation to Y that will make it approximately normal. For example, the natural log of income frequently normalizes the (usually pronounced) positively skewed income distribution.

Of course, one assumption common to all statistical inference is that the sample represents random information from a well-defined population.

The term *regression* is actually an abbreviation of the phrase **regression towards the mean.** These words mean that, in relative terms, the predicted variable is generally closer to the mean than the predictor variable. Stated differently, the predicted value of Y is generally closer to the mean of Y than is the observed value of X to its mean. This is easily shown using standard scores. Suppose the equation

$$Z_y = .52Z_x$$

adequately describes the relationship between two variables. Take the case where X is two standard deviations above the mean. In such a case, the predicted Y-score is just one standard deviation above the mean of Y. Note that the predicted Y-score is closer to its mean than is the X-score. Now remember that in standard form the slope of the regression equation is identical to the correlation coefficient (see equation 8.22). Thus the maximum possible slope is 1.0. In that limiting case, where X and Y stand in a perfect linear relationship to each other, there is no regression towards the mean. In all other instances, regression towards the mean occurs.

Observe the regression line in the scatter plot of Figure 8.2. Note that the lowest predicted values are higher than those observed, and, conversely, that the highest predicted values are lower than those observed. There is nothing mystical about this feature of the regression equation. This feature is simply built into the definition of the best straight line as the one that minimizes the squared error.

Is such a flatter slope desirable? In general, I would argue that it is. The rationale for such a conclusion rests on the assumption that the more extreme a score is, the less stable it is likely to be. This belief is based on the premise that an extreme score at a given point in time is the sum of two components: one genuine and one accidental. For example, the ten heaviest persons in any random sample have an extreme weight both because of their usual weight and because of unique factors operating to make these individuals particularly heavy at that particular time. The implication is that if you took the ten heaviest persons and weighed them again a month later, their *average* weight would be less. This average weight would now be closer to the *usual* weight. This is why I stated that extreme scores tend to be less stable.

This instability of extreme scores is at the root of the artifact usually referred to as the **regression fallacy**. This fallacy is likely in certain experimental settings. Let me take the weight example again to illustrate. Suppose I took a large sample of individuals, obtained their weight and then selected a sample of the most extremely overweight individuals for a special "treatment." Any treatment given, including no treatment at all, is likely to be "effective" in weight reduction of these individuals (i.e., to result in less extreme scores). Beware of diet claims concerning average weight reduction. The sample chosen was likely to have been extreme.

SPSS Instructions

Figure 8.6
SPSS Instructions for Obtaining Bivariate Plots

```
 1   DATA LIST FILE="dfoagg.raw" LIST
 2       /Numlic Vlength Bhp Tonnage.
 3   VAR LABELS
 4       Numlic  "Mean number of fishing licenses per vessel"
 5       Vlength "Mean vessel length"
 6       Bhp     "Mean British horsepower per vessel"
 7       Tonnage "Mean tonnage per vessel".
 8   PLOT
 9           /HSIZE=55
10           /VSIZE=25
11           /VERTICAL=MIN(20) MAX(40)
12           /TITLE="Fig. 8.1: Scatter plot"
13           /FORMAT=REGRESSION
14           /SYMBOLS= "."
15           /PLOT=vlength WITH numlic.
```

Lines 1-2 (Figure 8.6): Whenever raw data (rather than an SPSS system file) is used, the data must be defined by a DATA LIST instruction. The FILE="dfoagg.raw" part of the command informs SPSS that the data resides in a file of that name. The keyword LIST indicates that all the variables for each case are on a single line of information. That is, each line represents one case. Further, variables are separated from each other with either a blank or a comma. In the example supplied above, blanks were used to separate each variable. The final information, starting on the second line and beginning with a slash (/), assigns variable names to each of the variables on the data file being read. There are four variables in the data file. Variable names start with an alphabetic letter, must not exceed eight characters in length and must be composed of only alphabetic and numeric characters. The variable names are separated by blanks or commas.

Lines 3-7: These are the familiar VARIABLE LABELS. Here each of the short variable names is given an extended label. By default, the labels for the horizontal and vertical axes of the plots are taken from the information supplied by the VARIABLE LABELS instruction. Although these instructions are optional, they help document the output and therefore should ordinarily be included.

Line 8: This instruction invokes the PLOT procedure.

Lines 9-10: These are optional instructions which control the size of the plot. I wanted the plot to fit on a printed page. This was accomplished by setting the horizontal size (HSIZE) of the plot to fifty-five spaces (or columns). In similar fashion, the vertical size (VSIZE) was set to twenty-five lines (or rows).

Line 11: The PLOT procedure determines the lowest and highest values encountered for each variable and uses this information to provide numerical reference points at equal intervals along the X and Y axes. The numbers that result are sometimes not neat, round, whole numbers. By providing carefully chosen minimum and maximum numbers, control is retained over the reference numbers printed. A trial run of the data showed that the reference numbers for the Y-axes were not pleasing; by choosing a minimum value of twenty (which was somewhat lower than the actual minimum) and a maximum of forty, the vertical axis was given the desired reference values divisible by five.

Line 12: The optional TITLE subcommand produces a title for the plot. The desired title is enclosed in either single or double quotation marks. The title is printed, exactly as provided, at the beginning (or top) of the plot.

Line 13: This subcommand prints the symbol "R" on both the left and the right boundary of the vertical axis. Connecting the two symbols with a straight line locates the best-fitting least-squares regression line on the scatter plot. I have drawn this line in Figure 8.2.

Line 14: SPSS uses a combination of numbers and letters of the alphabet to indicate data points on the plot. With large data sets, multiple cases may fall at the same physical location. For this reason, SPSS has a default set of symbols to indicate how many cases fall at a given point. Thus, the symbol 1 by default indicates one case, 2 indicates two cases, and so on. These defaults can be changed with this subcommand. Since my data set was small, with no points overlapping, I chose to let a dot (.) represent one case. If I also wanted to change the symbol for two cases to an asterisk (*), the command would have been /SYMBOLS=".*".

Line 15: This is the only mandatory subcommand for the plot procedure. It informs SPSS which variables are to be plotted. Variables named before the WITH keyword are plotted on the vertical axis; those after this keyword are plotted along the horizontal axis. Where the PLOT procedure is used as a precursor to regression analysis, the dependent variable is conventionally plotted on the vertical axis and the independent variable on the horizontal axis.

The plot procedure also prints a variety of bivariate regression statistics such as the slope, Y-intercept, Pearson correlation, standard error of estimate, and significance level for evaluating the hypotheses that the population slope is zero.

Summary

- Increasingly in the social sciences, concern focuses on describing the form of the relationships among variables. The simplest form of relationship is linear. The simplicity and elegance of a linear model makes it enticing.
- A straight line can be drawn through any set of paired observations. A necessary first step therefore is to define and find the "best" straight line. The task of fitting a line through a set of data is called regression analysis. The **ordinary least squares** (OLS) criterion defines the best line as the one which minimizes the squared error around the regression line.
- Having defined a best line, it is important to develop a measure of the *goodness of fit* of the model being used, in this case, the OLS regression model. The coefficient of determination is such a measure. The coefficient of determination can be interpreted as the proportionate improvement of the OLS regression model over the base model. The base model simply uses the mean of Y as the predicted value of any case. It indicates the proportion of variance in the dependent variable explained by the independent variable.
- Regression analysis achieves its elegance by imposing restrictive assumptions on the data. Violation of these assumptions can produce profoundly misleading artifacts. It is therefore imperative that thorough analysis, using the techniques developed in the earlier chapters, be completed prior to attempting regression analysis.
- Preliminary analysis will provide useful clues to the presence and severity of problematic features of the data. In particular, univariate analysis of X and Y will indicate gross departures from normality, and the presence of outliers. A visual examination of the bivariate scatter plot would also show outliers and suggest the form of the relationship. The scatter plot is also useful for identifying deviant cases, i.e., cases with an unlikely combination of values. A plot of the conditional means will show marked deviations from linearity. The conditional standard deviations (produced by the SPSS means procedure) will suggest whether the homoscedasticity assumption has been violated.

- The distinction between sample statistics and population parameters introduced in Chapter 4 applies also to regression equations. The assumptions in regression analysis are particularly restrictive when sample data is used to make inferences about the population slope.
- Fruitful use of regression techniques is often possible even when some of the assumptions involved are known to be violated. Some of the assumptions, like uncorrelated error terms, are more crucial than others. Simulation studies suggest that OLS is robust with respect to violation of the homoscedasticity and conditional normality assumptions. As always, the important point is not whether certain assumptions have been violated, but whether the summarizing techniques being used provide valid insights into the phenomena under investigation. Having found, for example, that the assumption of homoscedasticity was violated in the party imagery example, support increased for the argument that political knowledge produced correct party imagery.

Notes

1. Where the number of cases is large, a plot of the conditional means is more likely to be fruitful. This is discussed later.
2. The SPSS instructions that produced a similar plot are presented at the end of this chapter.
3. Whether one divides by N or by $N-2$ depends on whether one is describing the sample or making inferences about the population. In the former case, dividing by N would be permissible. However, since most of the time the s_e is used to make inferences about the population, it is conventional to always divide by $N-2$. Remember that the same consideration applies to the concept of variance. When the concept of variance is used to describe a sample, the denominator is simply N. When the sample variance is used to estimate the variance of the population, the denominator is $N-1$, since one degree of freedom is lost in calculating the sample mean.
4. The mean of X and Y (2.66 and 31.27, respectively) is obtained by dividing the sum of X (31.89) and the sum of Y (375.27) by 12, the number of cases.
5. The minimal criterion for deciding that the regression model surpasses the base model is that the slope is statistically significantly different from zero. We will cover such tests later in this chapter. Additionally, we want to have substantially smaller errors in prediction. As we shall see, the coefficient of determination can be used for this purpose.

Key Terms

beta weights: An alternative name for *standardized regression coefficients*. By expressing the impact of all independent variables in standard deviation units, it becomes possible to assess the relative importance of each predictor variable.

coefficient of determination: In bivariate analysis, the square of the Pearson product-moment correlation coefficient, symbolized as r^2. In regression analysis, it is a measure of how good a fit to the data the regression equation provides, since it can be read as the proportion of variance in Y that is explained by X. When using regression equations, it is customary to report the coefficient of determination for each equation.

conditional normality: An assumption in regression analysis is that the distribution of Y is normal for every value of X. Violation of the conditional normality assumption affects tests of the significance of the slope. If the overall distribution of Y is not normal, then the conditional distributions will also not be normal.

explained variance: In regression analysis, the variance of Y is partitioned into two parts: the explained and the unexplained. The explained variance is the part that co-varies with X. It is the average squared deviation from the predicted value of Y to the mean of Y, i.e.,

$$\frac{\Sigma(\hat{Y} - \bar{Y})^2}{N}.$$

homoscedasticity: One of the assumptions in regression analysis is that the variance of Y for a given value of X is the same as the variance of Y for any other value of X. Homoscedasticity is the term used to signify such equal conditional variances. Violation of this assumption affects tests of the significance of the slope.

least-squares regression equation: The most common form of regression analysis. The name derives from its feature that the *squares* of the vertical distance between the observed and predicted values of Y are minimized in this approach.

linear equation: An equation consisting of two unknowns (the slope and the Y-intercept) that expresses one variable as a linear function of the other. All linear equations have the general form:

$$Y = bX + a$$

where b is the slope and a the y-intercept. By convention, Y is called the dependent variable and X the independent variable. In social science research, a linear form of relationship is often imposed on the data and then the fit is evaluated.

ordinary least squares (OLS): The most common form of regression analysis, in which the squared vertical distances between the observed and predicted values of Y are minimized.

predicted value of Y: In bivariate regression analysis, it is the value of Y predicted on the basis of the value of X. In least-squares regression analysis, the predicted value of Y minimizes the sum of the squared vertical distances from the observed value of Y.

raw equations: Regression equations expressed in their original units. That is, regression equations that are not expressed in standard deviation units. Raw equations are useful when commonly understood units of measures are involved, such as years, dollars, feet and pounds. They are also generally preferred when comparing identical equations in several subgroups or populations.

raw slopes: Slopes in regression equations that are expressed in their original units of measure. That is, slopes which have been estimated using the equation:

$$b = \frac{\sum(X - \bar{X})(Y - \bar{Y})}{\sum(X - \bar{X})^2}.$$

When phenomena are measured in widely understood units, such as dollars and years, raw slopes provide a convenient way of communicating regression results. Hypothetically, if the raw slope for predicting income from education were 3,000, we could phrase this result in ways such as: "Our analysis estimates that each additional year of education is worth $3,000 in increased earnings."

regression analysis: Statistical techniques used to produce a "best fitting" equation for a data set. A criterion for "best fitting" must be defined. The least-squared error is the most common criterion; in bivariate regression, it minimizes the sum of the squared vertical distances between the observed and predicted Y values.

regression fallacy: The fallacy of attributing the artifactual regression towards the mean to the substantive properties of the phenomenon. Thus, for example, if we predict the height of girls from the height of their mothers, we would predict that daughters are typically shorter than mothers, which is patently not the case. Conversely, if we "postdict" the height of mothers from those of their daughters, we would conclude the opposite, namely that mothers are shorter than daughters.

regression towards the mean: The feature in least-squares regression where the value of Y for any case will be closer to the mean of Y than that case is to the mean of X. It is important to recognize that this feature is built into the least-squares regression equation and is not a substantive feature of the phenomenon being investigated. Failing to recognize the artifactual basis of the regression effect results in the "regression fallacy."

scatter plots: A graphic display of bivariate numeric data. The values of one variable are represented along the X-axis, and the values of the other on the Y-axis. Each case is represented as a single point whose location is determined by the intersection of its X and Y values on the graph. With small to moderate sample sizes (perhaps less than 300 or so) and with variables that have a potentially large range (such as income), it is an excellent preliminary screen of the data, because it permits us to visualize the form of the relationship and to detect the presence of problematic outliers.

slope: One of two unknowns in the equation for any straight line. The slope informs us how many units of change in the dependent variable (Y) are produced by one unit of change in the independent variable (X). In least-squares regression, the slope turns out to be the ratio of the covariance of X and Y over the variance of X. For any two variables, there are two possible slopes, and they are unlikely to have the same value.

For example, the slope for expressing the "worth" of an additional year of education on annual income will be different from the slope expressing how much additional education is associated with a dollar.

standard error of estimate: In the context of regression analysis, the square root of the variance around the regression line. It can be thought of as the average amount of error in predicting Y from X. As such it is a measure of how poor the regression equation is for predicting Y. In symbolic form,

$$s_e = \sqrt{\frac{\sum(Y - \hat{Y})^2}{N - 2}}.$$

standardized equations: Regression equations in which all variables are measured in standard deviation units. In this form, the Y-intercept becomes zero and drops out of the equation. The slopes in standardized equations are often referred to as *beta weights*. In bivariate regression, the standardized equation is:

$$\hat{z}_y = rz_x.$$

standardized slopes: Slopes expressed in standard deviation units. They can be calculated from the raw slope if the standard deviation of X and Y are known through the following equation:

$$\hat{z}_y = b\left(\frac{s_x}{s_y}\right).$$

unexplained variance: That part of the variance of Y that is not accounted for by its relationship to the independent variables. Symbolically it is:

$$\frac{\sum(Y - \hat{Y})^2}{N}.$$

It is this quantity that is minimized in the least-squares regression equation. The unexplained variance can be thought of as arising from four factors: (1) measurement error in the variables involved, (2) non-linearity in the relationships (in general, having a form different from the one implied by the equation), (3) multiple causes (additional causes not included in the equation), and (4) indeterminacy in the dependent variable (the possibility that the phenomenon being investigated is intrinsically probabilistic).

Y-intercept: The value of Y when the value of the independent variable X is zero. In bivariate regression, this is where the straight line crosses the Y-axis, and hence its name.

Chapter 9

MODELLING AND MULTIVARIATE ANALYSIS

Until now, we have been limited to univariate and bivariate techniques. If we had wanted to see the interrelationships among three variables, we could have done so only by treating them two at a time. That is, we were restricted to showing sequentially how the first variable was related to the second or the third, or how the second was related to the third. In this chapter, we will learn techniques that will permit us to analyze three or more variables simultaneously.

Some of the most important questions in social science arguments cannot be assessed, or even addressed, with bivariate techniques. The meaning of an observed relationship between two variables emerges from, and is constrained by, the relationships of both to still other variables. An observed positive relationship may disappear when a third variable is simultaneously introduced into the analysis. Conversely, apparently unrelated events may suddenly show an association when another variable is entered into the equation. The main reason for this is that the relationships between two variables is affected by the nature of the relationship of both to other variables.[1]

The reason that bivariate relationships can be misleading is that the various independent variables are themselves interrelated. These interrelationships cannot be taken into account with bivariate techniques.

Precisely because they sever the connections among the independent variables, experimental designs are usually considered the paragon of scientific methods. In experimental designs, random assignment of subjects into control and experimental groups has the effect of severing the connection of other variables with the experimental treatment.

With "naturally occurring" data, we emulate random assignment by specifically incorporating into the analysis all of the important interrelationships among the variables. As we will learn in this chapter, we can statistically "control" variables that might produce misleading results (assuming that we know which variables those are, and that we have obtained measures of them in the study).

Arguments frequently link a variety of events together. We can extend the party imagery example in this way. It is plausible that education would "correct" party imagery: the higher the educational level, the more likely that subjective party imagery would be correct. One can postulate that the specific mechanism that links education with party imagery is political knowledge. That is, education is related to party imagery because education increases political knowledge. If we use arrows to symbolize causal links, the theoretical argument would look like Figure 9.1.

Figure 9.1

Political Knowledge as an Intervening Link Between Level of Education and Correct Party Imagery

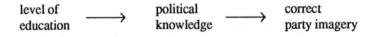

| level of education | $\longrightarrow$ | political knowledge | $\longrightarrow$ | correct party imagery |

In methodological parlance, political knowledge is considered an **intervening variable** between level of education and correct party imagery. Level of education is considered an **antecedent variable** to the relationship between political knowledge and correct party imagery. Additionally, the relationship between education and party imagery is indirect, because no arrow connects these two events directly.

If the argument outlined above is correct, several empirical results should follow:

- There should be a positive relationship between level of education and correct party imagery.
- There should be a positive relationship between level of education and political knowledge.
- The relationship between education and correct political knowledge should disappear when all three variables are analyzed simultaneously.

The reason for the last implication needs to be explained. As the argument is formulated, there is no direct link between education and correct party imagery. Think of the arrows as paths. The only path from education to party imagery is through political knowledge. Now imagine that a gate has been erected at political knowledge and that this gate is locked. In such a situation there is no possibility of getting to correct party imagery from education. This analogy points to a fundamental feature of multiple regression. Think of the slopes as paths. In multiple regression, each slope statistically "controls" for the other independent variables in the equation. These "controls" are analogous to gates. Including political knowledge in the equation "locks the gate" at that point. If the diagram is correct, it should then be impossible to get from educational level to correct party imagery. This "inability" to get from the antecedent to the dependent variable is represented statistically by a slope that is not significantly different from zero.

With this information, we are now in a position to develop the statistical manipulations that permit us to treat these three variables simultaneously.

Three-Variable Multiple Regression

The form of the **multiple regression equation** is a simple extension of the bivariate equation, namely:

$$\hat{Y} = b_1 X_1 + b_2 X_2 + a \qquad (9.1)$$

where X_1 = the first independent variable with a slope of b_1
$\quad\quad\;\; X_2$ = the second independent variable with a slope of b_2 and
$\quad\quad\;\; a$ = the Y-intercept (i.e., the point on the Y-axis where X_1
$\quad\quad\quad\quad$ and X_2 both equal zero).

In our case, $\hat{Y}$ is the predicted party imagery score, X_1 is political knowledge as measured by the number of names of premiers a respondent could identify, and X_2 is the respondent's level of education.[2]

A main difference from bivariate regression is that there are two slopes rather than one. This results in the prediction equation being a *plane* in three-dimensional space rather than a line in a two-dimensional one. We must now find the "best" plane. We will keep the same criterion for "best" as in bivariate regression, except that we will minimize the squared deviations from the regression plane. The quantity that we will minimize is still expressed as $\Sigma (Y - \hat{Y})^2$. We will now solve for the two slopes that jointly minimize these errors.

The notation used so far creates difficulties in the multiple regression case, since what we consider an "independent" variable at one point in the analysis may become a "dependent" variable in another. To avoid such confusion we will not distinguish between the dependent and independent variables by notation—we will simply number all variables as X_1, X_2, etc. The variable that happens to be on the left-hand side of the regression equation will simply be the dependent variable at that time. In multiple regression, each of the slopes statistically adjusts for the effects of the other independent variables in a given equation. To remind the reader that these are adjusted slopes, the equation will typically be written as:

$$\hat{X}_1 = b_{12.3} X_2 + b_{13.2} X_3 + a_1. \qquad (9.2)$$

The number after the point (.) in the subscripts indicates which variables are **statistically held constant** by that particular slope. In the equation above, the symbol $b_{12.3}$ means the slope of variable 2 on variable 1 controlling for variable 3. Conventionally, slopes in which other variables are held constant are referred to as **partial slopes**. Additionally, the number of variables held constant is designated as the **order of the slope**. Thus, a **zero-order slope** is one in which there are no statistical controls (i.e., the slope for simple regressions covered in Chapter 7); a **first-order slope** statistically controls for one variable, a second-order slope for two variables, and so on.

If we wanted to predict X_2 from X_1 and X_3, the equation would be:

$$\hat{X}_2 = b_{21.3}X_1 + b_{23.1}X_3 + a_2. \tag{9.3}$$

The first-order slopes can be found through a combination of the zero-order (only one independent variable) slopes. The equations are:

$$b_{ij.k} = \frac{b_{ij} - (b_{ik})(b_{jk})}{1 - (b_{jk})(b_{kj})} \tag{9.4}$$

$$b_{ij.k} = \frac{b_{ij} - (b_{ik})(b_{jk})}{1 - r_{jk}^2} \tag{9.5}$$

The slopes in these equations are the ones appropriate for raw data. Notice that they make some intuitive sense. In the numerator we take the zero-order slope and subtract from it a correction factor for the slopes of the control variable with the dependent and independent variables. In the denominator we have another correction factor for the correlation between the control variable and the independent variable.

Our first task, then, is to obtain the bivariate or zero-order slopes. We will need the following zero-order slopes in order to calculate the necessary first-order slopes: b_{12}, b_{13}, b_{23} and b_{32}. Both the raw and standardized slopes are given in Table 9.1.

Table 9.1
Raw and Standardized Zero-Order Slopes of Party Imagery (X_1), Political Knowledge (X_2) and Educational Level (X_3)

	Raw Slopes	Standardized Slopes
b_{13}	0.042	0.264
b_{23}	0.333	0.281
b_{12}	0.038	0.284
b_{32}	0.237	0.281

Source: 1984 CNES.

Using equation 9.4, we obtain the necessary first-order slopes:

$$b_{12.3} = \frac{(0.038) - (0.042)(0.237)}{1 - (0.333)(0.237)} = 0.031 \tag{9.6}$$

$$b_{13.2} = \frac{(0.042) - (0.038)(0.333)}{1 - (0.237)(0.333)} = 0.032. \tag{9.7}$$

The **standardized slopes** can be calculated from the raw slopes in a manner analogous to that used in the bivariate case:

$$b^*_{ij.k} = b_{ij.k}\left(\frac{s_j}{s_i}\right) \tag{9.8}$$

where $b^*_{ij.k}$ refers to the slope expressed in standard deviation units.

The standardized regression equation is:

$$\hat{Z}_{X_1} = 0.23 Z_{X_2} + 0.22 Z_{X_3}. \tag{9.9}$$

Although the partial slope of education on party imagery is smaller than the zero-order slope, it is clear from the standardized equation that it is far from zero. This shows that our argument is not substantiated. Education has both a **direct effect** and an **indirect effect** on party imagery. Stated differently, to some extent the effect of education on party imagery results from increased political knowledge. But education also has either an intrinsic (direct) effect or additional indirect effects through other variables not included in the argument so far. In causal diagram form, the evidence is consistent with the Figure 9.2.

For raw scores, the Y-intercept can also be calculated from the means and first-order slopes:

$$a = \bar{X}_1 - b_{12.3}\bar{X}_2 - b_{13.2}\bar{X}_3. \tag{9.10}$$

For the case at hand, the Y-intercept is 0.465. Thus the multiple regression equation, in raw form, is:

$$\hat{X}_1 = 0.031 X_2 + 0.032 X_3 + 0.465 \tag{9.11}$$

where $\hat{X}_1$ = the predicted proportion of correct party imagery,
X_2 = the number of premiers named, and
X_3 = educational level.

Figure 9.2
Causal Diagram Showing Education
to Have Both Direct and Indirect
Effects on Party Imagery

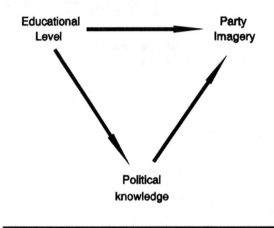

This equation can now be used to read the predicted party imagery scores for individuals with any combination of scores on political knowledge and educational level. For example, perfectly correct party imagery is predicted for an individual who has a university degree and who knows the names of all ten premiers, as is shown in the following:

$$\hat{X}_1 = 0.031(10) + 0.032(8) + 0.465 = 1.03. \qquad (9.12)$$

Of course, the highest possible score is 1.0, indicating perfect party imagery as measured here. Although a score of 1.03 is clearly impossible, this is not a huge problem since we have chosen the most extreme combination of respondent characteristics, which applies to only a few individuals. At the other extreme, in contrast, we would predict that about half the party imagery would be correct for a respondent who could not name any premiers and who has not completed grade school.

Partial Correlation

In Chapter 6, we documented that reported marital happiness was positively related to agreement on feelings after the birth of the first child but inversely related to the number of negative feelings reported. Furthermore, negativity and agreement were inversely related. Respondents who report positive feelings are more likely to agree on the feelings each experienced. The correlation between total negativity and total agreement is –0.51. It is this last relationship which creates the interpretive difficulties. In order to assess the relationship between agreement and marital satisfaction, we logically need to compare individuals who differ on proportion of agreement but have similar proportions of negative emotions. Stated differently, the question we need to answer is: "What is the strength of the relationship between agreement and marital satisfaction among couples who report the same proportion of negative emotions after the birth of their first child?" This question can be answered through **partial correlation**.

The logic of partial correlation is analogous to the partial slopes in multiple regression: in both instances we are looking at the effect of one variable on another while statistically controlling for the effect of additional variables. However, the question we are answering when using partial correlations is: "What is the strength of the linear relationship between given dependent and independent variables when adjusting for the effect of a third variable?" This adjustment is accomplished through some statistical manipulations, the nature of which needs to be understood. So let's develop the mathematical underpinnings to show more concretely how such adjustment is done.

We will take the example of agreement, marital happiness and negativity. What we want to know is the "true" effect of agreement on marital happiness, uncontaminated by the effect of negativity of emotions after the birth of the first child. I can state the question differently as "What is the strength of the relationship between agreement and marital happiness among couples who have experienced the same proportion of negative emotions after the birth of the first child?"

Obviously we cannot force all couples to have the same proportion of negative feelings. A theoretically possible solution is to take all couples who report no negative emotions and to compute the correlation between agreement and marital happiness among this subsample. Then take all those who report one negative emotion and repeat the process of computing the correlation between agreement and marital happiness, and then so on for each different number of negative emotions experienced. If all of these correlations were the same, we could just report one figure as the true correlation between agreement and marital happiness, having controlled for the impact of negative feelings. If they were not all the same, and they invariably would not be, we could take the *average* of these correlations, weighting the average by the number of observations that went into each of the separate calculations. This is in essence what a partial correlation is. Note that by taking the average of these correlations, we are essentially assuming that the various sizes of the correlations are unimportant, that they represent nothing more substantial than sampling fluctuations. Technically, we are assuming **additive effects** of the independent variables on the dependent variable. An alternative to this assumption is to conclude that the strength of the relationship between agreement and marital happiness depends on, or is contingent upon, the level of negativity. That is, we can postulate that there is an **interaction effect**. Let me emphasize that this latter possibility is ruled out when computing partial correlations, since they always provide a weighted average.

In short, the partial correlation coefficient is the average correlation between two variables that one would get if we computed it separately for very small intervals of the third variable.

To actually compute the partial correlations in this manner would be extremely tedious. Given that we are going to assume that the partial correlation between two variables is identical at all levels of some third variable, we can compute it much more simply. We want to obtain the correlation between agreement and marital happiness which is uncontaminated by negativity. What we will do is to first let negativity explain everything that it can about marital happiness. How can we do this? Well, we set up a least-squares regression between negativity and marital happiness. If we subtract the predicted marital happiness from the reported one, we have a figure that is independent of negativity since we have subtracted the amount that would be explained by negativity. This difference between the observed and the predicted score is called a **residual**. Similarly we will let negativity explain all it can about agreement. That is, we will compute a predicted agreement for each observation on the basis of that person's negativity. We then have a second residual, the difference between the predicted and the observed agreement, which will make the agreement score totally free of the effect of negativity. Now we have two residuals, one for marital happiness and one for agreement, and both of these residuals are freed of the effect of negativity. That is, they are the scores on agreement and marital happiness that remain after negativity has explained everything it could about these two variables. Having obtained two measures that are both independent of negativity, we can simply correlate these two using the usual correlation formula. The answer that we would get when we correlate the two residuals is the partial correlation of agreement on marital happiness controlling for negativity.

The complete procedure, using the general notation introduced earlier, would involve the following. We would like to obtain the partial correlation of variable X_1 with X_2 controlling for X_3. The symbol for such a partial correlation is $r_{12.3}$. The two subscripts before the point (.) are the variable numbers for the two variables for which we want to obtain a partial correlation. The subscripts after the dot refer to the variables being held constant. The first operation would be to get the predicted score of X_1 on the basis of X_3. This predicted score would be obtained using the ordinary regression equation:

$$\hat{X}_1 = b_{13}X_3 + a_1. \tag{9.13}$$

The residual for X_1 would then be $(X_1 - \hat{X}_1)$. In the same fashion we would obtain the predicted score of X_2 on the basis of X_3:

$$\hat{X}_2 = b_{23}X_3 + a_2 \qquad\qquad (9.14)$$

and the corresponding residual would be ($X_2 - \hat{X}_2$). The partial correlation is then defined in the traditional covariance manner. That is,

$$r_{12.3} = \frac{Cov[(X_1 - \hat{X}_1),(X_2 - \hat{X}_2)]}{\sqrt{Var(X_1 - \hat{X}_1)}\sqrt{Var(X_2 - \hat{X}_2)}}. \qquad\qquad (9.15)$$

This would still be a tedious way to compute a partial correlation, since it would involve solving two regression equations, computing predicted scores for each observation from both of these equations, obtaining deviations for each case, and then computing the correlation between these deviations. Fortunately, it is not necessary to go through all of these computations. They are presented merely to show the underlying logic of partial correlations. We would obtain precisely the same answer if we computed the partial correlation coefficient from the following equation, which is the one actually used:

$$r_{12.3} = \frac{r_{12} - (r_{13})(r_{23})}{\sqrt{(1 - r_{13}^2)(1 - r_{23}^2)}}. \qquad\qquad (9.16)$$

It may be difficult at first glance to see that this equation is derived from the equation for the residuals. However, a closer scrutiny shows that it makes some intuitive sense. In the numerator appears the total correlation between variable 1 and variable 2. Subtracted from this correlation is the product of the amount that variable 3 explains in variables 1 and 2. The denominator, which is always less than or equal to one, adjusts for the reduced variance in variables 1 and 2 that results from the fact that variable 3 explains part of the variance in both of these variables. In other words, in the numerator we subtract from the total correlation the amount that is explained by the relation of the control variable to each of the two variables. The denominator adjusts for the fact that a certain proportion of the variance in each of the two variables is explained by the control variable.

In summary, partial correlation involves the correlation of the residuals of two variables. The residuals are formed by taking the difference between the observed values and those predicted on the basis of the control variables. **Control variables** are defined as those variables which we hold statistically constant. The question we usually ask when we compute partial correlations is: "What is the 'true' strength of a given relationship, when by 'true' we mean the strength of the relationship when the effects of certain other variables (sometimes referred to as control variables) are statistically held constant?"

With this background, we are now in a position to compute the correlation between agreement and attraction (marital happiness), controlling for negativity.

Any of the partial correlations in columns 3 and 4 of Table 9.2 can be calculated from the zero-order correlations (remembering that the zero-order correlation between negativity and agreement is –0.51) Let's compute the correlation between a *wife's happiness in marriage* (1) and *agreement on feelings after the birth of the first child* (2), controlling for the *number of negative feelings* (3):

$$r_{12.3} = \frac{0.29 - (-0.41)(-0.51)}{\sqrt{1-(-0.41)^2}\ \sqrt{1-(-0.51)^2}}. \tag{9.17}$$

The correlation between agreement and marital attraction is reduced from 0.29 to 0.10 when the impact of negativity is controlled. Table 9.2 shows that a similar reduction occurs in all four instances. Indeed, none of the partial correlations (of marital attraction with agreement, controlling for negativity) is statistically significantly different from zero. Although the correlation between marital attraction and negativity controlling for agreement is also reduced, all of these latter partial correlations remain statistically significant. These results imply that the case for the similarity-attraction hypothesis is substantially weaker than it first appeared. One could develop a cogent argument that the similarity-attraction relationship is a spurious one, as diagrammed in Figure 9.3.

Table 9.2
Zero-Order and Partial Correlation Coefficients for Total Agreement and Total Negative Feelings Indices with Marital Harmony

| | Zero-Order | | First-Order | |
	Agreement	Negativity	Agreement[a]	Negativity[b]
Husband felt:				
Married Wrong Person	0.13	–0.27	0.01	–0.24
Happy in Marriage	0.31	–0.40	0.13	–0.30
Wife felt:				
Married Wrong Person	0.23	–0.31	0.09	–0.22
Happy in Marriage	0.29	–0.41	0.10	–0.32

[a] Controlling for negativity.
[b] Controlling for agreement.

Source: Fogarty, Rapoport and Rapoport (1971) and Baylin (1970).

Figure 9.3
The Similarity-Attraction
Hypothesis Modelled as a Spurious
Relationship

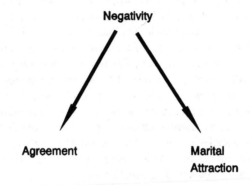

We must keep in mind in the above two equations that $\hat{Y}$ is predicted from
several independent variables. The resulting coefficient of determination informs
what proportion of the variance in the dependent variable results from its relationship
to all of the independent variables included in that particular multiple regression
equation.

Multiple Correlation

The **coefficient of determination** (the square of the multiple correlation coefficient)
serves to evaluate the overall multiple regression equation. Remember from
Chapter 8 that the coefficient of determination expresses the proportion of the total
variance in Y that is attributable to its relationship to X. If we let R represent the
multiple correlation coefficient, we have:

$$R^2 = \frac{\Sigma(\hat{Y} - \overline{Y})^2}{\Sigma(Y - \overline{Y})^2}.$$
(9.18)

As discussed in Chapter 8, this is equivalent to:

$$R^2 = 1 - \frac{\Sigma(Y - \hat{Y})^2}{\Sigma(Y - \overline{Y})^2}.$$
(9.19)

We must keep in mind in the above two equations that $\hat{Y}$ is predicted from
several independent variables. The resulting coefficient of determination informs
what proportion of the variance in the dependent variable results from its relationship
to all of the independent variables included in that particular multiple regression
equation.

We must also keep in mind that independent variables are seldom independent of each other. Rather, they are correlated to some degree. The stronger the correlations among the independent variables, the greater the interpretive difficulty. The standard errors of the partial slopes become extremely large as the correlations between the independent variables approach unity.[3] This is the problem of **colinearity.**

Particularly when the sample size is small, it is possible to obtain a misleadingly high R^2 since one degree of freedom is lost for every additional variable added to a multiple regression equation. This has the consequence of making it appear that more and more variance is explained as more and more variables are added to the equation, *even if all of the variables were totally independent of the dependent variable.* Whenever the number of variables in a multiple regression equation equals the number of cases, R^2 will equal 1.0, even if the variables are random numbers. As the number of variables approaches the number of observations, R^2 capitalizes more and more on chance fluctuations. For this reason, it is desirable to report the **adjusted R^2** whenever several models with varying number of independent variables are compared. As its name implies, the adjusted R^2 corrects for the capitalization on chance. The equation is:

$$Adjusted\ R^2 = R^2 - \left(\frac{k-1}{N-k}\right)(1-R^2).\qquad(9.20)$$

where k = number of independent variables, and
        N = number of cases.

Developing Models

Every regression equation implies a particular model of the world. Different equations therefore imply different visions of our world. In this section, I will postulate a number of different visions (or theories) relevant to a single topic. I will then translate these visions into the mathematical models implied. These different mathematical models will then be applied to a common set of data. This permits an assessment of the relative merits of the different models.

The topic I have chosen to model is male sex role values.[4] The statements in Figure 9.4 express different possible aspects of male sex roles. There is no doubt that humans will differ in the extent to which they would endorse any of these statements. These nine statements were asked as part of the 1980 Edmonton Area Studies. A seven-point Likert-type response format was provided, ranging from Strongly Disagree (1) to Strongly Agree (7). The sample consisted of more than five hundred adult residents of Edmonton. The spouses of 179 of the married (or common-law) respondents were also interviewed. For reasons that will become clear later, the sub-sample of 179 married or common-law couples will be crucial to developing and testing the various models.[5]

Most scholars recognize that sex roles form a loose constellation of more or less cohesive values. We would expect in our society, for example, that those who feel men shouldn't be ashamed of crying in front of others would tend to feel that it is all right for men to hug each other. Although the nine sex role statements are neither logically nor theoretically related to each other, each of them seems to have a traditional and a non-traditional side to it. To agree with the first six statements (and to disagree with the last three), I would suggest, is to hold traditional male sex role values. Conversely, to agree with the last three and to disagree with the first six is to hold non-traditional sex role values.

After reversing the direction of the last three items (so that a high score indicates a traditional sex role value), the internal consistency of these statements can be assessed. Cronbach's alpha is 0.65 and 0.72 for the husbands and wives in the married couples subsample. This is sufficiently high to permit the creation of an index consisting of the mean score on these items. At the same time, they are low enough to warrant replicating the analyses on the individual components to verify that the external consistency criterion is met.

Figure 9.4
Items for Measuring Male Sex Role Values

- If a man's wife or girlfriend is insulted by someone, he should always come to her defense, even if it means fighting.

- Men who don't like competitive sports, such as football or hockey, are lacking in masculinity.

- A husband should be entirely responsible for earning the living for a family (under ordinary circumstances).

- It is more important that a husband is ambitious than that he is kind and understanding.

- Whenever possible, a man should avoid having to work for a woman.

- The man should take the initiative in expressing physical affection.

- Men shouldn't be ashamed of crying in front of others.

- It's O.K. for men to show physical affection towards other men, such as hugging them.

- In a marriage, it is just as much a man's responsibility, as it is a woman's, to care for children.

Each of the models developed next will postulate one additional theoretical source of sex role values. I have given short descriptive labels to each of these sources. These labels should not be taken too seriously, because the theories corresponding to the labels are substantially more sophisticated than my treatment of them. The models are more like caricatures than expositions. Their advantage is that they show clearly how each theory implies certain equations and how different theories imply different equations.

Model I: Patriarchy

Some scholars argue that traditional sex role values are a manifestation of the patriarchal system. The Women's Movement has had as one of its aims the transformation of such values into ones more compatible with a feminist vision. To the extent that patriarchy was fostered by men and/or that the Women's Movement focused firstly on females, we would expect males to hold more traditional sex role values than females. The simplest way to express this mathematically is to predict that, on average, males would endorse these (recoded) statements more than females. That is:

$$\overline{X}_m > \overline{X}_f. \tag{9.21}$$

And indeed, on all nine issues, the responses of males were more traditional than those of females. The difference-o-means test would inform whether the patriarchy model is better than the base model (the base model denies the existence of "gendered" sex role values and is captured in the null hypothesis that the mean for males equals that for females). For all nine issues, the null hypothesis can be rejected using traditional levels of significance. On the index, the mean for the males was 3.25, and for the females it was 2.75. The associated t value was 7.03; the probability of a Type I error is thus less than one in a thousand. The difference-of-means test is diagrammed in the left half of Figure 9.5:

Figure 9.5
Patriarchal Sex Role Values in a Difference of Means and a Regresion Form

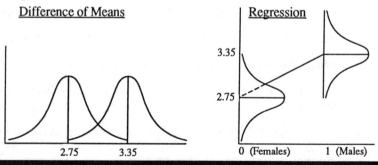

This way of modelling patriarchy does not permit an easy assessment of *how much* improvement the patriarchal model offers over the base model. It is possible, indeed preferable, to express the difference of means test in the form of a regression equation:

$$\hat{Y} = b(G) + a \qquad\qquad (9.22)$$

where $\hat{Y}$ = the predicted sex role value
        b = the least squares slope
        G = gender, scored so that 0 = females and 1 = males, and
        a = $\bar{Y}_f$ = Y-intercept.

Estimating the parameters of this equation for the main sample yields:

$$\hat{Y} = 0.60(G) + 2.75.$$

For females, the predicted sex role value score is the same as the mean female score, which is the same as the Y-intercept since $\hat{Y} = 0.60(0) + 2.75 = 2.75$. For males, $\hat{Y} = 0.60(1) + 2.75 = 3.35$, which is identical to the mean male score. Note that the unstandardized slope is identical with $b = \bar{X}_m - \bar{X}_f$. That is, the slope is identical to the numerator of the difference of means test.

The preceding illustrated that the bivariate regression (with the independent variable dichotomized as zero and one) is identical to a difference of means test. So far, one form has no advantage over the other. The advantage of the regression form can be seen when we express the equation in standard scores. The standardized slope is 0.32, which is the same as the Pearson correlation between gender and sex role values. Squaring this number to obtain the coefficient of determination indicates that gender accounts for just over 10 percent of the variance in sex role values. Expressing the relationship in a regression form rather than in a difference of means form permits an evaluation of how much the patriarchal model improves on the base model. The evidence is consistent with a patriarchal explanation, but such an explanation (at least in this crude form) leaves much unanswered. The regression form of the relationship is diagrammed in the right side of Figure 9.4.

Model II: Joint Reality Construction (JRC)

Joint reality construction was discussed in previous chapters as a possible alternative interpretation of the similarity-attraction relationship. Berger and Kellner (1964) posed the construction of a joint reality as the single biggest task confronting new relationships. Successful marriages, they argue, produce psychological havens where each partner confirms the positions taken by the other. Such confirmation is possible only when mutual definitions of "reality" have been created. To the extent that the marriage process is successful, it produces agreements between husband and wife.

If marriage is such a process of negotiated realities, then the sex role values of one spouse should be predictable from those of the other. This is captured in the simple bivariate regression:

$$\hat{H} = b(W - \overline{W}) + \overline{H} \qquad (9.23)$$

where $\hat{H}$ = the husband's predicted sex role value,
W = the wife's sex role value, and
$\overline{H}$ = the mean sex role value of husbands (also the Y- intercept).

In this context, we can think of the slope b as an "influence" coefficient. If the slope is zero, then wives have no influence on husbands (in the area of sex role values). The closer the slope comes to 1.0, the more influence wives exert on husbands. In the limiting case where $b = 1.0$, the sex role values of husbands are perfectly predictable from those of the wives. The square of the standardized slope would be the coefficient of determination, indicating the proportionate improvement of the JRC model over the base model. Just a reminder: the impact of measurement error in measuring the sex role values of either husbands or wives is to attenuate the slope, making it appear that fewer shared realities are constructed. I will come back to this point later.

In regression analysis, adding a constant to any of the variables does not affect the slopes, only the Y-intercept. Capitalizing on this, we can modify the above equation to capture simultaneously the patriarchy factor. If we were to measure husbands' sex role value relative to the mean sex role value of wives (i.e., to subtract $\overline{W}$ from H), then the Y-intercept would be the difference of means between husbands and wives. That is, $a = \overline{H} - \overline{W}$.

In this form, the Y-intercept captures the patriarchy model. The sex role values of husbands can be thought of as composed of two parts. The first part is that produced by joint reality construction. This is captured by the slope. The second part is that reflecting patriarchy. This is captured by the new Y-intercept. The two components are shown in Figure 9.6.

The ordinary least-squares (OLS) solution of equation 9.20 for the data at hand is:

$$\hat{H} = 0.50(W) + 0.51.$$

Note that in this form, the coefficient of determination is unaffected by the presence or absence of patriarchy. That is, gender does not affect the explained variance of husband's sex role values. It simply affects the Y-intercept.

Figure 9.6
The Regression Line Modelling Both Joint Reality Construction and Patriarchy

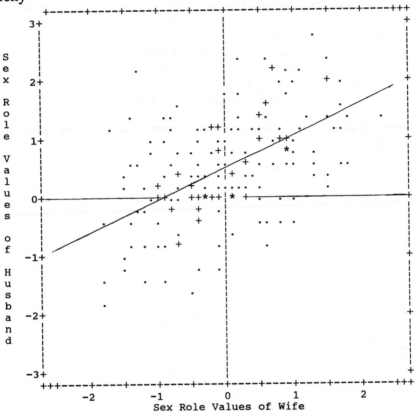

Model III: Social Class
Social class is to sociology what patriarchy is to feminist theory. In one form or another, social class is central to most sociological analyses. With respect to sex role values, it is sometimes argued that there is a male working class culture distinct from that of the middle class male culture. The male working class culture is thought to be particularly patriarchal.

The concept of social class is variously defined and consequently measured in disparate ways. Occupation is often regarded as a key aspect of social class. This aspect is more likely than education or income to differentiate working from middle class male subcultures.

The Pineo et al. (1977) coding scheme can be used to dichotomize the respondents as either working or middle class. Working class membership corresponds to blue collar occupations at a rank lower than foreman. Middle class occupations range from foreman to self-employed professionals.

Again, if we code the dichotomous class variable such that 0 stands for working class and 1 for middle class, the regression would be symbolized by two parallel lines, as in Figure 9.7.

To plot the simultaneous relationship of two independent variables on a dependent variable usually requires a three-dimensional diagram. When one of the independent variables is a dichotomy, as is the case here, the single regression equation can be drawn as two separate regression lines.

Figure 9.7
Plot of the Social Class Model

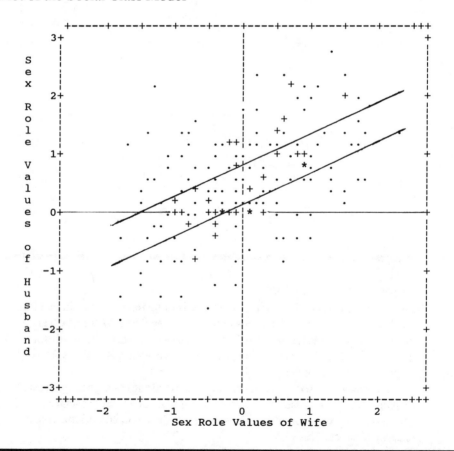

Sex Role Values of Wife

For the data at hand, the ordinary least-squares (OLS) estimates of the multiple regression equation is:

$$\hat{H} = 0.48(W) - 0.28(C) + 0.65.$$

where C = the dichotomous class variable.

For a working class couple (WC), this equation simplifies to:

$$\hat{H}_{wc} = 0.48(W) - 0.28(0) + 0.65$$
$$= 0.48(W) + 0.65$$

(since C equals zero, and any number multiplied by zero is zero). Clearly, this is a simple bivariate regression equation. For a middle class couple (MC), the equation also simplifies, but this time it becomes:

$$\hat{H}_{mc} = 0.48(W) - 0.28(1) + 0.65$$
$$= 0.48(W) + 0.37.$$

The two equations have identical slopes, but differ in their Y-intercept. Specifically, middle class males hold lower (i.e., less traditional) sex role values. That is precisely what the social class model envisioned.

The social class model improves on the previous models. An additional 2.4 percent of the variance in male sex role values is accounted for through this model.

Model IV: Class-Specific Marriage Styles
The results of the first three models are consistent with the following theoretical conclusions:

- Sex role values are gendered, with males advocating more traditional values than females.
- Sex role values are the product of a negotiated reality between spouses.
- Sex role values are differentiated by social class, with the middle class rejecting traditional values more than the working class.

These three models were captured using regression techniques. Underlying all such regression models is the additivity assumption. **Additivity** is fulfilled when the (unique) effects of several variables can be summed or added together. In this context, the antonym of additivity is interaction. When the effect of one variable depends on the value of a second variable, it is called an **interaction effect**. The class-specific marriage styles model postulates an interaction (or multiplicative) effect.

A number of scholars, e.g., Berger and Kellner (1964), suggest that middle class marriages have a different character than working class marriages. The difference of interest here concerns the importance of unity or a common front. Communicating and negotiating with each other as a means of constructing a shared view is thought to be prototypically a middle class feature. This class difference is caricaturized in the car seating arrangements when two couples spend an evening out. In the middle class case, one wife-husband pair sit in the front seat and the other pair sits in the rear seat. In the working class case, the two husbands sit in the front and the two wives sit in the back. Such seating arrangements symbolize the differential importance of conversation partners. How does this translate to an interaction effect?

The class specific marriage style argument postulates, among other things, that the influence the wives have on their husbands' sex role values depends on their social class. In middle class marriages, the influence of wives is felt to be greater than among the working class.

Statistically, interaction effects always require that two variables be multiplied by each other. Here's how Model IV would look:

$$\hat{H} = b_1(W) + b_2(C) + b_3(C \times W) + G.$$

The interaction effect is postulated to occur between social class and the wife's sex role values. That is, joint reality construction is postulated to feature middle class marriages more than working class marriages. This means that the slope for wife's influence on husband's sex role values is not a constant for the whole sample. Rather, two different slopes are necessary, one for the working class and the other for the middle class marriages.

The OLS solution for the above equation is:

$$\hat{H} = 0.37(W) - 0.27(C) + 0.24(C \times W) + 0.66.$$

Remembering that social class is a dichotomous variable (0 = working class, 1 = middle class), we can simplify the above equation by writing it separately for the two classes. For the working class, the equation becomes:

$$\hat{H}_{wc} = 0.37(W) - 0.27(0) + 0.24(0 \times W) + 0.66$$
$$= 0.37(W) - 0 + 0 + 0.66$$
$$= 0.37(W) + 0.66.$$

For middle class marriages we get:

$$\hat{H}_{mc} = 0.37(W) - 0.27(1) + 0.24(1 \times W) + 0.66$$
$$= 0.37(W) - 0.27 + 0.24(W) + 0.66$$
$$= 0.61(W) + 0.39.$$

Note that both the slope and the Y-intercept differ in the two equations. As expected, the slope expressing the wife's influence on the husband's sex role values is substantially greater in middle class marriages than in working class marriages. In addition, there is less gender difference in middle class than in working class marriages. This is manifested by the lower Y-intercept for the middle class cases. In short, the data is consistent with the postulation of distinct marriage styles by social class: middle class marriages are ones where more joint realities are constructed, resulting in both a more shared view and a less gendered view.

Although this model seems quite complex, it can be plotted in two dimensions if we use different symbols to represent middle class and working class couples. Figure 9.8 is an SPSS-produced plot. The symbols "w" and "m" identify working class and middle class couples, respectively (the symbol "$" is used by SPSS whenever more than one case occupies the same plotting space). The instructions that produced this plot are provided at the end of the SPSS regression instructions. I have superimposed the two regression lines that correspond to the class-specific marriage styles model. Note the substantially steeper slope for the middle class couples compared to the working class couples.

Each of the coefficients in the equation represents a specific substantive/ theoretical component:

- b_1 captures joint reality construction among working class couples,
- b_2 represents how much less gendered sex role values are in middle class than in working class families,
- b_3 informs how much more joint reality construction characterizes middle class marriages than working class marriages, and
- the Y-intercept (G) reflects patriarchy, the extent to which sex role values are gendered in working class marriages.

Model V: Social History

The final model introduces social history into the argument. Social commentators have postulated major changes in the distribution of sex role values in recent history. The social climate has changed, and with it, the values (but not necessarily the behaviour!) regarding appropriate sex roles. If that is true, it constitutes a major threat to the joint reality thesis. This change in social history provides an alternative rationale for the previously documented relationship between the sex role values of husbands and wives. The alternative interpretation involves the following steps:

- With the passage of time, sex role values have become less traditional.
- Humans are socialized to accept the prevailing values of their culture.
- Therefore older cohorts can be expected to hold more traditional sex role values than younger ones.
- Grooms tend to marry brides similar in age, or somewhat younger, than themselves.

- Therefore husbands and wives will hold similar sex role values (with wives being somewhat less traditional since they are somewhat younger), not because they have constructed a shared reality but because they have experienced a common social history.

An emphasis on individual maturation rather than on social history would lead to the same conclusion that the shared sex role values of husbands and wives are not due to joint reality construction. In any event, social history and/or individual maturation provides a plausible alternative interpretation to that of joint reality construction. Therefore the social history argument must be addressed. This can be done by adding the husband's age (A) as an additional independent variable to the previous ones:

$$\hat{H} = b_1(W) + b_2(C) + b_3(C \times W) + b_4(A) + G.$$

Figure 9.8
Plot of Class-Specific Marriage Styles

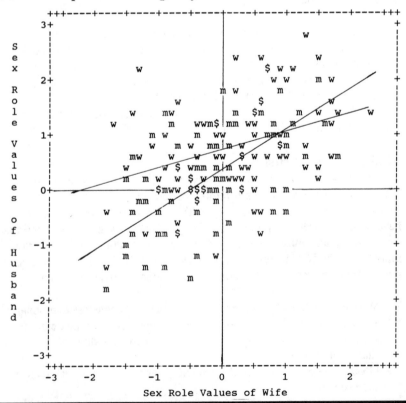

Remember that in multiple regression, each of the slopes is a partial slope. That is, each slope is adjusted for the effects of the other independent variables included in the equation. If the common social history (and/or maturation) is the sole cause of the shared spousal sex role values, then the slopes for the effect of wife's sex role value should disappear (i.e., become statistically insignificant). Table 9.3 summarizes the information for Models II to V.

Clearly, age is an important ingredient for understanding the sex role values of husbands. It adds over five percent to the explained variance of Model IV. Further, although introducing age reduced the slope for joint reality construction, the latter remains the single strongest effect. Furthermore, introducing age did not erase the interaction effect (if anything, the interaction effect became stronger). Thus the joint reality construction argument withstood the challenge of the social history interpretation, although it did suggest that joint reality construction is not as pronounced a feature as estimated by our previous models.

Further models could be developed. For example, it is likely that some individual characteristics such as education have an impact on sex role values. Such factors would simply be added to the regression equation. My concern was not to develop a full explanation of sex role values but rather to show how each multiple regression equation implies a particular explanation of some aspect of our world.

Before leaving the topic of sex role values and its various models, let's reflect on what methodological artifacts might be masquerading as substantive models. A methodological interpretation can be constructed to rival the class-specific marital styles argument. The pattern of the wife having less influence on the husband's sex role values in working class marriages than in middle class ones is precisely what one would expect if the sex role values indicators did not form as internally consistent an orientation among the working class as among the middle class. Such lack of cohesion would manifest itself as greater random measurement error among working class respondents. As documented in Chapter 7, the greater the measurement error in any variable, the less effect that variable will appear to have. This is because of greater regression towards the mean with increased measurement error. One simple test of this methodological interpretation is to compute the internal consistency reliabilities separately for working class and middle class respondents. This was done, providing mixed evidence for the "measurement error" hypothesis. Cronbach's alpha was 0.59 and 0.77 for working class husbands and wives, respectively, while for their middle class counterparts it was 0.69 and 0.71. Thus, consistent with the measurement error hypothesis, these sex role values were least internally consistent for working class husbands. However, and inconsistent with the measurement error hypothesis, these issues formed the most cohesive orientation among working class wives.

Table 9.3
Raw and Standardized Multiple Regression Slopes for a Variety of Models of Sex Role Values

		b_1	b_2	b_3	b_4	Adjusted R^2
Model II:	Joint Reality Construction	0.50 (0.51)	—	—	—	0.25
Model III:	Social Class	0.48 (0.48)	–0.27 (–0.16)	—	—	0.27
Model IV:	Class-specific Marriage Styles	0.37 (0.38)	–0.27 (–0.16)	0.24 (0.16)	—	0.28
Model V:	Social History	0.27 (0.28)	–0.27 (–0.16)	0.26 (0.17)	0.01 (0.24)	0.33

Note: (1) Numbers in parentheses are the standardized coefficients, and (2), for all coefficients in this model, $p < 0.05$.

Source: Edmonton Area Studies (1980).

The fact that these issues were most cohesive for the working class wives permits a second test between the "class-specific marriage styles" and the "measurement error" explanations. Since measurement error was no greater among working class wives than among either middle class husbands or wives, the wife's impact on her husband's responses to the individual sex role items should be about the same as that of middle class husbands and wives on each other. Such calculations were conducted and failed to support the measurement error interpretation. That is, the working class wife's impact on her husband's responses is consistently lower than is the case for middle class marriages. This suggests that joint reality construction is indeed more pronounced among middle class than among working class couples.

The fourth model, which introduced a social class interaction effect, has a direct bearing on the similarity-attraction hypothesis. This model showed that, with respect to sex role values, working class couples had more systematic disagreement and less of a shared reality than middle class couples. The greater systematic disagreement was manifested by the higher (more traditional) Y-intercept. The lesser shared reality was revealed by the lower slope for the wife's influence on the husband's sex role values. If these findings are manifestations of a general class difference in marriage styles, then it follows that there would be generally fewer agreements in working class than in middle class marriages. This should result in diminished wife-husband attraction among the working class. This expectation can be tested with the 1980 Edmonton Area Studies data. Figure 9.9 reproduces the two measures of attraction available in this data.

Figure 9.9
Items for Measuring Marital Attraction

- How many times in the past 12 months have you and your spouse discussed breaking up or ending your relationship?
  _____ time(s)

- The numbers on the following line represent different degrees of happiness in marriage relationships. Use the middle point, "Happy," to represent the degree of happiness of most marriage relationships. Which number best describes the degree of happiness in your relationship?

"Happy"

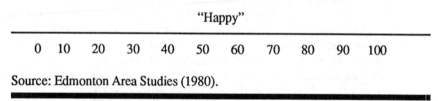

| 0 | 10 | 20 | 30 | 40 | 50 | 60 | 70 | 80 | 90 | 100 |

Source: Edmonton Area Studies (1980).

If joint reality construction is a feature of middle class marriages, then the similarity-attraction hypothesis would predict that the middle class couples would have discussed breaking up less frequently and would rate their marriage as happier than the working class couples. Although there is a slight tendency in the predicted direction, the class differences are well within the range of sampling fluctuations. One can imagine a number of reasons for this disappointing finding. Clearly, this negative finding introduces a puzzle that would need to be addressed by serious proponents of the similarity-attraction paradigm.

SPSS Instructions

Line 1 (Figure 9.10): The 1980 Edmonton Area Studies couples data resides on a file named "Eas80c.sys".

Lines 2-3: The missing values for the sex role values items are declared as zero. Var399 to var407 are the nine variable names for the husband's sex role values; var768 to var772 and var776 to var779 are the corresponding items for the wife's sex role values.

Lines 4-5: Three of the nine items are scored in the wrong direction with a low score implying traditional sex role values. This problem is eliminated by recoding the relevant items to make a high score imply traditional values.

Lines 6-12: Var316 contains a detailed four-digit occupation code. Lines 9 to 15 list all the middle class occupation codes which occurred in the sample and recodes them to a one. The missing values for this variable originally was a zero; line 11 recodes this to an 8888. This was a necessary step so that the (ELSE = 0) instruction in line 12 could be employed. This instruction asks SPSS to recode to zero all values of var316 that have not been listed up to that point in the recode instruction. This "trick" makes it unnecessary to list all working class occupation codes. But note that the missing values code had to be recoded prior to that point in time. Otherwise there would be no way to distinguish between a missing value and a working class occupation.

Line 13: Missing values are provided for the recoded occupation variable and var020 which contains the husband's age. (Note: In the system file, zero was declared a missing value for var316. If the new missing value instruction had not been provided, SPSS would treat all working class cases as missing cases. Note also that brief comments can be included at the end of any SPSS instruction by leaving a space after the instruction, followed by the characters /*.)

Lines 14-15: Two indices, intended to capture the sex role values of husbands and wives, are created using the MEAN function. This function calculates the mean of all the (non-missing) variables enclosed within the parentheses. I prefer to use the mean rather than the sum since the mean is not adversely affected by missing values. That is, it is meaningful to compare the mean index scores for individuals who responded to all, to eight or to only one of the nine sex role items. It would not be meaningful to compare the sums for such different cases.

Lines 16-17: The sex role indices are adjusted by subtracting the mean of the wive's scores from the score of every husband and every wife. Doing this permits us to interpret the Y-intercept as the gender effect.

Line 18: This instruction creates an interaction variable (named "ia") between occupation and wife's sex role values. The value of this interaction variable will be zero for all working class cases; for middle class cases, the value of this variable is identical to the wife's sex role value index score.

Lines 19-22: Extended labels are provided for all newly constructed variables. These appear in the printout, providing fuller documentation.

Lines 23-25: There are two important reasons for providing new value labels for var316. The first is that this variable has been recoded, so that the original value labels are incorrect. The second is that the PLOT procedure (lines 36-38) uses the first character of the value labels to identify the control values in the scatter plot. Given the value labels I have provided, a "w" will identify a working class case and an "m" will identify a middle class case.

Line 26: Lines 26 to 35 are the multiple regression procedure instructions that produced Models II to V. The keyword REGRESSION invokes the regression procedure. The optional DESCRIPTIVES keywork produced the means, standard deviations and intercorrelations of all the variables listed in line 27. The placement of this keyword is crucial. It must precede the VARIABLES subcommand.

Figure 9.10
SPSS Instructions for Obtaining Regression Models
of Male Sex Role Values

```
1   GET FILE "eas80c.sys".
2   MISSING VALUES var399 TO var407
3       var768 to var772,var776 TO var779(9).
4   RECODE var401,var402,var403,var770 TO var772
5       (1=7)(2=6)(3=5)(5=3)(6=2)(7=1).
6   RECODE var316
7       (2141 3111 1171 2142 THRU 2161 2311 2331 THRU 2733
8       1113 1130 THRU 1137 2183 2319
9       2117 2119 2165 2169 8535 9153
10      1119 1149 4170 4190 5130 5170
11      8160 8510 8580 8710 8780 9130 9170 9310 9530=1)(0=8888)
12      (ELSE=0) /*working class recoded as 0's.
13  MISSING VALUES var316 (8888) var020 (99).
14  COMPUTE hsrv=MEAN(var399 TO var407).
15  COMPUTE wsrv=MEAN(var768 TO var772,var776 TO var779).
16  COMPUTE hsrv=hsrv-2.875 /*subtract mean wsrv.
17  COMPUTE wsrv=wsrv-2.875 /*subtract mean wsrv.
18  COMPUTE ia=var316*wsrv.
19  VAR LABELS var316 "Social class"
20      hsrv "Sex Role Values of Husband"
21      wsrv "Sex Role Values of Wife"
22      ia "Interaction between class and wsrv".
23  VALUE LABELS var316
24      0 "working class"
25      1 "middle class".
26  REGRESSION DESCRIPTIVES
27      /VARIABLES=hsrv,wsrv,var316,ia,var020
28      /STATISTICS=R,CHA,COEFF
29      /DEPENDENT=hsrv
30      /ENTER=wsrv
31      /ENTER=var316
32      /ENTER=ia
33      /ENTER=var020
34      /RESIDUALS
35      /SCATTERPLOT (*PRE,hsrv)(*RES,*PRE).
36  PLOT
37      /TITLE="Figure 9.4 Plot of Class-Specific Marriage Styles"
38      /PLOT=hsrv WITH wsrv BY var316.
```

Line 27: The VARIABLES subcommand must list the names of all variables to be used in any of the regression equations that follow. Note that by default SPSS uses a listwise deletion in the regression procedure. This means that if information on a single variable is missing, the whole case is deleted from analysis. This feature can rapidly deplete the usable number of cases; hence care must be exercised in deciding how many and which variables are to be included in the list. Although the default treatment of missing cases can be overridden, this should not be done until a moderate level of competence in multiple regression analysis has been achieved. When using pairwise deletion of missing cases, for example, certain logical inconsistencies in the pattern of associations can result. This problem is of particular importance when causal inferences are being made. SPSS computes a variance-covariance matrix using all the variables listed on the VARIABLES subcommand. This permits efficient calculation of numerous regression equations using subsets of the variables listed.

Line 28: This is an optional command used to change the statistics that would be provided by default. In particular, I wanted information on how much the coefficient of determination changed between each of the models. This is not produced by default but is provided using the CHA option in the STATISTICS subcommand. The option "R" provides information on the coefficient of determination, and COEFF provides the raw and standardized regression coefficients (and their statistical significance) for all four models.

Line 29: One or more of the variables listed in line 27 must be declared as the dependent variable(s). For all of the models, the sole dependent variable is the husband's sex role values.

Lines 30-33: Each ENTER subcommand adds one or more independent variables to the regression equation. These four ENTER subcommands produced, in sequence, Models II to V.

Line 34: Regression analysis makes many assumptions about the data, violations of which can generate nonsense. Fortunately, SPSS can provide a number of diagnostic aids. One such set of aids is provided through the optional RESIDUALS subcommand. It is particularly useful for detecting deviant cases and violations of the assumption of a normal distribution of residuals.

Line 35: Up to six scatter plots can be obtained with the optional SCATTERPLOT subcommand. For each scatter plot desired, the two variables to be plotted are enclosed within parentheses. The first variable in each pair is plotted on the vertical dimension and the second along the horizontal. The REGRESSION procedure produces a variety of temporary variables whose names start with an asterisk. These can be used in the scatter plots. *PRE is the predicted score calculated by SPSS for each case; *RES refers to the residual, $Y - Y$. These temporary variables are for the last equation specified. I have requested two scatter plots, one plotting the relationship between the predicted and the observed sex role values; the other the relationship between the residuals and the predicted scores.

Lines 36-38: These instructions produced Figure 9.7. Note on line 38 the addition of the phrase "BY var316". This phrase differentiates the scatter plot points by social class position. Var316 acts as a control variable. As I stated earlier, SPSS uses the first character in the value labels for var316 ("w" and "m" for scores of 0 and 1, respectively) as the symbols for the value of the control variable.

SPSS Regression Printout

I have divided the regression printout into four sections, coresponding to the four types of subcommands: DESCRIPTIVES (Figure 9.11), ENTER (Figure 9.12), RESIDUALS (Figure 9.13) and SCATTERPLOT (Figure 9.14). For convenience in locating particular statistics in the regression printout, I have numbered the lines in each section and identified the section by taking the first letter of each subcommand. For example, D11 represents the eleventh line in the DESCRIPTIVES section.

Figure 9.11
SPSS Regression Output: DESCRIPTIVES

********** M U L T I P L E   R E G R E S S I O N **********

D1: Listwise Deletion of Missing Data

D2:   Mean Std Dev Label

		Mean	Std Dev	Label
D3:	HSRV	.509	.879	Sex Role Values of Husband
D4:	WSRV	.000	.892	Sex Role Values of Wife
D5:	VAR316	.503	.501	Social class
D6:	IA	–.061	.589	Interaction between class and wsrv
D7:	VAR020	41.249	15.170	Age of Respondent

D8: N of Cases = 177

D9: Correlation:

		HSRV	WSRV	VAR316	IA	VAR020
D10:		HSRV	WSRV	VAR316	IA	VAR020
D11:	HSRV	1.000	.505	–.224	.428	.394
D12:	WSRV	.505	1.000	–.137	.667	.372
D13:	VAR316	–.224	–.137	1.000	–.104	–053
D14:	IA	.428	.667	–.104	1.000	.219
D15:	VAR020	.394	.372	–.053	.219	1.000

Commentary on the DESCRIPTIVES Output

Line D1 (Figure 9.11: A reminder that the whole case was deleted if a missing value was encountered on any of the variables listed in the regression procedure.

Lines D2-D7: The variable names, their means, standard deviations, and extended labels are provided. The means and standard deviations should be examined closely for possible problems. For example, I subtracted the mean index score on the wives' sex role values from both husbands and wives. Therefore the mean for wives' sex role values should be 0.0, which it is (line D4). I am not aware of any reason for expecting substantially different degrees of consensus in sex role values between wives and husbands. Hence the standard deviation of the variables HSRV and WSRV should be quite similar, which they are. (If they had been very dissimilar, I would have checked the distribution of the individual items that make up the scale, as well as my instructions for computing the two indices. More likely than not, I would find that I made a silly mistake such as having listed the wrong variables for either husbands or wives.) Suppose, as a third possibility, that the standard deviation of age (line D7) were as high as 30. It is extremely unlikely that in a random sample the average difference in age between any two respondents is that high. If such a high standard deviation had been calculated for age, it is almost certain that I had failed to inform SPSS that values of 0, 88 and 99 should be considered missing. These extremely high and low numbers would increase the standard deviation enough to warn me that something was wrong. Any of these, and many other, problems can affect the regression results, often without the researcher being aware of the folly.

Line D8: Since listwise deletion of missing values can severely reduce the sample size, the actual number of cases used in the regression analysis is listed. This number should be compared to the total sample size to judge whether the reduction in sample size is tolerable.

Lines D9-D15: The zero-order correlation matrix should be examined closely. The pattern of correlations should correspond to the expectations developed during the preliminary analysis.

The correlations among the independent variables should also be assessed. Invariably these variables are not independent of each other. It is this feature of our social world that creates both interpretive and statistical difficulties. The statistical problem is called **colinearity** or **multicolinearity**. As the correlation between any one independent variable and one or more other independent variables increases, it becomes increasingly difficult to assess the unique effect each variable has on the dependent variable.

Suppose I had included the age of both wife and husband as explanatory variables. Since the correlation between the age of spouses is very high, the answer to what is the unique contribution of his age as opposed to her age is close to arbitrary. Correlations among independent variables as high as ± 0.80 are candidates for colinearity problems. In such instances it is frequently best to exclude some of the independent variables, such as either spouse's age. Colinearity manifests itself in relatively large standard errors. That's another way of saying that little confidence can be attached to the estimate of the unique contribution each variable makes. Where two independent variables are perfectly correlated, the standard error of both variables is infinity. Interaction variables have a built-in colinearity with the variables that comprise the interaction. Note (line D14) the high correlation ($r = 0.667$) between the interaction variable and the wife's sex role values. This is because the value of these two variables is identical for all middle class couples. For this reason, the standard error of the interaction effect is relatively large. I will return to this point later.

Figure 9.12
SPSS Regression Output: Equations

********** MULTIPLE REGRESSION **********

E1:   Equation Number 1   Dependent Variable: HSRV Sex Role
                                                    Values of Husband

E2:   Beginning Block Number 1. Method: Enter   WSRV

E3:   Variable(s) Entered on Step Number
E4:   1.. WSRV   Wife: Mean Sex Role Values

E5:   Multiple R   .50502
E6:   R Square   .25504   R Square Change   .25504
E7:   Adjusted R Square   .25079   F Change   59.91292
E8:   Standard Error   .76071   Signif F Change   .0000

E9:   F =   59.91292   Signif F = .0000

E10: — — — — — — — Variables in the Equation — — — — — — —
E11:   Variable   B   SE B   Beta   T   Sig T

E12:   WSRV   .497581   .064284   .505018   7.740   .0000
E13:   (Constant) .508794   .057179   8.898   .0000

E14:   End Block Number 1 All requested variables entered.

       *

E15:   Beginning Block Number 2. Method: Enter   VAR316

E16:   Variable(s) Entered on Step Number
E17:   2..   VAR316   Social class

E18:   Multiple R   .52868
E19:   R Square   .27951   R Square Change   .02446
E20:   Adjusted R Square   .27122   F Change   5.90770
E21:   Standard Error   .75026   Signif F Change   .0161

E22:   F =   33.75041   Signif F = .0000

********** MULTIPLE REGRESSION **********

E23:   Equation Number 1   Dependent Variable: HSRV   Sex Role
                                                        Values of Husband

E24:   — — — — — — Variables in the Equation — — — — — — — —
E25:   Variable   B   SE B   Beta   T   Sig T

E26:   WSRV   .476195   .064009   .483313   7.440   .0000
E27:   VAR316   −.276768   .113869   −.157904   −2.431   .0161
E28:   (Constant)   .647956   .080364   8.063   .0000

E29: End Block Number 2 All requested variables entered.

* *

E30:   Beginning Block Number 3. Method: Enter   IA

E31:   Variable(s) Entered on Step Number
E32:   3..   IA   Interaction between class and wsrv

E33:   Multiple R   .54205
E34:   R Square   .29382   R Square Change   .01431
E35:   Adjusted R Square   .28157   F Change   3.50639
E36:   Standard Error   .74492   Signif F Change   .0628

E37:   F =   23.99318   Signif F = .0000

E38:   — — — — — — Variables in the Equation — — — — — — — —
E39:   Variable   B   SE B   Beta   T   Sig T

E40:   WSRV   .370810   .084890   .376352   4.368   .0000

E41:	VAR316	-.273353	.113073	-.155955	-2.417	.0167
E42:	IA	.239770	.128046	.160669	1.873	.0628
E43:	(Constant)	.660899	.080090		8.252	.0000

E44:   End Block Number 3 All requested variables entered.

********** M U L T I P L E   R E G R E S S I O N **********

E45:   Equation Number 1   Dependent Variable: HSRV Sex Role
                                                 Values of Husband

E46:   Beginning Block Number 4. Method: Enter   VAR020

E47:   Variable(s) Entered on Step Number
E48:   4.. VAR020   Age of Respondent

E49:	Multiple R	.58757		
E50:	R Square	.34523	R Square Change	.05142
E51:	Adjusted R Square	.33001	F Change	13.50642
E52:	Standard Error	.71937	Signif F Change	.0003

E53:   F =   22.67237   Signif F = .0000

E54: — — — — — Variables in the Equation — — — — — — — — —

E55:	Variable	B	SE B	Beta	T	Sig T
E56:	WSRV	.272789	.086208	.276866	3.164	.0018
E57:	VAR316	-.272213	.109195	-.155305	-2.493	.0136
E58:	IA	.259005	.123765	.173559	2.093	.0378
E59:	VAR020	.014165	.003854	.244509	3.675	.0003
E60:	(Constant)	.077207	.176654		.437	.6626

E61:   End Block Number 4 All requested variables entered.

Commentary on ENTER Printout

Lines E1-E2 (Figure 9.12): An equation number is given for each dependent variable listed on the DEPENDENT subcommand. In addition, there are a number of different methods for entering or removing independent variables from an equation. When the researcher decides which variables should be entered, and in what order (rather than letting the computer decide on the basis of various statistical criteria), the ENTER subcommand is used. Each ENTER subcommand produces one additional equation with a common dependent variable, called a block by SPSS. Block 1, contained in lines E2 to E14, is the information for Model II, the joint reality construction model. It was produced by the instruction "ENTER=wsrv".

Lines E3-E4: Identifies the variable(s) entered in this step.

Lines E5-E7: The R and the CHA keywords on the STATISTICS subcommand produced this information about the strength of the relationships captured in the model. Note that the multiple R (line E5) is identical to the zero-order correlation beteen spouses' sex role values (line D12), since our first model is a bivariate rather than a multivariate one. The coefficient of determination is identified as "R Square" (line E6). Since this is the first model, R^2 is synonymous with the change in R^2.

Line E8: Reports the standard error (s_e).

Line E9: The statistical significance of the total regression equation, rather than its individual parameters, is calculated using the analysis of variance distribution. It is seldom useful.

Lines E10-E14: The COEFF keyword on the STATISTICS subcommand provides the slopes in both raw (labelled "B") and standardized form (labelled "Beta"), the Y-intercept (identified as "Constant" in line E13), the standard error of the slope and Y-intercept (labelled "SE B") and the statistical significance of the same, with the null hypothesis that the particular population parameter equals 0.0 (the columns labelled "T" and "Sig T" are the Student's t and associated probability, respectively). Line E12 provides all this information for "wsrv", the only variable introduced into the equation so far.

The Student's t value is obtained in the usual manner (distance from mean divided by the standard deviation of that distribution). Take the slope for "wsrv" as an example. The value of t is obtained by dividing the slope by the standard error of the slope (i.e., 7.440 = 0.497581/0.064284).

Lines E15-E29: Block 2 information, produced by the subcommand "ENTER=var316", gives us the social class model, Model III. Since this is the first multiple regression equation, a number of features should be pointed out:

- Social class increases the explained variance. The "R Square Change" (line E18) of 0.02446 is the difference between the R^2 of Model II (line E6) and Model III (line E18). This is a statistically significant increase in explained variance. From line E21 it can be seen that the probability that this increase is the result of sampling fluctuations is 0.0161.
- Since the standard error represents the average size of the residuals, these should decrease as our models become more powerful. Between Models II and III, the standard error decreased slightly from 0.76071 (line E8) to 0.75026 (line E21).
- The slope for WSRV in Model III (line E26) is not identical to the slope for this variable in Model II (line E12). This is because in multiple regression the slopes are adjusted for the effect of all other variables in the equation. To the extent that the independent variables are intercorrelated (i.e., are colinear), they will fluctuate as these other variables are introduced. The correlation between

social class and wife's sex role values is quite low ($r = -0.137$; line D13); hence the slope of WSRV is altered only slightly when social class (var316) is entered into the equation.

- When a single variable is added to an equation, the significance of the change in R^2 (line E21) is identical to the significance of the slope for the variable introduced (line E27).

Lines E30-E44: The "ENTER=ia" subcommand produced the information for the class-specific marriage styles model. Note that although the interaction variable increased the explained variance by more than one percent (line E34), the introduction of the interaction term does not reach the conventional significance level (line E42). Note in particular that the estimated standardized slope of the interaction effect (Beta = 0.160669; line E42) is slightly stronger than the standardized slope for occupation (Beta = -0.155955). Despite this, the interaction effect is not statistically significant, but the occupation effect is (compare "Sig T" column, lines E41 and E42). This is a manifestation of the colinearity problem whenever interaction variables are created, which I discussed earlier. This colinearity increases the standard error of the estimated slope, yielding less confidence that the unique effect is statistically significant.

Lines E45-E61: Two points are worth mentioning in the printout of the final model. First, note that the unstandardized slope for age is the lowest of all the variables included ($B = 0.014165$; line E59). Yet it is the second most powerful variable, as revealed by the standardized slope (Beta = 0.244509). This illustrates that the strength of a relationship is not easily determined from the unstandardized slopes, but the standardized slopes make for easy comparisons.

Secondly, although most of the time the slopes become weaker as new variables are introduced (since the slopes always take into account the intercorrelations of the independent variables with all other variables included in a given equation), this is not always the case. Note that the estimated slope for the interaction effect in the final model (line E58) is stronger than in the previous model (line E42). Indeed, the interaction effect reaches statistical significance in the final model, but not in the previous one. In the previous model the interaction effect was partially masked by the fact that in this sample, the middle class couples were somewhat younger than the working class couples. In the final model, this age diference is statistically adjusted and, in the process, the interaction effect is shown to be stronger. This reversal of significance (from insignificance to significance as variables are added) shows in still another way why theory needs to guide research.

Commentary on the RESIDUALS Printout

Lines R3-R8 (Figure 9.13): A number of summary statistics concerning the predicted scores (*PRED; line R4) and the residuals (*RESID; line R5) are provided: their minimum, maximum, mean and standard deviation. The identical information is provided for these two temporary variables after they have been converted to standard scores (*ZPRED and *ZRESID in lines R6 and R7). The lowest predicted sex role value score was –0.7647 and the highest was 1.6847. The mean predicted score should equal the mean observed score, and it does (compare line R4 with line D3). Comparing the same two lines, note that the observed standard deviation of HSRV is substantially larger than the standard deviation of the predicted scores (0.879 vs. 0.5164). This is the empirical manifestation of what is meant by the phrase "regression towards the mean."

The prediction of high and low scores was about equally successful (on line R6, the highest predicted score was 2.27 standard deviations above the mean; the lowest was 2.47 standard deviations below the mean). Similarly, comparing the standardized residuals (line R7), the worst case of overshooting the mark (i.e., where $Y > \hat{Y}$) was not much different from the worst case of undershooting ($Y < \hat{Y}$). Both of the above two findings suggest that the final model fits both high and low scorers about equally well (with the low scorers fitting just slightly better). The fact that no case falls more than three standard deviations from the predicted value indicates that there are no extreme outliers.

Line R9: The Durbin-Watson test is meaningful only when there is a sequence in the data, such as for time-series studies. It is a measure of auto-correlation and should be ignored for non-sequenced data.

Lines R10-R21: The ten cases with the largest residuals are identified. Deviant case analysis is frequently fruitful on these worst cases. A simple start would be to have SPSS list the values of all variables thought to be relevant for these cases of worst fit. Sometimes the ensuing "Gestalt" of the worst fit cases provides clues for necessary modifications in the analysis. Othertimes, it uncovers data entry errors.

Figure 9.13
SPSS Regression Output: RESIDUALS

`*********** MULTIPLE REGRESSION ***********`

R1:	Equation Number 1 Dependent Variable.. HSRV Sex Role Values of Husband				
R2:	Residuals Statistics:				
R3:	Min	Max	Mean	Std Dev	N
R4: *PRED	–.7647	1.6847	.5087	.5164	177
R5: *RESID	–1.6698	1.8695	.0000	.7111	177
R6: *ZPRED	–2.4661	2.2773	.0000	1.0000	177

```
R7:    *ZRESID        −2.3212        2.5987      .0000     .9886    177
R8:    Total Cases = 1.91044
R9:    Durbin-Watson Test = 1.91044
```

* *

```
R10:  Outliers - Standardized Residual

R11:      Case #            *ZRESID

R12:        161             2.59874
R13:        103             2.46705
R14:         85            −2.32120
R15:         77            −2.30320
R16:          3            −2.11830
R17:        101            −2.11625
R18:        167            −2.01525
R19:         40            −1.96611
R20:        157             1.96335
R21:         63             1.94093
```

```
R22:  Histogram - Standardized Residual

R23:  N Exp N          (* = 1 Cases,  . : = Normal Curve)
R24:  0    .14    Out
R25:  0    .27    3.00
R26:  1    .69    2.67 :
R27:  1   1.58    2.33 *.
R28:  2   3.23    2.00 **.
R29: 10   5.92    1.67 *****:****
R30:  6   9.71    1.33 ******     .
R31: 16  14.28    1.00 *************:**
R32: 15  18.80     .67 ***************     .
R33: 21  22.17     .33 *********************.
R34: 26  23.43     .00 **********************:***
R35: 27  22.17    −.33 *********************:*****
R36: 19  18.80    −.67 ******************:
R37:  9  14.28   −1.00 *********     .
R38: 11   9.71   −1.33 *********:*
R39:  6   5.92   −1.67 *****:
R40:  5   3.23   −2.00 **:**
R41:  2   1.58   −2.33 *:
R42:  0    .69   −2.67 .
R43:  0    .27   −3.00
R44:  0    .14    Out
```

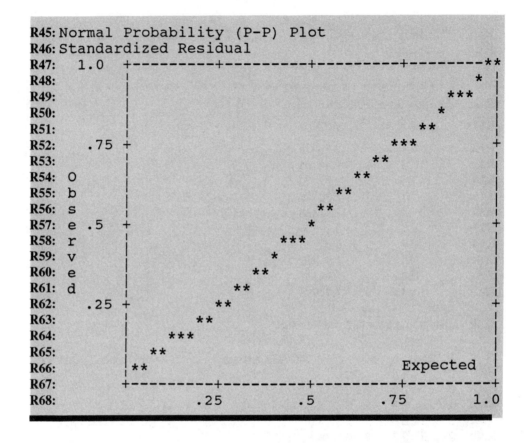

```
R45: Normal Probability (P-P) Plot
R46: Standardized Residual
R47:    1.0  +----------+----------+----------+--------**
R48:         |                                        *  |
R49:         |                                      *** |
R50:         |                                     *   |
R51:         |                                   **    |
R52:    .75 +                                 ***       +
R53:         |                               **        |
R54:  O      |                            **           |
R55:  b      |                          **             |
R56:  s      |                        **               |
R57:  e  .5 +                       *                 +
R58:  r      |                    ***                  |
R59:  v      |                  *                      |
R60:  e      |                **                       |
R61:  d      |              **                         |
R62:    .25 +            **                           +
R63:         |          **                            |
R64:         |        ***                             |
R65:         |      **                                |
R66:         |  **                        Expected   |
R67:         +----------+----------+----------+--------+
R68:                   .25        .5        .75       1.0
```

Lines R22-R44: Tests of hypotheses, such as whether certain slopes are significantly different from zero, require the assumption that the residuals are normally distributed with a mean of 0.0. Line R5 showed that the mean residual was indeed 0.0. The histogram provided here helps assess the normality assumption. The first column (labelled "N") indicates how many cases were observed with residuals of a given magnitude; the column labelled "Exp N" indicates how many cases would be expected to have a residual of that magnitude. The third column gives the standard score intervals for the residuals (ranging from -3.00 to +3.00 standard deviations plus outliers more extreme than that, identified simply as "Out." A normal distribution is superimposed on the observed distribution of residuals. In the case at hand, the assumption of normality of residuals is not seriously violated.

Lines R45-R68: The normal probability plot is an alternative method for depicting possible violations of the assumption of a normal distribution of residuals. The X-axis represents the cumulative expected (if normal) distribution of residuals. The Y -axis is the observed cumulative distribution. If the observed distribution were identical to the expected, a straight line from the bottom left to the top right diagonal would characterize the plot. Violation of normality would reveal itself as "bulges" or "depressions" from this diagonal line. These would indicate too many or too few residuals of that particular magnitude. A bulge near the middle, for example, would indicate there there are too many cases with normalized residuals around zero. The residuals for Model V fit very well. I have drawn in one comparison at the median of the expected distribution. By going up to the asterisks and then across to the *Y*-axis, we can read what the cumulative proportion of observed residuals is.

Figure 9.14
SPSS Regression Output: SCATTERPLOT

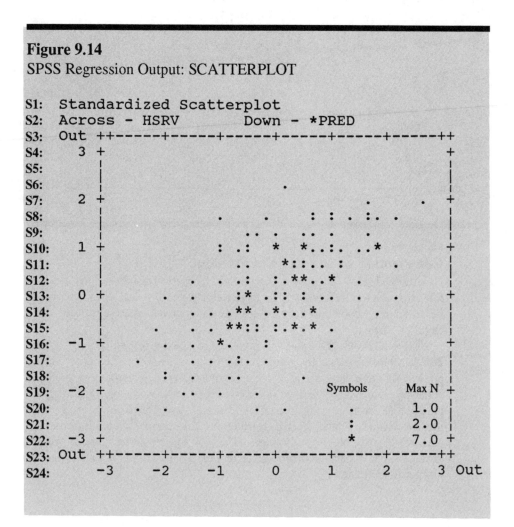

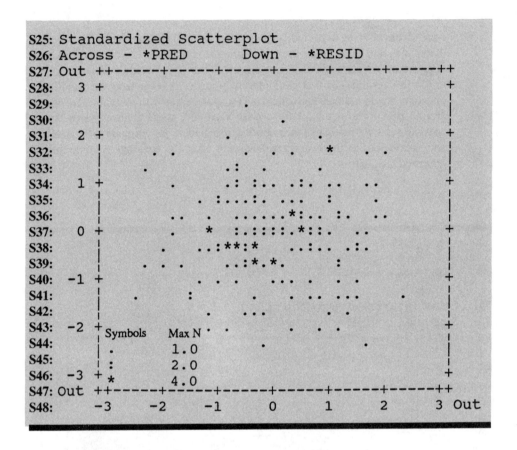

```
S25: Standardized Scatterplot
S26: Across - *PRED         Down - *RESID
S27: Out ++-----+-----+-----+-----+-----+-----++
S28:   3 +                                         +
S29:     |                    .
S30:     |                 .
S31:   2 +               .              .          +
S32:     |         . .       .   . .        *    . .
S33:     |     .            .:  .          .
S34:   1 +       .          .: :.. .:.  ..      . .  +
S35:     |                .  :....:. ...   :      .
S36:     |         . .    .  .......*:.. :.   ..
S37:   0 +         .    *    :..::::..*::.   ..       +
S38:     |           .    ..:**:.*    ..:... .:.
S39:     |       . . .        ..:*..*.      :
S40:  -1 +             . .       ...  .    . .        +
S41:     |       .          :         .     . ...
S42:     |                .        ...      . .
S43:  -2 + Symbols   Max N .  .         .   . .       +
S44:     |    .          1.0             .
S45:     |    :          2.0
S46:  -3 +  *            4.0                          +
S47: Out ++-----+-----+-----+-----+-----+-----++
S48:      -3    -2    -1     0     1     2     3 Out
```

Commentary on SCATTERPLOT Printout

Lines S1-S24: This is the scatter plot of the observed against the predicted sex role values. It was included to see if there was any area of "HSRV" where this model fit substantially worse than others. A visual examination does not suggest this is the case.

Lines S25-S48: This plot was produced in the hope that no pattern could be detected. This is a plot of the predicted against the residual sex role values. At any point along the X-axis, the proportion of points above and below zero should be about the same. Otherwise the residuals are likely not to be random. Furthermore, the average departure from zero of the residuals should be about the same at all predicted values. Funnel-shaped distributions, for example, would indicate that homoscedasticity has been violated. The plot appears to be without pattern, increasing one's subjective confidence that the final model is not an artifact of violated assumptions.

Summary

- Many scholarly arguments postulate explanations for observed relationships. That is, they suggest the reasons for the connection between events. To test the fruitfulness of these explanations usually requires multivariate analysis.
- The logic of testing explanations involves the use of "control" variables. These controls act like gates that can be closed along certain assumed "paths" connecting various events. If the connection between two variables is not severed when certain controls are introduced, then the control variables do not represent the causal mechanism or explanation for the observed relationship.
- Using the logic of statistical controls, the impact of agreement about the feelings experienced after the birth of the first child—and how difficult (negative) emotionally that experience was—on marital satisfaction was reassessed. The results were consistent with the interpretation that negative feelings both deterred the resolution of disagreements and resulted in marital dissatisfaction. They decreased the plausibility of the view that agreements are intrinsically rewarding.
- For any topic, multiple, more or less internally coherent, interpretive frameworks rival each other. For the topic of male sex role values, for example, feminist theorists might argue that the distribution of such values is a manifestation of patriarchy; classical sociologists might postulate omnipresent class effects; social construction theorists might see sex role values as the product of spouses' negotiation of a common definition of appropriate sex role behaviour; and historians might postulate a "Zeitgeist"—a forever-changing spirit of the times.
- The expectations from each of the interpretive frameworks can sometimes be modelled as a series of different multiple regression equations. The empirical results may show some of the frameworks to be compatible with each other for that topic, and others not. Thorough arguments show which interpretions are compatible and supported (i.e., each explains a different part of the phenomenon) and which remain rivals (i.e., both explain the same phenomenon, but the explanations are mutually exclusive).
- Multiple regression equations were developed for a number of the different interpretive frameworks for the distribution of sex role values. The findings support the following conclusions:

  - The gender effect expected from a patriarchal framework exists.
  - The class effect is also present in addition to the gender effect.
  - The social construction framework is compatible with both of the above frameworks.
  - However, the joint reality construction framework is less appropriate in working class than in middle class marriages.
  - The joint reality construction and the social history interpretive frameworks

rival each other. Taking social history into account suggests that joint reality construction is not as powerful an explanation as first appeared.
- Greater unreliability in the measurement of working class sex role values is *not* the reason for the documented class difference in the extent of joint reality construction.

- Sometimes the tests for a given interpretation are indirect. For example, the finding that middle class couples are more likely to have a common definition of appropriate male sex role behaviours has implications for the similarity-attraction hypothesis. The finding implies that middle class couples should be more attracted to each other. This expectation was not supported, creating a theoretical puzzle and diminishing the subjective confidence in the applicability of the similarity-attraction hypothesis to ongoing marriages.

- The models generated with multiple regression techniques make numerous assumptions about the data being used. Therefore these techniques should be used only after substantial familiarity with the data has been gleaned through sustained preliminary analysis.

- A number of diagnostic tools are available for assessing various assumptions made in regression analysis. These are available in SPSS and should always be used and carefully evaluated for clues to possible artifacts.

- A type of "deviant case analysis" can be conducted on the worst-fitting cases for the best-fitting model. This involves detailed examination of the profiles of the worst cases.

Notes

1. Technically, such problems are called "specification errors." This term takes on meaning in the context of causal modelling. In formal causal modelling, we postulate the nature of the relationships among all the important variables impinging on some ultimate dependent variable. By introducing all important variables simultaneously, we can address and remedy the difficulty created by the fact that the bivariate relationships may be misleading.

2. Level of education was measured by the following question "What is the highest grade or level of school you reached?" The response categories ranged from 1 (did not complete grade school) to 8 (completed university).

3. The denominator for the standard error of the slope includes a term that makes it approach zero as the correlation between the independent variables approaches one. The result is that the standard error approaches infinity under this condition.

4. A fuller discussion of the models and the data is given in Hofley and Thiessen (1985).

5. Additional information on sampling design and related methodological considerations can be obtained from the Population Research Centre, Department of Sociology, University of Alberta, Edmonton.

Key Terms

additive effects: In multiple regression, the condition where the effect of one variable on the dependent variable is the same for all values of other independent variables. Partial slopes are calculated on the assumption that the effects of the variables in the equation are additive. This assumption permits us to add the direct effects of the independent variables. Effects that are not additive are called interaction effects.

adjusted R^2: The proportion of variance accounted for by a set of independent variables after taking into account the loss in degrees of freedom occasioned by the number of independent variables included in the equation. This is calculated from the equation:

$$Adjusted\ R^2 = R^2 - \left(\frac{k-1}{N-k}\right)(1-R^2)$$

where k is the number of independent variables and N is the number of cases.

antecedent variable: In a multivariate causal chain, any variable that is at least one step removed from the phenomenon of interest; that is, where a minimum of two causal arrows exist between the antecedent variable and the dependent variable. A possible causal sequence is:

residential propinquity → similarity → attraction.

In this sequence, "residential propinquity" (a term used to denote how near to each other any two residences are) is the antecedent variable, because it is one step removed from the dependent variable, "attraction."

coefficient of determination: The proportion of variance accounted for by the least-squares regression equation. In the bivariate case, this is the same as the square of the Pearson product-moment correlation coefficient, r^2. In general, it is

$$R^2 = \frac{\sum(\hat{Y}-\bar{Y})^2}{\sum(Y-\bar{Y})^2} = 1 - \frac{\sum(Y-\hat{Y})^2}{\sum(Y-\bar{Y})^2}$$

where R^2 is the coefficient of determination in the multivariate case, Y is the observed value of the dependent variable, $\hat{Y}$ is its predicted value, and $\bar{Y}$ is its mean.

colinearity: Covariation among the independent variables included in a multiple regression equation. The greater the extent of such covariation, the more difficult it becomes to assess the relative effect of each variable because of increasingly large standard errors of the slopes. For this reason, it is generally advisable to delete one of any pair of independent variables whose absolute intercorrelation exceeds 0.90, or even 0.80, unless there are sound theoretical reasons for including both variables.

control variable: A variable that is either physically held constant (as in separate contingency tables for each of its values) or whose effects on a dependent variable are statistically controlled (as in partial correlations or partial slopes).

direct effect: The effect of an independent variable on a dependent variable that does *not* result solely from its relationship with other independent variables. In the causal sequence

$$\text{residential propinquity} \rightarrow \text{similarity} \rightarrow \text{attraction}$$

"residential propinquity" (living in proximity) is postulated to have a direct effect on "similarity"; "similarity" in turn is postulated to have a direct effect on "agreement." "Residential propinquity," however, does not have a direct effect on "attraction" (that would require another arrow going directly from "residential propinquity" to "attraction"). The usual test for a direct effect is a non-zero partial slope.

first-order slope: Any slope in which exactly one variable has been statistically held constant. The slopes in all three-variable multiple regression equations are first-order slopes. Example:

$$\hat{X}_1 = b_{12.3}X_2 + b_{13.2}X_3 + a.$$

As in the above equation, first-order slopes are symbolized by having exactly one subscript after the dot, indicating which variable is being held constant.

indirect effect: The effect a particular independent variable has on the dependent variable via its effect on intervening variables. In the causal sequence

$$\text{residential propinquity} \rightarrow \text{similarity} \rightarrow \text{attraction}$$

"residential propinquity" has an indirect effect on "agreement." To test for an indirect effect requires two steps: (1) there must be a non-zero bivariate slope between the variable in question and the intervening variable(s), and (2) the partial slope between the variable in question and the dependent variable becomes zero when the other (intervening) variables are statistically held constant. For the example at hand, (1) the slope between residential propinquity and similarity would be negative (the more distance between any two people's residences, the less the similarity) and (2) the slope between residential propinquity and attraction, controlling for similarity, would be zero (or, more accurately, not significantly different from zero).

interaction effect: The term used to designate situations where the effect of an independent variable on the dependent variable is not the same for different values of some other independent variable. Suppose we are interested in the effect of education and gender on earnings. From a "human capital" perspective, it is reasonable to expect earnings to increase with education. It is also well known that women earn less than men on average. An interaction effect would exist if the "worth" of education on earnings was different for women than for men, for example, if each year of education translated into average increased earnings of $1,000 for men but only $600 for women. Unfortunately, there are no clear empirical warning signs that a specific interaction effect needs to be incorporated into the regression model. Substantive and theoretical familiarity with the phenomena being investigated is usually required.

intervening variable: In a causal chain, a variable that is the effect of a prior variable and in turn is a cause of the next variable in the sequence. Take, for example, the possible causal chain

$$\text{residential propinquity} \rightarrow \text{similarity} \rightarrow \text{attraction.}$$

In this sequence, "similarity" is the intervening variable. As diagrammed, one of the (antecedent) causes of "similarity" is "residential propinquity." That is, people who live close to each other are likely to have similar material conditions of life, and thus similar attitudes, values and beliefs. Such similarity, according to the argument, creates mutual attraction.

multicolinearity: Substantial intercorrelation among a set of independent variables. It creates the same methodological problem as *colinearity*; the only difference is that the presence of even extreme multicolinearity may be difficult to detect. For example, the age of a respondent may have only a moderately high correlation with both "number of years living in an urban community" and "number of years living in a rural community." Yet together these three variables are perfectly multicolinear, since age is numerically identical to the sum of the other two variables. Hence, the multiple correlation of age with the other two variables is 1.0. At least one of these variables should be removed from any set of independent variables being used in a multivariate analysis.

multiple regression equation: Any regression equation in which there are at least two independent variables. The general form is:

$$\hat{Y} = b_1 X_1 + b_2 X_2 + \ldots + b_k X_k + a$$

where Y is the dependent variable, $X_1, X_2 \ldots X_k$ are the k independent variables, $b_1, b_2 \ldots b_k$ are the k slopes associated with the corresponding independent variables, and a is the Y-intercept.

order of the slope: The term used to designate how many variables are held constant in the regression equation. Thus the slopes in an equation in which exactly one variable is held constant would be called *first-order slopes*. The order of the slope is always one less than the number of independent variables in the equation.

partial correlation: The correlation between two variables, statistically adjusting for the effect of additional variables. Partial correlation coefficients tend to be quite similar to their corresponding standardized partial slopes, although the equations for the two are not identical.

partial slope: The term used to denote that the slope has been calculated adjusting for the effects of certain variables. In multiple regression, all slopes are partial slopes, because each is calculated with all other variables in the equation statistically held constant. By convention, partial slopes are designated in ways such as $b_{13.2}$ or $b_{42.31}$. The first subscript designates which variable (in a numbered list) is the dependent variable; the second subscript informs us with which particular independent variable the slope is connected; the subscripts following the dot indicate which variables have been statistically held constant in that equation. Thus, in the first example, the dependent variable is the first variable in the list, the slope is associated with the third variable, and the effect of the second variable is held constant. In the second example, the dependent variable is the fourth variable in the list, the slope refers to the effect of the second variable, and the effects of the third and first variable are (statistically) held constant.

residual: The difference between the observed and the predicted value of the dependent variable. Various features of the distribution of residuals are used as clues to possible problems in the regression model. Thus it is customary to look closely at extremely large positive or negative residuals on a case by case basis. Additionally, multiple regression assumes the residuals are normally distributed, and major violations of this assumption can be detected by plotting the residuals.

standardized slope: Slopes expressed in standard deviation units. Standardized slopes are also referred to as *beta weights.*

statistically held constant: Techniques to assess the direct effect of an independent variable. One approach is partial correlation, which estimates the strength of the relationship between two variables, adjusting for the effect of specified additional variables. Multiple regression offers a second approach in which each of the slopes is adjusted for the effects of all the other independent variables in the regression equation; that is, in multiple regression equations, each slope is calculated so as to statistically hold constant the effects of all other variables in that equation. An alternative approach is to physically hold constant the effect of a variable. This alternative requires one to estimate separately the strength of the relationship separately for separate values of the control variable. The advantage of physically holding a variable constant is that it permits us to detect interaction effects which would not be detected otherwise.

zero-order slope: A slope in which no variables are statistically held constant. Slopes for bivariate regressions are zero-order slopes. Example: In

$$Y = bX + a$$

the slope is of zero order.

References

Baylin, Lotte. 1970. "Career and Family Orientation of Husbands and Wives in Relation to Marital Happiness." *Human Relations* 23:97-113.

Berger, Peter L., and Hansfried Kellner. 1964. "Marriage and the Construction of Reality." *Diogenes* 46:1-24.

Blau, Peter. 1955. "Cooperation and Competition in a Bureaucracy." *American Journal of Sociology* 59:530-35.

Blumer, Herbert. 1948. "Public Opinion and Public Opinion Polling." *American Sociological Review* 13:542-49.

Buss, David M. 1989. "Preference Mechanisms in Human Mating: Consequences for Mate Choice and Intrasexual Competition." In Barkow, Jerome H., L. Cosmides and J. Tooby (eds.), *Evolved Mechanisms in Human Behavior and Culture*. Don Mills: Oxford Univerity Press, forthcoming (1992).

Byrne, Donn. 1962. "Response to Attitude Similarity-Dissimilarity as a Function of Affiliation Need." *Journal of Personality* 30:164-77.

Byrne, Donn. 1971. *The Attraction Paradigm*. New York: Academic Press.

Byrne, Donn, G.D. Baskett and L. Hodges. 1971. "Behavioral Indicators of Interpersonal Attraction." *Journal of Applied Social Psychology* 1:137-49

Byrne, Donn, O. London and W. Griffitt. 1968. "The Effect of Topic Importance and Attitude Similarity -Dissimilarity on Attraction in an Intrastranger Design." *Psychonomic Science* 11:303-4.

Byrne, Donn, C. Gouaux, W. Griffitt, J. Lamberth, N. Marakawa, M.B. Prasad, A. Prasad and M. Ramirez III. 1971. "The Ubiquitous Relationship: Attitude Similarity and Attraction." *Human Relations* 24:201-7.

Byrne, Donn, and W. Griffitt. 1966. "A Developmental Investigation of the Law of Attraction." *Journal of Personality and Social Psychology* 4:699-702.

Byrne, Donn, W. Griffitt, W. Hudgins and K. Reeves. 1969. "Attitude Similarity-Dissimilarity and Attraction: Generality Beyond the College Sophomore." *Journal of Social Psychology* 79:155-61.

Clore, G.L., and B. Baldridge. 1970. "The Behavior of Item Weights in Attitude-Attraction Research." *Journal of Experimental Social Psychology* 6:177-86.

Davis, Anthony, and Victor Thiessen. 1986. "Making Sense of the Dollars: Income Distribution Among Atlantic Canadian Fishermen and Public Policy." *Marine Policy* 10:201-14.

Deutscher, Irwin. 1966. "Words and Deeds: Social Science and Social Policy." *Social Problems* 13:235-54.

315

Fogarty, Michael, Rhona Rapoport and Robert Rapoport. 1971. *Sex, Career and Family*. London: George Allen and Unwin.

Hoffer, Eric. 1951. *The True Believer: Thoughts on the Nature of Mass Movements*. New York: Harper.

Hofley, John, and Victor Thiessen. 1985. "Bringing Men Back In: A Comparison of Husband/Wife Values Towards Male Roles." Paper presented at the 26th annual meeting of the Western Association of Sociology and Anthropology in Winnipeg, Manitoba, February 14-16, 1985.

Kohn, Melvin. 1969. *Class and Conformity*. Homewood, Ill.: Dorsey.

Krauss, R.M. 1966. "Structural and Attitudinal Factors in Interpersonal Bargaining." *Journal of Experimental Social Psychology* 2:42-45.

Lazarsfeld, Paul F. 1949. "The American Soldier: An Expository Review." *Public Opinion Quarterly* 13:377-404.

Laing, Ronald D. , H. Phillipson and A.R. Lee. 1966. *Interpersonal Perception*. New York: Springer.

Lambert, Ronald D., Steven D. Brown, James E. Curtis, Barry J. Kay, and John M. Wilson. 1986. *The 1984 Canadian National Election Study Codebook*. Waterloo: University of Waterloo.

Lenton, Rhonda L. 1990. "Techniques of Child Discipline and Abuse by Parents." *Canadian Review of Sociology and Anthropology* 27(2): 157-85.

Looker, E. Dianne. 1977. "The Role of Value Elements in the Intergenerational Transmission of Social Status." Unpublished Ph.D. dissertation, McMaster University.

McWhirter, R.M., and J.D. Jecker. 1967. "Attitude Similarity and Inferred Attraction." *Psychonomic Science* 7:225-26.

Moss, M.K. 1969. "Social Desirability, Physical Attractiveness, and Social Choice." Unpublished Ph.D. dissertation, Kansas State University.

Newcomb, Theodore M. 1956. "The Prediction of Interpersonal Attraction." *American Psychologist* 11:575-86.

Peterson, R.L. 1969. "A Videotape Analogue for Interpersonal Attraction Research." Unpublished master's thesis, Purdue University.

Pineo, Peter C., John Porter and Hugh A. McRoberts. 1977. "The 1971 census and the socioeconomic classification of occupations." *Canadian Review of Sociology and Anthropology* 6:162-78.

Popper, Karl R. 1963. *Conjectures and Refutations: The Growth of Scientific Knowledge*. London: Routledge and Kegan Paul.

Rapoport, Rhona, Robert N. Rapoport and Ziona Strelitz, with Stephen Kew. 1977. *Fathers, Mothers and Society*. New York: Basic Books.

Robinson, William S. 1950. "Ecological Correlation and the Behavior of Individuals." *American Sociological Review* 15:351-57.

Rosenthal, Robert. 1976. *Experimenter Effects in Behavioral Research*. New York: Irvington.

Schwartz, M.S. 1966. "Effectance Motivation and Interpersonal Attraction: Individual Differences and Personality Correlates." Unpublished Ph.D. dissertation, University of Texas.

Appendix A
Distribution of Chi-Square

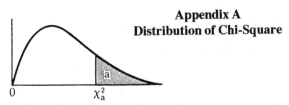

$a = .10$	$a = .05$	$a = .025$	$a = .010$	$a = .005$	df
2.70554	3.84146	5.02389	6.63490	7.87944	1
4.60517	5.99147	7.37776	9.21034	10.5966	2
6.25139	7.81473	9.34840	11.3449	12.8381	3
7.77944	9.48773	11.1433	13.2767	14.8602	4
9.23635	11.0705	12.8325	15.0863	16.7496	5
10.6446	12.5916	14.4494	16.8119	18.5476	6
12.0170	14.0671	16.0128	18.4753	20.2777	7
13.3616	15.5073	17.5346	20.0902	21.9550	8
14.6837	16.9190	19.0228	21.6660	23.5893	9
15.9871	18.3070	20.4831	23.2093	25.1882	10
17.2750	19.6751	21.9200	24.7250	26.7569	11
18.5494	21.0261	23.3367	26.2170	28.2995	12
19.8119	22.3621	24.7356	27.6883	29.8194	13
21.0642	23.6848	26.1190	29.1413	31.3193	14
22.3072	24.9958	27.4884	30.5779	32.8013	15
23.5418	26.2962	28.8454	31.9999	34.2672	16
24.7690	27.5871	30.1910	33.4087	35.7185	17
25.9894	28.8693	31.5264	34.8053	37.1564	18
27.2036	30.1435	32.8523	36.1908	38.5822	19
28.4120	31.4104	34.1696	37.5662	39.9968	20
29.6151	32.6705	35.4789	38.9321	41.4010	21
30.8133	33.9244	36.7807	40.2894	42.7956	22
32.0069	35.1725	38.0757	41.6384	44.1813	23
33.1963	36.4151	39.3641	42.9798	45.5585	24
34.3816	37.6525	40.6465	44.3141	46.9278	25
35.5631	38.8852	41.9232	45.6417	48.2899	26
36.7412	40.1133	43.1944	46.9630	49.6449	27
37.9159	41.3372	44.4607	48.2782	50.9933	28
39.0875	42.5569	45.7222	49.5879	52.3356	29
40.2560	43.7729	46.9792	50.8922	53.6720	30
51.8050	55.7585	59.3417	63.6907	66.7659	40
63.1671	67.5048	71.4202	76.1539	79.4900	50
74.3970	79.0819	83.2976	88.3794	91.9517	60
85.5271	90.5312	95.0231	100.425	104.215	70
96.5782	101.879	106.629	112.329	116.321	80
107.565	113.145	118.136	124.116	128.299	90
118.498	124.342	129.561	135.807	140.169	100

Appendix B
Normal Curve Areas

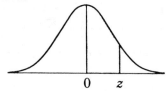

z	0	1	2	3	4	5	6	7	8	9
0.0	.0000	.0040	.0080	.0120	.0160	.0199	.0239	.0279	.0319	.0359
0.1	.0398	.0438	.0478	.0517	.0557	.0596	.0636	.0675	.0714	.0754
0.2	.0793	.0832	.0871	.0910	.0948	.0987	.1026	.1064	.1103	.1141
0.3	.1179	.1217	.1255	.1293	.1331	.1368	.1406	.1443	.1480	.1517
0.4	.1554	.1591	.1628	.1664	.1700	.1736	.1772	.1808	.1844	.1879
0.5	.1915	.1950	.1985	.2019	.2054	.2088	.2123	.2157	.2190	.2224
0.6	.2258	.2291	.2324	.2357	.2389	.2422	.2454	.2486	.2518	.2549
0.7	.2580	.2612	.2642	.2673	.2704	.2734	.2764	.2794	.2823	.2852
0.8	.2881	.2910	.2939	.2967	.2996	.3023	.3051	.3078	.3106	.3133
0.9	.3159	.3186	.3212	.3238	.3264	.3289	.3315	.3340	.3365	.3389
1.0	.3413	.3438	.3461	.3485	.3508	.3531	.3554	.3577	.3599	.3621
1.1	.3643	.3665	.3686	.3708	.3729	.3749	.3770	.3790	.3810	.3830
1.2	.3849	.3869	.3888	.3907	.3925	.3944	.3962	.3980	.3997	.4015
1.3	.4032	.4049	.4066	.4082	.4099	.4115	.4131	.4147	.4162	.4177
1.4	.4192	.4207	.4222	.4236	.4251	.4265	.4279	.4292	.4306	.4319
1.5	.4332	.4345	.4357	.4370	.4382	.4394	.4406	.4418	.4429	.4441
1.6	.4452	.4463	.4474	.4484	.4495	.4505	.4515	.4525	.4535	.4545
1.7	.4554	.4564	.4573	.4582	.4591	.4599	.4608	.4616	.4625	.4633
1.8	.4641	.4649	.4656	.4664	.4671	.4678	.4686	.4693	.4699	.4706
1.9	.4713	.4719	.4726	.4732	.4738	.4744	.4750	.4756	.4761	.4767
2.0	.4772	.4778	.4783	.4788	.4793	.4798	.4803	.4808	.4812	.4817
2.1	.4821	.4826	.4830	.4834	.4838	.4842	.4846	.4850	.4854	.4857
2.2	.4861	.4864	.4868	.4871	.4875	.4878	.4881	.4884	.4887	.4890
2.3	.4893	.4896	.4898	.4901	.4904	.4906	.4909	.4911	.4913	.4916
2.4	.4918	.4920	.4922	.4925	.4927	.4929	.4931	.4932	.4934	.4936
2.5	.4938	.4940	.4941	.4943	.4945	.4946	.4948	.4949	.4951	.4952
2.6	.4953	.4955	.4956	.4957	.4959	.4960	.4961	.4962	.4963	.4964
2.7	.4965	.4966	.4967	.4968	.4969	.4970	.4971	.4972	.4973	.4974
2.8	.4974	.4975	.4976	.4977	.4977	.4978	.4979	.4979	.4980	.4981
2.9	.4981	.4982	.4982	.4983	.4984	.4984	.4985	.4985	.4986	.4986
3.0	.4987	.4987	.4987	.4988	.4988	.4989	.4989	.4989	.4990	.4990
3.1	.4990	.4991	.4991	.4991	.4992	.4992	.4992	.4992	.4993	.4993
3.2	.4993	.4993	.4994	.4994	.4994	.4994	.4994	.4995	.4995	.4995
3.3	.4995	.4995	.4995	.4996	.4996	.4996	.4996	.4996	.4996	.4997
3.4	.4997	.4997	.4997	.4997	.4997	.4997	.4997	.4997	.4997	.4998
3.5	.4998	.4998	.4998	.4998	.4998	.4998	.4998	.4998	.4998	.4998
3.6	.4998	.4998	.4999	.4999	.4999	.4999	.4999	.4999	.4999	.4999
3.7	.4999	.4999	.4999	.4999	.4999	.4999	.4999	.4999	.4999	.4999
3.8	.4999	.4999	.4999	.4999	.4999	.4999	.4999	.4999	.4999	.4999
3.9	.5000	.5000	.5000	.5000	.5000	.5000	.5000	.5000	.5000	.5000

Appendix C
Percentage Points of the t-Distribution

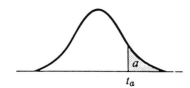

n	$a = .10$	$a = .05$	$a = .025$	$a = .010$	$a = .005$	df
2	3.078	6.314	12.706	31.821	63.657	1
3	1.886	2.920	4.303	6.965	9.925	2
4	1.638	2.353	3.182	4.541	5.841	3
5	1.533	2.132	2.776	3.747	4.604	4
6	1.476	2.015	2.571	3.365	4.032	5
7	1.440	1.943	2.447	3.143	3.707	6
8	1.415	1.895	2.365	2.998	3.499	7
9	1.397	1.860	2.306	2.896	3.355	8
10	1.383	1.833	2.262	2.821	3.250	9
11	1.372	1.812	2.228	2.764	3.169	10
12	1.363	1.796	2.201	2.718	3.106	11
13	1.356	1.782	2.179	2.681	3.055	12
14	1.350	1.771	2.160	2.650	3.012	13
15	1.345	1.761	2.145	2.624	2.977	14
16	1.341	1.753	2.131	2.602	2.947	15
17	1.337	1.746	2.120	2.583	2.921	16
18	1.333	1.740	2.110	2.567	2.898	17
19	1.330	1.734	2.101	2.552	2.878	18
20	1.328	1.729	2.093	2.539	2.861	19
21	1.325	1.725	2.086	2.528	2.845	20
22	1.323	1.721	2.080	2.518	2.831	21
23	1.321	1.717	2.074	2.508	2.819	22
24	1.319	1.714	2.069	2.500	2.807	23
25	1.318	1.711	2.064	2.492	2.797	24
26	1.316	1.708	2.060	2.485	2.787	25
27	1.315	1.706	2.056	2.479	2.779	26
28	1.314	1.703	2.052	2.473	2.771	27
29	1.313	1.701	2.048	2.467	2.763	28
30	1.311	1.699	2.045	2.462	2.756	29
inf.	1.282	1.645	1.960	2.326	2.576	inf.

Index